CRITICAL INSIGHTS

Gabriel García Márquez

CRITICAL INSIGHTS

Gabriel García Márquez

Editor
Ilan Stavans
Amherst College

Salem Press
Pasadena, California   Hackensack, New Jersey

Cover photo: AP/Wide World Photos

Published by Salem Press

© 2010 by EBSCO Publishing
Editor's text © 2010 by Ilan Stavans
"The *Paris Review* Perspective" © 2010 by Caitlin Roper for *The Paris Review*

∞ The paper used in these volumes conforms to the American National Standard for Permanence of Paper for Printed Library Materials, Z39.48-1992 (R1997).

Library of Congress Cataloging-in-Publication Data
Gabriel García Márquez / editor, Ilan Stavans.
    p. cm. — (Critical insights)
Includes bibliographical references and index.
ISBN 978-1-58765-634-7 (alk. paper)
    1. García Márquez, Gabriel, 1928—-Criticism and interpretation. I. Stavans, Ilan.
PQ8180.17.A73Z67346 2010
863'.64—dc22

                                                                    2009026436

PRINTED IN CANADA

Contents_____

Career, Life, and Influence_____

Critical Contexts_____

Critical Readings_____

Resources

About This Volume

Ilan Stavans

There are several compendiums in English about the life and work of Gabriel García Márquez, winner of the Nobel Prize in Literature in 1982, that help to amplify our understanding of his influence; among the most rewarding are those by Harold Bloom and Gene H. Bell-Villada. In selecting the essays for this volume, the objective has been to reach further and deeper into García Márquez's oeuvre while offering a panoramic view of its principal motifs and obsessions.

The piece by Amy Sickels delivers a general overview. It is followed by "The Master of Aracataca," a piece I wrote in 1993 for the journal *Transition* in which I follow the author's aesthetic arc from his literary beginnings as a journalist in Barranquilla and Cartagena, on Colombia's Caribbean coast, to the mature stories in *Strange Pilgrims*. In "Remedios the Child Bride: The Forgotten Buendía," Amy M. Green focuses on one of the most emblematic and endearing characters in *One Hundred Years of Solitude*, a female beauty whose physical presence literally hypnotizes those who see her. John Cussen sets out to understand the metabolism of García Márquez's only freestanding travelogue, *De viaje por los países socialistas*, the narrative of a ninety-day journey behind the Iron Curtain, written when García Márquez was around thirty. Cussen looks at the work through the prism of Miguel de Cervantes's *Don Quixote de La Mancha*, a book that, even if tangentially, is regularly invoked in any appraisal of the Colombian writer's impact on the Hispanic world.

The third section, "Critical Readings," contains ten essays, the themes of which range from Magical Realism to the tricks of autobiography as a literary genre. (In Spanish the word used for memoir is *memorias*, which means memories.) Gene H. Bell-Villada begins this section with his essay "The Master of Short Forms," in which he argues that García Márquez would have received some accolades for his short fiction even if he had not written his longer novels, and that his control of the genre of short fiction is undisputed. After Bell-Villada, Moylan C. Mills and Enrique Grönlund follow the style of Magical Realism as it mutates from the novella *Innocent Eréndira* to the cinematic adaptation of that work by Ruy Guerra. Next, Deborah Cohn argues that the works of modernists such as James Joyce and Virginia Woolf, and most emphatically William Faulkner's *As I Lay Dying, Absalom, Absalom!*, and *The Sound and the Fury*, influenced García Márquez's strategies of distorting time in *Leaf Storm*, an early novel where traces of Macondo are already on display.

Rosa Simas, in "A 'Gyrating Wheel,'" shows the fashion in which time in *One Hundred Years of Solitude* moves at once cyclically and synchronically and the extent to which the novel's first line is a map of its overall chronology. Following Simas, Brian Conniff articulates a suggestive thesis in "The Dark Side of Magical Realism." He asserts that the character of José Aureliano Buendía, through his quest for the philosophical stone and other myths connected with science and technology, showcases the disappointment in modernity as a synonym of progress felt throughout Latin America. In his essay "Superstition, Irony, Themes," Stephen M. Hart's aim is to vivisect the collateral that results from the encounter between irony and superstition in García Márquez's *Crónica de una muerte anunciada*.

Michael Palencia-Roth writes that the intertextual devices in *The Autumn of the Patriarch* juxtapose the work of Julius Caesar, Christopher Columbus, and Rubén Darío, enabling the reader to understand the lonesome life of the novel's dictator, his relationship to power, imperialism, and the aesthetic life. Following Palencia-Roth, Lourdes Elena Morales-Gudmundsson explores the connection between García Márquez's universe and the Bible. Her argument is that *No One Writes to the Colonel* and *The Autumn of the Patriarch* constitute a kind of "theology of justice" from García Márquez, one where the concepts of redemption, the Messiah, and the Antichrist are present. Next, M. Keith Booker suggests that *Love in the Time of Cholera* is filled with traps designed for a gullible reader. He argues that the novel is only superficially a romance between septuagenarians, with politics and history playing a crucial role in the narrative. Closing this volume, Efraín Kristal meditates on García Márquez's interest in Spanish Golden Age literary classics as well as on the author's political education, his debt to a Catalan mentor, and his adventures in bordellos. Kristal's thesis is that *Living to Tell the Tale* not only sanitizes García Márquez's life but also makes it impossible to pin him down.

It is no coincidence that *One Hundred Years of Solitude* receives more attention from the scholars gathered in this volume than any other of García Márquez's books. Indeed, since its publication in 1967, this masterful genealogical saga has monopolized people's attention for good reason. It is credited with bringing Latin American literature to the international stage. An effort of such magnitude requires a large reservoir of analysis to be fully appreciated. Every attempt has been made to balance the analysis here, however, not only in regard to García Márquez's production but also in the analytical tools used to map his legacy.

CAREER, LIFE, AND INFLUENCE

On Gabriel García Márquez_____

Ilan Stavans

Gabriel García Márquez (Colombia, b. 1927) is credited with almost single-handedly reinventing Latin America, a region that after World War II was seen by the industrialized nations as a backwater. Even those for whom this acknowledgment sounds grandiose agree that, at the very least, *One Hundred Years of Solitude* placed Spanish-language literature at the international level.

A journalist by training, García Márquez was still in his twenties when he began conceptualizing his mythical town of Macondo, and the Buendía family at the center of it, in stories and novellas such as *Big Mama's Funeral* and *No One Writes to the Colonel*. His vision did not coalesce until 1967, however, when his magnum opus was published by Editorial Losada in Buenos Aires. Within weeks, it hypnotized local audiences. Soon the novel was seen as the banner of "El Boom," an aesthetic and marketing Latin American literary movement that had started a bit earlier and for the next decade or so was the rubric under which a wealth of first-rate narratives from the Southern Hemisphere stampeded into bookstores everywhere. Participants of the movement include, in chronological order by their dates of birth, Julio Cortázar, José Donoso, Carlos Fuentes, and Mario Vargas Llosa. In time other authors joined the fiesta, from Manuel Puig to Isabel Allende. (Born in 1899, Jorge Luis Borges belongs to an earlier generation.) The signature style of "El Boom" became known as Magical Realism, a misnomer representing an artistic vision that exoticized the Americas through a combination of bizarre, nonrational imagery connected with dream sequences, a lush view of the ecosystem, an abundance of nonbourgeois sexual scenes, and straightforward realistic depictions of a society where modernity had arrived in incomplete fashion.

To some García Márquez appeared to have come from nowhere, although in fact his work was the by-product of an idiosyncratic Colombian novelistic tradition as well as close readings of Juan Rulfo's fiction in *Pedro Páramo* and the stories in *The Burning Plain*, an admiration for Borges's palimpsests, and the desire to produce a literature with ideological consequences. It resulted from the Colombian writer's emulation of U.S. authors such as John Dos Passos, William Faulkner, and Ernest Hemingway, and figures from other countries such as Knut Hamsun. Even the Bible, which the agnostic García Márquez approached as storytelling and not as a religious text, exerted a decisive influence.

Translated into more than three dozen languages, *One Hundred Years of Solitude* is as perfect a novel as is possible to imagine. For decades it has remained a steady international best seller. It has also become enormously influential among writers, leading to stirring genealogical sagas and inspiring writers from Toni Morrison to Salman Rushdie in exploring, in unconventional fashion, the crossroads where politics and literature meet. But while admiration for it has only grown with time (in my view, it ranks along with *Don Quixote de La Mancha* as the quintessential book of Hispanic culture, its language a testament to the versatility of Spanish some 350 years after Miguel de Cervantes released his masterpiece), García Márquez is far more than a one-book author. Aside from remaining active as a journalist, covering the Colombian drug cartel and other topics, and contributing influential op-ed pieces to newspapers on major issues of the day, he has produced superb, multifaceted fiction, as is clear in *Love in the Time of Cholera*, as well as an admirable autobiography, *Living to Tell the Tale*. He has also been active as a screenwriter and promoter of Latin American cinema. Plus, his friendships with Fidel Castro and members of Castro's Cuban regime turned him into a power broker during the Cold War.

When looking at the curve of García Márquez's career, it is obvious that the author has remained truthful to his humble origins in Aracataca, a small town on the Caribbean coast of Colombia. His early readings of U.S. writers such as William Faulkner defined him as a chronicler of a continent where modernity arrived halfheartedly and where collective memory was shaped by a history of submission to outside empires and corrupt politicians imbued in a culture of amorality, negligence, and contempt. His is a habitat known for overwrought emotions. (Colombia is known today for exporting prime-time *telenovelas*.) García Márquez, in his oeuvre, has paid equal attention to the private and the public domains. The internal lives of his characters are as rich as the colorful environment that surrounds them. What keeps his plots moving is a single feeling: a love that conquers all.

Another important factor in García Márquez's artistic development was his reading of Jorge Luis Borges's fictions. The cyclical patterns of time in his work and his attention to myth are ingrained in the weltanschauung of South America and the Caribbean, but they come too from Borges's affinities: the universe as a book, reality as a labyrinth, the inexorability of death, and the doppelgänger. Finally, there is the relevance of the Bible in his work. Although from early on, as a result of his socialist opinions, García Márquez has professed an anticlerical, even atheistic, stand, his creations are imbued with a biblical quality. The Buendías genealogy is marked by the prohibition against incest and the realization that everything the characters do has already been prefigured by the ghostlike figure of the gypsy Melquíades. Likewise, Santiago Nasar, the protagonist of *Chronicle of a Death Foretold*, is fated as a sacrificial lamb by the people in his town. And the late-awakening romantic attraction experienced by Florentino Ariza and Fermina Daza with the intrusion of Juvenal Urbino between them (the liaison is based in the actual relationship of García Márquez's own parents) has echoes of the ordeal of Abraham with Sarah and Hagar.

For all these reasons, the majority of people in Latin America approach García Márquez with utter reverence. In his native country he is seen as the second *Libertador*; the first being Simón Bolívar, who fought for independence against the Spaniards and dreamed of creating a continental republic. Of course, this is not to say that García Márquez is not bedeviled in intellectual and diplomatic circles. A few right-wingers see him as Castro's marionette, while others on the left accuse him of being inflexible in his views. Critics suggest that his literary output is repetitive, his dialogue stiff, and the spontaneity in his characters nonexistent. Yet it is among the subsequent literary generations where a refutation of García Márquez has been felt the strongest. The principal complaint is that Magical Realism as cultivated by him has taught editors and audiences to expect a formulaic depiction of Latin America replete with clairvoyant prostitutes, forgotten generals, epidemics of insomnia, and rainstorms of butterflies. In other words, that a more urbane, less mythical view of the region is of little interest abroad. The response of writers born from 1960 onward who belong to the McOndo group (Alberto Fuguet, Edmundo Paz-Soldán, et al.), and those in Mexico conglomerating around "El Crack" (Jorge Volpi and Ignacio Padilla, among others), has been to produce novels about the making of the atomic bomb, the climbing of the Himalayas, and the suspense that comes in a cyberthriller. Their mission is to prove that no topic is off-limits in Latin American fiction. For several of them, writing is a form of parricide.

The truth is that García Márquez, as is often the case with extraordinary artists, transcends his own circumstance. One does not need to know anything about his background, who his models are, or what aspirations nurtured his quest to enjoy his writing. *Madame Bovary* is equally enjoyable whether or not one knows a single thing about Gustave Flaubert. Likewise with *The Brothers Karamazov* and *Ulysses*. Thus, to those readers for whom García Márquez's literature is a source of unadulterated enjoyment, to be savored alone, like good wine, this volume is unnecessary. It is for the seasoned literature student that this critical artillery is meant.

Biography of Gabriel García Márquez_____

Roy Arthur Swanson

Gabriel García Márquez is among the major figures in the mid-twentieth-century surge of creativity that placed Latin America at the forefront of the global literary scene. García Márquez was born in Aracataca, a Colombian village on the Caribbean coast. He was the first of twelve children. Owing to his parents' indigence, he was reared by his maternal grandparents, who provided him with the stories, legends, and superstitions of Aracataca that would inform a number of his short stories as well as his monumental novel *One Hundred Years of Solitude*. He was sent to school at the age of eight, after the death of his grandfather. Completing his early and secondary education at Barranquilla and Zipaquirá, he matriculated in 1947 at the National University of Colombia in Bogotá.

During the 1940s he read the modern writers, especially Franz Kafka and William Faulkner. In his freshman year in Bogotá, he punctuated his law studies with reading fiction and publishing his first story, "The Third Resignation," a chilling Kafkaesque narrative about a comatose male who lives from the age of seven to the age of twenty-five in a coffin. During this time, a volatile conflict between Colombia's Liberal and Conservative parties culminated in 1948 with the assassination of Jorge Eliécer Gaitán, the Liberal presidential candidate, and initiated a decade of civil bloodshed known as *la violencia* (the violence). The university in Bogotá had closed during the preceding year, and García Márquez continued his studies at Cartagena, where he abandoned his legal studies to pursue journalism.

In 1950 he moved to Barranquilla and became a columnist for the newspaper *El Heraldo*. Four years later, he returned to Bogotá and became a writer for *El Espectador*, the newspaper that had published his first story. His determination to become a writer had been fostered by his admiration for Faulkner, and his first long fictional work, *Leaf Storm*, was published in 1955. Set during a funeral, it is a Faulknerian rendition of the thoughts that occupy the minds of the deceased's son, mother, and grandfather. In the same year, García Márquez was sent by *El Espectador* to Geneva, where he was left without resources after the military government shut down the newspaper. He then spent some three years in Paris, living in poverty and continuing to write. He traveled extensively to Europe, the Soviet Union, and Venezuela, where he edited *Momento* and, in 1958, married Mercedes Barcha. From 1959, the year of Cuba's revolution, until 1961, he worked as a journalist for Fidel Castro's news agency Prensa Latina. In 1961 he, with his wife and son, journeyed through Faulkner's South on a trip from New York to Mexico. Still in Mexico the following year, he saw the publication of eight of his stories in one volume.

After the publication of more stories and novellas, García Márquez was struck by an epiphany in 1965 while driving to Acapulco. He went into seclusion and emerged in 1967, having written *One Hundred Years of Solitude*, a novel that resists and revises conventional notions of temporality, morality, and the demarcations between life and death. The immediate international success of this novel established its author as a major figure of twentieth-century literature. In *One Hundred Years of Solitude* the history of the New World and of the human spirit is encapsulated in the generations of the Buendía family, the founders and chief residents of the fictional town of Macondo. In the novel the most ordinary events are related as though they were miracles, while ostensibly extraordinary events are presented as mere matters of fact.

García Márquez's distaste for dictatorships is evident in his writing. *The Autumn of the Patriarch* is largely based on the Venezuelan dictator of the 1950s, Marcos Pérez Jiménez. The novel's fictional counterpart is a grotesque whose atrocious tyranny is recorded in an unrelenting style that retains the humor of *One Hundred Years of Solitude* but darkens it with grisly and diabolic details. The regime of Augusto Pinochet in Chile is depicted as oppressive in *Clandestine in Chile: The Adventures of Miguel Littín*. García Márquez's pro-Marxist position is evident in this historically based first-person narrative of filmmaker Littín, who returned in disguise to Chile to compile a cinematic documentary of life under Pinochet twelve years after the violent over-throw of the Marxist president Salvador Allende in 1973.

While his views on world events are well known and have been pub-lished under fictional guise and in journalistic form since 1968, it is for his Magical Realism that García Márquez has won international ac-claim. He was awarded the Nobel Prize in Literature for 1982, and his *Love in the Time of Cholera* was well received upon its translation into English in 1988. Critics and reviewers continued their praise of his tal-ent and creative imagination upon the appearance of his short novel *Of Love and Other Demons*, which recounts a twelve-year-old girl's "pos-session" (the effects of an attack by a rabid dog) and a priest's being possessed by rabid love in his attendance on her. The novel, as R. Z. Sheppard notes, extends the gallery of Maconderos and maintains "the daring and irresistible coupling of history and imagination."

In his prologue to *Strange Pilgrims*, a collection of twelve short stories written between 1976 and 1982, García Márquez is explicit about his concept of nonlinear narrative: A "story has no beginning, no ending: it either works or it does not." Scholars continue to study the revolutionary art of García Márquez, and readers still delight in the strangely realistic humor of this artist, whom Thomas Pynchon once called a "straight-faced teller of tall tales."

From *Cyclopedia of World Authors, Fourth Revised Edition.* Pasadena, CA: Salem Press, 2004.

Bibliography

Bell, Michael. *Gabriel García Márquez: Solitude and Solidarity.* New York: St. Martin's Press, 1993. Explores García Márquez's works from a number of dif-ferent perspectives, ranging from comparative literary criticism to political and social critiques. Also included are commentaries on García Márquez's style that examine his journalism and his use of Magical Realism.

Bell-Villada, Gene H. *García Márquez: The Man and His Work.* Chapel Hill: University of North Carolina Press, 1990. Presents biographical information on García Márquez as well as analyses of his major works. Includes bibliography and index.

_____, ed. *Gabriel García Márquez's "One Hundred Years of Solitude": A Casebook.* New York: Oxford University Press, 2002. Collection presents a dozen essays on García Márquez's masterpiece, comprising a wide range of critical approaches.

Bloom, Harold, ed. *Gabriel García Márquez.* New York: Chelsea House, 1989. Collection of essays by eighteen critics, with an introduction by Bloom, on the fiction of García Márquez. Includes two studies of *Chronicle of a Death Foretold,* discussion of the influences on García Márquez's work of Kafka and Faulkner, analyses of narrative stylistics, and inquiries into the author's types of realism.

Byk, John. "From Fact to Fiction: Gabriel García Márquez and the Short Story." *Mid-American Review* 6 (1986): 111-116. Discusses the development of García Márquez's short fiction from his early imitations of Kafka to his more successful experiments with Magical Realism.

Gerlach, John. "The Logic of Wings: García Márquez, Todorov, and the Endless Resources of Fantasy." *Bridges to Fantasy.* Ed. George E. Slusser, Eric S. Rabkin, and Robert Scholes. Carbondale: Southern Illinois University Press, 1982. Argues that the point of view of "A Very Old Man with Enormous Wings" makes readers sympathize with the old man by establishing his superiority over the villagers.

González, Nelly Sfeir de. *Bibliographic Guide to Gabriel García Márquez, 1986-1992.* Westport, CT: Greenwood Press, 1994. Annotated bibliography includes works by García Márquez, criticism and sources of works about him, and an index of audio and visual materials related to the author and his works.

Hart, Stephen M. *Gabriel García Márquez: "Crónica de una muerte anunciada."* London: Grant & Cutler, 1994. A thorough critical guide to *Chronicle of a Death Foretold.*

McGuirk, Bernard, and Richard Cardwell, eds. *Gabriel García Márquez: New Readings.* New York: Cambridge University Press, 1987. Collection of twelve essays in English by different authors reflects a variety of critical approaches and covers García Márquez's major novels as well as a selection of his early fiction: *No One Writes to the Colonel, Innocent Eréndira,* and *Chronicle of a Death Foretold.* Also includes a translation of García Márquez's Nobel address and a select bibliography.

McMurray, George R., ed. *Critical Essays on Gabriel García Márquez.* Boston: G. K. Hall, 1987. A collection of book reviews, articles, and essays covering the full range of García Márquez's fictional work. Very useful for an introduction to specific novels and collections of short stories. Also includes an introductory overview by the editor and an index.

McNerney, Kathleen. *Understanding Gabriel García Márquez.* Columbia: University of South Carolina Press, 1989. Overview addressed to students and nonacademic readers begins with an introduction on Colombia and a brief biography. The five core chapters explain García Márquez's works in depth. Chapters 1 through 3 discuss three novels, chapter 4 focuses on his short novels and stories, and chapter 5 reviews the role of journalism in his work. Includes bibliography of critical works and index.

Minta, Stephen. *Gabriel García Márquez: Writer of Colombia*. London: Jonathan Cape, 1987. After a useful first chapter on Colombia, traces García Márquez's life and work. Focuses on the political context of *la violencia* in *No One Writes to the Colonel* and *In Evil Hour*. Includes two chapters on Macondo as García Márquez's fictional setting and another chapter with individual discussions of *The Autumn of the Patriarch*, *Chronicle of a Death Foretold*, and *Love in the Time of Cholera*. Includes select bibliography and index.

Oberhelman, Harley D. *Gabriel Gárcia Márquez: A Study of the Short Fiction*. Boston: Twayne, 1991. Argues that García Márquez's short fiction is almost as important as his novels. Suggests that his stories have the same narrative pattern as his novels. Includes five interviews with García Márquez and essays by four critics.

Solanet, Mariana. *García Márquez for Beginners*. New York: Writers and Readers, 2001. Part of the "Beginners" series of brief introductions to major writers and their works. Very basic, but a good starting point.

Williams, Raymond L. *Gabriel García Márquez*. Boston: Twayne, 1984. Offers a good introduction to García Márquez's works for the beginning student.

Wood, Michael. *Gabriel García Márquez: "One Hundred Years of Solitude."* New York: Cambridge University Press, 1990. Provides much of the background information necessary to an understanding of the history and cultural traditions that inform García Márquez's writings, including insight into the sociopolitical history of Latin America and biographical information about García Márquez himself.

the PARIS REVIEW

The *Paris Review* Perspective_____

Caitlin Roper for *The Paris Review*

"A novelist can do anything he wants so long as he makes people believe in it," Gabriel García Márquez said in his interview with *The Paris Review*. A deft, versatile writer, García Márquez has proved as capable at marshaling facts for a work of nonfiction as he is at making readers believe in the supernatural events that transpire in many of his novels.

García Márquez was born in Aracataca, Colombia, in 1927. After his parents moved away when he was two, he was raised by his grandparents in a home where storytelling was revered. His grandmother, Doña Tranquilina Iguarán, would spin supernatural yarns with a bluff directness, using an unchanging expression that García Márquez referred to as her "brick face." His grandfather, Colonel Nicolás Ricardo Márquez Mejía, would take the young García Márquez to the circus and the cinema, and would tell him tales of his service during the Thousand Days' War, the ferocious Colombian conflict of 1899-1902. The future novelist described his grandfather as his "umbilical cord with history and reality."

After abandoning early plans to study law, García Márquez started working as a reporter, eventually ending up at Bogotá's *El Espectador*. He composed a series of articles about the sinking of a Colombian naval vessel in which eight crewmen died. The navy claimed a storm was to blame; through extensive interviews with a young sailor who survived, García Márquez concluded that the sinking was caused by contraband that had been poorly secured to the ship's deck. His articles caused a public controversy because the sailor's account contradicted the government's official version of the event. The young reporter also got noticed for the style of his articles. "The sailor would just tell me his adventures and I would rewrite them trying to use his own words and in the first person, as if he were the one writing," García Márquez explained in his *Paris Review* interview. "Fiction has helped my journalism because it has given it literary value. Journalism has helped my fiction because it has kept me in a close relationship with reality." He admires the same ability to balance nonfiction and fiction in other writers. Discussing the origin of the insomnia plague in *One Hundred Years of Solitude* (1967), he said, "One of my favorite books is *The Journal of the Plague Year* by Daniel Defoe, among other reasons because Defoe is a journalist who sounds like what he is saying is pure fantasy."

While working as a reporter, García Márquez embarked on a self-directed literary education that featured formative encounters with the works of Joyce, Woolf, and Faulkner. He later described the visceral reaction he had while reading a borrowed copy of Kafka's *The Metamorphosis*: "The first line almost knocked me off the bed. I was so surprised. . . . I thought to myself that I didn't know anyone was allowed to write things like that. If I had known, I would have started writing a long time ago." But it was a return visit to Aracataca in his twenties that got him writing fiction again in earnest. "Nothing had really changed," he recalled, "but I felt that I wasn't really looking at the village."

> I was *experiencing* it as if I were reading it. It was as if everything I saw had already been written, and all I had to do was to sit down and copy what was already there and what I was just reading. For all practical purposes everything had evolved into literature: the houses, the people, and the memories. I'm not sure whether I had already read Faulkner or not, but I know now that only a technique like Faulkner's could have enabled me to write down what I was seeing. The atmosphere, the decadence, the heat in the village were roughly the same as what I had felt in Faulkner.

Upon his return to his home in the coastal town of Barranquilla, he wrote *Leaf Storm*, his first novella. He worried afterward that writing about his childhood was a means of avoiding the political reality of his country. "This was the time when the relationship between literature and politics was very much discussed. I kept trying to close the gap between the two." Hemingway was a powerful influence on the early story collections *No One Writes to the Colonel* and *Big Mama's Funeral*, as well as on the novella *In Evil Hour.* García Márquez refers to these books, which have none of the magical elements of his later work, as "journalistic literature."

It took García Márquez five years to write his next work of fiction after *In Evil Hour.* He hoped to write about his grandparents' home, but he couldn't find the right tone. He eventually discovered the solution by returning to his grandmother's "brick face." "She told things that sounded supernatural and fantastic," he remembered, "but she told them with complete naturalness. When I finally discovered the tone I had to use, I sat down for eighteen months and worked every day." The resulting novel, *One Hundred Years of Solitude*, sold millions of copies and made García Márquez a preeminent figure in world literature. The novel follows the Buendía family from the founding of a fictional South American town, Macondo, through many generations, a long war, and many transfigurations. It renders fantastical events in detail and with a bracing directness: "If you say that there are elephants flying in the sky," García Márquez explained, "people are not going to believe you. But if you say there are four hundred and twenty-five elephants flying in the sky, people will probably believe you."

At the end of his *Paris Review* interview, García Márquez claimed that receiving the Nobel Prize in Literature "would be absolute catastrophe," that it would "just complicate the problems of fame even more." But he conceded that he "would certainly be interested in deserving it." He received the prize the next year. Since then he has continued to straddle the line between journalist and novelist, following up novels such as *Love in the Time of Cholera* and *The General in His*

Labyrinth with nonfiction works like *Clandestine in Chile* and *News of a Kidnapping*. And although he is already one of the world's most celebrated living writers, García Márquez remains ever on the lookout for the masterpiece that might be just around the corner: "I'm absolutely convinced that I'm going to write the greatest book of my life, but I don't know which one it will be or when. When I feel something like this—which I have been feeling now for a while—I stay very quiet, so that if it passes by I can capture it."

Bibliography

Bell-Villada, Gene H. *García Márquez: The Man and His Work*. Chapel Hill: U of North Carolina P, 1990.

Caistor, Nicholas. "Gabriel García Márquez: Love, Passion and a Melancholy Man." *The Independent* (London) 23 Oct. 2004.

Kennedy, William. "A Stunning Portrait of a Monstrous Caribbean Tyrant." *The New York Times* 31 Oct. 1976.

García Márquez, Gabriel. "The Art of Fiction No. 69." Interview with Peter H. Stone. *The Paris Review* 82 (Winter 1981).

————. *Collected Stories*. New York: Harper & Row, 1984.

————. *Living to Tell the Tale*. New York: Vintage International, 2003.

————. *One Hundred Years of Solitude*. New York: Avon Books, 1970.

Gyllensten, Lars. "Presentation Speech, 1982." *Nobel Lectures, Literature 1981-1990*. Ed. Tore Frängsmyr and Sture Allén. Singapore: World Scientific Publishing, 1993.

Kakutani, Michiko. "Master of Magic Realism Works in Real Realism." *The New York Times* 19 June 1997.

Simons, Marlise. "The Best Years of His Life: An Interview with Gabriel García Márquez." *The New York Times* 10 Apr. 1988.

CRITICAL
CONTEXTS

Gabriel García Márquez:
Cultural and Historical Contexts_____

Amy Sickels

> Amy Sickels offers a time line of García Márquez's achievements, paying attention to the ways he has reacted, throughout his life, to important artistic and historical trends. She places the Colombian novelist firmly as a leader of the so-called Latin American Boom and recognizes his influence on a younger generation of the region's writers.   — I.S.

Gabriel García Márquez, the Colombian author of more than fifteen highly acclaimed books, is a Nobel laureate, master of Magical Realism, and one of the most the most widely read and critically acclaimed contemporary authors in the world today. His best-known work is *One Hundred Years of Solitude*; its popularity and critical success almost single-handedly fostered his international esteem. When *One Hundred Years of Solitude* was published, it shook apart the literary scene in Latin America, and soon its impact reverberated around the world. Critics also hold in high esteem García Márquez's *The Autumn of the Patriarch*, *No One Writes to the Colonel*, and *Love in the Time of Cholera*, as well as his memoir *Living to Tell the Tale*. García Márquez, who has become a symbol of contemporary Latin American literature, has had a great impact on the state of literature in both Latin America and abroad, influencing writers around the world.

To understand fully García Márquez's contribution to literature, one first must understand the personal, literary, and political landscapes that have shaped his work. Gabriel García Márquez was born on March 6, 1927, and spent most of his childhood living with his grandparents in Aracataca, Colombia, a small, dusty tropical town on the coast that he would later turn into the magical, doomed town of Macondo. A town grappling with poverty and abandonment, Aracataca was the site of the infamous Banana Strike Massacre in 1928, in which a U.S. corporation, the United Fruit Company, gave consent for the Colombian army to open fire on a workers' demonstration, murdering hundreds of workers. From an early age, García Márquez was aware of the political history and violence in his country; Colombia, like most Latin American countries, possesses a complicated, exhausting history of civil wars, dictators, coups d'état, and social revolutions. Yet growing up in Aracataca was also magical. García Márquez felt close to his grandfather, a steadfast Liberal who fought in the Thousand Days' War of 1899-1902 and would be the subject of his novel *No One Writes to the Colonel*. His grandmother also influenced him with her countless stories of ghosts and the dead. Between the violent war memories of his grandfather and the fabulous tales of his grandmother, García Márquez learned the art and power of storytelling at a young age.

García Márquez attended the Universidad Nacional in Bogotá to study law, but he spent most of his time reading literature and writing stories. A significant influence on his decision to become a writer was his reading of Franz Kafka's novella *The Metamorphosis*. In a *Paris Review* interview, he told Peter Stone that the first line of the story, in which Gregor Samsa awakens as a cockroach, "almost knocked me off the bed I was so surprised. . . . When I read the line I thought to myself that I didn't know anyone was allowed to write things like that. If I had known, I would have started writing a long time ago" (319). He was also inspired by the modernists, particularly by Virginia Woolf's use of interior monologue and, even more important, William Faulkner's narrative techniques, themes, and small-town settings. García Márquez's first novel, *Leaf Storm*, is his most Faulknerian in terms of plot pattern and style, echoing the narrative structures of *As I Lay Dying* and *The Sound and the Fury*. Macondo, the setting of his first four novels and *One Hundred Years of Solitude*, is comparable to Faulkner's mythical Yoknapatawpha County.

García Márquez developed as a writer during one of the most violent periods in modern Colombian history. After he dropped out of college, he spent the 1950s writing for various newspapers and living in

Europe. In 1955, *Leaf Storm* was published, marking the beginning of his literary career; however, not many people read the book, and he continued to make a living by writing for newspapers. He also worked on *In Evil Hour* and *No One Writes to the Colonel*, which were directly influenced by *la violencia* he had witnessed in Colombia and were more outwardly political than his first novel.

While in Europe, García Márquez interacted with other writers from Latin America, each of them regularly publishing work in the principal Spanish-language literary magazine, *Mundo Nuevo*. Several of these figures, including García Márquez, would make up the so-called Latin American Boom, a literary movement during the 1960s when Latin American fiction received much international recognition. The major players, in addition to García Márquez, were Julio Cortázar from Argentina, Carlos Fuentes from Mexico, and the Peruvian Mario Vargas Llosa. Their diverse work produced a superb body of literature that received impressive critical success and attention, and now some of these major novels are considered modern classics in the Hispanic world, including *One Hundred Years of Solitude*, Fuentes's *The Death of Artemio Cruz*, Vargas Llosa's *The Green House,* and Cortázar's *Hopscotch,* all of which are also in the process of being canonized in American, Latin American, and European academia. The Boom authors were not members of an organized movement, but they were grouped together as their work became well known around the world.

The Boom authors were influenced by modernism, leftist politics, and Latin American writers from the 1940s and 1950s, particularly the Argentine Jorge Luis Borges and Alejo Carpentier from Cuba, whose fiction reacted against traditional narrative form. Carpentier often used myths and Afro-Indian folk tradition in his work, and he is considered by some to be an early practitioner of Magical Realism. Borges was a stylistic innovator who employed techniques of detective fiction and fantastic literature and evoked themes of cyclical time and the universe as labyrinthine. Though García Márquez and other Boom writers disliked Borges's conservative politics, his work had a profound impact on them. In *One Hundred Years of Solitude*, García Márquez makes references to some of his literary forebears, including Borges, Carpentier, and Mexican author Juan Rulfo, who also influenced the style of Magical Realism with his single book *Pedro Páramo*.

Politics were of major importance to the Boom writers. The Boom occurred during the 1960s, between the populist regimes of the 1940s and 1950s, and the devastating wave of military dictatorships in the early to mid-1970s. The 1960s was symbolized in Latin America by hope and cultural innovations, and the Cuban Revolution played a big part in the Boom's formation. After right-wing dictatorships fell in both Venezuela and Colombia, the defeat of Cuba's dictator Fulgencio Batista followed. Fidel Castro had secretly returned to Cuba from exile, and with a small group of followers, including Che Guevara, he fought against the brutal regime of Batista. On January 8, 1959, Castro and his supporters entered Havana in triumph. Like many Latin American intellectuals and writers, García Márquez favored the socialist revolution and was an early ally of Castro. During this exciting period of political and cultural changes, a great amount of Latin American literature appeared, helping to create the Boom.

In the 1960s the success of the Latin American novel was recognized with zeal in the international world, and the Boom writers, including García Márquez, helped to develop Latin American literature. The authors benefited from English translations and the fact that their books were published in Europe and by Harper & Row in the United States, which helped to widen the readership. There were also important publishing houses based in Buenos Aires, Mexico City, Havana, and Santiago, Latin and South American cities that became strong cultural centers during this period. Furthermore, American and European universities began teaching the Latin American Boom authors, and scholars and critics took an interest in their work. Though the Boom writers' styles were quite different, many of their literary ideas were similar, as they experimented with forms of realism and narrative structure. The four main writers of the Boom—García Márquez,

Cortázar, Fuentes, and Vargas Llosa—along with several others, began to enjoy critical and commercial success both in Spanish and in translation.

Before *One Hundred Years of Solitude*, García Márquez wrote four books: *Leaf Storm*, *Big Mama's Funeral*, *No One Writes to the Colonel*, and *In Evil Hour*, for which he won the Esso Prize, a literary prize in Mexico. He was not well known outside of his small circle, however, and no one could have predicted the impact he would have on literature or foresee the international fame that was in his near future. After the Cuban Revolution, García Márquez was living with his family in Mexico, earning money by writing film scripts. He had not written any fiction for about six years. Then in 1965 he isolated himself to write the complete story of Macondo, which had been building in his head for so long that he wrote the novel in eighteen months. The novel chronicles the saga of the Buendías living in the mythical town of Macondo; as the town progresses from a primitive village to a modern town, it also suffers from the troubles experienced in Colombian (and Latin American) history.

Fellow Boom author Carlos Fuentes followed the development of the book closely and wrote an influential article in *Mundo Nuevo* praising the book before its publication, yet he too would be astounded by its runaway success. *One Hundred Years of Solitude* first appeared in Buenos Aires, Argentina, in 1967, and, in Vargas Llosa's words, its arrival provoked "a literary earthquake throughout Latin America." The publisher began with a modest printing of eight thousand copies, far more than any of García Márquez's others novels, and then quickly added new editions after the initial run was sold out within hours. In Latin America, García Márquez had become famous overnight; he was regarded as if he were a legendary soccer player or singer. When he visited Buenos Aires shortly after the book's release, people shouted support and applauded him.

Over the next two years, García Márquez's fame grew exponentially, not only in Latin America but throughout the international community. Sales of *One Hundred Years of Solitude* skyrocketed, and awards and honors rained down on the author. The novel has been translated into more than thirty languages and has sold more than twenty million copies; its critical acclaim and popularity have forever changed García Márquez's life. An epic novel about memory, community, myth, history, and nostalgia, *One Hundred Years of Solitude* is considered by many critics to be the greatest of all Latin American novels, with the story of the Buendía family functioning as a metaphor for the history of Latin America. Critic Gene H. Bell-Villada praises the novel "as a glorious instance of literature's possibilities, of what prose narrative can do for our imaginations and emotions, our politics and pleasures, our knowledge of life and our sense of humor" (204). The novel examines native and popular cultures as valid forms of knowledge and depicts the tension between the written and the oral word. Critics have praised the work as "biblical" in its scope, an epic that has delighted readers across the world, taking them through one hundred years of the lives of the Buendía family.

Unlike the other books of the Boom, *One Hundred Years of Solitude* moved beyond an academic audience and elite writing circles to reach popular audiences across the world. In Latin America, García Márquez gave literature to the people, as people from all socioeconomic classes and various backgrounds were reading the book and recognizing their world. Though several Boom authors were important during this period, *One Hundred Years of Solitude* was the only book that truly won popular and critical success. Immensely popular with Latin Americans, the novel also transcended any notion of regionalism, and it soon captured international attention.

García Márquez's technique for writing *One Hundred Years of Solitude* had a significant impact on contemporary literature, both in Latin America and around the world. García Márquez is often credited as the master of Magical Realism, the literary technique in which no distinction is made between reality and the fantastic. Magical Realism is a somewhat vague literary label that has been applied to many writers, including Franz Kafka, Salman Rushdie, Borges, Italo Calvino, Günter Grass, and Julio Cortázar, but García Márquez has emerged as the name most associated with the style. The movement itself is typically credited to García Márquez, although aspects of the technique appeared earlier, most notably in the work of Alejo Carpentier.

When he was working on the novel, García Márquez, who repudiates fantasy writing, did not set out to write a "Magical Realist novel." He simply wanted to capture the stories of his grandmother and the calm tone of her voice, without leaving the realm of reality. He has often said that if a writer makes something specific enough, he can make the reader believe anything, no matter how fantastic or exaggerated. For example, he told Peter Stone that he struggled with the scene of Remedios the Beauty ascending to heaven. Then one day he went outside and saw a woman hanging up the sheets to dry on a windy day: "I discovered that if I used the sheets for Remedios the Beauty, she would ascend. That's how I did it, to make it credible. The problem for every writer is credibility. Anybody can write anything so long as it's believed" (324). In Latin America, he has explained, Magical Realism is perfectly ordinary—the strangest, oddest things happen every day. By incorporating mythical elements into realistic fiction, García Márquez reveals both past and present problems in Latin America.

Most critics consider *One Hundred Years of Solitude* the greatest novel of the Boom, even though it may not be as structurally or technically complex as some of the other Boom books. Critic Philip Swanson considers the work to be more of a transition book, from Boom to Post-Boom. He argues that it contains many features of typical Boom books, including radical questioning of the nature of reality and literature's ability to describe it, yet is also a mostly linear narrative and an entertaining novel, which breaks with the elitism of typical Boom writing: "The novel, in other words, posits on the one hand a complex literary-intellectual problemization of the relationship between literature and reality; while on the other hand, it seeks to put forward a popular and in some ways authentically Latin American demystification of literature and reality" (86). No other book in the Boom garnered such support or popularity; it was a novel that had a significant impact on scholarship and readership around the world.

By the early 1970s, the unity among the writers of the Boom began to dissipate, and some of them were no longer friends or political allies. The hopeful myth that surrounded the Cuban Revolution began to fade away, symbolized when the poet Heberto Padilla was arrested in 1971, inciting an outrage. Sixty intellectuals who had supported the revolution signed an open letter to Fidel Castro, demanding Padilla's release. Several Boom authors, including García Márquez, signed the letter. Though the Boom reached its end, the major writers continued with stellar careers that show no signs of diminishing.

After the momentous success of *One Hundred Years of Solitude*, critics and audiences eagerly awaited García Márquez's next book. Initially, he planned to write this novel in a year; it actually took seven, during which time his fame continued to burgeon at a rapid speed. The long-awaited *The Autumn of the Patriarch* was published in 1975 and quickly sold half a million copies; however, its dense, difficult prose turned off many readers who had hoped to return to the magical world of Macondo. Structured in six unnumbered chapters comprising long, dense sentences, without separate paragraphs, it is a difficult book and somewhat inaccessible. Some critics also expressed disappointment at first; however, over time, opinion has changed and many consider this novel to be a major work of García Márquez's oeuvre as well as of contemporary Latin American fiction. "All of his works are well crafted; this novel is his most refined project of technical virtuosity," attests critic Raymond Leslie Williams (100).

During the late 1960s and early 1970s, several writers of the Boom published novels about dictators, a powerful subject for the region, as Latin America has a painful, long-standing history of tyrannical dictatorships. For example, in 1973 the democratically elected president of Chile, Salvador Allende, was overthrown and replaced by General Augusto Pinochet, a dictator who remained in power until the end of the 1980s and was infamous for torture and human rights abuses. *The Autumn of the Patriarch* is based on several dictators in Latin America. The General, the main character, is dead from the first line of the text, and the rest of the novel is told in flashbacks and a series of anecdotes that relate to the General, with none of them appearing in chronological order. Writing this novel allowed García Márquez to distance himself from the literary world of Macondo and also proved to critics his wide range of literary style and technical experimentation.

After this publication, García Márquez returned to journalism. In 1980, he began writing columns dealing with such subjects as the "disappearances" of intellectuals under the Argentine military regime, articles that were syndicated in a couple of dozen Latin American newspapers and magazines. His dedication to journalism has influenced many young journalists and writers in Latin America. In 1999, he purchased a struggling Colombian newsmagazine, *Cambio*, with his Nobel Prize money, and today the magazine continues to thrive. García Márquez's devotion to journalism and nurturing of young journalists is symbolized by his founding of the New Journalism Foundation, which has a school in Cartagena, Colombia, and sponsors workshops and scholarships throughout Latin America. His major link to journalism is politics, which has always informed not only his outlook on the world but also his writing.

Though it is for his long-lasting impact on literature that García Márquez is most widely known, he is also famous for his political ideologies and journalistic background. García Márquez has always been outspoken about politics. Early on in his career, he committed himself to several years of vigorous journalistic activity in support of revolution, and over the years, his fame and journalism have provided a platform from which he can fight against human injustices and support leftist causes. He has been outspoken about U.S. involvement in Colombia and other Latin America countries, and for many years he was denied a visa by the U.S. government. Though García Márquez is well respected for serving as an intermediary between governments and revolutionaries, he is often criticized in Latin America for remaining close to Castro; unlike many artists and writers who later changed their views about the Castro regime, García Márquez has always supported the Cuban Revolution.

Though García Márquez is a social critic in his fiction and assertively leftist in politics, his fiction is not didactic or overtly political. Turning to journalism instead of fiction to deal directly with political and social issues, García Márquez rejects social-protest literature, believing it limits artistic expression and freedom. Yet nearly all of his work addresses social-political concerns in some way—though often subtly. His fiction examines the realities of late-colonial and post-colonial history and cultures in the Americas while also exploring the truths and myths of national histories. Though critics focus on the Magical Realism of his work, García Márquez claims he writes "socialist realism," and critic Raymond Williams agrees: "*One Hundred Years of Solitude* might seem at first like a book of fantasy, but it is one of the most historical books of the Boom and it abounds in social and political implications" (96). Constant political discontent, national instability, and Colombian history and myths have shaped not only García Márquez's ideology but also the grand scope and depth of his fiction.

After a focus on journalism, García Márquez broke his literary silence with the publication of the highly acclaimed short novel *Chronicle of a Death Foretold*, based on a 1951 newspaper article involving honor and death in Colombia. Two million copies were printed in Colombia, Argentina, Spain, and Mexico. The novel, which consists of five untitled chapters, explores why an entire town allows a senseless murder to occur. It uses many conventions of the classical detective genre but also subverts these conventions and presents the sequence of events in reverse.

On December 5, 1985, a million copies of *Love in the Time of Cholera* were released in the world's four most populous Spanish-speaking countries. This book, one of García Márquez's most popular, is a love story based on his parents' courtship. One of his most straightforward and accessible narratives, it is also rich and artistic, and it received prominent critical praise in Latin America, Europe, and the United States—in the last, most notably with an enthusiastic review by the recluse novelist Thomas Pynchon in *The New York Times Book Review*. The novel, an extensive narrative, is also an intentional re-creation of romantic nineteenth-century realism. The plot follows the love story of Florentino Ariza and Fermina Daza over the course of sixty years, and love and aging are the main themes. The story is told by a single narrative voice, and the structure incorporates several temporal planes.

From 1989 through the 1990s, García Márquez published several highly acclaimed works of fiction and nonfiction, including *The General in His Labyrinth*, based on the life of Simón Bolívar; *Strange Pilgrims*, a collection of stories; and a well-received novel, *Love and Other Demons*, which centers on the transferring of burial remains from the crypt of an old convent, something the author had witnessed as a child. This was followed in 1996 with a work of journalism detailing the atrocities of the Colombian drug trade, *News of a Kidnapping*. In 2003, Knopf released the English translation of *Living to Tell the Tale*, the first of three projected volumes of memoirs. *Living to Tell the Tale* takes the reader from García Márquez's birth in Aracataca through his years as a journalist and artist in the 1950s.

For more than forty years, García Márquez has had a great impact on the scholarly and academic worlds. Numerous studies have been written about his work, both in Latin America and throughout the international community. One impressive early study was written by Mario Vargas Llosa; titled *García Márquez: Historia de un deicidio*, it is a 650-page examination of *One Hundred Years of Solitude*. Although for a number of years the majority of the scholarly attention focused on *One Hundred Years of Solitude*, hundreds of books and articles have now been published analyzing all of García Márquez's work. In the United States, many scholarly and critical studies have emerged in the past fifteen years; important critics include Gene H. Bell-Villada, Steven Boldy, Harley Oberhelman, and Raymond Williams.

García Márquez has been honored with the highest awards for his writing from the international community. *One Hundred Years of Solitude* won the Chianchiano Prize in Italy and the prestigious Rómulo Gallegos Prize. In 1981 García Márquez was awarded the French Legion of Honor, and in 1982 he received the Nobel Prize in Literature, the most prestigious recognition possible for a major writer. He was the fourth Latin American to win a Nobel Prize and the first Colombian. Colombia went wild with excitement, sending García Márquez off to accept the prize with an entourage of sixty dancers and musical performers to bring a tropical celebration to Sweden. García Márquez delivered a moving speech about the political tragedies of Latin America, and the Nobel Committee acknowledged García Márquez for his global readership and humanitarianism.

García Márquez's influence on other writers in Latin America, the United States, Europe, and across the globe has been significant and lasting. In the United States, García Márquez has been well received, to say the least. Before the Boom, in the twentieth century, it was typically the French who influenced American writers. When *One Hundred Years of Solitude* appeared in translation in the United States, it was something new and wholly different. American reviews of García Márquez's work are typically positive, and writers such as Robert Coover and John Barth have praised *One Hundred Years of Solitude* as brilliant literature. García Márquez's work has influenced such highly acclaimed American authors as Anne Tyler, Jonathan Safran Foer, Oscar Hijuelos, and fellow Nobel laureate Toni Morrison. Morrison's writing in particular, which focuses on the experiences of African Americans, blends fantastical and mythical elements with realistic depictions of racial, gender, and class conflict. The influences of both García Márquez and Faulkner are apparent in such Morrison novels as *Song of Solomon* and *Beloved*, in which the heavy weight of the past presses down on present reality.

García Márquez's literary influence also extends far beyond the United States. For example, his works have had an impact on British Indian novelist Salman Rushdie, whose novels weave mythology, pop culture, politics, and religions from around the world. García Márquez has also been a major influence on contemporary Chinese fiction, and echoes of his style can be detected in the work of the Nigerian poet and novelist Ben Okri, who describes both the mundane and the metaphysical.

The success of the Latin American Boom helped set the stage for the postmodern novel and the Post-Boom novel. The Boom itself changed the way Latin American culture and arts are perceived around the world and opened doors for many new writers. *One Hundred Years of Solitude* in particular, as a culmination of a modernist project, influenced the Latin American postmodern novel. Like Borges's work, García Márquez's writing was revolutionary and affirmed the power of invention. Of all the Boom writers in his generation, only García Márquez was a true Magical Realist. Now the stereotype that all Latin American fiction involves Magical Realism pervades much popular and critical opinion, which testifies to the strength of García Márquez's literary reputation. The critic Bell-Villada attests, "Because of the enormous reach of his reputation, García Márquez is now seen not just as another major author but as the prime symbol of the surge of creativity in Latin American letters in our time" (203).

In Latin America, writers cannot escape García Márquez's looming shadow, and his popularity and success are viewed as both blessing and curse. The style of Magical Realism is apparent in the work of writers such as Luisa Valenzuela and Isabel Allende, one of the first successful women novelists in Latin America. Allende's novels often focus on the experiences of women, weaving together myth and realism. *The House of the Spirits* (1982) concerns a cast of bizarre characters telling a story that covers several generations and includes psychic abilities, ghosts, and strange accidents. Allende is often compared to García Márquez, and critics have analyzed *The House of the Spirits* as a unique reworking of *One Hundred Years of Solitude*. Many Latin American authors have tried to free themselves from the shadow of García Márquez and from Magical Realism, including the critically acclaimed writers José Manuel Prieto, Horacio Castellanos Moya, and Francisco Goldman. Other Post-Boom authors include Antonio Skármeta, Rosario Ferré, and Gustavo Sainz, who have typically used a simpler, more readable style than the Boom authors or have returned to realism. Yet almost all Latin American writers have learned from García Márquez's imaginative oeuvre, and, in fact, he galvanized Colombian literature in a way that was unprecedented. For many writers in Latin America, García Márquez was the masterful Latin American writer of their youth, a hero and mentor who inspired many to pick up a pen. He raised the bar high with the quality of his novels, however, and each succeeding generation of Latin America authors runs the danger of being pigeonholed as writers of Magical Realism.

In Colombia and throughout much of Latin America, García Márquez is an icon. In Colombia, everyone knows who he is, and most people have read *One Hundred Years of Solitude*, or at least a story or newspaper article written by him; his work is very much in the public realm. García Márquez has greatly affected the reading public, specifically Latin Americans, who immediately respond to and recognize the world that he presents as their world—the social and cultural reality, and the specific history of their countries. Yet his work is also widely appreciated around the world by readers who can identify with the solitude suffered in modern times.

When *One Hundred Years of Solitude* was published, it first took Latin America by storm, and then the world, becoming an international best seller and establishing García Márquez as an inventive, epic novelist. No South American writer or literary novel from South America had ever had such an impact. *One Hundred Years of Solitude* and García Márquez's diverse, acclaimed work that followed have inspired a vast array of critical scholarship and inspired readers from around the world. García Márquez is considered one of the most significant authors of the twentieth century, and his work has influenced ideas about the novel, the technique of Magical Realism, and the power of imagination. It is difficult to imagine the contemporary novel without García Márquez. One of the most famous, beloved, and critically acclaimed literary writers alive today, García Márquez has greatly contributed to and rejuvenated contemporary literature.

Works Cited

Bell-Villada, Gene H. *García Márquez: The Man and His Work*. Chapel Hill: U of North Carolina P, 1990.

Stone, Peter. "Gabriel García Márquez." *Writers at Work: The Paris Review Interviews—Sixth Series*. Ed. George Plimpton. New York: Viking, 1984. 313-39.

Swanson, Philip. "The Post-Boom Novel." *The Cambridge Companion to the Latin American Novel*. Ed. Efraín Kristal. New York: Cambridge UP, 2005. 81-101.

Vargas Llosa, Mario. *García Márquez: Historia de un deicidio*. Barcelona: Barral Editores, 1971.

Williams, Raymond Leslie. *The Modern Latin American Novel*. New York: Twayne, 1998.

The Master of Aracataca _____

Ilan Stavans

My objective in this essay—the seed of a full-fledged biography—is to explore the way García Márquez navigates the crossroads where politics and literature meet. I argue that Macondo is the supreme accomplishment of his career and that everything that came before and after must be understood in relation to *One Hundred Years of Solitude*. The author's artistic capital is on astonishing display in *Love in the Time of Cholera*, which is more than a romance between septuagenarians, but even this novel pales in comparison to the Buendía genealogy.   — I.S.

The invention of a nation in a phrase . . .
                    —Wallace Stevens

For God's sake!—quick!—quick! put me to sleep—or, quick!—waken me!—quick!—I say to you that I am dead!
                    —Edgar Allan Poe

Honor to whom honor is due: Gabriel García Márquez, whose labyrinthine imagination has enchanted millions worldwide since 1967, when his masterpiece *One Hundred Years of Solitude* was first published in Buenos Aires, has reinvented Latin America. Macondo, his fictional coastal town in the Caribbean, has become such a landmark—its geography and inhabitants constantly invoked by teachers, politicians, and tourist agents—that it is hard to believe it is a sheer fabrication.

What makes this south-of-the-border Yoknapatawpha irresistible is the idiosyncrasy of its inhabitants, who often defy the rules and principles of Western civilization. As V. S. Pritchett once argued, the Colombian novelist "is a master of a spoken prose that passes unmoved from scenes of animal disgust and horror to the lyrical evocation, opening up vistas of imagined or real sights which may be gentle or barbarous." A parade of both gentleness and barbarity, Macondo makes beauty of chaos. García Márquez's fictional topos makes Latin America's ancient battle between the forces of progress and those of regression, between civilization and anarchy, look like a mere theatrical prop—an adjuvant to art.

John Updike put it simply: García Márquez dreams perfect dreams for us. But not always, we must qualify—in fact, quite rarely. For the radiant glare of his finest work has obscured the dismal truth: García Márquez's literary career is curiously disappointing. Aside from his masterpiece, his writing often seems uneven, repetitive, obsessively overwritten, forced: cynical in ways even this master of the cycle never intended.

Perhaps it couldn't have been otherwise. So arrestingly powerful is his magnum opus that all beside it looks pallid. I shall never forget the suggestion of a celebrated Uruguayan colleague, who argued at a writer's conference that, after 1967, García Márquez's annus mirabilis, it would have been best had he mysteriously vanished, become prematurely posthumous. This was an unfair, strange, even villainous thought, no doubt, but one that spoke to the curiously monotonous nature of the Colombian's art.

Whatever the lapses of his pen, however, there can be no doubt as to his stature. Alongside Miguel de Cervantes, he is considered today the premier Hispanic writer, *Don Quixote of La Mancha* and *One Hundred Years of Solitude* being the most durable and widely read best sellers in the Spanish-speaking world, with billions of copies in print and translations into every imaginable language. Who would have thought that this obscure journalist of *El Espectador* in Bogotá (a city he considers "the ugliest in the world"), an admirer of Graham Greene, Virginia Woolf, and William Faulkner, could end up traveling to Stockholm in 1982 to receive the Nobel Prize for literature—and this on the basis of a single genealogical narrative?

Indeed, critics such as Irving Howe, Tzvetan Todorov, and Emir Rodríguez Monegal claim García Márquez has helped renew the novel as a literary genre. And so he has. After the earlier legacy of the high modernists had almost reduced the form to a philosophical battlefield where, it sometimes seemed, only pessimistic insights were worth writing about, he has imbued prose fiction with a sense of wonder and joy that is both critically and popularly acclaimed around the world. John Leonard believes you emerge from the Colombian's marvelous universe "as if from a dream, the mind on fire. A dark, ageless figure at the hearth, part historian, part haruspex, in a voice by turns angelic and maniacal, first lulls to sleep your grip on a manageable reality, then locks you into legend and myth." Alfred Kazin compared his masterpiece to *Moby Dick* and Mario Vargas Llosa calls his ex-friend "a total novelist"—able to encapsulate, through words, the complexities of our vast universe. It's hard to imagine a modern voice with more echoes.

But aside from the memorable Buendía saga—its intricate structure destined to remain a much-envied model of creative intelligence—will readers ever witness another achievement of this order? Can García Márquez ever stop imitating, even plagiarizing, himself as he has frequently done since the mid-seventies? Is the sense of déjà vu conveyed by his post-1967 titles a normal reaction to the decades-long accumulation of his literary talent, the audience always sensing an inevitable return to the same set of metaphors, once fresh and now trite? Or is it that any writer at any given time, Shakespeare aside, is capable of handling only a limited number of ideas and images and that the Colombian has used and abused them all? Can *One Hundred Years of Solitude* leave room for another *coup de maître*?

It could be argued, of course, that García Márquez, more than many, has earned the right to repeat himself. Since *Leafstorm*, a novella he began at age nineteen (later collected with a handful of stories and printed in English in 1972), a dozen volumes by the Colombian have become available in the United States. (Spanish editions of his books include some twenty different titles, including volumes of journalistic pieces and screenplays.) Prolific as he is, his settings, from Macondo to a fictionalized Magdalena River, inhabit a region only about fifty square miles long; very rarely does he place a story line elsewhere—say in Mexico, Chile, or Europe. His characters share provincial values in a universe where memory and modernity are antagonists; García Márquez specializes in making the so-called Third World look exotic and anachronistic, in touch with nature and its own roots. His exuberant, grandiloquent style, however, reveals a writer who spends his life creating one sublime book—a book of books whose pages reflect all things at all times, the sort of conceit to which Walt Whitman was devoted.

What's most puzzling, to my mind at least, is that, in spite of his dazzling international esteem, García Márquez remains a literary subject in search of a biographer. While discussions of his work exist in profusion, his intellectual odyssey remains in shadow, as does his carefully guarded private life. We don't even know for sure in what year he was born. In 1971 Vargas Llosa published an ambitious and voluminous literary study of him, *History of a Deicide*, the first seventy pages of which gave the most accurate profile of García Márquez up to that time; but political differences between the Peruvian and the Colombian kept the volume out of print and unavailable, and today the document seems hopelessly dated. In 1983, a volume of conversations with his longtime friend Plinio Apuleyo Mendoza, shedding light on his intellectual anxieties, came out in England. Otherwise, what little is known about this man remains scattered in interviews (with William Kennedy, with Ernesto González Bermejo, with Harley D. Oberhelman, and with some thirty others) and reviews in literary journals and yellowing newspaper pages.

To complicate matters further, García Márquez, a sly humorist, often enjoys deceiving interviewers by revamping his own life story, giving out confusing information and spinning anecdotes and gossip to evade answers. Unfortunately, nothing remotely resembling a true literary biography, à la Leon Edel's *Henry James* or Carlos Baker's *Ernest Hemingway*, is available, while only a few scholarly volumes on the writer's life and work have been published by scholarly imprints, including essay collections put out by the University of Texas Press and G. K. Hall. Thanks to the Colombian's loquacious tendency to embellish the past, even the circumstances surrounding the composition of *One Hundred Years of Solitude* remain shrouded by myth. Ever since 1967, it would seem, García Márquez has been busy fabricating his own eternity. A biographer is needed to bring perspective to his story, at once to render his aspired heroism in human scale and to render his routine existence in the form of narrative art. For the biographer's craft, at its best, is one that at once reduces and magnifies its subject, discovering the ordinariness within the art, but also making art of that very ordinariness.

A serious consideration of García Márquez's ups and downs would probably divide his years into five parts. The first part, 1928 to 1954, includes his birth and childhood years in Aracataca, his adolescence in Bogotá, his early stories, his years in Cartagena as a law student and journalist, and his writing for Bogotá's newspaper *El Espectador.* The second part, 1955 to 1966, takes us from his first published novel, *Leafstorm (La hojarasca)*—encompassing the influences of Joseph Conrad, Faulkner, Hemingway, Graham Greene, and John Dos Passos on his work, Colombia's political upheaval in the mid-fifties, and his travels to Paris and marriage to Mercedes Barcha—to the publication of his celebrated novella *No One Writes to the Colonel (El coronel no tienen quién le escriba).* The third part, 1967 to 1972, includes the origin, impact, and contribution of García Márquez's magnum opus, *One Hundred Years of Solitude (Cien años de soledad)*; the writer's friendship with famous Latin American intellectuals like Julio Cortázar, Álvaro Mutis, Mario Vargas Llosa, and Carlos Fuentes; his permanent residence in Mexico City and Cuba; and his increasing international stardom. The fourth part, 1973 to 1982, spans the years between his stunning success and his reception of the Nobel Prize for literature, just after the publication of *Chronicle of a Death Foretold (Crónica de una muerte anunciada).* And the fifth part, from 1983 onward, begins with García Márquez's second major work, *Love in the Time of Cholera (El amor en los tiempos del cólera*), and includes his mature political views and friendship with Fidel Castro, his semibiographical account of Simón Bolívar's last days in *The General in His Labyrinth* (*El general en su laberinto*), his fight against cancer, the shaping of his "European" short stories in the collection *Strange Pilgrims* (*Doce cuentos peregrinos*), his physical and creative decline, and his own attempt to write an all-encompassing memoir.

Yet what the neatness of this or any other schematism leaves out are the ambiguities that attend the pivotal events of his life, especially his formative years and the period in which he wrote *One Hundred Years of Solitude*. So I want to indicate, however sketchily, the difficulties of examining the intricate relation between his life and craft, if only to help point the way toward the route future biographers might follow.

The very first mystery to address is his elusive date of origin. According to some accounts, Gabriel García Márquez—or simply Gabo, as his friends like to call him—was born on March 6, 1928, in Aracataca, a small forgotten town on Colombia's Caribbean coast, but a lack of official documents makes it hard to confirm this information. The writer himself claims he is not sure of the precise birth year, and his father, Gabriel Eligio García, known as Dr. García by friends and acquaintances, maintains that it was 1927, before a famous banana workers' strike that agitated the entire region. What is certain is that he came to this world a couple of decades after his country, once part of a region called New Granada, which included Panama and most of Venezuela, had undergone the far-reaching and thoroughly exhaustive War of a Thousand Days (1899-1902), which resulted in the deaths of more than 100,000 people.

He was an opinionated, intelligent, highly imaginative boy. Legends and myths, ubiquitous in his childhood, are the stuff Latin America's collective past is made of, a region where History is malleable—always adjusted to the needs of the regime in power. During García Márquez's early years, numerous stories about brave army men still circulated, including one about the liberal Colonel Rafael Uribe

Uribe—a model for Aureliano Buendía, one of the main protagonists of *One Hundred Years of Solitude*—who had lost a total of thirty-six battles and still remained quite popular. The colonel's pair of identical last names recalls the endogamous marriages that plague the Buendías' chronology, where cousins marry each other and have children with pig tails. Indeed, what García Márquez did was to transmute the fictions that surrounded him into literature: his originality is based on the artful redeployment of the flamboyant creations that inhabit Hispanic America's popular imagination. Everything he saw and heard was eventually recorded in his early literary works, given its most crystalline shape in his 1967 masterpiece, and then revamped in subsequent works.

Throughout the nineteenth century Colombia, which became a republic in 1886, has been filled with political unrest; partisan division along conservative-centrist and liberal-federalist lines would not infrequently erupt into civil war. After the War of the Thousand Days, when the conservatives emerged victorious, the regime of General Rafael Reyes (1904-10) ushered in a boom of banana plantations along the Magdalena River, the place where *The General in His Labyrinth* and other titles are set. Many foreign companies settled down in the region, including the United Fruit Company, which had 3,000 employees in 1908, more than a fourth of the whole banana workforce.

Flush with newfound prosperity, Aracataca was a place where, it was remarked, prostitutes danced *cumbias* at the side of arrogant tycoons. "With the banana boom," the writer would later recollect, "people from all over the world began to arrive at Aracataca and it was very strange because in this little town in Colombia's Atlantic coast, for a moment all languages were spoken." A couple of decades later, with the growth and expansion of organized unions from Mexico to Argentina, and after the creation of Colombia's Socialist Revolutionary Party, a bloody massacre took place in Ciénaga. The army used machine guns to disperse striking banana laborers near a train station. Hundreds died, perhaps thousands. The event was retold through stories and folksongs time and again while García Márquez was still young. It took hold in his memory and would eventually make for a powerful scene in *One Hundred Years of Solitude*: scores of bodies of United Fruit toilers lie motionless on the battlefield after an unsuccessful strike and are then piled in a train. The next day, nobody in Macondo acknowledges the tragedy and many even insist that it never happened.

Dr. García, the novelist's father, had a total of fifteen children, three the result of extramarital affairs. One of these three, a daughter, was raised by his wife, Luisa Santiaga Márquez Iguarán, much in the way Úrsula Iguarán, the matron at the heart of Macondo, takes upon herself the raising of the vast bastard descendants of Colonel Aureliano Buendía. Gabriel was oldest of the legitimate branch, most of whom share his left-wing politics, although a few of his siblings, like their dad, are *gordos*, or conservatives. As García Márquez has said in public statements, *Love in the Time of Cholera*, his 1986 romance in which an old couple reunites after persistent passion and decades of separation, is based on his parents' relationship. Before getting married, Dr. García was a telegrapher. (Indeed, telegraphs and other forms of pre-Second World War wire communication are ubiquitous in his son's oeuvre.) After strong opposition from Luisa Santiaga's family—her parents, probably the most aristocratic couple in Aracataca, were first cousins—they married, and Dr. García and his wife left their then only son Gabriel to the care of the child's paternal grandparents because the father wanted to improve his economic situation. The newlywed couple lived in numerous towns throughout the Caribbean coast. Dr. García eventually received a degree in homeopathic medicine in Barranquilla. Afterwards, while studying for four years at the medical school of the Universidad de Cartagena, he became a pharmacist.

After ten years of separation, Gabriel was reunited with his parents, and during 1939-50, the family, already numerous, settled in Sucre, a port town in Bolívar Province, a place where several of his novels would be set, including *No One Writes to the Colonel*. But soon they had to move again because another doctor had settled in the same town and taken most of Dr. García's clientele. Around 1951 (some say it was 1950), the family moved to Cartagena, where the father, in spite of his unfinished course in clinical medicine, finally received an M.D. and maintained his own practice for decades. Luisa Santiaga, the novelist's mother, a spirited, strong-willed woman with a liberal upbringing—her father, Nicolás Márquez Iguarán, an army man, fought on General Rafael Uribe Uribe's side—is said to have been quite intuitive. She won the lottery several times based on information she claimed to have gotten in dreams.

In interviews and autobiographical pieces, García Márquez has said that his first eight years of life were the most crucial and memorable. At twelve months of age, when his parents left Aracataca, he went to live in his grandparents' home, a place, he says, full of ghosts. In Luis Harss's volume of narrative portraits *Into the Mainstream*, the novelist describes his new tutors as superstitious and impressionable people.

> In every corner [of the house] there were skeletons and memories, and after six in the evening you didn't dare leave your room. It was a world of fantastic terror [in which] there were coded conversations. . . . There was an empty room where Aunt Petra had died. And another one where Uncle Lázaro passed away. Thus, at night you couldn't walk because there were more people dead than alive. I remember [an] episode well, one that captures the atmosphere of the house. I had an aunt. . . . She was very active: she was doing something else at home all the time and one day she sat down to sew a shroud. I then asked her: "Why are you sewing a shroud?" "Because I'm going to die, my boy," she answered. When she finished sewing her shroud, she lay down and died.

In 1969, a Bogotá journalist who traveled to Aracataca discovered that García Márquez's childhood house was being devoured by ants and covered with dust. Just like the Buendía mansion, and, for that matter, all of Macondo, it was condemned to perish.

Death, a common, banal fact in Latin America, was a preoccupation of the novelist. Aunt Petra's end and others sharply more violent color his work: colonels agonizing before firing squads, corpses found in a huge palace, a killing solved by a private eye. Memory, in García Márquez's view, is synonymous with redemption: to remember is to overcome, to defeat the forces of evil. Lust, illusion, corruption, and the recalcitrance of barbarism are also at the core of his work. These themes, openly or otherwise, are frequently intertwined with another pressing subject: a sharp critique of institutionalized religion. His attack on the Catholic church is not surprising when one considers the fact that García Márquez completed primary and high school in a private Jesuit institution in Zipaquirá, near Bogotá, a place where his mother's liberal views and his own frequently clashed with institutional dogmas. Priests and clerical acolytes are often portrayed by him as distant, corrupt, ill-informed, or simply lazy. In the story "Tuesday's Siesta" (*La siesta del martes*), a woman and her daughter arrive in a small town to pay last respects to Carlos Centeno, the woman's only son, who became a thief in order to support the family. The response she gets from the local priest is not only cold but offensive: he refuses to help her; when he finally agrees to give her the keys to the cemetery, it is only after asking her for charity.

Such a jaundiced view of matters ecclesiastical is, of course, unsurprising from a leftist. And yet García Márquez, it should be made clear, does not attack God or human spirituality; his target is the clerical hierarchy. In his universe the Almighty is alive and well, and, one senses, possessed of literary talents. After all, couldn't *One Hundred Years of Solitude* be read as a daring rewriting of the Bible? Floods, prophesies, sin and condemnation, epic wars and the abuse of power, hero worship and romance—the elements are all there, and so are the theological and teleological undertones. Both the Bible and the Colombian's masterpiece intertwine the individual and the collective in a concrete, urgent fashion with images that seem tangible, real.

Indeed, García Márquez's imagination, since early on, has been graphic: scenes, however surrealistic, always have an incredible immediacy. This fact is important when one considers García Márquez's lifelong passion for the movies. He is founder and executive director of Cuba's Film Institute in Havana, to which he often donates the profits of his films. His interest in the silver screen dates back to when he worked for Mexico's J. Walter Thompson advertising agency. He wrote commercials and was enchanted with the filmmaking process. "To write for the movies," the Colombian once reflected, "one needs great humility. That distinguishes it from the literary endeavor. While the novelist sitting at the typewriter is totally free and in control, the screenwriter is only a piece in a complex machinery and thus the target of contradictory special interests." Aside from his youthful work as a film reviewer for newspapers in Barranquilla and Bogotá, his numerous film projects began when he collaborated with Carlos Fuentes and others in adapting Juan Rulfo's *El gallo de oro* (*The golden rooster*), and include such titles as *Time to Die*, directed by Arturo Ripstein; *Patty My Love*; Alberto Isaac's *No Thieves in This Town*; and Juan Rulfo's *Pedro Páramo*. Later he would also shape the screenplays of *Difficult Loves*, a series made for Spanish TV, as well as *Chronicle of a Death Foretold* and *Eréndira*. Nor can I forbear mention of *Clandestine in Chile: The Adventures of Miguel Littín*, a journalistic piece on his friend the filmmaker Littín and his secretive journey to Augusto Pinochet's Chile in the mid-eighties. (After the downfall of Salvador Allende, García Márquez publicly swore he would not write again until Pinochet gave up power. As it turns out, the dictator had more endurance than the author.)

Many of his adaptations and screenplays originated in short stories and vice versa; a few, in prose form, are collected in *Strange Pilgrims*, conceived as "mere entertainments," to use Graham Greene's fashionable term, and unified by the common theme of investigating the lives of Latin Americans transplanted to Europe—the New World inhabiting the Old. One of them is "The Summer of Miss Forbes" (*El verano de la Señora Forbes*), directed by Jaime Humberto Hermosillo, about a

German nanny who, in taking care of a pair of children in Sicily, kills herself in an apocalyptic act of unresolved sexual passion; another is "I Only Came to Use the Phone" (*Sólo vine a usar el teléfono*), about a young wife mistaken as a lunatic and imprisoned in a psychiatric home.

But García Márquez's vivid imagination reaches beyond the screen. Consider the extraordinary metafictional imagery in *One Hundred Years of Solitude*. In the last few pages, Aureliano Babilonia, the last in the Buendía lineage, whose first member is found tied to a tree and whose last is eaten by ants, discovers the lost manuscripts of the gypsy Melquíades. Like *Hamlet*'s play-within-a-play and Cervantes's novel-within-a-novel, García Márquez introduces a text that can be read "as if it had been written in Spanish," in which the very novel the reader holds in hand is included. What follows is Gregory Rabassa's superb translation:

> It was the history of the family, written by Melquíades, down to the most trivial details, one hundred years ahead of time. He had written it in Sanskrit, which was his mother tongue, and he had encoded the even lines in the private cipher of the Emperor Augustus and the odd ones in the Lacedemonian military code. The final protection, which Aureliano had begun to glimpse when he let himself be confused by the love of Amaranta Úrsula, was based on the fact that Melquíades had not put events in the order of man's conventional time, but had concentrated a century of daily episodes in such a way that they coexisted in one instant.

It's a passage that recalls Borges's tale "The Aleph," in which the Argentine narrator discovers, hidden in a Buenos Aires basement, a magical object capable of turning past, present, and future into one single unifying moment. But García Márquez's passage, although intertwining spiritual elements, also has a concrete, visual, cinematographic texture: the act of reading, the sudden discovery of death, the past as a bewitchment. Perhaps that's why García Márquez has stated he will never sell the movie rights to *One Hundred Years of Solitude*, for the novel is already a film. By contrast, Isabel Allende's 1982 best-selling genealogical novel *The House of the Spirits*—a novel that suspiciously resembles the Colombian's masterpiece and could almost be considered a trivialization of his trademark style—is, after a highly competitive auction, being directed by the Danish filmmaker Bille August, a concession to the imposing ways of mass culture.

Of course, one could argue that although *Don Quixote* has been adapted to the screen time and again, its sheer literary force remains intact, as enchanting as when first written half a millennium ago. Could Anthony Hopkins play the role of Aureliano Buendía and Vanessa Redgrave that of Úrsula Iguarán on location somewhere in the Amazon? Can actual vistas of the jungle do justice to García Márquez's colorful, baroque style? Most devoted fans hope it will never happen, but sooner or later they are likely to be betrayed. It won't matter, though. In keeping with the metaphysical transmutation any literary classic undergoes with time, the book's mesmerizing Biblical images are somehow already no longer the property of the author but of language and tradition.

To return to his formative years, García Márquez was still twenty years old in 1948 when another tragic clash between conservative and liberal parties took place, again costing hundreds of thousands of lives. On April 9, Jorge Eliécer Gaitán, ex-mayor of Bogotá and the Liberal Party's populist presidential candidate, who had defended the workers in the strike of 1928, was assassinated. The event, known as *el bogotazo*, inaugurated a decade-long period generally referred to by Colombians as *la violencia*, chaos and disorder prevailing in rural areas. The year before, García Márquez had enrolled as a law student at the National University, and it was around that time that he met Plinio Apuleyo Mendoza, a strong supporter of his talent, whom he would reencounter in Paris in the late fifties. At age nineteen, García Márquez wrote, in the fashion of Maupassant's "Le Horla," his first short story, to my knowledge still untranslated into English, "La tercera resignación" ("The Third Resignation"), published in *El Espectador*. The violence that surrounded him at the time left a profound scar. The National University was temporarily closed, and he had to move to Cartagena, where his family had resettled. He entered the local university and, in order to support himself, began his career as a journalist in *El Universal*.

Not much else is known about his beginnings, making the job of a biographer all the more urgent: to dig—to recover, uncover, and discover; to trace lost steps on the map of the subject's existence. Why did García Márquez select law as a profession? Why not a medical career, like the novelist's father, Dr. García? (The doctors in his plots are, in the Flaubertian manner, always representatives of science and modernity.) The relationship between oral storytelling and literature is at the core of his craft. When did he decide to sit down and write? Was he politically active as a student? Did he perceive literature as an instrument to educate and enlighten the masses and to further a process of social revaluation and reconstruction? (This view of literature's purpose is in fashion at the time and was later debated by Jean-Paul Sartre and Albert Camus in a controversy with far-reaching effects in Latin America during the late fifties and early sixties.) Did he have any direct confrontations with the government and the armed forces, a rite of passage decisive for most intellectuals in the region?

What is sure is that around 1948 he began reading Faulkner, a turning point in his career. Literature would become his sole passion. His goal now was to build an architecturally perfect, fictional universe that most of his ghosts and fears could inhabit, a mirror of the reality that daily overwhelmed him. Faulkner immediately became his secret personal tutor. For Faulkner had, in one novel after another, devoted all his creative energy to investigating the historical wounds of the Deep South—and those wounds are not unlike Latin America's: the acceptance of collective defeat and the adjustment to external colonizing forces and the phantoms of history. At the same time, Faulkner's fictional constellation seemed autonomous and self-sufficient. Besides, his introspective, experimental, Rashomon-like style appealed greatly to the Colombian fabulist.

He started by reading *A Rose for Emily*, which had recently been published in a poor Spanish translation. (García Márquez's English is weak.) Based on a July 1949 newspaper review by the author, critics like Jacques Gilard and Raymond L. Williams claim it was the Colombian's first encounter with the southern U.S. writer, an interest that would evolve into a lifelong fascination. Today, out of saturation perhaps, the Colombian claims he is no longer able to read good old Faulkner. Still, the encounter with the Yoknapatawpha saga changed his view of literature forever. "When I first read [him]," he would later say, "I thought: I must become a writer." A similar Faulknerian impact, by the way, transformed the Uruguayan Juan Carlos Onetti and the Peruvian Vargas Llosa, to name only a few Latin Americans with a Faulkernian drive. More than a decade later, around 1961, García Márquez, married and with a son (he has two, one of them a writer in his own right), traveled by bus from New York to Mexico through the Deep South "in homage to Faulkner." Segregation reigned, and the family encountered signs that read "No Dogs and Mexicans Allowed" and were frequently not allowed to stay at hotels.

Two other U.S. authors commanded an overwhelming influence across the Rio Grande in the fifties: Hemingway and John Dos Passos. With respect to the latter, one can point to García Márquez's interest in cruel realism; but it was the former who truly influenced him by teaching precision, objectivity, and directness in style. Literature and journalism, he understood, were brothers. Indeed, as was the case with the author of *The Sun Also Rises*, the impact of the Colombian's journalistic writing on his future artistic development was enormous. He learned to write in short, clear sentences. But unlike Hemingway, who claimed journalism could kill a writer's career, García Márquez not only saw the trade as essential in the shaping of a novelist's style but also needed it as a source of income until book royalties began to come in, well into his forties.

In 1952 he began writing for *El Heraldo* in Barranquilla and became part of the so-called Barranquilla Group, a gathering of intellectuals who read and discussed Hemingway, Virginia Woolf, Faulkner, Erskine Caldwell, and Dos Passos. (The group included two aspiring writers who would eventually leave a mark on Colombian letters, although never with the impact of García Márquez: Álvaro Cepeda Samudio and Germán Vargas.) Already in his mid-twenties, García Márquez began to take himself seriously as a writer. He was constantly publishing short stories in newspapers and magazines, and even finished a first novel, *La casa* (*The house*), which Buenos Aires's Losada, the prestigious imprint responsible for the works of the River Plate luminaries Borges and Adolfo Bioy Casares, rejected after one of its editors told García Márquez he had no talent as a writer and should devote himself to something else. The novel, known today as *La hojarasca*, has an unquestionably Faulknerian style: its plot is told from three different viewpoints—that of a father, his daughter, and his grandchild—and circles around the funeral of a doctor who had been hated by everybody in town and who, at the end of his life, had become a recluse. As William Kennedy has argued, the protagonist's personality recalls Rev. Gail Hightower of *Light in August*.

It is an interesting fact about the world of letters into which García Márquez emerged that, with very few exceptions, Colombian literature was, and remains, largely undistinguished. When García Márquez was born, José Eustasio Rivera, author of the country's heretofore most famous work *The Vortex*, was dying. Besides his, few names are worthy of notice: Jorge Isaac, author of the best-seller *Maria*, the *modernista* poet José Asunción Silva; the eccentric Porfirio Barba Jacob; Eduardo Caballero Calderón, author of *The Noble Savage*; and that's about all. Recently, however, another name has emerged: Álvaro Mutis, who, as it turns out, is a key figure in García Márquez's artistic progress. He invited García Márquez to return from Cartagena to Bogotá to write for *El Espectador*, and, after his acceptance, they became good friends. In the early sixties, García Márquez sent Mutis, who was in a Mexican prison, two of his short stories, which his friend in turn showed to the journalist Elena Poniatowska. Later, after a few mishaps, she and Mutis managed to convince the Universidad Veracruzana Press to publish them, alongside other tales, as *Big Mama's Funeral*, for which the author got an advance of a thousand pesos. Published in 1962, the book's first printing of 2,000 copies took years to sell.

As a belated expression of deeply felt gratitude, García Márquez dedicated *The General in His Labyrinth* to Mutis, for having given "me the idea for writing this book." The novel, to my mind one of the writer's most sophisticated and accomplished, studies the last few days of Simón Bolívar, who, on December 10, 1830, soon after he had dictated his last will and testament and a physician had insisted that he confess and receive the sacraments, said: "What does this mean? . . . Can I be so ill that you talk to me of wills and confessions? . . . How will I ever get out of this labyrinth!" In the section "My Thanks," García Márquez writes:

> For years I listened to Álvaro Mutis discussing his plan to write about Simón Bolívar's final voyage along the Magdalena River. When he published "El último rostro" ["The Last Face"], a fragment of the projected book, the story seemed so ripe, and its style and tone so polished, that I expected to read it in its complete form very soon afterwards. Nevertheless, two years later I had the impression that he had regarded it to oblivion, as so many writers do with our best-loved dreams, and only then did I dare ask for his permission to write it myself. It was a direct hit after a ten-year ambush.

The Bolívar novel, rather poorly received in the United States because of its abundance of historical data and a period setting that many Anglo-Saxons found unappealing, created a huge controversy in South America. There Venezuelan and Colombian politicians attacked it as "profane," claiming García Márquez was defaming the larger-than-life reputation of a historical figure who, during the nineteenth century, struggled to unite the vast Hispanic world. But Mutis, the author's ideal reader, is known to be very fond of the book. That alone made García Márquez happy.

While working for *El Espectador*, García Márquez wrote a series of fourteen semijournalistic pieces, composed in the first-person voice of a twenty-two-year-old mariner, that chronicled the episode of a shipwreck in which eight crew members were left alone at sea. Only one, Luis Alejandro Velasco, survived, and he became a national hero. According to the official version, bad weather had caused the tragedy, but when assigned to investigate the details, the novelist discovered the boat was carrying *contrabando*—smuggled items: television sets, refrigerators, and laundry machines brought from the United States. Dictator Rojas Pinilla had allowed only pro-government newspapers to cover the event. Although the Velasco celebration had diminished by the time García Márquez published his articles, they became a public sensation and an embarrassment to the government in power. A Barcelona publishing house reprinted the serial in book form in 1970 as *The Story of a Shipwrecked Sailor*, a volume that, had readers never seen the Colombian's name on the cover, would frankly have passed without pomp and glory as a forgettable and poorly structured report.

The year 1955 was among the most decisive in the novelist's life. When he was twenty-seven, a small Bogotá house, Ediciones Sipa, finally decided to publish his first novel under the title *La hojarasca*. Reports of the early critical and commercial reaction are ambiguous, and García Márquez has only added to the uncertainty. In an interview, he claimed it sold some 30,000 copies, but some sources, including Vargas Llosa in *History of a Deicide*, claim it elicited very small interest and passed largely unnoticed.

An indication of the book's poor reception was the writer's reaction: as often happens to South American first-time novelists, García Márquez felt depressed and swore never to write again. Ironically, this wasn't another of his histrionic gestures. His trust in literature actually diminished as he became increasingly conscious of his personal needs in the future: he would have to support himself and a family, and writing novels didn't seem like a money-making venture, at least not at the time. Fortunately, fate managed to stimulate him by other means. That same year he was awarded a prize by Bogotá's Association of Artists and Writers for his story "Un día después del Sábado" ("A Day After Saturday"), and while the amount of money he received was small, his name and photograph circulated in newspapers. To add to the excitement, his editor at *El Espectador* had earlier decided to send him to Geneva as a foreign correspondent. He would leave his native town for Europe, where the literary careers of those from south of the Rio Grande have always been forged.

Things in Colombia changed drastically the moment he left. The overall reach of *la violencia* was omnipresent, and soon the military regime of Gustavo Rojas Pinilla, a merciless *caudillo*, closed down *El Espectador*. The old battle between federalists and centralists took a high toll, and nobody was immune from the violence. García Márquez arrived in Europe excited to be an independent young man in a strange and glamorous place, and ready to seize the opportunity to perfect his craft as a novelist. But now, suddenly, he was left out in the cold. He had been staying at Hôtel de Flandre in the Latin Quarter, where he waited for a check from the newspaper to come in the mail. For obvious reasons, none arrived. In time he would owe the management some 123,000 francs. Since he was on good terms with the hotel administration, he was allowed to stay for a little while, in spite of some clients' complaints of his typing after midnight. He then managed to travel to Rome, where he participated as a student at the Centro Sperimentale di Cinematografia—where Manuel Puig would later enroll—and finally moved to Paris. The legends about his Parisian stay conform to the stereotype of the down-and-out litterateur: he had a hard time making ends meet, and in one instance was seen collecting empty bottles at garbage cans to exchange for extra centimes to buy food.

And yet the European years proved to be very fruitful, in part because he finished *No One Writes to the Colonel* and *In Evil Hour*, published, respectively, in Medellín by Aguirre Editor in 1961 and in Madrid by Talleres de Gráficas Luis Pérez the year after. These titles, together with *Big Mama's Funeral*, form a unified whole. "I tried to put in them everything I knew," he said later. But after a painful artistic struggle, he gave up the encyclopedic approach to narrative: "It was too much accumulation." He thus cut sections, expanded chapters, and turned ideas into short stories. (Robert Coover believes the conflict between "the realistic" and "the fantastic" is never adequately worked out in these works.) Away from Latin America, his imagination had begun to metamorphosize his past, his native culture, into the stuff of myth. Distance distorted the actual size and value of things, misforming them into pieces of a personal puzzle. Through literature, he could revisit the ghosts of his grandparents' home. He could re-create the violence he had witnessed by invoking plots where brave military soldiers are forgotten by their army peers. Years later, when a journalist asked him to summarize the region's idiosyncratic nature, he answered with the following tale set in a small rural town in Colombia: At around ten o'clock, two men parked a truck outside a boarding school and said, "We've come to pick up the furniture." No one knew if they were supposed to come, but the principal allowed them in, the furniture was placed in the truck, and the two men left. "Only later people found out they were thieves."

García Márquez returned to South America in 1956. He made a quick stop in Colombia to marry Mercedes Barcha, then moved to Caracas, Venezuela, where he worked for *Momentos* and *Elite*. Together with Apuleyo Mendoza, García Márquez traveled back and forth through Eastern Europe and the Soviet Union in 1957 and produced a report in ten installments, more anecdotal than political, for the magazines *Elite* in Venezuela and *Cromos* in Bogotá, under the general title of *Noventa dias en la cortina de hierro* (*Ninety days on tour through the Eastern Block*). Among other places, he visited East Germany, Czechoslovakia, Poland, and Russia.

Upon his return, he went to London to learn English, then to Venezuela, and finally to Mexico. At thirty-one, he was enchanted by the Cuban Revolution and began working for Cuba's press agency, Prensa Latina, a job he performed for two years. He was stationed in New York to cover the United Nations General Assembly, but after a while his relationship with the news agency deteriorated and he quit. García Márquez's role in modern politics is evident in his left-wing views, his solid friendship with Fidel Castro, and his defense of Latin America. "I have firm political beliefs," he once told Luis Harss, "but my views of literature change with every digestion." In his Nobel acceptance speech to the Swedish Academy in 1982, he said: "Latin America neither wants, nor has any reason, to be a pawn without a will of its own; nor is it merely wishful thinking that its quest for independence and originality should become a Western aspiration." Often he has acted as intermediary between human rights commissions and the Havana regime, as in the celebrated Heberto Padilla affair, in which a Cuban poet, imprisoned for betraying his country's national security, was freed after many pleas from, among others, Susan Sontag and Robert Silver, editor of the *New York Review of Books*, thanks in part to García Márquez, who persuaded a reluctant Castro to let him go.

Some have criticized García Márquez for at once being a devoted Fidelista and having two mansions, one in Havana and the other in Mexico City, in the exclusive southern San Angel section. Don't his material circumstances contradict his ideological beliefs? García Márquez turns to another subject every time the question is asked. But this apparent tension between lifestyle and politics is prevalent among famous Latin American intellectuals of the seventies: to act as the voice of the people, to attack the government, to promulgate left-wing views has never required that one's daily domestic life be reduced to the bare essentials. It's an irony that becomes all the more evident among exiled scholars and writers who for decades have portrayed the United States as an imperialist aggressor but who, when the time comes to escape from a repressive regime, avail themselves of the safe haven offered by the U.S. academy: a comfortable salary at a college or university.

García Márquez, in many ways, epitomizes this outrageous behavior. While he never stayed at an American campus for a long period of time because of problems with the Immigration and Naturalization Service, he is a symbol of lavish lifestyle and anachronistic Franciscan principles: the revolutionary struggle amid champagne glasses.

After his stay in New York, García Márquez settled in Mexico and was largely inactive as a writer, devoting himself exclusively to gestating Macondo in his own mind. His novella *In Evil Hour* had won an obscure prize, sponsored by Esso in Colombia. Through an ambassador, he was sent word that the award would be his if he agreed to eliminate a couple of "nasty" words: "prophylactic" and "masturbate." In reply, he agreed to censor only one, whichever the ambassador wished. The transcript was sent to Spain to be printed, and a copy editor, to make the style Iberian, changed the wording of his sentences. When García Márquez saw the final product, he was furious. In the Mexican edition of 1966 and the one he considered "official," he added an author's note stating that the text had been restored to its original form.

The mythical Macondo acquired its structure in the stories of *Big Mama's Funeral*. Critics mistakenly claim *No One Writes to the Colonel* and *In Evil Hour* take place in it, when, in fact, as George R. McMurray has shown, their setting is a town, probably Sucre, farther inland in the coastal region. In their exuberant *Dictionary of Imaginary Places*, Alberto Manguel and Gianni Guadalupi describe Macondo "as a Colombian village founded in ancient times by José Arcadio Buendía, whose boundless imagination always stretched farther than the inventiveness of nature." Its apex occurs between 1915 and 1918, during the height of the banana plantations. Toward the east, as Manguel and Guadalupi have mapped it, the town is protected by a high and forbidding range of hills and, toward the south, by marshes covered with a kind of vegetable soup. Toward the west the marshes give way to a large body of water in which cetaceans of delicate skin, with the face and torso of a woman, lure sailors with their firm and tempting breasts. To the north, many days' march away through a dangerous jungle, lies the sea. Among Macondo's most notable events is the unusual insomnia epidemic that strikes the entire population: the most terrible effect isn't the impossibility of sleep—because the body does not tire either—but the gradual loss of memory. When a sick person becomes accustomed to staying awake, memories of his childhood start to vanish, followed by names and concepts of things. With self-reflecting mirrors and all, the novel's self-reflecting ending is simply remarkable:

> Macondo was already a fearful whirlwind of dust rubble being spun about by the wrath of the biblical hurricane when Aureliano shipped eleven pages so as not to lose time with facts he knew only too well, and he began to decipher the instant that he was living, deciphering it as he lived it, prophesying himself in the act of deciphering the last page of the parchments, as if he were looking into a speaking mirror. Then he skipped again to anticipate the predictions and ascertain the date and circumstances of his death. Before reaching the final line, however, he had already understood that he would never leave that room, for it was foreseen that the city of mirrors would be wiped out by the wind and exiled from the memory of men at the precise moment when Aureliano Babilonia would finish deciphering the parchments, and that everything written on them was unrepeatable since time immemorial and forever more, because race condemned to one hundred years of solitude did not have a second opportunity on earth.

The legend behind the final shaping of Macondo has come to be referred to, by García Márquez and others who know him, simply as "the miracle." It took place in 1965, on the road from Mexico City to Acapulco in the family's Opel. Suddenly, as the writer puts it, the entire first chapter appeared to him, and he immediately felt he was prepared to write the rest of the story. Afterwards he told an Argentine friend that if he had had a tape recorder in the car, he would have dictated the chapter right then and there. Instead of continuing on to Acapulco, he decided to turn around and seclude himself completely for a year. He asked Mercedes, his wife, not to interrupt him for any reason, especially where bills were concerned, and indeed she protected him fully. When the novel was finished, the García Márquezes were $12,000 in debt; to tide themselves over, Mercedes had asked their friends for loans (according to Vargas Llosa, it was around $10,000). Soon rumors of the book's qualities began to circulate: Carlos Fuentes and Julio Cortázar, who had read pieces of the manuscript before it was finished, were so excited they praised it highly in articles and reviews. And so, by the time *One Hundred Years of Solitude* was published in May 1967 by Editorial Sudamericana, it ignited the literary world, and García Márquez, at thirty-nine, became an instant international celebrity. The first edition sold out in a few days, and the novel sold half a million copies in three and a half years, a huge sum for any Spanish book anywhere in the Hispanic world. He immediately began to receive honorary degrees and prizes: the Rómulo Gallegos award; the Prix du Meilleur Livre Étranger in France; the Italian Chianchiano Prize; the Neustadt Prize by the magazine *Book Abroad* (now *World Literature Today*); the National Book Award to Gregory Rabassa for the English translation; and, a bit more than a decade later, the Nobel Prize. (Five Latin Americans have now received it: before him, Gabriela Mistral, Pablo Neruda, and Miguel Ángel Asturias; after, Octavio Paz.)

Does someone capable of creating a book of such caliber have a second such opportunity on earth? Having set the standard sky-high, he has written nothing since 1967 that seems fully satisfying. While some maintain that a bad García Márquez is extraordinary by other people's standards, it is clear that the Colombian has always been haunted by his masterpiece's overwhelming success. His method of writing has also changed over the decades. He can spend long seasons without putting a word on paper, and then, during creative periods, write eight to ten pages each day from sunrise to noon. His paragraphs are extremely polished, the opposite of André Breton's idea of automatic writing, which Jack Kerouac and the Beat Generation took to an extreme. The dialogue is infrequent but crisp and full of parables and metaphors. In the age of mechanical typewriters and liquid corrector, he claims to have rewritten *No One Writes to the Colonel* a total of nine times. "I had the impression I was writing it in French," he once said, as if after so many rewritings his native tongue had become alien to him, and pure technique ended up shaping the book. He took a similar approach with future books, until the late seventies, when he bought a word processor. Considered by many his second best title—a distant second, though—*Love in the Time of Cholera* was published in 1985. It is a romance of sorts (according to Salman Rushdie, "a masterful revamping of the genre") encapsulating the affair of García Márquez's parents from their youth to their eighties. Written with the help of a computer, the book retains his typically labyrinthine paths of fantasy, but the texture seems a bit removed, less immediate than that in *One Hundred Years of Solitude*. The protagonists are Fermina Daza, who is married to Doctor Juvenal Urbino de la Calle, and Florentino Ariza, who has a crush on her that lasts, in one of the novelist's typical phrases, "fifty three years, seven months, and eleven days." Many biographical elements are included: the telegraph, a Flaubertian doctor who functions as a voice of reason, a critique of religion, and an unrelenting love beyond all odds.

A succession of repetitive, structurally overdone narratives has steadily issued from the Colombian's pen since 1967. Predictably, their reception nevertheless has been enthusiastic, as if anything produced by García Márquez, no matter the quality, is to be applauded. The truth is, his magnum opus had satisfied and engrossed so many readers that each new narrative became legendary even before it could reach the bookstores.

The novelist's lifelong interest in continental history is apparent in his 1975 experimental novel *Autumn of the Patriarch*, a favorite of such postcolonial critics as Edward Said but, to my mind, too allegorical, too boring. The book was also a disappointment to those expecting another installment of the Buendía saga. One of about a half a dozen Latin American narratives about dictators (others include Alejo Carpentier's *Reasons of State*, Augusto Roa Bastos's *I, the Supreme*,

Tomás Eloy Martínez's *The Perón Nobel*, and Miguel Ángel Asturias's *El Señor Presidente*), the novel deals with a tyrant's relentless desire to accumulate power and narrates his obsessive love affair with Manuela Sanchez, the status of "civil sanctity" given to his ailing mother, and his final demise. Already close to his hundredth birthday, he marries Leticia Nazareno and has a child with her, only to find mother and child assassinated, their bodies ripped apart by dogs at a public plaza. Contrary to common belief, García Márquez did not base the story and its protagonist solely on Gustavo Rojas Pinilla and his military regime in Colombia but also on the Venezuelan *caudillo* Juan Vicente Gómez. "My intention," he once said, "was always to make a synthesis of all the Latin American dictators, but especially those from the Caribbean."

Another unbalanced text is *Chronicle of a Death Foretold*, published in 1981, shortly before the announcement of the Nobel Prize. Built as a detective story in reverse, it describes the assassination of Santiago Nasar, accused of deflowering Angela Vicario, who is hence unable to marry Bayardo San Román. Everybody in town knows Nasar will be killed, but nobody does a thing. The story is told from the point of view of a journalist, a chronicler who years later returns to the place to unveil the truth. As Raymond L. Williams has shown, the novella is based on real events reported by *El Día* in Bogotá in 1981:

> In the municipality of Sucre . . . the elders still remember with horror the rainy morning of January 22, 1951, in which a young man . . . Cayetano Gentile Chimento, twenty-two years old, medical student at the Javeriana University in Bogotá and heir of the town's largest fortune, fell butchered by machete, innocent victim of a confused duel of honor, and without knowing for sure why he was dying. Cayetano was killed by Víctor and Joaquín Chica Salas, whose sister Margarita, married the previous day with Miguel Reyes Palencia and returned to her family by her husband the same night of the marriage, accused Cayetano of being the author of the disgrace that had prevented her being a virgin at her marriage.

García Márquez re-creates the events by mixing sex and exoticism, and filtering it all through the surreal prism of his imagination. According to William H. Gass, the novel is not told but pieced together like a jigsaw. The result, although entertaining, is another minor work in the novelist's corpus.

In some ways a remarkably ordinary man by all accounts, the Colombian is, and will always be, an object of rumors. According to Roger Straus, when, to celebrate the centennial of the world's most important awards, the Nobel committee decided to invite every awardee from around the globe (paying handsomely for everybody's room and board), García Márquez alone refused the invitation—unless he received a payment of $10,000, which was not forthcoming. But perhaps the most convoluted of the legends surrounding him is his friendship with Mario Vargas Llosa. They met in Caracas and moved together to Bogotá and Lima, where they participated in a symposium on the novel (published as *The Latin American Novel: A Dialogue* [1968]). Alongside José Donoso, Fuentes, and Cortázar, they are part of the so-called Latin American boom of the sixties. The Peruvian, of course, wrote the previously mentioned *History of a Deicide*, a 667-page literary study of the Colombian's life and oeuvre, submitted originally as a doctoral dissertation at Madrid's Universidad Central. They shared a room in Mexico's capital, but then, some time in the seventies, a fight erupted at Cine Lido, in which Vargas Llosa punched García Márquez for circulating tales about an (unconfirmed) extramarital affair with a Nordic model. Since then, they have not spoken to each other. Others claim it was their politics that created a rupture: after the 1959 Cuban Revolution, Vargas Llosa, like Octavio Paz, slowly grew disenchanted with Fidel Castro's worldview and soon became an enemy, his ideology today being center-right.

As the leading voice of the Latin American narrative boom of the sixties, García Márquez is the decisive force and influence behind Salman Rushdie, Anton Shammas, Isabel Allende, Oscar Hijuelos, Laura Esquivel, and scores of other writers who came to prominence from the seventies onward. His craft so uniquely mixes magic, hyper-realism, and exotic dreamlike images that one could thank him for having finally put Latin America, long a forgotten part of the world, back on the map. Of course, by the same token, one could also accuse the Colombian of having distorted the hemisphere's reality by reducing it to a theater of clairvoyant prostitutes, opinionated matrons, and corrupt generals. He turned Latin America into a distraction—a chimera, a magical creation.

Today, unfortunately, his decline is not only creative but physical. Around 1991 news began to circulate that García Márquez was sick with cancer. In spite of his reclusiveness, the Associated Press announced a serious medical operation in Colombia. How serious the illness was is anybody's guess. In fact, when *Strange Pilgrims*, an unremarkable compilation of tales written from 1974 on, appeared a year later, people talked about a hidden desire on his part to sum up, to leave the desk clean. His next project, his American editor claims, is a memoir. Although in photographs and public appearances the writer looks healthy, what is unquestionable is his exhaustion. Since *Love in the Time of Cholera* and perhaps even before, he has not seemed at the peak of his power; his creativity seems diminished by an exhausted imagination.

And yet, anybody ready to count him out makes a big mistake. In early 1994, for instance, in a renewed display of stamina, he published a short novel: *Del amor y otros demonios*. Set on the Caribbean coast during the colonial period, it describes a passionate affair, under the shadow of the Church, between a young girl, Sierva María de Todos los Angeles, a saint adored for her many miracles but who supposedly was possessed by the devil, and her exorcist. While García Márquez's story is engaging and well-crafted, it ultimately becomes a showcase of his recent excesses: an overly compressed style that creates a sense of suffocation in the reader, a plot that seems flat, and a lack of spontaneity in the prose that ends up undermining any kind of suspense.

The rumor that he is writing a memoir, which he once claimed in an

El País interview would be structured theatrically and not chronologically, raises the expectation of his turning his personal odyssey into literature; and it is obvious that the Colombian himself understands now the imminence of his fate. The closeness of death provides an opportunity for him to wrap up and reshape reminiscences, to translate the past into a historical record. He is ready to consummate his act of fabricating his own heroic destiny by stamping his signature on everything he did and did not do, or preferred never to have done. But most important, he, the person and the persona, knows he has already entered the pantheon of literary giants and wants full control, in death as in life, of everything that has to do with his life and craft. The Hispanic world keeps a double standard regarding biographies and autobiographies. As is the way with confessional genres, they do what Hispanic society otherwise wholeheartedly discourages: to make public what is private, to forsake intimacy for extroversion. And yet, the extraordinary attention that the narrative boom of the sixties received has persuaded many to control memory, to stop cultural thieves from dismantling the mythical aura with which experiences were lived: José Donoso has written a personal recollection of the boom years, originally published in English in *TriQuarterty*; Heberto Padilla did his part in *Self-Portrait of the Other*; in 1993, Mario Vargas Llosa wrote *The Fish in the Water*, a self-serving study of his first twenty-two years, including a detailed recollection of his campaign as a presidential candidate in 1990; Borges, in collaboration with Norman Thomas Di Giovanni, wrote his "Autobiographical Essay" for the *New Yorker*, and Reinaldo Arenas, the talented Cuban exile who died in New York City, denounced every one of his enemies in *Before Night Fall*. As a fiesta of intellectual rebirth, the sixties and seventies in Latin America are emerging as one of the most exciting periods in the region's cultural history. And García Márquez's authoritative voice is probably destined to become the chronicle against which everything else is to be judged. Yet biographical accounts revisiting the period, in Spanish or for that matter any language, are almost nonexistent: Emir Rodríguez Monegal wrote *Jorge*

Luis Borges: A Literary Biography for Dutton in 1978, but that's about it. While Norman Mailer, a lover of scandals, has already been written about in several biographies, official and unauthorized—as have Paul Bowles, Saul Bellow, and J. D. Salinger—south of the Rio Grande, little, if anything, has been written about Julio Cortázar, an experimentalist who wrote "Blow-Up" and died in 1984, Manuel Puig, and Juan Rulfo, not to mention Fuentes, Vargas Llosa, and, of course, the creator of Macondo himself.

Physical or creative decadence aside, *One Hundred Years of Solitude*, which, in John Barth's words, is "as impressive a novel as has been written so far in the second half of our century and one of the splendid specimens of that splendid genre," will no doubt remain resplendent with prestige. Its existence alone more than justifies the Colombian's days and nights. John Leonard once wrote that "with a single bound García Márquez leaps onto the stage with Günter Grass and Vladimir Nabokov, his appetite as enormous as his imagination, his fatalism greater than either." If it weren't for this larger-than-life novel, Latin America's prominence on the literary map would be much diminished. And if he has often failed to live up to the supernal standards he set himself, that achievement alone ought to keep García Márquez on the bookshelves of humankind for a long time to come. Redemption through a single artistic stroke, the overcoming of death through memory: What else can a writer desire?

First published in *Michigan Quarterly* XXXIV, 2 (Spring 1995). From *Art and Anger: Essays on Politics and the Imagination*, 41-67. Copyright © 1996 by the University of New Mexico Press. Reprinted by permission.

Remedios the Child Bride:
The Forgotten Buendía_____

Amy M. Green

In the constellation of women in *One Hundred Years of Solitude*, Remedios the Beauty, in contrast with the matriarch Úrsula Iguarán and the clairvoyant prostitute Pilar Ternera, is among García Márquez's most celebrated creations. Amy M. Green's analysis focuses on the character's name as well as on her actions. Remedios "drives the village's men to insanity and the women to distraction as they try to cover her nudity." She represents purity, even a celestial virginity, yet, in Green's view, Remedios's quiet presence drowns beneath the weight of other, more emphatic characters.   — I.S.

Colonel Aureliano descends into an intense infatuation with the youngest Moscote daughter, Remedios. Although the narrator claims that after Aureliano met Remedios, the Buendía "house became full of love" (65), Aureliano acts more like a man fascinated by something shiny, new, and untouched. Lust might be a better descriptor than love. As much as Aureliano turns her into a sort of child-doll-wife, Remedios ironically moves her own collection of dolls into the marital bedroom, presumably to admire their delicate beauty but where they remain well past her death until they turn into a moldering, rotting pile. Aureliano at first appears motivated by a desire to craft a wife entirely by his own hand and force of will. After all, he teaches the young girl to read and write and thus immediately has the power to restrict or recommend various reading materials. Although Aureliano never physically or emotionally mistreats his young wife, and perhaps García Márquez wants the reader to take this point cynically, as Remedios dies early on in their marriage, he nonetheless assumes the role of father-husband-teacher. However, García Márquez resists turning Remedios into an infantile, victimized child, although those elements certainly surround her marriage to Aureliano, given that he waits until the moment she reaches sexual maturity and then immediately claims her as wife. Instead, Remedios emerges as a strong young woman versed in proper behavior and seemingly possessed of the means to unite the fragmented pieces of the Buendía family. However, such a task falls far beyond the grasp of any female character in the novel, even the hyper-controlled Fernanda and the omnipresent Úrsula. The women attempt to maintain home and hearth throughout the novel while the men wander, battle, and perish violently, but the members of each successive generation of Buendías emerge as "degenerated forms" (Taylor 101) beyond the help of any matriarchal force. Remedios, a selfless force of light in the Buendía household and representative of a true source of redemption for the family line, therefore must not only perish shortly into her marriage to Aureliano but also must fail to leave a lasting legacy for the Buendías to come. Her regenerative potential as woman and wife can never come to fruition.

Remedios dies in grotesque fashion, "soaked in a hot broth which had exploded in her insides with a kind of tearing belch . . . with a pair of twins crossed in her stomach" (86). Although she will hardly be the first casualty of the story, her death strikes the reader as especially vivid. García Márquez provides horror for nearly every sense, from touch to smell, sound, and sight. Little Remedios, who just a short time earlier triumphantly paraded the soiled panties heralding the coming of her first period, now lies a broken and twisted heap of flesh corrupted by sexual contact with Aureliano. Furthermore, she dies with her unborn children inside of her, taking with her the only possibility of passing down her genes into the next generation. Certainly, her young body did not yet have the physical stamina needed to carry twins to term, regardless of the onset of menstruation. Yet on a deeper level, her death signals the loss of the possibility for the Buendías to rise up out of the cycles of insanity, violence, and solitude that have plagued them generation after generation. Remedios serves as a bridge across the solitary world of the tree-bound José Buendía, for example, through the simple act of bringing him a large slice of wedding cake even though he remains physically separated from the ceremony. She also focuses Aureliano's attention, at least for a time, away from revolution, war, and whores.

Her lasting influence, however, proves fleeting. Úrsula demands that Remedios's daguerreotype be placed prominently on display, but the ensuing generations cannot connect with the past. Instead, "they were never able to connect her with the standard image of a great-grandmother" (88) and thus begin to regard her as a sort of curiosity rather than as the self-possessed young woman who honored José Buendía and, for a time, lessened the feuding between Rebeca and Amaranta. The daguerreotype fixes her in history, but in the worst possible way. She exists forever as an anachronism, the strange little woman whose dolls rot away unused. The newer generations can forge no tie to this aspect of their aspect, and thus her influence remains confined to the boundaries of a picture frame wherein her history both begins and ends. Colonel Aureliano attempts to hurry along the burying of Remedios's memory by demanding that Úrsula burn "the poems inspired by Remedios" (124). His demands, however, do not stem from an overwhelming sense of grief. Of the loss of his wife, Colonel Aureliano feels only "a dull feeling of rage that gradually dissolved in a solitary and passive frustration" (94). By seeking to burn written acts of commemoration of his relationship with Remedios, the Colonel loosens the ties of her calming influence and places himself in a prime position to beget seventeen sons by different mothers.

As with other characters in the novel, Remedios does have her name passed down twice, albeit to frustrating ends. Fernanda opts to name her daughter Renata Remedios instead of Remedios, relegating the namesake to the middle position, easily and often forgotten. The second namesake, Remedios the Beauty, emerges as a bizarre creature "thought to be mentally retarded" (163). She spends her days playing with her own excrement, reveling in her nudity, and driving the men of Macondo wild with the odor that exudes, saintlike, from her body.

However bizarre her behavior may be, Remedios the Beauty is only mistaken for being mentally defective. Instead, she chooses at some level to cast off the external trappings of society and plays only by her own rules. She cuts her luxurious mane of hair short so as not to be bothered with having to maintain it. Later, when forced to cover her nudity, she eschews fashionable clothing in favor of a simple cassock. Remedios the Beauty tempts men and drives them in some cases to their deaths, but without any conscious action on her part. Of all the characters in the novel, Remedios the Beauty best escapes the chains of society and of the troubled Buendía legacy. She is "apparently a being totally lacking in the capacity for memory" (Taylor 102) and thus she transcends the weight of the history eating away at women like Fernanda and Úrsula. Thus, Remedios the Beauty leaves the novel by ascending to the heavens while clutching a bed sheet, leaving no physical memorial behind.

Certainly, Remedios the Beauty does not in any way provide peace to the Buendías as she drives the village's men to insanity and the women to distraction as they try to cover her nudity. Tellingly, the nearly wild Remedios the Beauty, whose "deadly nature reveals itself through fragrance" (Hoffman-Jeep 290), ascends into the heavens bodily and unscathed, rather than Fernanda, genuinely devout if not severe and cold. There exists something reminiscent of the serpent and Eve-as-temptress conflated together about Remedios the Beauty. After all, consciously or not, she lures men to their doom, tempting them with the possibility of sex yet ultimately gifting them with frustration or death. However, for Remedios the Beauty to be a true temptress would require that she be conscious on some level of the power she wields. Unlike the serpent in the Garden, she makes no verbal enticements. Macondo's men come to Remedios the Beauty, and sometimes their doom, solely on their own and need no persuasion to do so. She remains unconnected to all those around her, even family, and as such "is also a *reductio ad absurdum* of the notion of the intrinsic merit of virginity" (Penuel 558). She does not participate in the daily life of

Macondo and does not serve as an example to the village's young women. She remains a virgin, but without any understanding of the power inherent in that status, or of the lengths the men of the town would go to claim her virginity. She lives a life of her own choosing and thus escapes the shackles of history.

García Márquez's choice of the name "Remedios," which translates to "help" or "remedy," proves insightful for an understanding of both young Remedios and Remedios the Beauty within the context of *One Hundred Years of Solitude*. The name proves more potent still owing to its association with the Virgin Mary, often referred to as *Nuestra Señora de los Remedios*. This association with the Virgin Mary and the implication of her holy intervention makes little Remedios all the more tragic. Not only does her premature marriage to Colonel Aureliano rob her early of her virginity, but also her valiant attempts to save the family ultimately prove fruitless. Remedios the Beauty, virginal only through the stalwart attempts of Fernanda and Úrsula to keep at bay the local men who might otherwise have taken her by force, provides an ironic connection to the Virgin Mary. Like Mary, Remedios the Beauty ascends bodily into heaven, a mark of holding great favor with the divine. However, Remedios the Beauty never displays the level of religious devotion Fernanda does. The reader can only imagine Fernanda's internal dialogue and sense of entitlement as Remedios the Beauty waves goodbye as she travels upward to heaven. Remedios the Beauty certainly does not make any attempt to redeem the Buendía line, nor does she add to it with her own progeny.

García Márquez provides the possibility for family peace and solidarity in the strangest of packages through Remedios the child bride. By first having her die with her children in her womb, then later by depicting her increasing lack of influence over the family, the author demonstrates the power of solitude. Nearly all the novel's characters participate in or contribute to "a lack of consciousness . . . [the] incapacity to see economic, political, and cultural structures behind the apparent reality and activities of daily life" (Taylor 98), and their collective power proves overwhelming. Remedios's gentle ministrations to the family and her quiet presence drown beneath the weight of the Buendía legacy.

Works Cited

García Márquez, Gabriel. *One Hundred Years of Solitude*. 1967. New York: HarperCollins, 2006.

Hoffman-Jeep, Lynda. "Plotting a Misogynistic Path to Christian Dior's Poison." *Western Folklore* 55.4 (Autumn 1996): 281-96.

Penuel, Arnold M. "Death and the Maiden: Demythologization of Virginity in García Márquez's *Cien años de soledad*." *Hispania* 66.4 (Dec. 1983): 552-60.

Taylor, Anna Marie. "*Cien años de soledad*: History and the Novel." *Latin American Perspectives* 2.3 (Autumn 1975): 96-112.

García Márquez's Investigation of Cold War Soviet Europe:
Its Cervantine Invocation_____

John Cussen

In an analysis of one of García Márquez's lesser-known works, his travelogue of a ninety-day journey behind the Iron Curtain, John Cussen looks at the narrative—though not exclusively, avoiding overemphasis—through the prism of *Don Quixote de La Mancha*, a book frequently invoked, by way of comparison, in any appraisal of the Colombian writer's oeuvre. — I.S.

The early reference to Miguel de Cervantes's *Don Quixote de La Mancha* in Gabriel García Márquez's Cold War travelogue *De viaje por los países socialistas: 90 días en la cortina de hierro* [*A Journey Through the Socialist Countries: 90 Days Behind the Iron Curtain*] alerts us to the breadth of quixotic principle that has for several centuries infused travel writing texts. In other words, it calls to mind the countless travel-text protagonists who have stood on the fault lines that separate fact and fiction, observation and illusion, individual/observed truth and official/cultural truth, and so on, and, as a result, not known in which direction they were turned. The reference also recalls *Don Quixote*'s prima facie moral warnings regarding the danger of believing what one reads and the danger of going anywhere with fixed ideas. These themes, which are pervasive in the whole history of travel writing, are also among García Márquez's primary concerns in *90 días*. Finally, the allusion notifies us of the fact that, through much of his journey, García Márquez is not traveling alone. He has a foil, albeit a like-minded one, a fellow leftist and *mamagallista* against whose observations and prejudices his own might be checked. This last feature of *90 días* puts it in one of travel writing's understudied sectors, namely, accounts of journeys made by a traveler and his or her sidekick.

The reference is slight but unmistakable. It occurs in the text's second paragraph, in which the narrator identifies himself and his companion travelers:

> Eramos tres a la aventura. Jacqueline, francesa de origen indochino, diagramadora en una revista de París. Un italiano errante, Franco, corresponsal occasional de revistas milanesas, domiciliado donde lo sorprenda la noche. El tercera era yo, según está escrito en mi pasaporte. (9)

> [We were three in this adventure. Jacqueline, a French girl of South Asian origin and a graphic artist for a Parisian magazine. An errant Italian, Franco, a freelancer to Milanese magazines, housed wherever the night surprised him. The third was myself, so subscribed in my passport.]

At the outset of any *aventura*, the word *errante*, for Spanish speakers as much as for English speakers, calls to mind Cervantes's Don Quixote, "el ingenioso hidalgo de la Mancha" [the ingenious gentleman of La Mancha], whose eyes notoriously played second fiddle to his book-inspired visions. I say "for Spanish speakers as much as for English speakers" because, of course, the word with a more direct Cervantine lineage would be *andante*, as in *caballero andante* [knight errant]; however, *knight errant*'s ubiquity in English-language references to the roving protagonists of medieval romances as well as to Don Quixote himself, coupled with the same term's frequent reversion to Spanish as *caballero errante*, warrant our thinking of the Don when García Márquez identifies his traveling companion as an *errante*. Also, of course, over *andante*, *errante* has the advantage of the additional connotations *misguided*, *delinquent*, and *self-absorbed*, all of which play some role in Franco's characterization. In short, from the moment the word *errante* appears in *90 días* through to the end of the text's Russian chapters (after which Franco is no longer involved in the book's action), we are inclined to think of the errant Italian freelancer as a version of the know-it-all squire of La Mancha, and to think of the quiet but observant narrator (García Márquez himself)—a workaday Colombian journalist with a peasant's moustache, rough dress, and zero pretensions (*90 días* 19)—as a descendant of Sancho Panza.

Other component pieces of *90 días*'s first chapters confirm the identification: "La ultima aldea del mundo occidental" (10) [The last village on the western frontier] resembles in its provincialism the whole of La Mancha, but most especially it has the feel of Don Quixote's unnamed homeplace, the "somewhere in La Mancha" whose name the *Quixote* narrator "does not care to remember" (I, 1; 19). In its surreal forsakenness, "la zona de nadie" [the no-man's land between West and East] and the miles of uncultivated terrain that succeed it (11) also look like the preternatural Manchegan mythscape. When his road divides in four, the Don memorably cedes the reins to Rocinante (I, 1; 34). Similarly, "en Alemania Oriental," says García Márquez, "se tiene la impresión de haber equivocado la ruta y de viajar por una autopista que no conduce a ninguna parte" (17) [in East Germany you feel as if you've lost your way and taken a highway that leads to nowhere]. Again, just as Don Quixote, his placaters, and his provokers all behave irrationally in La Mancha's archetypal landscapes (McKendrick 224-225), so, too, "en la frontera nos hacemos los locos" [in the frontier we go crazy], says Franco (11). Franco meets a girl in a tavern, and his heart rushes into his head (6). In the presence of women García Márquez, on the other hand, is like Sancho (I, 33 and II, 33), circumspect and deferential. He and they talk honestly to one another, with sex's spark of hope, perhaps, but not with its disorientations. He genuinely learns from them. Like the taverns in *Don Quixote*, those in *90 días* are home to deception and self-confession. Both Sancho Panza (II, 68; 903) and García Márquez (16) slump down and sleep without remorse whenever they are so inclined.

On the other hand, I would not wish to overstate the linkages between *90 días* and *Don Quixote*. To do so would be to mischaracterize García Márquez's early and only freestanding travel book, a work of more transparent journalistic than novelistic character. A serialized, ten-chapter, news-periodical travelogue, later published in book format with an additional eleventh chapter, *90 días* is not, to be sure, *Don Quixote*'s hall of mirrors, seventh degree of separation reunion, Arab's portfolio, farce, or tragedy. It is, instead, a more or less factual—yet also cobbled and fictionalized—account of three journeys into Soviet Europe and Russia made by its author during the era of his semi-exilic European sojourn from 1955 through 1957. On the first of those journeys, from Paris to East Germany, he was accompanied by his friend Plinio Apuleyo Mendoza, a Venezuelan journalist, and Mendoza's sister, Soledad. Later, after passing through Czechoslovakia, he and P. Mendoza attended an international youth festival in Moscow. Traveling alone, he made trips to Poland and Hungary. In the resultant group of serialized newspaper reports, García Márquez changed his companions' names in order to protect them and their families in South America from accusations of communism.

Other features of the trip were altered for thematic reasons. For one, García Márquez reorganized his journey's itinerary in order to alternate descriptions of failed Marxist states—East Germany and Poland—with the thriving countries of Czechoslovakia and Russia. For another, in both the original ten-installment, newsmagazine version of *90 días* and its later eleven-chapter book format, he so positioned the Russian chapters, anchored by his pilgrimage-like visit to Stalin's tomb, as to achieve a climactic, end-of-journey effect. Similarly, the book text's last chapter about conditions in Hungary after its 1956 revolution is strategically placed. "La moraleja es más bien clara," says Pedro Sorela, chronicler of García Márquez's early career. "En el socialismo hay problemas pero siempre se pueden resolver de una forma política" (200). [The moral is clear. With socialism there are always problems, but they can be resolved by politics.] Again, the subtitle affixed to the text's book version—*90 días en la cortina de hierro*—is more rhetorically than factually composed. For sure, neither the text's episodes nor the author's three real-life journeys took place in anything like three months. Therefore, we are safe in assuming that the title is designed to resonate with titles such as Jules Verne's *Around the World in Eighty Days*, in which case it anticipates both the book's epic and mock-epic contents, or, another possibility, it is designed to resonate with titles like fellow journalist Nellie Bly's *Around the World in Seventy-two Days*, in which case it speaks to journalism's inherently sensationalistic tendencies, a recurrent theme in García Márquez's nonfictional prose.

Few are *90 días*'s other transparently novelized features; indeed, one could argue that García Márquez has insufficiently fictionalized his text. In any event, beyond the early Cervantine invocations in character and in setting that I have just described, García Márquez does not conspicuously novelize his characters. Jacqueline (Soledad) is not Dulcinea del Toboso, though she does add a catalytic feminine element to the journey's first lugubrious inn scene, as well as to a subsequent tavern episode. Further, her presence is negligible in the text, not because parallels with *Don Quixote* require her absence but because in actual fact Soledad did not accompany her brother and his journalist friend in their later travels. In the steppes, Franco does not "cut capers" and act like a madman because he has read of prior tourists in Eastern Europe so behaving, though he does fall victim once to a woman's beauty. Again, García Márquez has not been seduced into the journey by promises of an island, though class differences between him and Franco are discernible. Once more, as history requires, in Poland and Hungary Franco drops completely out of the text, so there is no Quixote/Panza reverberation in those chapters. In Russia, Franco's is a marginal, subdued presence; again, little two-traveler reverberation is found in those pages.

Still, the salutatory *errante* of *90 días*'s second paragraph is an unmistakable *Quixote* reference. It is, on one hand, a telling suggestion of García Márquez's frame of mind as he begins traveling and writing his first and only travel book; on the other hand, it is a summoning bell clap at the work's outset, alerting readers to the text's Cervantine dynamics. Further, though it is only a light, introductory chime tap, one whose ring gradually fades, it alerts readers to the agency of at least three quintessentially Quixotian dynamics in the text: the tension between reality and illusion, the importance of the protagonist-sidekick relationship, and the author's awareness of print materials'—especially official, propagandistic print materials'—deceptions. Or, if we imagine the invocation from the writer's perspective, it is the first-page authorial tremor that courses through García Márquez's nervous system as he begins his journey into the bifurcated, Cold War planet's oft-maligned, ill-lit, and forbidding Soviet sector and/or begins writing his first travel book. As he goes into his journey/text, he anticipates dream-like scenes; he is wary of the West's and the Soviet's mind-altering propaganda; and he is glad for the company of a traveling companion against whose perceptions he can measure his own. In sum, he feels the quixotic principles that have for several centuries infused travel writing texts.

But why, then, is Franco *un italiano errante* rather than *un español errante*, as the reference to Cervantes's hero would seem to require? In a necessary coda to this essay, I explain why—because tremors emanating from the works of archetypal travel writer Dante and counter-cultural journalist Malaparte also course through García Márquez's nerves as he begins traveling and writing—and I explain, too, how García Márquez succeeds in investing Franco with three antecedent prototypes without cluttering his text's allusional mapping. However, before going to those materials, we move first to the question of the allusion's importance regarding *90 días*'s contemporary scholarly understanding and then to the fuller, more solid presentation of this essay's basic insight, namely, that the allusion represents García Márquez's insight that to write a book of travel is to take on the issues of reality versus illusion, of truth versus text, and of ego versus perspective that are archetypally handled in the fictional travel novel *Don Quixote*.

Import: *90 días*/García Márquez

What are the scholarly arguments about *90 días* that the recognition of this midcentury travel text's Cervantine features helps settle? About *90 días* and about the thirty-year-old García Márquez who wrote it, scholarship has put forward two contending opinions. On one side, foundational García Márquez biographer Mario Vargas Llosa (1971) and his late-century successor Dasso Saldívar (1997) have written that the Colombian journalist in para-exile, an ingrained deplorer of the Western, capitalist hegemony and an alleged *comunista*, succeeded in putting aside his core neocolonial antipathies as he traveled through Europe's Soviet sector. He succeeded, they say, in opening himself up to his journey's lessons and succeeded, thereby, in constructing an eminently fair and varied travel text (Vargas Llosa 52). For Vargas Llosa and for Saldívar the evidence of García Márquez's impartiality is in the quantity of social ills he spots and reports in Europe's Soviet sector. In the following passage, for example, Saldívar calls our attention to the quantity of negatives in García Márquez's account of his crossing from West to East Berlin:

> Los guardias de la frontera le parecieron 'inhábiles y medio analfabetos'; el director de aduanas era 'rústico en formas y maneras'; por la mañana, los alemanes orientales le parecieron 'gente estragada, amargada, que consume sin ningún entusiasmo una espléndida ración matinal de carne y huevos fritos'; . . . a excepción del 'colosal mamarracho' de la avenida de Stalin, donde vivían los once mil obreros del privilegio burocrático, la mayoría de los berlineses orientales residían todavía en los edificios sin reconstruir, y eran 'sordidos' y consumían 'artículos de mal gusto' y 'de una calidad mediocre'; y le resultó 'incomprensible que el pueblo de Alemania Oriental hubiera tomado el poder, los medios de producción, el comercio, la banca, las comunicaciones, y sin embargo fuera una pueblo triste, el pueblo más triste que yo había visto jamás.' (353-54)

[The border guards seemed to him "incapable and semi-illiterate"; the customs director "was a rustic in his manners and procedures"; in the morning East Germans seemed to him "a devastated, bitter people who consumed without the least bit of enthusiasm a splendid morning ration of meat and fried eggs"; . . . in contrast with Stalin Avenue's "colossal sight," where eleven thousand workers of the privileged bureaucracy worked, the majority of Eastern Berliners still lived in unreconstructed buildings; they were "unwashed" and they bought "unappealing goods of mediocre quality"; in sum, he found it "incomprehensible that the people of East Germany had taken hold of the power, the means of production, commerce, banks, communications, and nevertheless were a sad people, the saddest people [he] had ever seen."]

On the other hand, others say that García Márquez's fairness is feigned and that his ultimate reconciliation of the gap between his leftist leanings and his observations—the notion that the Soviet Union's exported social structures were not genuinely Marxist but, instead, Marxism's catastrophically defensive antithesis—is facile. This sounds like a negative judgment, and it is when delivered by Sorela, who metes out to the young Colombian only the damning credit of having achieved "una honestidad periodistica dificilmente igualable entre los periodístas de izquierda de esa época" (200) [a level of honesty only arduously achieved by leftist journalists of the era], following this narrow commendation with several paragraphs descriptive of *90 días*'s reportorial deficiencies, among them, an inaccurate description of the Berlin Wall, exaggeration of the Soviet sphere's accomplishments, rationalization of its failures, and complete whitewash of Stalin's malevolence (200-205). In contrast, Jacques Gilard, the editor of García Márquez's early journalism, sees virtue in García Márquez's supposed refusal to admit disillusionment as he travels through a disappointing Eastern Europe. This refusal demonstrates his allegiance to his people's and his continent's anti-imperial values. Says Gilard, "A nivel humano, cultural, político, García Márquez sólo había viajado a confirmar lo que ya sabía. Antes de partir era ya todo un latinoamericano" (in García Márquez, *De Europa* 19). [On individual, cultural, and political levels, García Márquez went to Europe only to confirm what he already knew. . . . Before he left he was already through and through a Latin American.]

Importantly, Gilard lists the contents of García Márquez's "already knew": "el estancamiento de Europa, el ascenso del socialismo, el despertar de las colonias, más allá de su América subdesarrollada" (19) [Europe's exhaustion, socialism's ascent, and the colonies' awakening, Latin America's undeveloped nations among them]. To that list, we might add Sorela's itemization of the same: ideological optimism, faith in the revolutionary process, anti-imperialism, and anti-Yankeeism (200). However, we do even better to recall the historic and personal sources of García Márquez's core political beliefs—in other words, the imbibed facts of his continent's, his people's, and his own history. Among other things, as a Colombian he had absorbed the story of Theodore Roosevelt's fomentation of separatist movements in what was once Colombia's Isthmus of Darien in order to set up there a puppet state amenable to his canal plans. In his autobiography, *Living to Tell the Tale*, García Márquez blames this land grab for much of Colombia's isolation from the larger world community (450). As a native of Aracataca, he had internalized the story of nearby Ciénaga's 1928 Banana Strike, which ended with the massacre of hundreds, perhaps thousands, of Colombian plantation workers by troops shooting on behalf of U.S. economic interests; and as a South American, he had contemplated to their abysmally offensive core dozens of other historic instances of North American heavy-handedness in the geopolitical region that was his birthplace. Then, too, there was the horror of *la violencia*, which raged savagely in the seven years prior to the *El Espectador* reporter's departure. To this conflagration's Conservative side, the United States contributed at the very least its alarmist anti-Communist, Cold War rhetoric. Again, García Márquez came to maturity as nativists and Marxists around the world developed the political philosophies and revolutionary rhetorics that would support anti-Western liberation movements as diverse as Sandino's, Perón's, Abbas's, Sukarno's, Ho Chi Minh's, Nasser's, and Nkrumah's (Westad 72-110). He was born two years after Fidel Castro, in the same year as Che Guevara. For all of these reasons, García Márquez went to Europe "ya todo un latinoamericano," as Gilard says, and neither the wonders of Western Europe's reconstruction nor the debacle of a counter, Soviet empire's social and political misadministration in Eastern Europe could cause him to budge from his opinions.

No, says the Cervantine allusion on *90 días*'s first page. Going into his East European tour, García Márquez was at the very least aware of ideology's and travel's inimicality. Also the invocation tells us that he was prepared to be disoriented by his journey. Lastly, it tells us that he will travel more like Sancho Panza than Don Quixote, attentive to reality as he meets it, rather than to his own favored construct of reality.

There is another reason we bother today to return to García Márquez's Cold War travel text: because it helps settle a broader, parallel debate regarding the author's politics in general. On this broader plane the question is whether or not García Márquez's leftism, anti-imperialism, and anti-Yankeeism are inordinately adamantine—that is, whether or not they prevent him from thinking freely, seeing the world as it is, and writing a fiction commensurate with the world's political complexity. The specifics of this debate—rooted in García Márquez's writings and behaviors—can be read elsewhere (Bell-Villada; Stavans; Webb; Anderson, Simons). Suffice it to say that García Márquez's detractors in this regard are ambulatory. Characteristically, for example, they turned commemorations on the occasion of *One Hundred Years of Solitude*'s fortieth publication year into "a referendum on his ideology," says Ilan Stavans, and, more important, they are dependably quick to notice passages in the writer's fiction that seem more driven by his ideology than by his fiction's organic movements. Such is the reaction of *The National Review* critic Selden Rodman to the passage in

The General in His Labyrinth in which the dying Bólivar advises his aide Iturbide, "Don't stay with Urdaneta [Bolívar's friend and successor in Bogotá] and don't go with your family to the United States. It's omnipotent and terrible, and its tale of liberty will end in a plague of miseries for us all." The slight to the United States is gratuitous, Rodman says, an emanation of García Márquez's antipathy for "the bogeyman [us]" (89).

Spotting the Cervantine arrangements of a García Márquez travel text of fifty years ago will not settle the question of his politics' ordinate or inordinate influence on his fiction, but it will establish the fact that at a telling moment in his early career he made an honest effort to let go of his principles and to allow himself to experience the disorientations of a reality that challenged his politics.

Import: The Travel Genre

Lastly, we go back to *90 días*'s Cervantine invocation and arrangements because they call our attention to *Don Quixote*'s overlooked archetypal position in Western print culture's post-Renaissance travel writing tradition. Long overdue in travel writing scholarship is the pluralizing of the term "quixotic principle" and its application to the travel genre. Some background: Though the thought underlying the term *quixotic principle*—that all novels are in one way or another variations of Cervantes's masterpiece—was far from original to him, its first articulation is usually credited to Harvard English professor Harry Levin and his 1970 essay "The Quixotic Principle: Cervantes and Other Novelists." Indeed, as Levin defines the principle, he quotes George Bernard Shaw: The quixotic principle is "the rivalry between the real world and the representation that we make of it for ourselves" (58). Thus, any work of fiction whose conflict is engendered by its protagonist's failure to understand or deal adequately with the world he or she inhabits is essentially a Cervantine novel. In the case of *Don Quixote*, the hero gets a false sense of reality because he reads too much chivalric fiction. Levin draws from his midcentury bank of curricular and continental novels to demonstrate how many have been the landmark fictional protagonists whose lives might basically be described as efforts to move walls that refuse to budge.

One might repeat and update Levin's demonstration by citing novels more familiar to contemporary undergraduate readers and grouping their protagonists according to the personal or social attributes that lead them to know less or want more than their life stations require. To begin, *innocence* complicates the life of *Great Expectations*'s Pip, who knows too little about women, as well as that of *Pride and Prejudice*'s Elizabeth, who knows too little about men. *Faith in one's national mythology* causes *Babbitt*'s George F. to confuse happiness with financial achievement and domestic orderliness, while faith in their national beliefs moves both Fielding and Heaslop of *A Passage to India* to underrate the racism that is an operative ingredient in their own behaviors. *Mania* proves fatal for *Crime and Punishment*'s Raskolnikov, who, as a boost to his ego, fixates on murdering an elderly pawnbroker, and for *The Mosquito Coast*'s Allie Fox, whose obsessive distaste for American convenience and french fries causes him to abscond to South America. Novels that feature a hero and sidekick owe a particular debt to Cervantes (Dickens's *Pickwick Papers*, Twain's *Adventures of Huckleberry Finn*, Rowling's Harry Potter books), as do those that recount the misdeeds of characters whose ill-disciplined natures are inflamed by the reading of books or the watching of movies (Flaubert's *Madam Bovary* and Puig's *Betrayed by Rita Hayworth*), as do those, too, that present themselves as lost manuscripts or novels within novels (Hawthorne's *The Scarlet Letter*, Nabokov's *Lolita*, and García Márquez's *One Hundred Years of Solitude*).

Apart from the occasional employment of the adjective "quixotic" to describe travel writers and their journeys, contemporary travel writing scholarship has not paid much attention to *Don Quixote*'s archetypal place in the genre's culture. A cross-referenced search of the terms "*Don Quixote*" and "travel writing" in the Modern Language Association's electronic bibliography, for example, yields zero results. Replace the second term with "travel literature" and the results increase to four. Hulme and Youngs's *The Cambridge Companion to Travel Writing* names Cervantes in a sentence devoted not to his novel's archetypal influence on the genre but rather to chivalric literature's "more invisible" influence on imaginative travel than on actual travel texts (25). Almost as bad, Jennifer Speake's three-volume *Literature of Travel and Exploration: An Encyclopedia* contains no *Don Quixote* or Cervantes entries, though listings are granted to other imaginative writers whose nonfictional works have so inscribed themselves on Western civilization's cultural consciousness as to become archetypal texts, exercising their influence on travel's nonfiction writers as well as its fiction practitioners, among them Homer's *Odyssey*, Chaucer's *Canterbury Tales*, Dante's *La divina commedia*, Defoe's *Robinson Crusoe*, Swift's *Gulliver's Travels*, Verne's *Around the World in Eighty Days*, and Conrad's *Heart of Darkness*.

Welcome, then, is García Márquez's *errante*, for, in addition to signaling the importance in *90 días* of the three quintessentially Cervantine dynamics that function in his text, it reminds us of their importance in the whole history of the genre.

Beware the Printed, Official Text

Prominent in *Don Quixote*—as it has been in the whole history of travel writing, and as it is in *90 días*—is the admonition here used as a subhead: Beware the printed, official text. In *Don Quixote* Cervantes issues this warning against the literary genre that his own work parodies, that is, against the books of chivalry whose excessive reading causes the hidalgo Alonso Quixano's "brains to dry up" and, as the narrator says, to have "the strangest thought any lunatic in the world ever had, which was that it seemed reasonable and necessary to him, both for the sake of his honor and as a service to the nation, to become a knight errant and travel the world with his armor and his horse to seek adventures and engage in everything he had read that knights errants engaged in" (21). Also, as a result of spending too much time with these books, Quixano (now Don Quixote) sees the world and its every movable and immovable feature through chivalry's prism. He sees inns as castles, prostitutes as maidens, windmills as giants, monks as enchanters, herdsmen as unworthy knights, and Maritornes, the lusty, yet ugly, Asturian maid on her way to a muleteer's cot, as a love-smitten princess. These are his misperceptions because these are the images that have been planted in his head by books.

To make matters worse, his book-learned delusions are for two reasons impervious to correction: first, because his native ingeniousness makes him capable of reconstructing any and all real-world facts in the light of the chivalric world that he prefers, and second, because the books have also furnished his mind with an explanation of last resort, the notion of wicked enchanters. Supplied with this latter notion, his mind writes off as enchanters' delusions any real-world object or event that proves impervious to his reconstructions. Thus, because he has read deeply in books that do not merit his attention, delusions become reality and reality becomes a delusion in Don Quixote's mind. Of course, Cervantes has also written into his novel a fondness for chivalric literature and for the values its works encapsulate. However, when all is said and done in the novel—that is, after Don Quixote has been defeated by Sanson Carrasco posing as the Knight of the White Moon and has been obliged as a consequence to retire for one year from knight errantry (II, 64), and after the thus dispirited Don Quixote has heard the Lazarus-like Altisidora's description of hell as a place where devils play pelota with books "apparently of wind and trash" (II, 70), and, lastly, after Don Quixote's (now Quixano's) deathbed speech in which he proclaims his judgment "restored, free and clear of the dark shadows of ignorance imposed on it by [his] grievous and constant reading of detestable books of chivalry" (II, 74; 935)—it is clear that the book *Don Quixote*'s stronger purpose is not to commend books of chivalry but to indict them (Durán 91).

Another layer of Cervantes's caution against books can be discerned in the disparaging uses his *Quixote*'s Part II makes of Avellaneda's spurious sequel. The efforts that Don Quixote and Sancho make to lift from their personal histories the lies imposed on them by Avellaneda's sequel are authorially opportunistic, humorous, and entertaining, but they are also an expression of Cervantes's sense of having been wronged by a book (Durán 129). Again, the point should be made, too, that Cervantes's concern about the pernicious influence of books, particularly romances, was not his alone. "The matter was one of considerable importance in the Counter-Reformation, especially in Spain," wrote E. C. Riley more than forty years ago. "In the century or more since the invention of printing the size of the reading public had enormously increased. The Church was naturally sensitive to the effects of literature on men's minds, and there was a wide awareness, not confined to the Church, of the power of literature and art to influence men's lives" (131). Now, in the early twenty-first century, we are inclined to think of a progressive Cervantes, of a Cervantes whose attitude toward books was less reactionary than the Church's, but contemporary scholarship that insists on locating him in his historical context continues to see Cervantes as genuinely concerned about books' power to turn hearts and minds away from their God-given purposes (Close 3-4). Also there is no gainsaying the genuineness of the work's last chapter, in which Alonso Quixano expresses his deathbed relief that his head is free of the "detestable books of chivalry," and no gainsaying either the attribution of some of that genuineness to his author Cervantes.

In the history of travel writing, this Cervantine principle—beware the printed text—may be interpreted in several ways. First, it may be taken as applying to the literalness with which misleading travelers' reports—based in fantasy, in misperception, in nationalism, in face-saving, or in pre-Enlightenment epistemology—were often read in Europe. Exemplary in this regard is Sir Walter Ralegh's *The Discoverie of the Large, Rich, and Bewtiful Empyre of Guiana* (1596). Because

Ralegh located El Dorado on Lake Parime, far up Guyana's Orinoco River, in his *Discoverie*, the fabled city appeared on England's and other nations' maps for two centuries, that is, until Alexander von Humboldt proved its nonexistence in his Latin America expedition of 1799-1804.

Second, the Cervantine admonition may be taken as referring to the undue influence that prior travel texts often worked on newer. Columbus's *Diario*, his journal of the first voyage (1492-93), for example, exhibits this trait. Echoes of both Mandeville and Marco Polo filter through his descriptions of the Caribbean islands, although, of course, neither ever traveled from Europe westward into the Atlantic (Hulme and Youngs 3). Similarly, Ralegh relied heavily on Spenser's *The Faerie Queen* in casting himself as a secular knight on a golden quest undertaken in his queen's honor. Though few today would read Ralegh's *Discoverie* as nonfiction, in its own day it was taken at near face value.

Finally, and most important, the Cervantine principle might be taken as referring to the several centuries of colonial and imperial travel accounts whose disastrously false Eurocentric premises and equally disastrous Eurocentric confirmations legitimated that continent's five centuries of high-handed imperial enterprise. More than anything else, the colonial discourses inscribed wittingly and unwittingly in European travel texts of the modern era—from roughly 1400 forward—have been the scorned subject of the late twentieth century's burgeoning of travel writing scholarship. A representatively disturbing text among those deconstructed is Henry Morton Stanley's *In Darkest Africa* (1890), which, though appalling by our contemporary understandings of race and empire, was a best-seller in its own day, and, no doubt, catastrophically influential in shaping Western perceptions of Africa and of Africans (Carr 75).

In *90 días*, the Cervantine warning has two applications. First, the entirety of García Márquez's text rides on the conviction that both the West's and the Soviet's accounts of Eastern Europe are largely propagandistic, and, for that reason, absolutely unhelpful in the true knowing of the place. Indeed, this warning, more than the writer's analysis of an exported Soviet Marxism in Europe, is the travelogue's key theme. Its first articulation is struck no later than in the first chapter's title—"La cortina de hierro es un palo pintado de rojo y blanco" ["The Iron Curtain Is a Stick Painted Red and White"]—and in the work's first paragraph, which like the title, debunks the Western-promulgated myth of an apprehensible iron curtain stretching from the Baltic to the Adriatic Sea:

> La cortina de hierro no es una cortina ni es de hierro. Es una barrera de palo pintada de rojo y blanco como los anuncios de las peluquerías. Después de haber permanecido tres meses dentro de ella me doy cuenta de que era una falta de sentido común esperar que la cortina de hierro fuera realmente una cortina de hierro. Pero doce años de propaganda tenaz tienen más fuerza de convicción que todo un sistema filosófico. Veinticuatro horas diarias de literatura periodística terminan por derrotar el sentído común hasta el extremo de que uno tome las metáforas al pié de la letra. (9)

> [The iron curtain is not an iron curtain. It's a red and white stick like a barbershop pole. After having spent three months behind this curtain, I understand now that the expectation that the iron curtain should actually be an iron curtain goes against common sense. However, twelve years of tenacious propaganda are more persuasive than a philosophical system. When all is said and done, a daily twenty-four hours of journalistic literature so thoroughly defeats common sense that one ends up understanding metaphors literally.]

Countless examples of both the West's and the East's Cold War, propagandistic efforts follow this overture. To begin, the Western warnings the travelers receive at the outset of their journey (10) turn out to be completely false. Their cameras and watches are not confiscated. In the 600 kilometers that separate the West-East border from West Berlin, they do find a gas station, as well as a serviceable restaurant. In that territory they are not machine-gunned by Russians. Further, says García Márquez, West Berlin is not a European city but, instead, an absurd, characterless Potemkin village, "una enorme agencia de propaganda capitalista" (25) [an enormous agent of capitalist propaganda], built to offer an appearance of fabulous prosperity in the face of East Berlin's less showy achievements. "Los turistas norteamericans la invaden en verano, se asoman al mundo socialista, y aprovechan la oportunidad para comprar en Berlin Occidental artículos importados de los Estados Unidos que allí son más baratos que en Nueva York" (24). [North American tourists invade the city in the summer, are scared by the socialist world's proximity, and take advantage of the opportunity to buy in West Berlin articles imported from the United States that are cheaper here than in New York.]

The title of *90 días*'s second Czechoslovakia chapter also speaks to a Western myth. The title, "La gente reacciona en Praga como en cualquier país capitalista" ["People in Prague React Just Like People in Capitalist Countries"], counters the Western contention that Czechs' professions of contentment with the socialist system are fraudulent. No, says García Márquez, "no encontré ningún checo que no estuviera más o menos contento con su suerte" (63) [I didn't find a single Czech who was not more or less content with his life]. Finally, and most important, he reports of the Russians that "son leales a su gobierno" (143) [they are loyal to their government] and completely unaggressive: "No hubo un solo indicio de agresividad" (143). Casually inserted into his narrative, these remarks by García Márquez have as their deliberate purpose the refutation of Western propaganda.

In *90 días* García Márquez also criticizes the Soviets for meddling with the truth. In East Berlin, legal controls on currency exchanges, for example, are an empty show. Although the law prohibits the spending of East German marks (currency) carried into the country from abroad, the law is a face-saving governmental charade. In East Germany, the South American trio spend their imported monies abundantly and in open sight (30). Again, for the sake of show, the Soviets have spent too much in the construction of East Berlin's showpiece street, Stalin Avenue. East Berliners themselves say, "Con lo que costaron las estatuas, los mármoles, el peluche y los espejos, habría alcanzado para reconstruír decorosamente la ciudad" (28). [With the money spent on statues, monuments, ornaments and mirrors, the entire city could have been decoratively reconstructed.] Further, in Poland, García Márquez is told by an Italian who once attended a Warsaw festival, "Para hacernos creer que en Polonia hay libertad religiosa, abrieron las Iglesias y pusieron por todas partes funcionarios públicos disfrazados de curas" (56). [In order to make us believe that there is religious freedom in Poland, officials open all the churches and place in them public workers disguised as priests.] In Russia, which García Márquez otherwise praises, he spots several egregious manifestations of the government's heavy-handed efforts to manage information content: radios with just one station, carrying exclusively, of course, the government's official radio programs (120), Russian citizens paid by the government to hand out gifts to visiting Westerners (127), and a collective farm's administrator who has apparently come to believe his government's absurd propaganda, namely, that his farm's pathetically antiquated showcase milking machine is superior to any used in the West, and, another lie, it was invented by Russians (174).

The second application in *90 días* of the Cervantine admonition against trusting what one reads is contained in García Márquez's cautious, studious, and reflective attitude as he travels. This attitude has its roots in his abundant awareness of the several fraudulent texts to which he, the traveler and journalist, is susceptible. One such text is the one I have just been describing, governments' propagandistic efforts. As a result of such propaganda, traveling in any country is for García Márquez "un viaje peligrosa para un periodística honesto: se corre el riesgo de formarse juicios superficiales, apresurados, y fragmentarios, que los lectores podrían considerer como conclusiones definitivas" (55) [a dangerous journey for an honest journalist: for he runs the risk of forming superficial, pressured, and fragmentary judgments that readers can take for definitive conclusions]. Another deceptive text is travel itself, which invariably jumbles reality and illusion indiscriminately and, thereby, disorients the traveler. Lastly, by creating Franco, García Márquez admits his awareness of his politics' ability to get between him and reality. Awareness of these false texts' potency, as I have begun to show, is a Cervantine awareness; it is the awareness that inspires *90 días*'s second paragraph's *errante*.

Illusion Versus Reality

Though *Don Quixote* was far from the first creative work to have handled the theme of the confusing interplay of reality and illusion, for the richness and the variety with which it handles the subject it has become Western literature's touchstone text regarding this issue (Mancing 96). The most famous of the ways in which the novel concretizes the theme has already been described, namely, Don Quixote's transforming of himself and of the world around him into the set pieces of chivalric romances. However, the book illuminates the theme in other ways, too. It shows us that the mind can be confused by many more things than an excess of bad reading. Frustrated desire, for example, will cause people to see things as they are not. Because he is fifty and unmarried, because his other sexual opportunities are either taboo ("a niece not yet twenty" [19]) or unattractive ("a housekeeper past forty" [19]), and because his life is sterile, Quixano transforms the peasant woman Aldonza into the damsel of his sublimated dreams. Sancho's perceptions of reality, too, are a function of his desire. Though he should know better than to accept Quixano's account of himself as a dubbed and authorized knight, he does so on the slimmest of chances that his master will be able to deliver on his promise of an island. In several instances, most notably in the Cave of Montesinos chapters (II, 22-23), the novel makes the point that dreams and reality are damnably interchangeable. Then there are the illusions inflicted by others. To cover for a lie that he has told his master, Sancho tries to persuade Don Quixote that three farm girls on jackasses are Dulcinea and two maids in waiting (II, 10). To make their sport, the Duke and Duchess enlist their retinue in staging elaborate scenes that play on Don Quixote's lunacy and Sancho's simplicity (II, 30-57; 69-70). They do so either because, like Don Quixote, they have read too many books of romance and lost their sense of other people's real pains or because they are malicious or because their unearned exalted stations in life make them feel as if they can tamper with other people's lives. Maliciousness and arrogance, says the novel, also disconnect one from reality. Lastly, if we consider that all these confusions of illusion and reality come raining down in their fullest measure on Don Quixote's and Sancho's heads once they leave home, once they begin traveling, then we can see why *Don Quixote*'s archetypal communication to the travel genre is a reminder to its writers that to travel is to become confused about the distinction between reality and illusion.

It is a communication that travel writers have heard. Countless are the pages in travel literature's large library of books in which travelers lose hold of the distinction between reality and illusion. I will not attempt here a typology of such pages—distinguishing, for example, deliriums incurred by stress from others incurred by wonder from others occasioned by loneliness, and so on—but, instead, just offer three illustrative examples. The first comes from Flaubert's 1849-1851 passage through the Middle East, during which he cultivated an affair with the harem beauty Kuschiuk Hanem. As did many of Egypt's exotic sights, the juxtaposition of filth and beauty on the woman's person had an exhilarating, disorienting effect on the Frenchman. In a letter to Louise Colet, he described as pleasurable the sight of insects on his harem mistress's body: "You tell me that Kuschiuk Hanem's bugs degraded her in your eyes; but that is what delighted me" (qtd. in Starkie 181).The arduousness of a camel journey, on the other hand, caused T. E. Lawrence in his *Revolt in the Desert* (1927) to describe himself as feeling as if he were "dividing into parts":

Step by step I was yielding myself to the slow ache which conspired with my abating fever and the numb monotony of riding to close up the gate of my senses. . . . Now I found myself dividing into parts. There was one which went on riding wisely, sparing or helping every pace of the wearied camel. Another, hovering above and to the right, bent down curiously and asked what the flesh was doing. The flesh gave no answer, for, indeed, it was conscious only of a ruling impulse to keep on and on; but a third garrulous one talked and wondered, critical of the body's self-inflicted labour, and contemptuous of the reason for effort. (191)

Lastly, a combination of psychological factors and physical stress seems to cause Russell Banks's vision of a Slovenian woman near the summit of Aconcagua, the highest peak in the Andes. In "Fox and Whale, Priest and Angel," Banks writes:

My thoughts were broken by the appearance of a stranger next to me, a climber with a backpack and parka, crampons and an ice ax, just like us, but a young woman and, most strange, alone. . . . She sat down beside me and unwrapped a fruit bar and shared it with me. She was a lovely dark-haired woman, in her mid-thirties perhaps, with an easy smile. I asked her why she was here, and in a soft Balkan or Eastern European accent she answered that she was meeting a friend. (27)

In *90 días*, too, instances of travel's disorienting conflations of reality and illusion are numerous. Of his shocked entrance into a remote roadside restaurant in East Germany, García Márquez writes, "Nunca olvidaré la entrada a este restaurante. Fue como darme de bruces contra una realidad para la cual yo no estaba preparada" (18). [I will never forget (our) entrance into that restaurant. It was like being thrown facedown against a reality for which I had never been prepared.] He goes on to compare the sight before him—East Germans catatonically eating breakfast—to his witnessing of a Naples scene in which a casket was lowered by ropes out of a window while the frenetic widow pulled her hair out in the street below. The bizarre juxtaposition of images in this description reveals the degree of García Márquez's disorientation. No less unnerving is his experience of East Berlin: "Quienes no tienen las claves de esa ciudad donde nada es completamente cierto, donde nadie sabe muy bien a qué atenerse y los actos mas simples de la vida cotidiana tienen algo de juego de manos, viven en un estado de ansiedad permanente. Se sienten en un barril de pólvora" (30). [Those who don't have the keys of this city where nothing is completely certain, where no one knows to what to attend, and in which even the simplest acts of daily life involve trickery—those unfortunates live in a state of permanent anxiety. They feel like they are sitting in a barrel of dust.] Again, he says of another macabre bar scene that it "was a setting suited for opium" (38). On a lighter note, he experiences a surreal moment when he realizes that no one in media-controlled Russia knows who Marilyn Monroe is: "Es indefinable la sensación que produce hacer un chiste sobre Marilyn Monroe y que la concurrencia se quede en las nubes. Yo no encontré un soviético que supiéra quién es Marilyn Monroe" (146). [The sensation produced by making a joke about Marilyn Monroe that no one understands is indefinable. I didn't find a single Soviet who knew who Marilyn Monroe was.]

It would not take much work for me to cite still more surreal and disorienting moments in *90 días,* so many are they in the text. However, more important than completing the list of examples is repeating their significance: they suggest García Márquez's genuine political instability as he traveled in Soviet Europe and Russia. Also, they confirm his awareness of the commonness of illusion-reality moments in travel writing, and they contribute to our notion of his connecting with Don Quixote and Cervantes as he began to travel/write Soviet Europe.

The Traveler's Sidekick

About the pair Don Quixote and Sancho: the two are opposites; the two are mirror images of one another. They are knight and squire, master and servant, teacher and disciple, idealist and pragmatist, spirit and matter, saint and sinner, grace and works, duelist and second, actor and understudy, bachelor and delinquent husband, lunatic and keeper, artist and artisan, *letrado* and illiterate, poet and hack, man and shadow, ego and alter ego, inspiration and temptation, Scholastic philosopher and folk philosopher, hunter and scavenger, father and son, husband and wife (Durán 110; Close 55), Christian and pagan, catechist and catechumen, Jesus and Peter. As Howard Young says, "The day in and day out record of their friendship, which occupies ninety per cent of the novel, involves the exploration of a relationship that evokes the gamut of human relations. The two comrades deceive each other, mock each other, forgive each other, argue about the state of the world, provoke each other to extreme exasperation" (378), and most wondrous of all, in the course of the novel, they switch roles, Sancho becoming ever more Quixote-like and Don Quixote becoming ever more Sancho-like, until, at novel's end, as seminal interpreter Salvador de Madariaga has pointed out, much that has distinguished them is now exchanged, including their speech patterns. Thus, a "quixotized" Sancho announces his and his master's homecoming with a florid orison: "Open thine eyes, O desired country, and behold thy son Sancho Panza, returning to thee . . . ! Open thine arms, and receive likewise thy son Don Quixote." And thus, too, a humbled Quixote dies with a peasant's proverb on his lips: "There are no birds this year in the nests of yesteryear" (qtd. in Madariaga 185).

So varied and comprehensive is their relationship that virtually all subsequent fictional pairs (Crusoe and Friday, Tom and Huck, Thelma and Louise) are thought to draw from this resource. This phenomenon applies even more so to travel literature, whose every paired set of travelers is invariably compared to Don Quixote and Sancho. Indeed, the one shelf of travel literature texts on which *Don Quixote* has been accorded an archetypal spot by scholarship is the shelf of two-traveler texts. On that shelf *Don Quixote* is seen as anticipating the rest of the shelf's books not only in their travelers' number but also in the peculiar qualities of the pairs' relationships. Johnson and Boswell of Boswell's *The Journal of a Tour to the Hebrides with Samuel Johnson, Ll.D.* (1785), for example, are teacher and disciple as well as indestructible conviction and timid impressionism, as are Don Quixote and Sancho. Twain and Mr. Harris of Twain's *A Tramp Abroad* (1880) are traveler and hired factotum, as are Don Quixote and Sancho. Also they match the Spanish pair inasmuch as Twain responds hyperbolically to everything he sees in Europe, whereas Harris is offended only by European customs that inconvenience him personally. Even mixed-gender pairs are anticipated by the Quixote-Panza team. Ella K. Maillart, the Panza figure of her own *Forbidden Journey: From Peking to Kashmir* (1937), for example, claims to have chosen Peter Fleming as her traveling companion, rather than vice versa (8); however, it is clear by the journey's end that she has done so for his dashing, quixotic airs, for his invincible self-assurance, and for the high self-esteem that he emanates and that she lacks.

The Franco-García Márquez relationship draws from two dynamics of the Quixote-Panza combination: those of leader/follower and dogmatist/skeptic. As regards leadership, it is Franco who, like Don Quixote, initiates the whimsical, albeit threatening, journey into Soviet Europe. Franco, explains García Márquez, had purchased for the summer a French auto and, not knowing what do with it, proposed, "Let's go see what's behind the Iron Curtain" (9-10). En route, Franco drives, or, if Jacqueline takes the wheel, he sits in the front passenger seat "para evitar que se durmiera" (16) [to guard against her falling asleep]. Again, when García Márquez hesitates in applying for a visa to attend the Moscow folklore festival for fear that the authorities will control their foreign visitors' activities, Franco determines that there will be plenty of opportunity to slip away from the official scenes and to get out on the street to meet ordinary Russians, and, thus, the decision is made to go to Moscow. In each of these situations García Márquez is, like Sancho, the follower.

Much more important from a thematic perspective is Franco's and

García Márquez's repetition of Don Quixote's and Sancho's performance as know-it-all and skeptic. By this dynamic I refer to the countless times in *Don Quixote* that Sancho questions his master's statements. When Don Quixote says that he sees giants, Sancho tells him that he is not looking at giants but at windmills (I, 8). When Don Quixote says that in imitation of a renowned knight he will eat no bread nor lie with a woman until he takes revenge on a wrongdoer, Sancho tells him that's not a good idea: "Your grace should send such vows to the devil" (I, 10; 73). When Don Quixote finds consolation for his bruises in the notion that "there is no memory that time does not erase, no pain not ended by death," Sancho responds quite practically, "What misfortune can be greater than waiting for time to end [my pain] and death to erase it?" (I, 15; 107). In *Don Quixote* such dialogues serve many purposes, but chief among them is to contrast the idealistic and practical approaches to life.

A similar, though less pronounced, contest of opinions goes on between Franco and García Márquez in *90 días*, though there is virtually no distinction in their ways of looking at reality and though Franco's opinions are more often accepted by García Márquez than quarreled with. In their three or four conversations, one detects that Franco and García Márquez are practitioners of *mamagallismo*, a Colombian term used to describe the knowing, conspiratorial, coded, conversational manner of two socially undistinguished friends whose shared belief is that the government is telling them lies and the government doesn't give a damn about them. In much of his journalistic prose, it is said, García Márquez achieves this *mamagallista* tone in his postings to his readers. In *90 días,* Franco and García Márquez's shared first belief is that both the Western and Soviet hegemonies would like to deceive them. This shared understanding is seen most clearly in two of the conversations in which García Márquez speaks first. For example, on their first arrival in Eastern Europe, when García Márquez smells food and says to Franco, "Los comunistas también comen" [The communists also eat], Franco responds in true *mamagallista* fashion, "Sí, a pesar de lo que dice la propaganda occidental" (12) [Yes, in spite of what the Western propaganda says]. Or, again, when García Márquez says about a particularly dismal bar that he feels as if he has been in the place before, Franco answers, No, "lo había leido en alguna novela existencialista" (37) [you read it in an existentialist novel]. In the second example, the *mamagallista*'s shared disdain is for all those authoritative literary voices that tell them that existentialist literature is important.

More important than these exchanges in terms of establishing García Márquez's intellectual honesty are those in which Franco speaks first, usually expressing an opinion about Soviet Europe. These exchanges are important because they symbolically create some distance between García Márquez and his own near-instinctive core political beliefs, and, thus, they make credible opinions like those of Vargas Llosa and Saldívar that the young Colombian journalist did indeed think through his judgments about Soviet Europe without being inordinately ruled by his own core political beliefs. Truth be told, García Márquez usually responds positively to Franco's statements, with only the pause of a thought between his confirmation and Franco's original statement. When the latter states, for example, that there will be time and opportunity to sneak around Moscow during the folklore festival, García Márquez puts the festival's impossibly crowded itinerary together in his head and agrees that Franco is right (57). Later, when Franco suggests that their understanding of Leipzig will forever be controlled by the dismal impression of their arrival in "illuminación triste y la llovizna" (64) [sad light and drizzle], García Márquez keeps quiet but agrees.

However, there is one occasion when he rejects Franco's observation, and it is doubly significant. The pair are again in a café, this time in Prague, Czechoslovakia, a city and a country that García Márquez likes for disproving by its air of contentment the Western propaganda that all Soviet-controlled European countries are sad. And, indeed, in this bar everyone seems contented. The revelers are dancing and drinking as freely and happily as if they were at a Colombian dance. During a break in the action, García Márquez says to Franco, "No encuentro

ningún indicio de la diferencia de sistema" (65). [I don't see any difference between the two systems (capitalist and Marxist).] However,
Franco responds, "Look at the singer's nylons." When García Márquez
notices that the nylons are torn, he rejects Franco's inference that the
partying masks poverty: "Yo protesté: no podía partirse un pelo en
cuatro para descrubrir las fallas de un sistema. En París hay una multitude de hombres y mujeres que duermen en las aceras envueltos en
periódicos, aún en invierno, y sin embargo no se ha hecho la rev-
olución" (66). [I protested: You can't split a hair in four in order to discover a system's faults. In Paris multitudes of men and women sleep on
the pavements wrapped in newspapers, even in winter, and still they
don't make a revolution.] But Franco insists that he is right: "Para una
mujer que se preocupa de su suerte una media raída es una catástrofe
nacional" (66). [For a woman who survives by her appearance, a torn
stocking is a national catastrophe.] Later in the evening, when another
woman goes to exceptional lengths so as not to tear her stockings,
Franco is proven to be right. Thus, the incident emblematizes the real
difference that García Márquez sets up between himself and his political opinions before invariably owning them. That is the anecdote's first
significance, but, as I say, it contains a second—in the fact that the
woman who is exceptionally cautious with her stockings is a woman
who so turns Franco's head that he fails to notice her husband and invites her out. Thus, the anecdote suggests Franco's likeness with Don
Quixote. He, too, is a man confused about women.

Coda: Why Is Franco Italian?

Lastly, if Franco plays the role of Don Quixote in *90 días*'s allusional patterning, then why is he Italian? Because García Márquez's
nerves are alive to two other authorial antecedents, apart from Cervantes. The more familiar is *La divina commedia* author Dante Alighieri.
His name comes to mind because his *Commedia*—like Cervantes's
Quixote (like Homer's *Odyssey*, More's *Utopia*, Defoe's *Crusoe*,

Behn's *Oroonoko,* Swift's *Gulliver,* Gogol's *Dead Souls*, and other creative texts)—has so inscribed itself on Western civilization's cultural
consciousness as to become an archetypal travel text, exercising its influence on travel's nonfiction writers as well as on its fiction practitioners. Dante also comes to mind as a Franco antecedent because he is
twice referenced in *90 días*, implicitly in the "letrero alarmante"
[alarming sign] that García Márquez reads as he and his companions pass through the Brandenburg Gate from West to East Berlin—
"Attention, you are now entering into the Soviet sector" (25-26)—and
explicitly in García Márquez's appalled exclamation a few pages later
upon spotting for the first time in an East Berlin tavern's rear quarter
the surreal, unnatural consequences of the Soviet Union's misguided
application of Marxist principles in Eastern Europe. He terms the
scene, in which men and women drunk unto prostration attempt "to
perform scenes of love," "una laberíntica mezclona de la Divina
Comedia y Salvador Dalí" (39) [a labyrinthine mix of *Divine Comedy*
and Salvador Dalí elements]. With equivalent aptness García Márquez
might have hung similar references to Dante on any of several subsequent *90 días* episodes, in particular, on those in which he feels himself
searching for truth in unsanctioned, beyond-the-pale places or feels
himself disheartened by scenes of human stultification. For this reason,
Dante is the first likely source of Franco's Italianness.

The second is the Italian soldier, war correspondent, journalist, and
novelist Curzio Malaparte (1898-1957). So colorful was his career, so
varied, brave, and unpredictable his opinions, so hallucinatory and yet
profound his prose, so maverick and yet admired his work, it is not a
stretch of the imagination to think that the younger García Márquez
would identify with him and, therefore, imaginatively invest his *90
días* travel companion with Malaparte's nationality and profession.
Also, like Dante, Malaparte is mentioned twice in *90 días*. In the first
reference, García Márquez is struggling to describe in credible words
the unspeakable realities whose remnants he tours in Auschwitz, when
he says to himself that he will have to "ask Malaparte's permission" to

write what he wants to write (110). In other words, his plan in describing the scene is to realize his own version of one of Malaparte's famed hallucinatory episodes. In the second instance, García Márquez is wakened on a Ukrainian train by a stench so insufferable that he imagines it to be the very smell described by Malaparte in his "most famous chapter" (122), *Kaputt*'s second chapter, "Horse Kingdom." Thus, references to Malaparte in *90 días* signify "exemplary travel writer of the macabre and of the surreal." However, since this is what an allusion to Dante also signifies, and since this is one of the meanings invested in references to *Don Quixote*, the need to choose among the three as Franco's prototypical original disappears. Franco is, to some extent, all three; however, he is mostly a Quixote figure, because in that role he carries three buckets for García Márquez: blurrer of the real and imagined, know-it-all, and sidekick's leader.

Works Cited

Anderson, Jon Lee. "The Power of García Márquez." *The New Yorker* 27 Sept. 1999: 56-71.

Banks, Russell. "Fox and Whale, Priest and Angel." *The Best American Travel Writing 2001*. Ed. Paul Theroux. Boston: Houghton Mifflin, 2003.

Bell-Villada, Gene H. *García Márquez: The Man and His Work*. Chapel Hill: U of North Carolina P, 1990.

Carr, Helen. "Modernism and Travel (1880-1940)." *The Cambridge Companion to Travel Writing*. Ed. Peter Hulme and Tim Youngs. New York: Cambridge UP, 2002. 70-86.

Cervantes, Miguel de. *Don Quixote*. Trans. Edith Grossman. New York: Harper-Collins, 2003.

Close, A. J. *Miguel de Cervantes: "Don Quixote."* New York: Cambridge UP, 1990.

Durán, Manuel. *Cervantes*. New York: Twayne, 1974.

García Márquez, Gabriel. *De Europa y América, 1955-1960*. Ed. Jacques Gilard. Barcelona: Bruguera, 1983.

_____. *De viaje por los países socialistas: 90 días en la cortina de hierro*. 7th ed. Cali, Colombia: Ediciones Macondo, 1980.

_____. *Living to Tell the Tale*. New York: Knopf, 2003.

Hulme, Peter, and Tim Youngs, eds. *The Cambridge Companion to Travel Writing*. New York: Cambridge UP, 2002.

Lawrence, T. E. *The Revolt in the Desert.* New York: George H. Doran, 1927.

Levin, Harry. "The Quixotic Principle: Cervantes and Other Novelists." *The Interpretation of Narrative: Theory and Practice.* Ed. Morton Bloomfield. Cambridge: Harvard UP, 1970.

McKendrick, Melveena. *Cervantes.* Boston: Little, Brown, 1980.

Madariaga, Salvador de. *Don Quixote: An Introductory Essay in Psychology.* 1934. London: Oxford UP, 1966.

Maillart, Ella K. *Forbidden Journey: From Peking to Kashmir.* London: William Heinemann, 1937.

Mancing, Howard. *Cervantes' Don Quixote: A Reference Guide.* Westport, CT: Greenwood Press, 2006.

Riley, E. C. "Literature and Life in *Don Quixote.*" *Cervantes: A Collection of Critical Essays.* Ed. Lowry Nelson, Jr. Englewood Cliffs, NJ: Prentice-Hall, 1969. 123-36.

Rodman, Selden. "The Conqueror's Descent." *The National Review* 15 Oct 1990: 87-89.

Saldívar, Dasso. *García Márquez: El viaje a la semilla—la biografía.* Madrid: Alfaguara, 1997.

Simons, Marlise, "A Talk with Gabriel García Márquez." *The New York Times Book Review* 5 Dec 1982.

Sorela, Pedro. *El otro García Márquez: Los años difíciles.* Madrid: Mondadori, 1988.

Speake, Jennifer. *Literature of Travel and Exploration: An Encylopedia.* 3 vols. New York: Fitzroy Dearborn, 2003.

Starkie, Enid. *Flaubert: The Making of the Master.* New York: Athenaeum, 1967.

Stavans, Ilan. "García Márquez's 'Total' Novel." *Chronicle of Higher Education* 15 June 2007: B9.

Vargas Llosa, Mario. *García Márquez: Historia de un deicidio.* Barcelona: Barral Editores, 1971.

Webb, Jason, "Writer Stays True to Beleaguered Castro." *The Guardian* 30 Apr. 2003. http://www.guardian.co.uk/world/2003/apr/30/books.booksnews

Westad, Odd Arne. *The Global Cold War: Third World Interventions and the Making of Our Times.* New York: Cambridge UP, 2005.

Young, Howard. "Game of Circles: Conversations Between Don Quixote and Sancho." *Philosophy and Literature* 24.2 (2000): 377-86.

CRITICAL
READINGS

The Master of Short Forms_____

Gene H. Bell-Villada

Gene H. Bell-Villada offers a detailed analysis, examining both style and content, of García Márquez's short fiction, from his early efforts in the volume *Big Mama's Funeral* to the pieces collected in the Spanish edition of *Innocent Eréndira*. Although the examination does not delve into the short-fiction output of the author's mature years (*Pilgrim Stories*, for instance), the reader comes out with a clear, sustained understanding of the strategies and structures employed. Ernest Hemingway is listed as a major influence, and Bell-Villada points to traces of Macondo and of certain motifs in *One Hundred Years of Solitude* in "Tuesday Siesta," "One Day after Saturday," and "Big Mama's Funeral." He also reflects on *No One Writes to the Colonel*, which belongs to the in-between genre of the novella. It remains to be discussed how the sparse, restrained strokes that García Márquez employs in his short fiction give place to the baroque, abundant vision of his larger narratives. — I.S.

Had García Márquez never put any of his novels to paper, his shorter fiction would have still gained him some niche in literary history. Already in 1967 the Uruguayan Writer Mario Benedetti was to observe that "some of the stories gathered in *Big Mama's Funeral* can be considered among the most perfect instances of the genre ever written in Latin America."[1] We might venture yet further and say that those pieces, along with the novella *No One Writes to the Colonel* and the stories collected in *Innocent Eréndira*, put García Márquez in the company of such acknowledged masters of short fiction as Chekhov, Mann, Joyce, Cheever, or Grace Paley.

The author cites Hemingway as the chief influence on his own story writing. The admission is borne out by the pieces themselves, with their spare, minimal prose that captures life's little disturbances and moments of solitude, evokes major emotion in a snatch of dialogue or in the slightest of gestures. García Márquez remarked in 1950 that "the North Americans . . . are writing today's best short stories" (*OP*, 1:324), and Hemingway in this regard served him as much as mentor as did Faulkner and Woolf for his longer works. Particularly influential was Hemingway's "iceberg" theory of the short story—often cited by García Márquez—whereby the author makes visible only one-seventh of what is to be communicated, the other six-sevenths lying implicitly beneath the narrative's surface.

The stories offer pleasures of a sort different from those we know from *One Hundred Years of Solitude*. They are miracles not of mythic sweep but of understatement, conjuring up as they do the subtle, small-scale, mostly interpersonal upsets and triumphs of common village folk—the sleepy priests, pool-hall souses, provincial wheeler-dealers, troubled but stouthearted women, and the abandoned, the mismatched, or the bereaved. In later pieces, García Márquez will emerge with his visionary side full-grown and include fantastical materials—a wizened angel or a ghost ship. But there is a key element never absent from the Colombian author's stories, be they "magical" or realistic: the climate of his world. Every one of these short pieces has at least a reference either to the intense daytime heat or the tropical rain and its effects on characters' lives (their slowness in midafternoon, their ill health in rainy season).[2] The consummate craft of the narratives should also be noted: García Márquez typically spends weeks or even months on a single short story, feeling pleased when completing just two lines in a day.

The slim volume *Los funerales de la Mamá Grande* (*Big Mama's Funeral*) stands quietly as the budding Colombian's first work of genius. The miracle is that we have the stories at all. When García Márquez finished work on its eight pieces in 1959 he made little effort at seeking publication and mostly consigned them to his suitcase. (These were his wandering years.) He did submit "Tuesday Siesta" to a story contest in Caracas, where it rated not so much as an honorable mention.[3] When his friend Álvaro Mutis happened to be spending time in a Mexico City prison, Gabo got a note from the jailbird asking for "something to read." He sent the stories to Mutis, who in turn would loan them to the young Mexican writer Elena Poniatowska, she then absentmindedly misplacing the manuscript. She happened upon the stories again a year later and returned them to Mutis, who succeeded in placing the collection with the University of Veracruz Press in 1962. García Márquez received a one thousand peso advance, approximately one hundred U.S. dollars at that time. The volume was issued in two thousand copies, sales being slow until the changes wrought by *One Hundred Years*.[4] Today the stories are classics in their own right.

Though García Márquez made "Macondo" synonymous with his territory, the only three of his short stories set in that fabled land are "Tuesday Siesta," "One Day after Saturday," and "Big Mama's Funeral." The others in this volume unfold in a settlement known simply as "el pueblo," "the town," the setting as well for *No One Writes to the Colonel* and *In Evil Hour*. The two municipalities are distinct. "The town" finds itself in a "lull" from political violence and has its own recurring cast of characters—the corrupt mayor, the rebel dentist, Mina and Trinidad, the Montiels—who occasionally allude to Macondo as a slightly remote place.[5] "The town" also has running through it a river large enough to serve as port, and is modeled after Sucre, where the boy Gabo lived in 1936 following the death of his grandfather. Macondo by contrast has the surrounding banana fields and a hotel outside the railroad station, but only vague, distant memories of plantation violence and no central waterway, based as it is on Aracataca, with its marginal stream alongside the village cemetery.

"Tuesday Siesta," which opens the volume, is García Márquez's favorite short piece. It was inspired by the boyhood memory of a woman and a little girl he had seen carrying an umbrella in the afternoon sun (a common enough sight in Aracataca), and someone remarking to him "She's the mother of that thief" (*OG*, 35; *FG*, 26). In the story she is an outsider who has come determined to argue with the priest and, ultimately, face all of Macondo in order to visit the grave of her only son, recently slain in the act of trying to rob the widow Rebeca.

García Márquez's sure hand is already in evidence in this initial story. The "Tuesday" of the title places the action during an ordinary weekday; "Siesta" evokes the suffocating heat and spectral silence. The authority of the woman is immediately established in her erect posture on the train and in her four initial utterances, all of them motherly commands. At the priest's house she will insist on seeing him and then state her business outright: "The keys to the cemetery." When reiterating her son's name, she adds his second surname and thus indirectly asserts her own identity. (The hint throughout is that there may be no father.) To the aging cleric's sanctimonious query about putting her hapless son "on the right track" the woman counters, "He was a very good man" and compares her boy's thieving to the greater evils of his boxing, while the little daughter interjects her one forceful comment about his battered teeth. The two females thus present a common front against the tired, drowsy priest, who is able to respond only with a formula to the effect that "God moves in mysterious ways" (rendered by J. S. Bernstein as "God's will is inscrutable").

By the end of the story all of Macondo has found out who this woman is, but neither their hostility nor the hot sun can daunt her— "We're all right this way" is her parting remark. Though the narrative breaks off at the very moment when she and her daughter step out onto the street, the author has masterfully set things up so that we know that the two will hold their own against the unfriendly stares and, with quiet dignity, succeed in their mission and even catch their return train thereafter. The nameless mother in "Tuesday Siesta" is one of García Márquez's most memorable figures of womanly strength, and the story's plot shows at work the simple power of parental solidarity and moral authority.

"Artificial Roses" has unusual art and subtlety, even for García Márquez. On the surface it tells of young Mina's not being able to attend mass owing to some wet sleeves, but the real core is the subsequent standoff with her blind grandmother over her secret amour. (The ostensible bone of contention between them is the damp pair of detachable sleeves, which Mina was to put on just before entering church, so as to comply with priestly rules that bar admission to women with bare arms.) The story is notable for two master strokes. First, the reason for the conflict takes place "offstage"; when Mina steps out she will briefly see her boyfriend; he abandons her on the spot and she dashes home. We find this out in the terse, minimal dialogue with her friend Trinidad:

> "What's the matter?" [Trinidad] said.
> Mina leaned toward her.
> "He went away," she said.
> Trinidad dropped the scissors on her lap.
> "No."
> "He went away," Mina repeated.
> . . .
> "And now?"
> Mina replied in a steady voice. "Now nothing."
>
> (*FMG*, 120-21; *CS*, 180-81)

The remainder of the story tells of Mina's rage at being jilted, an anger she will cruelly take out on her grandmother.

The second beauty of this story is that the reader learns most everything via Mina's grandmother who, though blind, knows that Mina at bedtime turns on the flashlight, writes until dawn, and breathes heavily, that Mina has just broken her morning routines and gone to the toilet twice (the second time, we saw, to discard his letters), and that young, innocent Mina's truculent obscenity is her first ever (a reflex expression of her fury). In all, it is a classic portrait of tender but prickly adolescence confronted by aged wisdom and solidarity (the grandmother stands up for Mina when the latter's more shadowy mother makes inquiries). Mina's name, presumably a nickname for

"Belarmina," further suggests slightness and delicacy. The presence of four women and no visible men in a narrative in which a male sparks the crisis is a special touch, and the artificial roses with which Mina earns her living symbolize aptly the illusoriness of her love.

Few novels can capture as economically the tensions of political conflict as do the four pages of "One of These Days," with the yearning for revenge already hinted at in the title's set phrase. The atmosphere of violence is soon established when the eleven-year-old son of the town dentist casually relays to him the death threat from the mayor—the comic, innocent irony is self-evident—and is further heightened when the dentist checks his own revolver in the drawer. The ragged appearance of the mayor's right cheek, however, quickly reverses the roles: he desperately needs the dentist's expertise. Now our good dentist literally has the upper hand, and will give orders to his hapless patient and also extract political vengeance by skipping the anesthetic (the medical reasons he cites are wickedly spurious). The moment of truth comes with the climactic cold pain suffered by the mayor—brought on by a little flick of the dentist's wrist even as he laconically claims retribution for the mayor's victims. (The Spanish original follows the phrase "twenty dead men" with the direct address "Lieutenant," thus revealing that the town is living under barracks dictatorship.)

In the end, however, the mayor reestablishes his rule with a casual (if respectful) military salute and his concluding quip about his shady finances. This latter reference contrasts sharply with the drab austerity of the dentist's office, a poverty registered midway through the story by the roving eyes of the mayor-as-patient. The dentist of course could have assassinated the martinet at this point, though the action would be dishonorable and out of character, and he has had his small victory instead. But it's all a brief respite; no sooner is the mayor on his feet than things are reverting to the status quo ante.

"Baltasar's Marvelous Afternoon" movingly and comically depicts the clash between a naive artist and the ways of the world. Its modest thirty-year-old carpenter (the combined age and occupation are significant) has the pride of a craftsman, but no notion either of the beauty of his handiwork or of the extent of his genius. While his wife Úrsula sees merely the large size of the birdcage he has made, and many villagers care only about its sale value, a cultured Dr. Giraldo and maybe Mrs. Montiel do sense its aesthetic worth and high artistry. Being a man of his word, however, Baltasar declines the opportunity to sell the work to the appreciative doctor, and later just gives it away to the boy Montiel simply because he had promised it to him. All this is in deliberate contrast with the sordid ambience of the Montiel household and its boorish tightwad of a tyrant, "obese and hairy" like a beast, who struts about in his underwear, brutalizes his child, calls Baltasar's cage a "trinket," and both starts and finishes his character role with voluminous shouting (his final word is a vulgarism). The son himself, when he cannot have his way, weeps frantically—and tearlessly, having learned a few lessons in control from his imperious father.

The generosity of Baltasar ultimately carries the day: he refuses to tell the disappointing truth to the jubilant villagers (his perceived victory over Montiel being perceived as theirs too) and moreover he treats for beers and music the whole night. (Never having consumed alcohol before, he now experiences his coming-out party.) Though he ends up drunk in the gutter, minus his wristwatch and shoes, he has had his moment of glory, complete with cheering crowds and women's kisses.

"Montiel's Widow" is a kind of sequel to "Baltasar": the tyrant, having disregarded doctor's orders, has died of a fit of rage. The story tells two tales, foregrounding that of the widow—a naive, superstitious, self-pitying innocent who remains blissfully unaware of her man's criminality. Being completely subservient to and even disdained by him, she herself has no identity—her name is never revealed. Because of her proper upbringing and her lack of contact with reality, she cannot handle Montiel's empire, which quickly goes to ruin. Only the loyal Mr. Carmichael keeps her afloat; the one thing the widow seems capable of is biting her nails, an appropriately childish and self-indulgent act. To add to the ironies, her children are settled in Europe as beneficiaries of Montiel's gangsterism, and they piously scorn the violence in their native homeland. (The obscene postscript in the daughter's letter has presumably been added on the sly by a prankster in Paris.) The widow's concluding vision of Big Mama is a fantastical, symbolic, oneiric representation of her own impending death.

The story also tells, retrospectively, of Montiel's rise to power and of the townspeople's ongoing reaction to him. Originally a barefoot bumpkin, he gained his wealth and influence as informer for the "brutish" military mayor (the dental patient from "One of These Days," no doubt). Understandably, Montiel's early demise goes unmourned by the villagers and his boorish taste is made manifest in the "mausoleum adorned with electric-light bulbs and imitation-marble archangels." These pages show the sheer genius of García Márquez at work. What could have been a fairly ordinary tale about a banal manipulator who comes into his own during *la Violencia* here takes on a formal and emotional richness by being recounted as a postmortem flashback from the perspective of his ever-loving wife (in many ways just another of his victims). "Montiel's Widow," it bears mention, contains in microcosm what will be the plot and structure of *The Autumn of the Patriarch*: the death of a mediocre oaf and local despot who achieved power by collaborating with military occupiers. As is the case with the best of García Márquez, the story is funny in a bittersweet way.

The two lengthiest narratives in *Big Mama's Funeral* are also the weakest. "One Day after Saturday," however, was García Márquez's first mature story, with physical geography, personal voice, and, smiling irony all now sharp and clear in their contours. It deservedly won in 1955 a prize granted by the Bogotá Association of Writers and Artists.[6] Set in Macondo some years after the banana-company massacre, it conjoins three different plots: the plague of dead birds that upsets the widow Rebeca, the swift mental deterioration of the ninety-four-year-old Father Antonio Isabel, and the hapless country boy who finds himself stranded in Macondo and, worse, has gone and left his mother's phony retirement papers on the disappearing train. The three characters are touchingly comical and sad, trapped as they are within their obsessions and limits, and unsettled by their encounters with reality's fantastical little surprises.

Their several lives converge in the climactic scene in church, with a dizzy Father Antonio pronouncing his daft Sunday sermon on the Wandering Jew, a disquieted Rebeca scurrying up the aisle with her arms outstretched and her bitter face turned upward, and a presumably bewildered youth seated in the rear, he and Rebeca both strangers to each other yet taken note of by the priest in his transports. The cryptic ending, however, redeems Father Antonio as he destines the collection plate contents for the wayward young man, who most needs the support and solidarity. The cleric thus performs a useful if eccentric deed on this "day after Saturday," when one of yesterday's mishaps is alleviated if not resolved. Knowing García Márquez's subsequent work, one can assume that in the wake of Father Antonio's act of charity the villagers' lives will revert to their humdrum ways, their gossip enriched by remembrances of this extreme episode.

The central plot of "There Are No Thieves in This Town" is too slight for the story's twenty-six pages, though the repercussions are broad enough. Dámaso's impulsive burglarizing of the only three billiard balls from Don Roque's pool hall seriously dampens the townsmen's leisure time and moreover brings about the cruel and undeserved punishment of the scapegoated Negro. But Dámaso's equally impulsive attempt at sneaking back the three balls after hours is, as Don Roque tells him, the act of "a fool," and the ultimate irony is that he will now be wrongly blamed for the theft of the two hundred pesos too.

The best thing about the story is its portrayal of the twenty-year-old Dámaso and his relations with others. A classic pretty-boy type who spends three laborious hours trimming his mustache and combing his hair, he is the sort of fellow whose appeal to women—whether the youthful whores or his maternal, practical, thirty-seven-year-old wife Ana—is precisely his being a handsome, useless, loutish dreamer lucky enough to live off his movie-star good looks. (There is no mention of him working.) The nameless tart at the dance hall actually pays for his dinner and treats him to free sex. Meanwhile a pregnant Ana has the run of the household money.

Dámaso moreover is an astoundingly primitive macho figure whose very first act on arriving home from the burglary is to grab Ana by her chemise and lift her bodily, and whose final act before departing for the pool hall is to thwack her on the ear. At home he likes playing the boxer; at the dance hall he picks a fight with a traveling salesman (because he objects to the man's teeth), declines the girl's offer of food ("we men don't eat"), and refuses to pay for the check with a dismissive "I don't like queers." In addition, the story evokes the dictatorship, ever briefly, in the prostitute's allusion to the mayor's having ransacked Gloria's room and extorted twenty pesos in reprisal for her defense of the black man's innocence (*FMG*, 46; *CS*, 125). As the title might suggest, "There Are No Thieves in This Town" is unusually encompassing and conveys the spirit of street life, of crowds gathered in public places. The length of the story, however, is a flaw.

Both in its panoramic range and its high-pitched prose the story "Big Mama's Funeral" presents a complete break with others in the collection, its form as well as content looking forward to the author's two greatest novels. The piece is told in the highly oral style of a public storyteller or carnival barker, who leans on his "stool against the front door," intent on preempting "the historians." The high pomp of the opening lines ("absolute sovereign," "died in the odor of sanctity") is already being deflated in the very third word of the story ("incrédulos," translated by J. S. Bernstein as "the world's unbelievers"). Similarly, the ending of the Spanish version echoes the closing phrase ("por los siglos de los siglos," "world without end," rendered by Bernstein as "forever and forever") of the venerable "Glory be to the Father," itself also spoofed in advance with the narrator's allusion to the sanitation workers "who will come sweep up the garbage from the funeral."

The content of "Big Mama's Funeral" comprises the unnamed republic's highest reaches of political power—all branches of government, broad sectors of the economy, wise doctors of laws, the Metropolitan Cathedral—and crowns it all with a state visit by the pope, who "honored with his Supreme Dignity the greatest funeral in the world." Throughout the piece this display of authority is self-parodied with such less lofty matters as the matriarch's dying burp, "the historic blahblahblah" that unfolds even as her corpse rots in the 104° heat, or the heirs' rapid ritual of carving up her wealth among themselves. The basic plot is one that García Márquez would repeatedly make the most of: the death of a powerful personage and its consequences for society. Big Mama's own riches originated in a royal decree from the founding of the colony, and under her fabulous rule have grown to encompass holdings that take her three hours to enumerate—the five townships, 352 tenant farms, and a vast array of connections including paramilitary forces (her gun-toting nephew Nicanor), the church (Father Antonio), the health system (the antiquated family doctor and his monopoly), and even the public festivals that happen to have coincided with her birthday.

All this, however, is only a starting point. It is García Márquez's imagination that now soars and takes common political muckraking to inspired heights of vision, grandeur, and wit. Big Mama's power, we are told, takes in "the waters, running and still" as well as the "roads, telegraph poles, leap years, and heatwaves" (*FMG*, 189; *CS*, 186). From there it is only a further step to the climactic and wonderfully funny paragraph itemizing her "invisible estate" via those thirty-nine set phrases and clichés—for example, "the colors of the flag," "the free but responsible press," "the Communist threat"—that typify the Colombian elite and Latin American oligarchies (*FMG*, 137; *CS*, 192). That catalog, moreover, is but one of many—some short, some long—that help give the narrative its grandiose, mock-heroic, tongue-in-cheek quality. (It is as if Whitman had been a satirist.) The story's second paragraph already unfurls a brief geographic-cum-populist registry, but the fun with lists truly begins with the inventory of foods sold at

Big Mama's birthday celebrations, rises to a feverish pitch with the roll call of occupations (a touching tribute to the trades of the humbler folk all over small-town Colombia), and reaches a level of explosive farce in the hilarious parody of beauty queens "of all things that have been or ever will be." (Even today, it should be noted, the Colombian daily press regularly carries reports of beauty contests.)

On one level "Big Mama's Funeral" expectedly depicts the economics of power and its shadier practices—for example, the old matriarch's secretly arming her supporters while publicly assisting her victims, or the dead electors who miraculously cast their votes. But it also skillfully captures and satirizes what is often missed even in the best analyses or narratives of politics: namely, the organized appearance and show of power, the visual panoply along with the orchestrated language, the "words, words, words" of power. Once the "heroine" has died, the story passes in review a full battery of ways in which secular and spiritual power visibly and audibly manifest themselves—the solemn gatherings of dignitaries and of worshipful crowds, but also the telling little details such as those busts of Greek thinkers, or, in a more comic-strip vein, those drum rolls onomatopoeically rendered ("ratatat"). Politics in "Big Mama's Funeral" is as much a matter of visual spectacle as it is that of lethal guns or physical property.

When García Márquez was writing "Big Mama's Funeral," no pope had ever so much as set foot in a Latin American country, and the president of Colombia was tall and thin. In order to avoid accusations of excess topicality, García Márquez purposely portrayed his fictional president as bald and chubby. The author's prophetic side, however, once again became manifest when, for the first pontifical visit to Latin America, Pope Paul VI chose Colombia in 1968. The visit inevitably brought out all possible public fanfare—and the president at the time was in fact bald and chubby.

* * *

The novella *No One Writes to the Colonel* originated in Paris as an episode within García Márquez's flawed full-length novel *In Evil Hour*. The materials took on a life of their own and became this little masterpiece, the author's first mature and achieved longer work, as subtly understated as any of the best realistic stories in *Big Mama's Funeral*, and as seriocomical. At the same time the length allows for a larger and fuller town portrait, and a more exhaustive treatment of the narrative's three interlinking subjects: fighting cock, military dictatorship, and the old couple's solitude and hunger.

Some of the chief topics are established from the start. The report of scarce coffee in the opening line informs us of the couple's impecunious state. The soon-to-arrive rains of winter will exacerbate the wife's asthma and the colonel's constipation (the latter ailment to be vividly rendered). The initial full event in the story is a funeral for the town trumpeter, which prompts painful reminiscences of their own dead son from the two, as well as the colonel's sober observation that it is the first death from natural causes in years (a hint at obscure violence, and concretely at *la Violencia* for Colombian readers). These themes will consistently dominate the novella's fifty-some pages.

The story first of all provides a masterful, bittersweet portrait of the hungry and lonely couple, he seventy-five, she presumably in the same range. Their son, murdered by the military nine months earlier, had been their sole support—hence her wistful remark, "We are the orphans of our son" (*CNT*, 21; *NWC*, 11). With the colonel's copartisans all either exiled or dead (some violently), the very title conveys both his isolation—the original actually signifies "The Colonel Has Nobody to Write Him"—and his empty pockets. Of course the item of mail most awaited by the colonel is the fabled notice of a government pension, five decades overdue and now quite urgent. On four different Fridays we see him heading down with the highest of expectations to the river port or the post office, only to have his hopes dashed by a terse "Nothing for the colonel." His only consolations are the friendly camaraderie and loans of newspapers from the wise, kindhearted doctor (who also furnishes him medical treatments "on credit").

The figure of the colonel is among García Márquez's most memorable and touching exemplars of human innocence: an ex-soldier yet gentle, timid, wide-eyed, dreamy; unable to counter the wiles of the trickster Don Sabas yet himself blessed with reservoirs of self-irony and belief that are all but wondrous; peaceable, yet ultimately stubborn enough to say "no" to the sale of the rooster, and then end up pronouncing the most unforgettable final line in all prose fiction. (That closing noun is particularly ironic, given his earlier-expressed aversion to obscenity, as well as his excretory incapacities.) His wife, similarly, is another for Gabo's gallery of shrewd, strong-willed, loyal women; it is she who consistently manages to round up food and at one point elicits from him the jovial hyperbole, "This is the miracle of the loaves and fishes" (*CNT*, 34). She cuts his hair, suggests ways of securing money, and indeed rather treats the colonel like a child.[7] Only in the bitter quarrel between them in the last pages will the colonel take a firm stand and rebel. Notwithstanding this tense and electrified finale, *No One Writes to the Colonel* gives us one of the fullest and most loving (if unsentimentalized) portraits of conjugal life in modern literature since Joyce and Beckett.

Directly related to the couple's economic straits and marital discord is the sinister military dictatorship, about whose existence we learn piecemeal, in bits and fragments: the nightly eleven o'clock curfew, the casual talk about censored press and absent elections, the routine church bannings of movies, the hints about the governmental origins of Don Sabas's ill-gotten wealth, the clandestine leaflets that are now and then slipped to the protagonist, and the lightning police raid on the pool hall, with its mute, climactic confrontation between the colonel and the very man who had shot the old couple's son. As in *One Hundred Years*, the public and the private are expertly integrated and fused.

The decisive touch of genius in *Colonel*, however, is the fighting cock, a dominant presence from the second page on through the last, and a living symbol for most everything that is positive in the story.

The bird represents the couple's loved and departed son (to whom it belonged), the young people in town (who like just staring at it, and feed it), the colonel's hopes for income from the cockfights in January, and last but not least the ordinary people who congregate in the cockpit (and who, not just incidentally, oppose the military). At one point some youths "kidnap" the bird for a trial fight, and the colonel will chance by and see his rooster in the pit, expertly rebuffing its adversary's every blow. The audience naturally goes wild with cheers and applause both for the rooster (a good one) and its owner, claiming the two for "the whole town" but secretly giving vent to collective solidarity. Hence, though a bone of contention at home, the rooster remains to the colonel his source of personal worth as well as his chief affective link with the community. The figure of the bird thus helps unite the many narrative strands; without it the story would have been just another tender and smiling-sad portrait (if first-rate) of a small town's dignified poor.

At the end of that crucial episode at the cockpit, the bird is duly returned to the colonel. The escapade occurs, significantly, in the last of the novella's seven unnumbered "chapters," where the drift of the narrative makes a radical turn toward the better, even the joyous and luminous.[8] The weather at the start of the section is beautiful and clear. The colonel for the first time shrugs off his "hardened" wife's nagging complaints and he simply bypasses the post office. The newly arrived circus brings a festive atmosphere, prompting his memories of happier days with family and comrades. Now the colonel feels "no regrets," sleeps a "remorseless sleep," and firmly decides that "nothing about the rooster deserved resentment." All of this prepares us for the extensive final scene in which he shoos off the gawking kids, gently announces to his wife that "the rooster's not for sale," and resists every one of her nightlong importunities and worries (however legitimate they may be). Next morning, Sunday, he arrives at that fresh, bright moment of eschatological revelation and scatological eloquence with which the novel disyllabically ends.

With its gray weather, physical discomfort, and economic deprivation, *Colonel* could have been a heavy and oppressive piece, redeemed only by its closing chapter. What further saves it is its sudden surges of humor, many of them from the protagonist himself, who, for example, confronts the rooster and declares sententiously, "Life is tough, pal," and later warns the staring children, "Stop looking at that animal. Roosters wear out if you look at them so much." In reply to someone's remark about his thinness he self-deprecatingly likens himself to a clarinet. He takes some small joy in noting that his wife's momentary posture reminds him of the fellow on the Quaker Oats label. And he lyrically celebrates life as "the best thing that's ever been invented." There is also the comical portrait of Don Sabas's eccentric and neurotic wife, with her dreams of the dead, or the truly magical account of thunder that "entered the bedroom and went rolling under the bed, like a heap of stones." These humorous flashes regularly offset the potential bitterness of García Márquez's spare novella of solitude and empty stomachs. Where Knut Hamsun's *Hunger* has its intensely brooding, subjective, "Nordic" anguish, García Márquez's shorter book has its more benevolent, multigenerational, collective, "tropical" levity.

In later years García Márquez would more or less repudiate this phase in his evolution as a writer. He came to see the stories, with their "immoderate zeal for visualization," as excessively influenced by the cinema, and in *Colonel* in particular, he said, "I can see the camera. At that time . . . I was working like a filmmaker" (*OG*, 45; *FG*, 33), and was therefore taking into consideration such filmic concerns as the frame, the minutiae of pacing in dialogue and action, and the exact number of steps a character might happen to walk.[9] Back in 1956, of course, García Márquez had served his brief spell as a film student in Rome; not accidentally, these shorter works—what with their subject matter of humble folk in small towns, and their uncondescendingly objective approach mingled with an ironic affectiveness—happily suggest some fruitful lessons learned by the journeyman Colombian from the early neorealist films of de Sica and Fellini. Of all of García Márquez's work, his first neorealist short pieces are the most purely visual, a tendency he would eventually abandon in *One Hundred Years of Solitude*, where visualization for its own sake is minimal and the narrative-structural patterning holds full sway over the verbally descriptive.

Still, these tales are classics of their kind, and if a ripe and full-bodied history of Macondo is a more properly "literary" way of doing fiction, the stories' quiet understatement and their insight into character earn them their secure place in literature. Gabo the young realist is as much the wise artist as is García Márquez the master fabulator.

* * *

The story that shows García Márquez on the verge of disclosing the magic of Macondo is "The Sea of Lost Time," written in 1961, printed the next year in the magazine of the National University of Mexico (followed thereafter by the author's three-year writer's block), and first gathered in 1972 in the Spanish volume *Innocent Eréndira*. The setting is an arid and impoverished seaside hamlet on the edge of the Guajira desert, and the plot is threefold: the fragrance of roses that wafts in from the ocean and pervades everything, the arrival of tall and ruddy-faced Mr. Herbert with his philanthropic schemes, and the long swim to ocean's bottom and discovery of a live sunken city as well as a "sea of the dead" with its corpses perfectly intact. The action is experienced largely through protagonist Tobías, a happy innocent along the lines of carpenter Baltasar or the rooster-colonel.

With its insertion of fabulous materials into a commonplace reality, "The Sea of Lost Time" constitutes a breakthrough for its author. First, the daily life of the coastal village is lovingly captured, with its somewhat soured, mostly elderly inhabitants (who also find their consolation in each other), its open-air games of checkers, and the sad brothel with its gramophone and sad, nostalgic, shellac records. The broad intrusions of fantasy owe their success to a minor-magical texture already present at all levels of the narrative. The story has a smiling quality, filled as it is with jokes, dozens of them, ranging from comical exchanges and one-liners in the dialogue to small events, such as the brief, cartoonlike account of a dark rain cloud that first hangs over the sea but forthwith "descended, floated for a while on the surface, and then sank into the water" (*CE*, 31; *CS*, 217). Mr. Herbert himself is a fantastical entity whose public routine brings out people's extraordinary sides, notably Patricio's forty-eight bird calls. And there are the sudden incidences of pure magic—Clotilde has to "brush the smell [of roses] away like a cobweb in order to get up" (*CE*, 29; *CS*, 216), or, because Mr. Herbert asleep uses up the air in Jacob's room, "things had lost their weight and were beginning to float about" (*CE*, 40; *CS*, 225). This is as funny a story as García Márquez ever wrote, and the fanciful humor together with the mysterious smell of roses further prepares us for the astounding vision with which the piece ends.

In retrospect the story is, in content at least, a preliminary sketch for *One Hundred Years of Solitude*. There is the unnamed priest who, soliciting money for a church, actually rises physically off the ground, though the event is not made much of. Old Jacob's wife Petra, anticipating her death, prepares her husband's widower outfit—a harbinger of Amaranta's sewing of her own death shroud. The scene in which Tobías visits the unfortunate young prostitute (herself an early version of innocent Eréndira) has descriptions of sweat-soaked sheets and murky air to be retained verbatim when Aureliano visits the same whore in Macondo. Mr. Herbert, here a do-gooder who ends up appropriating Don Jacob's modest house, is a tamer precursor of the shady tinkerer by the same name, who applies the full battery of Yankee technology to a Macondo plantain and serves as advance guard for the fruit company. The conjugal life of a practical Clotilde and a dreamer Tobías who happens to be right anticipates that of Macondo's first couple, while their frolicsome sexuality gives a foretaste of the joyous eroticism to be unleashed throughout those *One Hundred Years*. The ending of the story is as apocalyptic as Macondo's, though watery rather than windy, and not so much biblical as Dantean in overtones, the sea of the dead having "so many of them that Tobías thought that he'd never seen so many people on earth" (*CE*, 43; *CS*, 227), like the city in Eliot's *Waste Land*.

Still, "The Sea of Lost Time" is more striking and novel a story than it is thoroughly successful. There are three plots in search of a suitable central image or character, the figures of Tobías and his wife not sufficing to unify all of the divers strands. In addition, the gentle though conventional narrative style fails to do justice to the bold and unsettling subject matter (as Vargas Llosa first noted).[10] The long, spacious paragraphs of the later García Márquez would eventually emerge as the medium far more appropriate to his complex, panoramic, magical vision. One sees here notable strides in García Márquez's developing imaginative gifts without a corresponding advance as yet in verbal craft and conception.

* * *

The other short stories in the Spanish (not the English) collection *Innocent Eréndira* all have fantastical materials in common, the author thus further reapplying the lessons he had assimilated and mastered in *One Hundred Years*. At the same time the narratives have moved north, away from the nameless port and the ancestral Macondo, both of which were inland settlements. The towns now have marine locations on the edge of the Guajira desert. The landscape is correspondingly barren. No bananas grow here; even flowers are a rare and precious commodity.

The new settings express García Márquez's aim at the time of becoming more broadly a writer of "the Caribbean," its geography already being reimagined by him in his novel (then in progress) about a dictator, with an unnamed republic that combines Venezuelan and Colombian features, and a horizon that ranges from the colonial Guianas to the Gulf of Mexico. Moreover, three of the stories are evidently stylistic exercises, practice studies for *The Autumn of the Patriarch*, having as they do the winding syntax and the mid-sentence shifts in pronoun-subjects so intimidating to first-time readers of that book.

"The Last Voyage of the Ghost Ship" in fact consists of a single long sentence, as will be the case with the final chapter of *Patriarch*, though its youthful protagonist and occasional narrator here lives the solitude not of power but of abandonment and alienation. He is fatherless at the outset; his mother soon dies in a freak accident; he survives on the fish he pilfers from docked trawlers, and is despised by the townsfolk, who ostracize him and beat him up. From the start, however, he is determined to prove that his nocturnal sightings of a wandering transatlantic cruiser are not a mere phantasm of his mind. ("Now they're going to see who I am," the story opens—a defiant phrase that reappears fourfold.) And though the boy too had initially "thought it was a dream," at the end, from a rowboat, he guides the ocean liner on a halter, and an omniscient narrator tells in dramatic detail of the "living ship" that crashes right onto the shore and lights up the town as the villagers stand and stare in disbelief.

The "aluminum" hulk itself is precisely described, with some freight ("fighting bulls"), an ill passenger, and captain and pilot alluded to in passing, its physical dimensions ("twenty times taller than the steeple and some ninety-seven times longer than the village") ingeniously spelled out, and its 90,500 champagne glasses, now reported as destroyed. The ship even has a name, *Halácsillag*, Hungarian for "Star of Death," García Márquez purposely having chosen a word from a language of a landlocked nation.[11] In all, the story is a suspenseful, luminous account of a lonely truth being vindicated by its lone and ardent knower, who acts to bring and impose that truth, with smashing success, onto those who had once dismissed and scorned him.

The setting already looks forward to *The Autumn of the Patriarch*, with pan-Caribbean allusions to Hindu shops, Dutch Negroes, and Guianese smugglers, fearsome memories of pirate William Dampier (to be evoked on the very first page of the later novel), and suggestions of Cartagena in the references to distant colonial fortifications and an old slave port across the bay. "The Last Voyage of the Ghost Ship" also has recognizable flashes of its author's humor, such as the brief history of a "murderous" rocking chair so old it can no longer give rest. The piece itself seems inspired by a short narrative of Hemingway's, "After the Storm," set along the Florida Keys and written in long, sinuous sentences untypical for the U.S. author. Hemingway's pugnacious and resentful narrator happens upon a sunken ocean liner, "the biggest I ever saw in my fife," where he glimpses "a woman inside with her hair floating about." The story has further magical intimations—"There was a million birds above and all around"—without reaching the subjective heights of García Márquez's six-page sketch.[12]

"Blacamán the Good, Vendor of Miracles" is the one mature García Márquez story narrated exclusively in the first person. It likewise anticipates *The Autumn of the Patriarch*, not only in its dense prose and its chief setting (a fictional port city called Santa María del Darién) but also in the key role played by U.S. Marines, who are present at the start and later reinvade, "under the pretext of exterminating yellow fever" (an evident play on our Panamanian adventure). The story's first few pages are a masterful portrait of the roving con artist, Blacamán the *Bad*, from his colorful outfit of white suspenders and jingle bells to his street-hawker routine and actual sales of "suppositories that turned smugglers transparent." He has been at large since the days of the Imperial viceroys whom he used to embalm (thus being roughly as old as the patriarch), and now singles out the youthful "idiot-faced" narrator—a doppelgänger figure to be self-styled Blacamán the Good—and takes him on as an assistant. We follow the pair on their comical picaresque adventures along the coast, with a brief wink at Chaplin's *Gold Rush* when, in the ruins of a colonial mission in the Guajira, the twosome dine on boiled leggings.[13]

The story is by and large convincing until the moment when the pliant narrator, during a brutal torture session at the hands of his master, accidentally revives a dead rabbit and gains the power to rebel. He breaks off on his own and soon becomes enormously rich as Blacamán the Good, miracle-healer cum resuscitator and all-purpose wheeler-dealer. Years later he reencounters Blacamán the Bad in lesser straits, who dies of poison in a final performance—only to be kept sealed in an armored tomb and periodically brought back to horrific life there by his vengeful, erstwhile aide. But alas, the narrative in these last pages turns static and loses in cogency. The transition to Blacamán the Good's new life is abrupt and without explanation, and the narrator's recounting of his own daily latter-day successes lacks any tension, coming as it does not from a situation of ongoing conflict but of secure power. "Blacamán" is probably the most promising yet in the end the least effective of García Márquez's later fictions.

In "The Handsomest Drowned Man in the World," the only entity with a name is the eponymous cadaver, whom the villagers choose to call "Esteban." (The Catholic church's first martyr, we may recall, was St. Stephen.) When his tall, strong, broad-shouldered, lifeless body is washed ashore near a seafaring hamlet of "twenty-odd houses," the irruption from another, remote, unknown world excites the romantic, myth-producing imaginations of the sad and isolated townsfolk. He strikes them as proud, "the most virile and best-built man they had ever seen," and from there they infer for him the power to stop the winds and call fish from the sea. The women in particular fantasize about him, alive and polite as a fellow villager in their lives, and inasmuch as it is they who prepare his corpse for sea burial, they grow particularly attached to their ideas and images of him. The males by contrast get to feeling jealous and look forward to his being returned at last to the deep.

If the women's collective role in this story shows mythmaking's more specifically erotic side, in the ritual ocean burial the affective bonds are extended and "all the inhabitants of the village became kinsmen." Hints at Odysseus's adventure of the sirens help place the incident of Esteban within a larger ancestral continuum of seafaring fable. Through these intimations of a greater and more beautiful cosmos the villagers are reminded of "the desolation of their streets" and (by extension) of their lives. And so we probably can trust the omniscient narrator's prediction that the inhabitants, in response, will thence beautify and make fertile their hamlet, and give it some fame as "Esteban's village." In some of his best long narratives García Márquez forged a kind of fantastical history; here we see him experimenting in turn with a fantastical anthropology, as it were, a "folklore science-fiction" that speculates on the humbler origins and organizational powers of a commonly created and shared popular myth.[14] García Márquez the socialist well knows that the imagination and its dreams are as crucial a force in political life as is economic fact.

"A Very Old Man with Enormous Wings" is subtitled "A Tale for Children," but what fairy-tale characteristics it has are affectionately parodied throughout. On one hand, there is unmistakable magic in the arrival of the winged humanoid, the apparent angel who seems to have crash-landed in the courtyard of Pelayo and Elisenda, a modest rural couple living in a coastal village. On the other hand, everything about the visitor completely contradicts our standard, mythified, Western image of God's angels. Rather than stereotypically young, heroic-looking, and blond, with sumptuous garments and wings all in white, García Márquez's mysterious stranger is dressed in rags, is nearly bald and toothless, and has soiled "buzzard wings" strewn with parasites. His being temporarily lodged in the chicken coop further detracts from the dignity we normally expect of otherworldly creatures.

At the same time the official emissaries of the Catholic faith show their comic limitations. Father Gonzaga may bear the name of a legendary Jesuit saint and hero, and indeed he is a robust former woodcutter, but his expectation that the angel should know Latin as "the language of God" demonstrates his innocence of scriptural Hebrew and Greek. Meanwhile, in perfect medieval fashion, the learned argufiers in Rome debate endlessly as to whether the man in question possesses a navel or speaks Aramaic (the language Jesus probably spoke), and they even ask how many times—that old Scholastic chestnut—the stranded angel could fit on the head of a pin! (The simplest solution, of course, would be for the churchmen to betake themselves to the Caribbean village and use the evidence of their eyes and ears; but their Scholastic doctrine has yet to catch up with the empirical method.) Still, it cannot be denied that the visitor has the divine capacity to perform miracles, however skewed they be—such as giving a blind man three new teeth or having sunflowers sprout on a leper's sores. Perhaps they are practical jokes he plays on the gawking townspeople.

For the ordinary folk in this story—their notions as well as their ailments—come across as equally comical: the rustic who thinks the angel should be "mayor of the world," or the invalid woman who counts her heartbeats, or the Portuguese man disturbed by the noises of the stars. García Márquez's humor with his fictive villagers, it should be noted, is mostly gentle and good-natured. The only dark moment comes toward the end, when Pelayo and Elisenda, having gotten rich from exhibiting "their" angel, now build a mansion, and she wears satin shoes and fine silks. In the meantime the very source of their wealth is shooed around and out of the house by Elisenda with her broom, to be finally consigned to the shed. His wings are healing, however, and one spring day he flies off just as Elisenda is peeling onions (the same effect of Fernanda's sheets in *One Hundred Years*), and the onetime moneymaker-turned-nuisance recedes as "a dot on the horizon of the sea" before he disappears for good. Without demonstrating the aggressive satire of Luis Buñuel in movies such as *Simon of the Desert* or *The Milky Way*, García Márquez shares in the great Spanish film director's laughing sensibility.

The name of the story "Death Constant beyond Love" is a bittersweet pun on the title of what may be the most famous single sonnet in Spanish, Francisco de Quevedo's "Love Constant beyond Death," with its closing conceit, often casually quoted, about the lover's dust that will remain forever in love ("polvo seré, mas polvo enamorado"). García Márquez's prose narrative, by contrast, tells of the grim reality of love cut off by anticipated death. No doubt, Senator Onésimo Sánchez is cynical and corrupt to the core, and the illusory props of his electoral campaign neatly symbolize the empty ritualism of his speeches and slogans. And yet one cannot but feel touched by his desire for simple companionship with the young, smooth-skinned, Afro-

French beauty Laura Farina during his last few months alive (even if at the expense of his family and reputation). To add to the ironies, he gains "the woman of his life" only by finally giving in to a long-standing request from Laura's criminal father for a phony residence card. Love thus flowers thanks to a secret and sordid deal.

While the art of "Death Constant" recalls that of García Márquez's earlier realist pieces, its politics are not those of military dictatorship but of the quadrennial electoral rite, not of guns or repression but of the circus and spectacle, not of rifle-butts and fear but of the horse-trading, hucksterism, and sheer inertia of the patronage machine. At the same time, from the first line to the last the narrative is one of love and politics, sex and power—the two grand themes of *The Autumn of the Patriarch*. The senator's cultured cosmopolitanism and mostly happy family life, it should be noted, do set him apart from the animal crudity and vulgar greed of the nameless Caribbean despot, but both in the end inspire in us an understanding pity.

Abbreviations

CE = *La increíble y triste historia de la cándida Eréndira y de su abuela desalmada*. Barcelona: Barral Editores, 1972.

CNT = *El coronel no tiene quien le escriba*. Mexico City: Editorial Era, 1972.

CS = *Collected Stories*. Translated by Gregory Rabassa and J. S. Bernstein. New York: Harper & Row, 1984.

FG = *The Fragracle of Guava: Plinio Apuleyo Mendoza in Conversation with Gabriel García Márquez*. Translated by Ann Wright. London: Verso, 1983.

FMG = *Los funerales de la Mamá Grande*. Buenos Aires: Editorial Sudamericana, 1970.

NWC = *No One Writes to the Colonel and Other Stories*. Translated by J. S. Bernstein. New York: Harper & Row, 1968.

OG = *El olor de la guayaba: Conversaciones con Plinio Apuleyo Mendoza*. Barcelona: Bruguera, 1982.

OP = *Obra periodística*. Vol. 1, *Textos costeños*. Edited with an Introduction by Jacques Gilard. Barcelona: Bruguera, 1981.

Notes

1. Benedetti, "García Márquez o la vigilia dentro del sueño," p. 184.
2. Ibid., p. 182.
3. Vargas Llosa, *García Márquez*, p. 58.
4. Ibid., pp. 65 and 73.
5. Benedetti, p. 183.
6. Vargas Llosa, p. 43.
7. René Prieto, "The Body as Political Instrument," pp. 37-38.
8. Ibid., p. 37.
9. Durán, "Conversaciones con Gabriel García Márquez," in Rentería Mantilla, *García Márquez habla de García Márquez*, p. 31. Torres, "El novelista que quiso hacer cine," in ibid., p. 46.
10. Vargas Llosa, p. 476.
11. Cobo Borda, "Piedra y Cielo me hizo escritor," p. 36.
12. Hemingway, "After the Storm," in *Short Stories*, pp. 374-75.
13. For a fine discussion of this story see McMurray, *Gabriel García Márquez*, pp. 120-24.
14. For an examination of possible mythic sources for this story, see Speratti-Piñero, "De las fuentes y su utilización."

Works Cited

Benedetti, Mario. "García Márquez o la vigilia dentro del sueño." In *Letras del continente mestizo*, pp. 180-89. Montevideo: Arca, 1967.

Cobo Borda, Juan Gustavo. "Piedra y Cielo me hizo escritor." *Cromos* (Bogotá), 28 April 1981, pp. 30-36.

Durán, Armando. "Conversaciones con Gabriel García Márquez." *Revista Nacional de Cultura* (Caracas), año 24, vol. 29, no. 185 (July-September 1968): 23-34. Reprinted in *Sobre García Márquez*, edited by Pedro Simón Martínez (q.v.), pp. 31-41. Reprinted in *García Márquez habla de García Márquez*, edited by Alfonso Rentería Mantilla (q.v.), pp. 29-35.

Hemingway, Ernest. *The Short Stories of Ernest Hemingway*. New York: Macmillan, 1987.

McGuirk, Bernard, and Richard Cardwell, eds. *Gabriel García Márquez: New Readings*. New York: Cambridge University Press, 1987.

McMurray, George R. *Gabriel García Márquez*. New York: Frederick Ungar, 1977.

Martínez, Pedro Simón, ed. *Sobre García Márquez*. Montevideo: Biblioteca de Marcha, 1971.

Prieto, René. "The Body as Political Instrument: Communication in *No One Writes to the Colonel*." In *Gabriel García Márquez: New Readings*, edited by Bernard McGuirk and Richard Cardwell (q.v.), pp. 33-44.

Rentería Mantilla, Alfonso, ed. *García Márquez habla de García Márquez*. Bogotá: Rentería Mantilla Ltda., 1979.

Speratti-Piñero, Emma Susana. "De las fuentes y su utilización en 'El ahogado más hermoso del mundo.'" In *Homenaje a Ana María Barrenechea*, edited by Lía Schwartz Lerner and Isaías Lerner, pp. 549-55. Madrid: Castalia, 1984.

Torres, Miguel. "El novelista que quiso hacer cine." *Revista de Cine Cubano* (Havana), 1969. Reprinted in *García Márquez habla de García Márquez*, edited by Alfonso Rentería Mantilla (q.v.), pp. 45-48.

Vargas Llosa, Mario. *García Márquez: Historia de un deicidio*. Barcelona: Barral Editores, 1971.

Magic Realism and García Márquez's Eréndira_____

Moylan C. Mills and Enrique Grönlund

Moylan C. Mills and Enrique Grönlund offer a brief history of how the concept of Magical Realism evolved, its connections to surrealism, German Post-Expressionism, and the prologue to Alejo Carpentier's novel *The Kingdom of This World*. They then study the way García Márquez manipulates the technique in his novella *Innocent Eréndira*, especially in the cinematic adaptation by Ruy Guerra. They comment on the author's career as a screenwriter and the devices he has employed to translate the exotic and mystical from the page to the screen. Following the tracks of critics such as Stephen M. Hart and Luis Leal, Mills and Grönlund conclude that Magical Realism "allows us to see the fantastic within the real and not apart from it."   — I.S.

"Magic realism" is a term that has developed a certain voguish contemporary usage to describe such diverse artistic achievements as the novels and stories of John Cheever, the theatrical spectacles of Martha Clarke, and the recent Robert Redford film *The Milagro Beanfield War.*

"Magic realism," however, has been used most often in recent years as a critical term that describes a certain approach to subject matter and style found in the fiction of a number of Latin American novelists, notably in the work of pre-eminent Colombian writer and 1982 Nobel laureate Gabriel García Márquez, author of *One Hundred Years of Solitude*, *Chronicle of a Death Foretold*, *Love in the Time of Cholera*, and *Eréndira*. In recent years, too, Latin-American filmmakers appear to have drawn inspiration from the magico-realist approach to fiction. Since García Márquez is also a screenwriter, having adapted a number of his literary works into cinematic form, it might be of interest to examine the idea of "magic realism" from the vantage point of *Eréndira*, both the 1972 novella and the 1981 film treatment of the novella.

The Incredible and Sad Tale of Innocent Eréndira and Her Heartless Grandmother[1] begins when Eréndira's wind of misfortune causes a lighted candle to reduce to ashes the mansion of moon-like concrete in which she lives with her unmerciful grandmother. The grandmother, with sincere pity, informs the ninety-pound fourteen-year-old virginal Eréndira that life will not be long enough to pay her back for the mishap. And pay, Eréndira does. Over the next six years, she is forced to sell her body to countless men—day in, day out—as she and her grandmother criss-cross the desert, setting-up shop at arid outposts that border on barely civilized locales.

As the debt lessens and the grandmother's wealth increases (thanks to the girl's growing renown), their surroundings improve accordingly. Peasants are hired as servants; the living quarters are made lavish and comfortable; the grandmother's wardrobe grows more grotesquely regal; and the litter upon which the grandmother is transported becomes more majestic.

While awaiting their turn with Eréndira, the customers are entertained by hired musicians, some of whom charge more for playing waltzes because these songs are sadder; the customers also have access to food and drink provided by local entrepreneurs; and they can have their likenesses rendered by an enigmatic photographer who poses Eréndira's clientele against make-believe backgrounds made of cardboard and cloth.

Each successful stop brings new wealth to the grandmother and new levels of glitz and glitter to the carnival-like atmosphere. Eréndira herself becomes a living legend, an erotic icon.

One day Eréndira is kidnapped and held captive by self-serving missionaries bent on showing the path of righteousness to the young girl. Her grandmother, furious that her source of income has been taken from her, plots to achieve Eréndira's release. When her freedom has been secured, Eréndira is once again set up in her carnal occupation.

On another occasion, Eréndira meets the angelic Ulises, a strange young man whose father cultivates oranges that have diamonds inside instead of pits. Ulises, madly in love, wishes to rescue Eréndira from her doomed life. His presence and pleading words seem to awake

Eréndira to the reality of her situation, and she and Ulises plot the demise of the grandmother. In the end, on the third try, Ulises finally succeeds in killing the old woman. Covered in the oily, green blood of the grandmother, Ulises watches helplessly as a suddenly mature Eréndira runs off, carrying her grandmother's vest filled with gold ingots, never to be seen nor heard from again.

The beauty of the story, of course, lies in the descriptions, the atmosphere, the dialogue, the wondrous happenings, all of which combine to create a kaleidoscopic tapestry that many readers and critics would call "magic realism." Myriad articles have been written, books published, and conferences organized, all for the sole purpose of establishing a concrete definition of the controversial oxymoron "magic realism." Therefore, because "magic realism" is an appellation that apparently defies one exclusive definition, it might be more useful in a discussion of García Márquez's work to outline some of the outstanding characteristics of "magic realism" and to examine their presence in the works to be discussed.

The term "magic realism" was coined in 1925 by the German art critic Franz Roh in order to help define German Post-Expressionist painting. Roh used the term to describe a "magic insight into an artistically produced, unemphatically clarified piece of reality."[2] As critic Juan Barroso VIII has observed, reality becomes a concrete whole as a result of an objective process of transformation that emanates from the spirit of the object being created. In addition, according to Barroso, a more mysterious, deeper sense of meaning than it might otherwise have is bestowed on the finished creation, causing the viewer to respond to the wonderment of the object itself.[3]

In a retrospective study of German Post-Expressionism, published in 1983, Seymour Menton has pointed out the following characteristics which serve better to focus Roh's definition: 1) Reality is portrayed so overwhelmingly realistically that it is rendered illusive; 2) Ordinary material things are instilled with seemingly magical powers, yet remain easily identifiable; 3) Objective perspective becomes the basic point of view; 4) "Coldness" is a major component; that is, the works lack passion; they appeal intellectually, not emotionally.[4] Thus, Menton argued that magic-realists strove " . . . to portray the strange, the uncanny, the eerie, and the dreamlike—but not the fantastic—aspects of everyday life."[5]

Although Menton's observations focus upon German Post-Expressionist painting, other critics have discovered similar attributes in Latin American magic-realist fiction written over the past forty and some odd years. It is important to keep in mind that it is primarily, but not exclusively, in Latin American literature that "magic realism" has been so affectionately embraced. It can be found in works such as *The House of the Spirits* by Isabel Allende, *Dona Flor and Her Two Husbands* by Jorge Amado, *The President* by Miguel Ángel Asturias, *The Kingdom of This World* by Alejo Carpentier, *Hopscotch* by Julio Cortázar, *I, the Supreme* by Augusto Roa Bastos, *Pedro Páramo* by Juan Rulfo, and of course, *One Hundred Years of Solitude* by García Márquez.

In the prologue to *The Kingdom of This World*, published in 1949, the great Cuban novelist Alejo Carpentier felt compelled to explain the reality of Latin America as he saw it and proceeded to label this reality "lo real maravilloso." According to Carpentier, what is wondrously real is the incongruous amalgam of the American continent: its diverse racial roots and ethnic cultures, its improbable history, its marvelous flora and fauna, its discontinuous geography, all of which create an ontology which never fails to surprise whenever it reveals itself. Carpentier sees Latin American reality as being so infused with an inherent telluric wonderment that writers need not conjure artificial adornments in order to express this element. Once it reveals itself, the writer should describe the reality as it is.[6] Obviously, to Carpentier, this regional presence is a key component of the concept of "magic realism."

A number of critics of Latin American literature have contributed valuable observations in their quest toward a better understanding of "magic realism." The following are some of the most salient ones.

Angel Flores in his seminal essay of 1955 concluded that a "meticulous craftsmanship" and attention to style are the vehicles through which the "common and everyday" are transformed into the "awesome" and the "unreal." As such, "the unreal happens as part of reality," all quite logically.[7]

James Irby in 1957 proposed that "magic realism" is a peculiarly Latin American style which "blends the fantastic and the real," often transforming the latter into something extraordinary, anamorphous, and phantasmagorical which is infused with a sense of determinism (García Márquez's solitude?). Furthermore, Irby recognized an emphasis on the telluric nature of the magic-realist existence, as well as the use of colloquial language by the authors.[8] In *Eréndira*, the novella, in addition to the ever-present desert and the ubiquitous "wind of misfortune," Irby's observations are powerfully evoked by the grandmother's "sterile breath,"[9] by the fact that spirits are "dulled by the dust and sweat of the desert,"[10] as well as by a whorish Eréndira who " . . . made up her face [with] . . . posthumous make-up . . . in the style of sepulchral beauty . . . [that also included] artificial fingernails and . . . artificial eyelashes."[11]

Seymour Menton noted in a 1964 study that a magical quality is "achieved by juxtaposing scenes filled with very realistic details with completely fantastic situations."[12] This quality is exemplified in the novella in a description of the grandmother's plight following the kidnapping of Eréndira by the missionaries. The grandmother is shown as she camps outside the fortified mission:

Early that morning the grandmother slept less than before. She lay awake pondering things, wrapped in a wool blanket while the early hour got her memory all mixed up and the repressed raving struggled to get out even though she was awake, and she had to tighten her heart with her hand so as not to be suffocated with the memory of a house by the sea with great red flowers where she had been happy. She remained that way until the mission bell rang and the first lights went on in the windows and the desert became saturated with the smell of the hot bread of matins. Only then did she abandon her fatigue, tricked by the illusion that Eréndira had got up and was looking for a way to escape and come back to her.[13]

E. Dale Carter suggested in 1966 that "magic realism" possesses an allegorical quality, as well as a sense of time and space which is contrary to normally accepted standards.[14] With regard to time, for example, García Márquez points out the eerily ethereal quality of the grandmother's advice to Eréndira when she advises Eréndira to " . . . sleep slowly so that you won't get tired, because tomorrow is Thursday, the longest day of the week."[15] In addition, García Márquez distorts chronological time on occasion by means of hyperbole. For instance, the author notes that "Eréndira needed six hours just to set and wind the . . . numerous clocks of unthinkable sizes and shapes."[16]

Luis Leal in 1967 pointed out that in "magic realism," unlike in fantastic literature, mysteries do not intrude on accepted reality from some nether dimension, but are rather an intrinsic part of that reality. The magic-realist writer, Leal stated, confronts reality in order to extract and capture those mysteries which, since they are innate to the reality, need not be explained nor justified.[17] Thus, the mysteries of reality are presented in a mostly matter-of-fact manner, suggesting a kind of "pre-scientific" view of reality,[18] according to critic Hilda Perera. Ulises, the love-smitten, wingless angel who frees Eréndira from her enslavement, and his mother engage in the following perfectly normal drama:

When Ulises returned to the house with the pruning tools, his mother asked him for her four o'clock medicine, which was on a nearby table. As soon as he touched them, the glass and the bottle changed color. Then, out of pure play, he touched a glass pitcher that was on the table beside some tumblers and the pitcher also turned blue. His mother observed him while she was taking her medicine and when she was sure that it was not a delirium of her pain, she asked him . . .

"How long has that been happening to you?"

"Ever since we came back from the desert," Ulises said. . . .

In order to demonstrate, one after the other he touched the glasses that were on the table and they all turned different colors.

"Those things happen only because of love," his mother said.[19]

A short while later, having noticed Ulises's inability to eat bread, the mother explains that "people who are lovesick can't eat bread."[20]

These ideas of Luis Leal have been examined and developed in the mid-nineteen seventies by Lucila-Inés Mena, who has applied to them Tzvetan Todorov's theories on fantastic literature.[21]

Vicente Cabrera and Luis González-del-Valle argued in 1972 that magic-realist reality is conceived by means of a process that first invents the irreal, then elevates the irreal to a level of acceptable truth. Thus, reality is re-created artistically, not merely injected with magical elements.[22]

More recently, in 1983, Stephen Hart emphasized that in

> . . . the magical-realist universe . . . nothing is supernatural or paranormal without being at the same time real, and vice-versa. [Since] the world of magical realism is at once natural and supernatural [whenever the laws of nature appear to go askew,] . . . the supernatural is presented in a natural, matter-of-fact manner . . . [making] the most magical happenings seem believable.[23]

Hart's essence is captured in Garciá Márquez's description of the locale wherein the grandmother's abode is situated: "The house was far away from everything, in the heart of the desert, next to a settlement with miserable and burning streets where the goats committed suicide from desolation when the wind of misfortune blew."[24]

For the purpose of summarizing the aforementioned remarks, it seems most appropriate to refer to the conclusions reached by Juan Barroso VIII in his thorough 1977 study of "magic realism" and the works of Alejo Carpentier. Barroso identified three major schools of thought vis-à-vis "magic realism." They are the following: a) that which views "magic realism" as an artistic attempt to capture the mystery behind the reality; b) that which views "magic realism" merely as an artistic technique; and c) that which views "magic realism" as a Latin American phenomenon that focuses on the continent's "cultural syncretism" as its major theme.[25]

It is important to note that the major works that best reflect "magic realism" in Latin American literature have fused these three schools, resulting in the literary triumphs of, for example, García Márquez, Amado, Cortázar, and Allende. Furthermore, the characteristics of "magic realism" are easily discernible in contemporary works of fiction by non-Latin American writers, a point that will be addressed later in this essay. Interestingly enough, Gregory Rabassa, translator of *One Hundred Years of Solitude* into English, claims that the first magical realist was the renowned Cervantes, himself.[26]

Also, following the dicta of Italian art critic Massimo Bontempelli in the early Thirties, it can be unequivocally stated that most of the generally accepted characteristics that help define "magic realism" are readily discovered in other artistic media, not just in painting, as Franz Roh has argued. Thus, a case can be made that the attributes of "magic realism" can be found in poetry, the novel, and most certainly in film.

García Márquez, himself, has been fascinated by film for most of his life. From a relatively young age, he has maintained a strange love/hate relationship with the film medium. He was obsessed early on with movies and was determined to be a screenwriter even before he found fame as a novelist. As we know, García Márquez wrote the screenplay for *Eréndira* and most recently co-wrote the script for the 1988 film *Un señor muy viejo con unas alas enormes* (*A Very Old Man with Enormous Wings*), based on his short story of the same title. García Márquez's earliest scripting efforts, however, were a total disaster. In fact, he describes his relationship to film in this manner: "The cinema and I are like an ill-matched married couple—I can't live with it and I can't live without it."[27]

In the mid-1950s, García Márquez went to Rome to write film criticism. Because of his intense interest in cinema, he began to study film at the Centro Sperimentale. However, because he was primarily drawn to screenwriting, he was disappointed by the technical and directorial emphasis of the program and left after one year. During this time, however, he did get a chance to work with screenwriter Cesare Zavattini and director Vittorio De Sica.

Following several years in Paris and New York, García Márquez settled in Mexico in 1961, determined at last to be a successful screenwriter. He waited two years before getting the chance to collaborate with Carlos Fuentes on *El gallo de oro*, based on a short story by Juan Rulfo. During this time, García Márquez worked on a number of other projects, most notably with Fuentes on the adaptation of Rulfo's *Pedro Páramo*, which Fuentes—after viewing the result—claimed was the major disaster of modern Mexican cinema.[28]

Now profoundly disillusioned, García Márquez returned to a novel that he had been working on since the age of 19, a novel that he called the very opposite of cinema, a work which he completed in 1967, *One Hundred Years of Solitude*.

Apparently, García Márquez wrote the tale of Eréndira and her grandmother as an original screenplay during the middle 1960s. When a film did not materialize immediately, García Márquez used the tale as a single paragraph in *One Hundred Years of Solitude*. He subsequently constructed a novella from his screenplay. Since he is reported to have lost the original script, when *Eréndira* was filmed in 1981, he had to reconstruct the scenario from memory.

The film, directed by Ruy Guerra, follows the novella quite faithfully, or perhaps it's the other way around. The major addition to the film is the expansion of the role of Senator Onésimo Sánchez. In the novella, there is a mere mention of the Senator as an official who can supply the grandmother with a letter attesting to her moral integrity, thus smoothing her progression through the desert to the sea. In the film, the Senator is given a speaking role in two major sequences and is played by the well-known European actor Michel, also known as Michael Lonsdale.

Interestingly enough, several of the magical realistic manifestations take place in the film during the scenes which feature the Senator, who is characterized by García Márquez as a world-weary, cynical politician, part charlatan, part visionary, trying to bring water and natural rejuvenation to the desert region. And it is the youthful freshness of Eréndira—sent by the grandmother to entice the Senator into providing the desired letter of transit—who brings the lonely, despairing Senator a temporary relief from his own parched existence. Another reason for the enlargement of the Senator's role may have been García Márquez's desire to point up the political implications of his material, the wretched economic conditions and the deceit of the administrative officials—social comment that García Márquez has added to the screenplay.

Several other changes that García Márquez has made between the novella and the film have no doubt been prompted by the needs of the cinematic medium. For instance, both the novella and film focus on the metamorphosis of Eréndira from a sleepwalking slave completely subservient to her grandmother's wishes—note her zombie-like reply of "Sí, abuela," "Yes, grandmother," that runs like a metronomic leitmotif throughout the story—to a mature woman ready to assume her own identity and to take control of her own destiny. In the film, this metamorphosis is symbolized by Eréndira's palm, which is blank when the audience initially meets her and which magically grows lines after the death of her grandmother. In the novella, it is Eréndira's face that matures and becomes lined. No doubt García Márquez realized that creating changes in a hand rather than on a face was a technical accomplishment easier to achieve on screen. Too, the basic idea of gaining a "life-line" and a "love-line" is given more impact when a hand receives this natural marking.

Another addition to the film is an expansion of the grandmother's dialogue while she consumes the poisoned birthday cake. It is quite probable that García Márquez wished to elongate this scene in order that this attempt on the grandmother's life have maximum cinematic impact. And indeed the scene does enthrall the audience because the grandmother, in extreme close-up, hungrily devours the poisoned cake, shoving it into her mouth with both hands, making all the more graphic both her greed and her indestructibility. This representation of greed parallels a moment at the beginning of the film in which the grandmother greedily shoves chocolate candy into her mouth while reminiscing about her long-lost youth.

Of course, the most significant feature of the film and the element that places it squarely in the category of "magic realism" is its at once grotesque and almost otherworldly *mise en scène*. From the opening shots, the audience is titillated by the grandmother's grandly rococo mansion, replete with gaudy theatrical trappings, fanciful Victorian bric-a-brac, artificial flowers—not one, but hundreds—and her pet ostrich. There are also the grandmother's eccentric and extravagant costumes, composed of feathers, brocade wraps, fringed shawls, and vests filled with gold ingots.

Always García Márquez and Guerra treat the *mise en scène*, no matter how bizarre, as a very natural element of the narrative. García Márquez and Guerra are telling the viewer that these rooms, these vistas are the real and natural environment of Eréndira and her grandmother. This viewpoint is evident in Guerra's depiction of the vast landscape of ruin and destruction following the devastating fire that sets in motion the curse that condemns Eréndira to a life of prostitution. Too, there is the gigantic cardboard steamship that the Senator sets up as a backdrop for his political speeches which promise water for the drought-stricken country. This ship of hope, belching black smoke that is stoked from behind the cardboard superstructure, is an outlandish, but nevertheless impressive vision that awes the local peasants, just as the Senator intended. Only the grandmother refuses to be taken in by the Senator's tactics, as she skewers the sham display with her comment that it is "the same old shit."

When the company of black-robed missionaries rises up from the desolate landscape to interdict the grandmother and her entourage and to kidnap Eréndira, the audience is struck by this awesome and sudden appearance of the missionaries and is unsure whether the missionaries' arrival is an encouraging or evil omen. The fantastic atmosphere in the film is further enhanced by the rituals of the mission to which Eréndira is taken, rituals which puzzle and intrigue Eréndira, and by the mad frenzy with which Ulises, Eréndira's young lover, sets about his sworn task of murdering the grandmother.

As usual in the realm of "magic realism," there are the strange incidents accepted as wholly natural, such as the oranges that grow diamonds at their core, the ordinary drinking glasses that light up in brilliant colors when Ulises touches them, and the great gobs of hair that the grandmother pulls from her head upon discovering that her hair can be ripped out by the handfuls. All of these incidents in the film follow similar incidents in the novella, but the film makes these occurrences even more wondrous through their vivid realization on-screen.

The *mise en scène*, the atmosphere, the incidents in the film are all treated as if they were normal ordinary occurrences, thus, "magic realism" pushes the film into a kind of surreal world. And in fact, it was Stephen Hart of the University of Cambridge who commented on the correlation between surrealism in art and "magic realism."[29] A major difference, however, is that "magic realism" does not focus on the psychological elements that are often associated with surrealism.

In the novella, the grandmother is shown as rapacious, demanding, essentially heartless, determined to control all destinies that have contact with her. The grandmother has these same traits in the film. However, in the novella, she is described as very fat. In the film, this crucial role is taken by international screen star Irene Papas, who is lean and almost strikingly attractive in an androgynous sort of way. Her facial features, heavily made up, are strong; her voice is low and resonating. It is probable that Guerra, the director, or perhaps García Márquez, chose Papas for this central role because she projects a cruel ferocity and a fierce capacity to devour all who thwart her will, attributes that perfectly suit the character. Fatness connotes softness, as well as eccentricity. Papas avoids any sense of softness, unless it is a self-pitying and cloying attempt on the part of the grandmother to relive her former triumphs and defeats. Her larger-than-life freneticism is evidenced in her nightmarish caterwauling as she sleeps and in the superhuman way in which she fights off Ulises as he repeatedly stabs her, finally subduing her, though he is covered with the green slime that oozes from her body and cascades from her mouth during the death struggle.

Papas is perfect casting for the role, as are the other principals who embody García Márquez's characters. Claudia Ohana captures Eréndira's innocence and zombie-like acquiescence to the degrading situations thrust upon her by her grandmother. And Oliver Wehe is the very incarnation of Ulises, the "angel without wings," who becomes the instrument of Eréndira's liberation, her angel of freedom. All three actors give their characters outsize personalities; they perform at an exaggerated level in order to point up the characteristics that provide the central conflict in the material and lead to the subsequent resolution of that conflict.

Ruy Guerra and his production team have used their craft with evident care to translate García Márquez's adult fable to the screen. One must credit Guerra for recreating the hypnotic pace of the novella with his long-in-duration shots which match with uncanny precision the theme of Eréndira sleepwalking through the torture of her life, suppressing the feelings that, if awakened, would bring her unbearable pain. When he needs to push the cinematic pace to a frenzy, as he does in the rape sequence, Guerra can quicken his editing in order to heighten the impact of Eréndira's degradation. Guerra also lingers in extreme close-up on the glowering features of Irene Papas, underscoring her gluttony and greed and her monstrous and inhumane domination of Eréndira. Guerra's close-ups of the child-like features of Eréndira create sympathy; his close-ups of the grandmother induce repulsion.

Guerra also uses sound expressively. García Márquez's "wind of misfortune" that sets in motion Eréndira's fate is palpably present during the film's opening sequence, as the glasses and cups and bric-a-brac and chandelier crystals in the grandmother's house all clink and tremble in unison, suggesting a strong sense of foreboding. Similarly, Guerra and his designers, Pierre Cardiou and Raine Chaper, create a veritable torrential downpour that accompanies Eréndira's ravishing. In fact, Guerra's *mise en scène* continually underlines the awful excesses of nature, the foreboding wind, the tragic fire, the unrelenting rain, the sterile desert, and finally, the nourishing ocean. These heightened effects, all of course suggested by García Márquez in the novella, are utilized by Guerra to establish indelibly the mystery and magic of the real world as envisioned by García Márquez.

The at once fetid and desiccated atmosphere of the novella remains intact in the film, as does the language of the novella, the elliptical language that García Márquez uses as he twists his comments just enough so that their offbeat references at one and the same time *do* and *do not* make sense, as when the grandmother advises Eréndira to take the artificial flowers outside for a breath of fresh air or to sleep slowly so as not to be too tired in the morning or to water the graves of her father and grandfather or when Ulises's mother notices that he has been avoiding bread and concludes that he must be in love because people who are lovesick cannot eat bread. The incongruities of language and action in both the novella and film also create a kind of bizarre humor that keeps the grotesqueries from becoming too overwhelmingly disturbing.

Just as "magic realism" has been a major influence on Latin American literature, "magic realism" has also been a major stylistic device used in Latin American films, most notably *Xica da Silva*, *Macunaíma*, *Dona Flor and Her Two Husbands*, and *Bye, Bye Brasil*. García Márquez's taut fable *Chronicle of a Death Foretold*, definitely created in the magical realistic mode, has recently been fashioned into a film that is currently in worldwide distribution. And as previously mentioned, a film adaptation by García Márquez of his short story "A Very Old Man with Enormous Wings" debuted at the Venice Film Festival in September, 1988.

To examine in depth the manifestations of "magic realism" in Western literature and film would warrant a major study. Although the dominant strain in American and European literature during the 19th and the better part of the 20th centuries has been that of naturalism and realism, there have been, however, certain writers and subsequently certain filmmakers who appear to fall under the magical-realist rubric. In American literature, mention can be made of Southern writers such as Truman Capote in *Other Voices, Other Rooms*, Carson McCullers in *The Ballad of the Sad Café* and *Reflections in a Golden Eye*, and Flannery O'Connor in *Wise Blood*. Magic-realist attributes can be found in John Barth's *The Floating Opera* and *The Sot-Weed Factor* and John Cheever's "The Swimmer" and *Bullet Park*, as well as T. Correghesan Boyle's *Water Music* and *World's End*. Recently, critics have found evidence of "magic realism" in William Kennedy's *Quinn's Book*. In European literature one might mention the fiction of Kafka with *The Metamorphosis* and of Günter Grass with *The Tin Drum* or more recently Patrick Susskind with *Perfume*. In Great Britain, one might suggest the fiction of Ronald Firbank with *The Eccentricities of Cardinal Pirelli*, of Lawrence Durrell with *The Alexandria Quartet*, of William Golding with *The Lord of the Flies*, of Jonathan Barnes with *Flaubert's Parrot*. In addition, one might add the tales of Denmark's Isak Dinesen as exemplified by "Babette's Feast." Both Italian author Umberto Eco in *The Name of the Rose* and Portuguese novelist José Saramago in *Baltasar and Blimunda* express the influence of "magic realism."

In film, certainly one might consider the work of Werner Herzog in *Aguirre: The Wrath of God* and *Fitzcarraldo*, of Luis Buñuel in *Viridiana* and *The Discreet Charm of the Bourgeoisie*, of Rainer Werner Fassbinder in *Querelle*, and most certainly of Federico Fellini in, for example, *Satyricon*, *Juliet of the Spirits*, and *Amarcord*. Because of the strong realist tradition in American films, it is more difficult to find evidence of "magic realism" in the work of American directors, but one could cite a number of films directed by Francis Ford Coppola, most notably *Apocalypse Now*, *Rumblefish*, and *One from the Heart*. One might include Steven Spielberg's *ET*. And certainly the recent controversial film from David Lynch, *Blue Velvet*, could be considered. Even Robert Redford's new film *The Milagro Beanfield War* could be analyzed for its magic-realist influences.

What do David Lynch and Federico Fellini and García Márquez and Ruy Guerra have in common? They and other artists have utilized a style or mode based on realism, but obviously pushing beyond realism, in order to explore the awful and magnificent mysteries and magicalities of the daily round. In the example under discussion, *Eréndira*, García Márquez and Guerra have created a fable of liberation, of the journey that Eréndira and all sentient beings must take beyond the dehumanizing curse and the enslaving witch to self-awakening and eventually to self-realization. As critics Stephen Hart and Luis Leal have pointed out, "In the magical-realist novel [and by extension the magical-realist film], mystery palpitates with the real rather than descending sporadically upon it." Hart and Leal agree that these works allow "us to see the fantastic within the real and not apart from it."[30] *Eréndira* in both its incarnations—novella and film—is a supreme example of the magical-realist view of the world in all its bizarre and wondrous manifestations.

From *Literature Film Quarterly* 17, no. 2 (1989): 113-122. Copyright © 1989 by Salisbury State University. Reprinted by permission.

Notes

1. Gabriel García Márquez, "The Incredible and Sad Tale of Innocent Eréndira and Her Heartless Grandmother," trans. by Gregory Rabassa. In *Collected Stories* (New York: Harper & Row, Publishers, 1984) 262-311.

2. Quoted in Seymour Menton, *Magic Realism Rediscovered, 1918-1981* (Philadelphia: The Art Alliance Press, 1983) 19.

3. Juan Barroso VIII, *Realismo mágico y lo real maravilloso en El reino de este mundo y El siglo de las luces* (Miami: Ediciones Universal, 1977) 14-15. This book's thorough investigation of criticism on "magic realism" has been invaluable to this essay.

4. Menton 21-22.

5. Menton 13.

6. Alejo Carpentier, *El reino de este mundo*. In *Obras completas de Alejo Carpentier*, vol. 2, 2nd ed. (Mexico: siglo veintiuno editores, sa, 1983) 13-18. Carpentier concludes his essay asking: "But what is the history of the American continent if not a chronicle of the wondrously real?"

7. Angel Flores, "Magic Realism in Spanish American Fiction," *Hispania*, 38, No. 2 (May 1955) 187-92.

8. See Barroso, pp. 26-28. Original source: James Irby, *La influencia de William Faulkner encuatro narradores hispanoamericanos* (Mexico: Editorial Mimeográfica de Juan Ruiz Belazco, 1957).

9. García Márquez 295.

10. García Márquez 281.

11. García Márquez 272-73.

12. Quoted in Barroso, p. 29. See Seymour Menton, *El cuento hispanoamericano: antología crítica histórica*, vol. II (México: Fondo de Cultura Económica, 1964).

13. García Márquez 284.

14. See Barroso, p. 31. Original source: E. Dale Carter, *Magic Realism in Contemporary Argentinian Fiction* (Los Angeles: University of Southern California Press, 1966). Carter's ideas are reiterated in his "Breve reseña del realismo mágico en hispanoamérica, *"Ocho cuentos hispanoamericanos,"* Antologiá del realismo mágico* (New York: The Odyssey Press, 1970).

15. García Márquez 295.

16. García Márquez 263-64.

17. Luis Leal, "El realismo mágico en la literatura hispanoamericana," *Cuadernos Americanos*, 153, No. 4 (julio-agosto 1967) 230-35.

18. Hilda Perera, *IDAPO: El sincretismo en los cuentos negros de Lydia Cabrera* (Miami: Ediciones Universal, 1971) 103.

19. García Márquez 288.

20. García Márquez 289.

21. See Lucila-Inés Mena, "Hacia una formulación teórica del realismo mágico," *Bulletin Hispanique*, 77, No. 3-4 (juillet-decembre 1975), pp. 395-407, and "Fantasía y realismo mágico," in *Otros mundos, otros fuegos: fantasía y realismo mágico en Iberoamérica*, ed. by Donald Yates (East Lansing: Latin American Studies Center of Michigan State University, 1975) 63-68.

22. Vicente Cabrera and Luis González-del-Valle, *La nueva ficción hispano-americana a través de Miguel Ángel Asturias y Gabriel García Márquez* (New York: Eliseo Torres, 1979) 17-18.

23. Stephen Hart, "Magical Realism in Gabriel García Márquez's *Cien años de soledad*," *INTI: Revista de Literatura Hispánica*, No. 16-17 (Fall-Spring 1982-1983), pp. 37-52. This article also discusses the role of scientific explanations.

24. García Márquez 264.

25. Barroso 42-43.

26. Paul Gray, "Bridge over Cultures," *Time* 132 (11 July 1988) 75.

27. Julianne Burton, "Learning to Write at the Movies: Film and the Fiction Writer in Latin America," *The Texas Quarterly*, 18 (Spring 1975) 92.

28. Burton 96.

29. Hart 40-41.

30. Hart 40.

"The Paralysis of the Instant":
The Stagnation of History and the Stylistic Suspension of Time in Gabriel García Márquez's *La hojarasca*

Deborah Cohn

Deborah Cohn places the influence of William Faulkner on García Márquez alongside the influence of James Joyce and Virginia Woolf. She analyzes *La hojarasca* (*Leaf Storm* in English) as a Faulknerian experiment, especially as echoes of three books: *As I Lay Dying*, *Absalom, Absalom!*, and *The Sound and the Fury*. She focuses on the distortion of historical chronology in internal monologues and other ways in which García Márquez collapses time into a continuous present. Cohn uses these links to meditate on the fatalism that permeates this early narrative about Macondo. — I.S.

Gabriel García Márquez's first novel, *La hojarasca* (1955), has often been deemed "too Faulknerian," and García Márquez himself criticized for not yet having developed a voice of his own, differentiated from that of the southerner.[1] To be sure, García Márquez's early journalistic writings clearly reflect his fascination with Faulkner: in April of 1950, he called the southerner "lo más extraordinario que tiene la novela del mundo moderno" [the most extraordinary thing that the novel of the modern world offers],[2] and predicted that the Nobel Prize Selection Committee would, lamentably, bypass Faulkner and choose instead to honor the Venezuelan Rómulo Gallegos that year, in the same way that it had previously overlooked James Joyce in favor of Pearl S. Buck, and for the same presumably shortsighted reasons that it had withheld the honor from Marcel Proust and Virginia Woolf. Happily, several months later García Márquez was proven incorrect, and in an article commemorating the choice of Faulkner, he essentially congratulated the Committee for having chosen "el novelista más grande del mundo actual y uno de los más interesantes de todos los tiempos"

(1980, 494; the greatest modern novelist and one of the most interesting of all times).

As should already be apparent, though, these same essays also express García Márquez's keen interest in other modern writers, most frequently the aforementioned Joyce, Proust, and Woolf, as well as Kafka. He saw in their works and techniques the potential to renovate Colombian literature. "Todavía no se ha escrito en Colombia la novela que esté indudable y afortunadamente influida por los Joyce, por Faulkner o por Virginia Woolf" (A novel unmistakably and fortunately influenced by Joyce, Faulkner or Virginia Woolf has yet to be written in Colombia), he wrote in another article that year. He continues:

> Y he dicho "afortunadamente," porque no creo que podríamos los colombianos ser, por el momento, una excepción al juego de las influencias. . . . Faulkner mismo no podría negar la que ha ejercido sobre él, el mismo Joyce. Algo hay—sobre todo en el manejo del tiempo—entre Huxley y otra vez Virginia Wolf [*sic*]. Franz Kafka y Proust andan sueltos por la literatura del mundo moderno. Si los colombianos hemos de decidirnos acertadamente, tendríamos que caer irremediablemente en esta corriente. Lo lamentable es que ello no haya acontecido aún. (1980, 269)

> [I say "fortunately" because I don't think that Colombians can, at this time, be exceptions to the game of influence. . . . Faulkner himself would not be able to deny Joyce's influence in his work. There is something—especially in the use of time—between Huxley and, again, Virginia Woolf. Franz Kafka and Proust have been let loose in the literature of the modern world. If Colombians are to decide, we will have to fall into this current. It's simply a pity that this has not yet happened.]

He further deems these authors' lack of influence "una de las mayores fallas de nuestra novela" (1980, 269; one of the greatest flaws of our novel).

In this essay, I plan to explore how in his first novel García Márquez

---

undertakes the task of steering the Colombian novel in a new direction through his experimentation with one of the fundamental underpinnings of the realist novel: linear time. I will show how he suspends the forward movement of time in *La hojarasca* in the experiences of the individual characters and of the town of Macondo, and how his treatment of time reduplicates at the level of form the historical and social circumstances of a town in which the passage of time no longer has any significance. I will begin this project with a brief overview of García Márquez's relationship to the Euro-American modernists,[3] and, especially, to Faulkner and his vision of history, thereby situating him within his international literary context. Subsequently, I will establish points of contact between *La hojarasca* and works by Faulkner, Joyce, and Woolf,[4] with the ultimate goal of demonstrating how García Márquez incorporates, transforms, and, on occasion, undermines, stylistic innovations associated with modernism.

Numerous studies have been written on the influence of the modernists on the development of contemporary Latin American fiction. Comparisons to Joyce are relatively infrequent and tend to focus on his technical influence,[5] whereas studies of the influence of Woolf[6] and Faulkner address these authors' stylistic and thematic appeal to Latin American writers. Faulkner's legacy to and appropriation by the latter has been the central focus of the majority of these essays,[7] for reasons that will now be sketched briefly. Despite Faulkner's assertion that there is "no such thing as a regional writer, the writer simply uses the terms he is familiar with best" (1959, 95), the southerner can hardly be said to have cast his homeland as a simple bridge between regional reality and universal truths. Faulkner may well have invoked the world outside of the South, but the tales of Yoknapatawpha County simply cannot be reduced to a microcosm of the general upheavals of recent world history, for the author relied on history's traditional role as *magistra vitae* to draw attention to subjects of vital importance to the South. The universalizing humanist of later speeches and interviews is belied, then, by the "regional writer" whose concern with race, miscegenation, and prejudice, with the aftermath of the Civil War and the emergence of the New South, and with the divergent perspectives vying to be recognized as proffering the definitive version of the South's history, responds directly to social and political issues plaguing the "postage stamp of native soil" from whence he hailed (1956b, 255).[8]

I have argued elsewhere that the technical innovations of literary modernism provided Latin American authors with instruments that they felt allowed them to forge a style that they could consider their own (Cohn 1997). Above all, though, it was the symbiosis of subject and style that they perceived in Faulkner—in the Faulkner who was both modernist *and* southerner, in his carefully negotiated dialectic of the universal and the regional, in the acute consciousness of the South's past in its present that was rendered grammatically in sentences which encompass past, present, and future—that they found particularly pertinent to their efforts to describe the traumatic histories of their own nations. Indeed, García Márquez himself has rendered homage to Faulkner for precisely this concordance of form and content, and for its appropriateness to his own project:

El método "faulkneriano" es muy eficaz para contar la realidad latino-americana. Inconscientemente fue eso lo que descubrimos en Faulkner. Es decir, nosotros estábamos viendo esta realidad y queríamos contarla y sabíamos que el método de los europeos no servía, ni el método tradicional español; y de pronto encontramos el método faulkneriano adecuadísimo para contar esta realidad. (García Márquez and Vargas Llosa 1968, 52-53)

[The "Faulknerian" method is very effective in describing Latin American reality. Unconsciously, that was what we discovered in Faulkner. That is, we were seeing this reality and wanted to tell it, and we knew that the method of the Europeans didn't work, nor did the traditional Spanish method; and suddenly we found the Faulknerian method extremely accurate for describing this reality.]

Hence García Márquez joined with many of his fellow Latin American authors in embracing Faulkner as one of their own: "El Condado Yoknapatawpha tiene riberas en el Mar Caribe, así que de alguna manera Faulkner es un escritor del Caribe, de alguna manera es un escritor latinoamericano" (1968, 52-53; Yoknapatawpha County has banks on the Caribbean Sea; so in some way Faulkner is a writer of the Caribbean, in some way he is a Latin American writer).

Faulkner's influence on García Márquez in particular has been by far the favorite topic of this branch of inter-American comparative studies.[9] The parallels between the lives and works of the two Nobel Prize laureates are varied and intriguing: both were raised in traditional rural communities, impoverished and ravaged by war, and consumed by nostalgia for the past and its lost prosperity; the experiences of these communities, in turn, serve as the models for Yoknapatawpha County and Macondo, respectively, and for the changing orders which beset them; both often construct their narratives as family sagas; both address problems of innocence, honor, and guilt, of prejudice and violence, racial tensions and incest. Critics have focused on these similarities, but many also foreground the common attitudes towards time, history, and historical consciousness that pervade their works.[10] García Márquez's debt to Faulkner's treatment of time is evident both at the level of style and in the very stories he tells of people and towns struggling under the weight of their pasts and of issues that have continued to affect them into the present (Cohn 1997, 159-60).

Bearing these issues in mind, I would like to explore the levels at which the influence of Faulkner and other modernists operates in *La hojarasca* and, in particular, in the novel's representation of time and history.[11] From the use of multiple narrators to the italics which denote the embedding of a character's words in the thoughts of another, or (more important to a discussion of similarities in the two authors' treatment of time) which signal the flashbacks indicating the shifting of a character's thoughts from the present to the past, Faulkner's influence pervades the novel's form. *La hojarasca* is most frequently compared to *As I Lay Dying* (1930), for both novels center on a dead figure (the doctor and Addie Bundren, respectively) and the difficulties incurred while honoring a promise made to the deceased concerning their burial. There is also the undeniable (but less frequently noted) Faulkner of *Absalom, Absalom!* (1936): both novels are set against an historical backdrop of civil war and cycles of prosperity and decline; both rely on the same nonlinear narrative strategy of delaying the disclosure of critical information to the reader, impeding the reconstruction of events both private and historical; the questionable and enigmatic financial transaction between Mr. Coldfield and Colonel Sutpen, of which marriage to the daughter is a by-product, is reduplicated in García Márquez's Colonel's similarly unexplained deal with his future son-in-law; and the wisteria which signals the transitions from past to present in Miss Rosa's sections has its counterpart in the jasmine plant which is a living reminder of Isabel's dead mother.

Several even more critical parallels are to be found with *The Sound and the Fury* (1929). The perspective of the youngest narrator of *La hojarasca* is, like that of Benjy Compson, severely limited: Isabel's ten-year-old son is able to understand only what he can see, hear, smell, and touch, and his comprehension of time is similarly limited to that which is most immediate, that is, to the hours of the day and the days of the week. García Márquez's text also exhibits a view of humankind and, more importantly, an obsession with time that are strikingly similar to those of Quentin Compson. In the first place, Quentin's observation that "Father was teaching us that all men are just accumulations dolls stuffed with sawdust swept up from the trash heaps where all previous dolls had been thrown away" (1956a, 137) exactly encapsulates the description of Macondo given in the preface of *La hojarasca*: "En menos de un año [la hojarasca] arrojó sobre el pueblo los escombros de numerosas catástrofes anteriores a ella misma, esparció en las calles su confusa carga de desperdicios. Y esos desperdicios . . . [transformaron a Macondo] en un pueblo diferente y complicado, hecho con los desperdicios de los otros pueblos" (1986, 7; "In less than a year it sowed over the town the rubble of many catastrophes that had come before it, scattering its mixed cargo of rubbish in the streets. And all of a sudden that rubbish . . . changed [Macondo] into a different and more complex town, created out of the rubbish of other towns" [1972, 1]). Second, in the same way that time pursues Quentin—from the ticking of the clock (the "mausoleum of all hope and desire" [Faulkner 1956a, 59]) which opens his section to the final interior monologue which is sandwiched in between the tolling of bells on the three-quarter hour—determining the course of his section and day alike, *La hojarasca*, as I shall discuss in greater detail presently, begins and ends with references to the hour, is punctuated throughout by queries about the time, and similarly juxtaposes clock time with the interior time that strives to sidestep it.

The situation of the frame tale of *La hojarasca* on a specific day and date, and the use of multiple narrators, might on the surface also seem indebted to the structure of *The Sound and the Fury*, which is divided into four sections, each of which takes place on a different day and has a different narrator.[12] The restriction of the duration of García Márquez's novel to a single day, however, inscribes it in another tradition, one that Faulkner himself had drawn on: that of the novel-in-a-day, exemplified by Joyce's *Ulysses* (1922), which takes place on June 16, 1904, and Woolf's *Mrs. Dalloway* (1925), set on a day in mid-June soon after the end of World War I. In this genre, the action of the frame tale takes place within the formal unity of time marked by one calendar day. However, in keeping with modernist explorations of alternative modes of representing time, these novels encode a deliberate refutation of linear chronological time, for the psychological time of memory and speculation extracts the individual from clock time and injects years of experiences—past, present, and future—into the frame. All time (including, according to some interpretations, the rise and fall of humanity) is thus condensed into a single day through the experiential and extended present of the narrative focalizer. The frame of *La hojarasca* is even narrower than this: it takes place between 2:30 and 3 p.m. (the hour noted by several of the Gospels as that of the death of Christ) on Wednesday, September 12, 1928. Even this extreme brevity, however, does not impose any limits on the contents: García Márquez condenses approximately forty years of events (*fabula*)—from 1885, the beginning of the liberal wars in Colombia and the foundation of Macondo, through the arrival of the Colonel and his family and, later, the doctor, in the town, to the prosperity and decline ushered in by the banana company, the prohibition against the burial of the doctor, and the novel's narrative present—into thirty minutes of *sujet*. This of course anticipates the concentration of one hundred years into a single instant in Melquíades's manuscript in *Cien años de soledad*.

García Márquez carries out his distortion of linear historical time through the interior monologues that record the narrators' thoughts, and through the composite effect of the many monologues. The extent of the narrators' frames of social and historical reference differs significantly, and is almost immediately delimited by their reactions to the first chronological indicator, the sound of the train's horn, which marks 2:30. Isabel's young son, who remembers only the most recent past, thinks of his friends at the schoolyard and their daily rituals. Isabel, whose scope includes her personal and family history and the town's social codes, but who is only able to identify events as having taken place before or after one another (Ashok 1988, 18),[13] thinks that "a esta hora todo Macondo está pendiente de lo que hacemos en esta casa" (García Márquez 1986, 20; "at this moment all of Macondo is wondering what we're doing in this house" [1972, 9]). Finally, the Colonel, whose active participation in the doctor's and Macondo's past grants him the broadest temporal range (Sims 1976, 813), responds by explicitly situating the novel's events in historical time for the first time: "'Son las dos y media', pienso. *Las dos y media del 12 de setiembre de 1928; casi la misma hora de ese día de 1903 en que este hombre se sentó por primera vez a nuestra mesa y pidió hierba para comer*"

(1986, 32; "'It's two-thirty,' I think. *Two-thirty on September 12, 1928; almost the same hour of that day in 1903 when this man sat down for the first time at our table and asked for some grass to eat*" [1972, 17]).[14] The Colonel's noting of the hour problematizes linear narrative time by establishing the simultaneity of his monologue with those of his daughter and grandson, effectively collapsing all of them into the same brief moment which ends at the sound of the horn. Moreover, through his reference to the past, the character with the broadest historical perspective paradoxically expands the narrative's temporal scope to condense even more time into that single instant. Also, the italicized identification of a moment of contact between the past and the present precipitates a flashback in which the Colonel relives the past, extending the present backwards, and making it seem as if time has not passed. By the end of the first chapter, then, the sense of time as a continuous present which is the setting for the rest of the novel has been established.

The repeated references to the hour which open and close the novel—a similar exchange is recorded in the final monologues of mother and son at 3 p.m.[15]—correspond to another narrative strategy that García Márquez employs to subvert the passage of time at the level of the novel's structure. Like refrains, the repetition of a thought or dialogue or the repeated narration of the same scene both prevents the narrative from advancing and precludes a linear reading of the text: the reader must read backwards and forwards at once in order to locate all of the iterations of a refrain and establish the relative chronological order (or contemporaneity) of the monologues in which they appear. While examples of this technique abound,[16] the descriptions of Adelaida (the Colonel's wife and Isabel's stepmother) seem to best exemplify the novel's correlation of theme and style. Adelaida's resentment of the doctor demonstrates that she continues to dwell on his affront, obsessing about the past rather than engaging with her present reality. After he leaves the house, she prohibits anyone from ever entering his room again, as if she were trying to stop time in it at the moment of the insult; paradoxically, this has the effect of reifying the memory of the doctor rather than eradicating it for, as Isabel observes, the room "seguía siendo como algo suyo, como un fragmento de su personalidad que no podía ser desvinculado de nuestra casa mientras viviera en ella alguien que pudiera recordarlo" (1986, 88; "was still like something of his, a fragment of his personality which could not be detached from our house while anyone who might have remembered him still lived in it" [1972, 50]). Also, in her narration of the events precipitating the doctor's departure, Adelaida refers eight times to the eight-year period that the doctor had enjoyed her hospitality, reflecting her inability to let go of his unpaid debt (1986, 99-105; 57-62); moreover, Isabel describes her stepmother's attitude while recounting the events as if she were "viviendo de nuevo los episodios de aquella noche remota en que el doctor rehusó atender a Meme" (1986, 103; reliving the events of that remote night when the doctor refused to attend to Meme [translation mine]). Finally, both the Colonel and Isabel offer the same final image of a disillusioned, demoralized, and defeatist woman—the emblem of Macondo as a whole, as we shall see—who has given up fighting and hoping, and declared that "'Me quedaré aquí, aplanada hasta la hora del Juicio'" (1986, 143, 152; "'I'll stay collapsed here until Judgment Day'"; [1972, 86, 92]). By impeding the forward movement in the story, these textual repetitions can be understood as functioning as narrative correlatives to Macondo's stagnation, and to the emotional paralysis of its inhabitants.[17]

Adelaida's attitude is shared by other characters who are similarly unable to extricate themselves from the past or for whom the future only holds death. This fatalism, and the sense of predetermination that it complements, also presupposes a concept of time which is not linear: foreknowledge of the future requires that it somehow be present and identifiable in the present which, as a result, either offers premonitions of death or, conversely, appears to be the inevitable fulfillment of a fate determined in the past. On the one hand, on viewing the doctor's body, the boy first becomes aware of his own mortality. Moreover, his mother fears that heredity will determine the course of her son's life, that his physical resemblance to his father foreshadows a shared fate: "Mi hijo va a disolverse en el aire abrasante de este miércoles como le ocurrió a Martín. . . . Serán vanos todos mis sacrificios por este hijo si continúa pareciéndose a su padre" (1986, 137-38; "My son's going to dissolve in the boiling air of this Wednesday just as it happened to Martín. . . . All my sacrifices for this son will be in vain if he keeps on looking like his father" [1972, 82-83]). Also, Isabel is frequently told that she resembles her dead mother, who herself had been "martirizada por la ocupación de una muerte que se había compenetrado con ella en nueve meses de silencioso padecimiento" (1986, 48; "martyrized by the occupation of a death that had taken her over during nine months of silent suffering" [1972, 28]). The mother's embodiment of the principles of life and death further threatens to infect Isabel, who, when trying on her wedding dress, glimpses her own death: "Y ahora, viéndome en el espejo, yo veía los huesos de mi madre cubiertos por el verdín sepulcral. . . . Yo estaba fuera del espejo. Adentro estaba mi madre, mirándome, extendiendo los brazos desde su espacio helado, tratando de tocar la muerte que prendía los primeros alfileres de mi corona de novia" (1986, 108; "And now, looking at myself in the mirror, I saw my mother's bones covered by the mold of the tomb. . . . I was outside of the mirror. Inside was my mother, alive again, looking at me, stretching her arms out from her frozen space, trying to touch the death that was held together by the first pins of my bridal veil" [1972, 63]). The premonition is so strong that she later comments that the wedding dress could serve her as a shroud, in the same way that her mother had been buried in her gown. On the other hand, the death of the doctor is described variously as the predetermined culmination of the twenty-five years since his arrival at Macondo and as the event that the town had been awaiting for ten years. Isabel and the Colonel also view their—and the town's—present predicament as similarly preordained: they characterize it as "una tarea largamente premeditada" (1986, 18; a chore long since prepared for [translation mine]), a "castigo . . .

escrito desde antes de mi nacimiento" (1986, 22; "punishment . . . written down from before my birth" [1972, 11]), the "eslabonado cumplimiento de una profecía" (1986, 121; "linked fulfillment of a prophecy" [1972, 71]), and "la fatalidad [que] había empezado a cumplirse" (1986, 123; "fate [that] had begun to be fulfilled" [1972, 72]). Because the townspeople's lives are oriented towards the realization of what is already a foregone conclusion, and not towards effecting change, the time between beginning and end is effectively obviated before an action even starts because it is of no consequence to the outcome.

García Márquez uses two additional related mechanisms to collapse all time into a continuous present. This first is what Mario Vargas Llosa, in his early work *García Márquez: Historia de un deicidio*, labels "hyperbaton," the inversion of the order of disclosure of cause and effect, which grants the novel "su transcurrir circular de realidad donde el tiempo se halla suspendido o aun abolido" (1971, 284; its circular course, belonging to a reality in which time is suspended or even abolished). Hence the event which precipitates the injunction against the doctor's burial is alluded to three times in the Colonel's first monologue, but not explained until his last monologue. The disclosure clarifies the present predicament, but does not change it; also, rather than moving the narrative action any further into the future, it only expands the past, expounding upon what is already known, what has already happened. Second, García Márquez casts events which were recent in relation to the narrative present as meant to have taken place long before, and whose deferral had prolonged a period of time which should have ended. The Colonel, for example, claims that in 1918, the doctor was already "*un cadáver al que todavía no se le han muerto los ojos*" (1986, 135; "*a corpse whose eyes still haven't died*" [1972, 80]), and reiterates after his death that "este hombre había empezado a morir desde mucho tiempo atrás, aunque habían de transcurrir aún tres años antes de que esa muerte aplazada y defectuosa se realizara por completo" (1986, 151; "this man had begun to die a long time back, even though three years would pass before that postponed and defective death would [take place] completely" [1972, 91]). The doctor's death can be seen as analogous to the town's own situation, which essentially consists of waiting for its destiny to catch up to it. As Isabel comments, "Sacudida por el soplo invisible de la destrucción, también [nuestra casa] está en víspera de un silencioso y definitivo derrumbamiento. Todo Macondo está así desde cuando lo exprimió la compañía bananera" (1986, 153-54; "Shaken by the invisible breath of destruction, [our house] too is on the eve of a silent and final collapse. All of Macondo has been like that ever since it was squeezed by the banana company" [1972, 93]). Moreover, the doctor's death had now deprived the town of the only event that it still looked forward to.

The fatalism which leaves the townspeople passively awaiting their obliteration is the obverse of the nostalgia which has prevented them from ever fully letting go of the past to live in the present. When the Colonel and his family first moved to Macondo, then a burgeoning town, they were, Meme claims, unable to let go of the past that they had (not) left behind: "la llegada . . . fue la de una familia devastada, aferrada todavía a un reciente pasado esplendoroso" (1986, 44; "Their arrival . . . was that of a devastated family, still bound to a recent splendid past" [1972, 25]). Like Aeneas carrying his household gods with him as he fled Troy, the Colonel's family traveled with trunks "llenos con la ropa de los muertos anteriores al nacimiento de ellos mismos, de los antepasados que no podrían encontrarse a veinte brazas bajo la tierra . . . y hasta un baúl lleno de santos con los que reconstruían el altar doméstico en cada lugar que visitaban" (1986, 44; "full of clothing of people who had died before they'd been on earth, ancestors who couldn't have been found twenty fathoms under the earth . . . and even a trunk filled with the images of saints, which they used to reconstruct their family altar everywhere they stopped" [1972, 25]). But whereas Aeneas transported the gods to Rome to establish continuity between the world that he had left and the new community that he was to lead into the future, once settled in Macondo, the family's saints and luggage only served as anchors which kept them focused on the past, denied them a present, and further prevented them from leaving Macondo even after the town died. "Estamos atados a este suelo por un cuarto lleno de baúles," Isabel explains, "estamos sembrados a este suelo por el recuerdo de los muertos remotos cuyos huesos ya no podrían encontrarse a veinte brazas bajo la tierra" (1986, 155; "We're tied to this soil by a roomful of trunks. . . . We've been sown into this soil by the memory of the remote dead whose bones can no longer be found twenty fathoms under the earth" [1972, 94]).

Macondo's future is engraved on the faces and packed in the trunks of the members of the Colonel's household, foreshadowed from the town's earliest days. Thus does Isabel's description of Meme several years after she had moved in with the doctor echo the latter's own previous description of the family: "Nuestras vidas habían cambiado, los tiempos eran buenos . . . pero Meme vivía aferrada a un pasado mejor" (1986, 46; "Our lives had changed, the times were good . . . but Meme lived bound to a past that had been better" [my translation]). And this attitude is generalized throughout the town after the departure of the banana company: "Aquí quedaba una aldea arruinada . . . ocupada por gente cesante y rencorosa, a quien atormentaban el recuerdo de un pasado próspero y la amargura de un presente agobiado y estático" (1986, 132; "A ruined village was left here . . . occupied by unemployed and angry people who were tormented by a prosperous past and the bitterness of an overwhelm[ed] and static present" [1972, 79]). Macondo clings to the past in the face of a desolate present and thus also forfeits its future. Here, too, García Márquez's description of a region with a history of war and devastation, and of the paralysis wrought by memory may be partly indebted to his fascination with Faulkner's depictions of characters oppressed and suppressed by the past. Like Quentin Compson, whose "very body was an empty hall echoing with sonorous defeated names; [who] was not a being, an entity, he was a commonwealth . . . a barracks filled with stubborn backlooking ghosts" (Faulkner 1972, 12), the inhabitants of Macondo are "gente . . . devastada por los recuerdos" (García Márquez 1986, 155; "people devastated by memories" [1972, 94]), held in place by their ancestors' trunks, and one step away from the jasmine plant—the reification of memory—whose perfume continues to pervade the house nine years after it is uprooted. As Ada remarks, "'con los jazmines sucede lo mismo que con las personas que salen a vagar de noche después de muertas'" (1986, 80; "'The same thing happens with jasmines as with people who come out and wander through the night after they're dead'" [1972, 46]).

In *La hojarasca*, then, García Márquez replaces chronological progression—both narrative and experiential—with "la parálisis del instante" (1986, 77; "the paralysis of the instant" [1972, 44]), the prolongation of a moment which stretches to encompass the minute, lifetime, or novel separating cause and effect. This sense of time finds its counterpart in the boy's perception of "el minuto que no transcurre" (1986, 24; "the minute that doesn't pass" [1972, 12]), and in the "tiempo . . . de afuera" (1986, 73), the external time that Isabel distinguishes from interior, subjective time, and which, because she explicitly equates it with movement, she claims has stopped. "Mientras se mueva algo," she thinks, "puede saberse que el tiempo ha transcurrido. Antes no. Antes de que algo se mueva es el tiempo eterno" (1986, 77; "When something moves you can tell that time has passed. Not till then. Until something moves time is eternal" [1972, 43]). And almost nothing in the novel, from the corpse to the narrators who sit still and wait, to the dust that covers the room and the ruined town, moves. And this stagnation is rendered as eternity, which is thereby deprived of its transcendence. Herein lies the key to deciphering the novel: Isabel's understanding of objective time is reduplicated structurally in the refrains and duplicate descriptions that hinder the forward movement of the narrative. Vargas Llosa establishes the link between repetition, movement, and time beautifully. "El uso repetido de imágenes o de adjetivos en torno a cada personaje," he writes, representa formalmente lo que para el coronel y los suyos es la naturaleza humana: repetición eterna. En este mundo donde nada cambia—ni el individuo, ni las clases, ni las relaciones—, donde no hay libertad, no existe, propiamente hablando, un transcurrir . . . ¿Cómo se puede entender el tiempo en esta realidad? Como algo circular: cada minuto contiene a los otros, el final está en el principio y viceversa. Así lo intuye el coronel: el destino final de Macondo está escrito en su origen. El tiempo, desde el punto de vista de la historia social o individual, no es retroceso ni avance, sino movimiento en redondo. . . . Hay una circulación que se parece al estatismo, en la que presente—los tres personajes, quietos en torno al cadáver—y pasado—todos los antecedentes de esa situación—se confunden: el pasado no precede al presente en la ficción, coexiste con él, mana de él mismo. *La hojarasca* comienza y termina en la inmovilidad. (Vargas Llosa 1971, 273-74)

[The repetition of images or adjectives to describe each character represents formally what human nature is to the colonel and his family: eternal repetition. In this world where nothing changes—not the individual, nor classes, nor relations—where there is no liberty, the passage of time does not, properly speaking, exist. . . . How can time be understood in this reality? As something circular: each minute contains the others, the end is in the beginning, and vice versa. That's how the colonel understands it: Macondo's final destiny is written in its origin. Time, from the point of view of social or individual history, does not move forwards or backwards but, rather, in a circle. . . . There is a certain circular movement that appears static, in which the present—the three characters, sitting still by the cadaver—and the past—all that had led up to this situation—merge: the past does not precede the present in this fiction, it coexists with it, it emanates from it. *La hojarasca* begins and ends with immobility.]

Repetition is not progress. By continuously returning to a point in the past, then, the textual repetitions hold the narrative steady at a single moment, entrenching it in a time that is already paralyzed.

In keeping with the modernist search for the universal, the eternal, and the constants in human experience across time, Robert Sims has argued that García Márquez sets the stories of the doctor and Macondo in a "continuous present that becomes timeless . . . which dissociates them from past, present and future, plac[ing] them in an ahistorical context" (1976, 812). Moreover, he avers that what he identifies as circular time, in contrast to that discussed by Vargas Llosa, "allows Macondo to exist as a place without beginning or end . . . [and] adds a vital, temporal dimension to the creation of the myth of Macondo that becomes a place where [in the words of Carlos Fuentes] 'todo puede recomenzar'" (1976, 816-17; "everything can begin anew"). Quite to the contrary. The structuralist approach that Sims takes here is simply untenable. The atemporality that he describes does not affirm the viability of myth but, rather, is only the sense that time has ceased to be important precisely because history has already happened in and to Macondo, and that the only possible change left is for the apocalyptic wind to raze a town that has already been set aside with all the others "que han dejado de prestar servicio a la creación" (García Márquez 1986, 153; "that have stopped being of any service to creation" [1972, 93]). The tragedy of Macondo is, after all, determined by a historically-specific force: it is not Fortune but, rather, the fortune brought and taken away from Macondo by the banana company that brought about the town's ultimate downfall. One might argue that García Márquez ascribes to *la hojarasca*—also called *el ventisquero*, *la tempestad* and *la avalancha* [the blizzard, tempest, and avalanche]—the generic qualities of a Fate which is unstoppable, and whose effects are compounded by the decline brought about by the passage of time. Certainly his characterization of the leaf storm as a world-upside-down deliberately inscribes it within the classical tradition of the plague, from Sophocles' *Oedipus the King* to Daniel Defoe's *Journal of the Plague Year* (both favorite works of García Márquez), and thus enhances its almost mythical status, while the constancy of the force that recreates Macondo in the image and likeness of the towns that it has already destroyed likewise allows it to be viewed as an atemporal phenomenon. But it is ludicrous to attempt to reduce Macondo to an abstract mythical essence by distilling it from its historical context. The timeless and the timely are inextricable here: the chronological specificity of the novel, its situation in 1928, the same year as the strike and massacre of United Fruit Company workers in Colombia which plays such an important role in *Cien años de soledad*, rejects any attempt to dehistoricize the banana company and the ravages that it effected.[18] And, as García Márquez has commented on numerous occasions, Macondo is in many respects a fictionalized representation of a geographic and historical reality. Thus, the leaf storm remains—at least in part—the historically-based cipher of imperialism and neocolonialism. The repeated exercise of its powers stops time from progressing in Macondo, in the same way that the repetition of a phrase or scene detains the forward movement of the narrative, but it hardly grants the town the possibility of regeneration or vitality. Moreover, it further dooms the townspeople by infecting them with an attitude towards time that deprives them of the belief in a future in which their efforts would bear fruit and, by extension, of the will to rebuild.

> "Hace diez años, cuando sobrevino la ruina," the Colonel avers, "el esfuerzo colectivo de quienes aspiraban a recuperarse habría sido suficiente para la reconstrucción. Habría bastado . . . comenzar otra vez por el principio. Pero a la hojarasca la habían enseñado a ser impaciente; a no creer en el pasado ni en el futuro. Le habían enseñado a creer en el momento actual y a saciar en él la voracidad de sus apetitos." (1986, 147)

> ["Ten years ago, when ruin came down upon us, the collective strength of those who looked for recovery might have been enough for reconstruction. All that was needed was to . . . start again from scratch. But they'd trained the leaf storm to be impatient, not to believe in either past or future. They'd trained it to believe in the moment and to sate the voracity of its appetite in it."] (1972, 89)

In the end, Macondo remains enslaved to its belief in a fate that it has in part invented for itself, and which it uses to justify its continued failure to move from paralysis into the future.

The sense of confinement by history and time constitutes one of the most significant differences between the novel-in-a-day as practiced by Joyce and Woolf on the one hand and García Márquez on the other, even as if reaffirms the affinities in the world views of the Colombian and Faulkner. Joyce and Woolf used the genre to demonstrate how psychological time was able to transcend the strictures imposed by the clock, while mythical and biblical references similarly connoted the continuity of cultural paradigms over and despite the passage of time. García Márquez's recourse to the Antigone legend (in the epigraph) and to the plague motif do situate *La hojarasca* within a long-standing cultural tradition. However, the novel's limited temporal frame rejects a sense of freedom from time by underscoring the entrapment of its subjects in the present. The narrators' attention wanders to the past, but repeatedly returns to the point of departure; all describe the same scene, and recount the events of the same half-hour. The narrative present is further deprived of a future: except for the boy's thoughts of going out with his friends after leaving the doctor's house, reflecting a limited ability to conceive of the immediate future, all of the monologues are retrospective, only able to recall the past. Also, rather than extend the narrative frame beyond its 3 o'clock endpoint, they only describe actions which have already been narrated, or which are long completed. The backward movement of interior time eludes the limits of chronological time, then, intertwining past and present, but only to enclose both characters and collectivity in a time which is static, and to prolong interminably the (objectively) brief period spent waiting. As we have seen, the narrative is repeatedly dragged back to the same point, suspending the diachronic action in the framing story. In the end, the narrators have yet to leave the house which, like the man who had inhabited it, had for years been closed off from the town and fresh air alike. They, like Macondo and the novel itself, have no future.

Critics often compare García Márquez's notions of time to those of Henri Bergson. Like the French philosopher, he depicts time not as a continuum, but, rather, as duration, as a past which creeps up on and encompasses the present and future. This understanding of time is also found in Faulkner, who admitted to having picked and chosen from Bergson's ideas. But we also find in Faulkner a view of time diametrically opposed to that of Bergson which may well have appealed to García Márquez. Where Bergson held that life is flux, a process of constant change and becoming, a never-completed movement towards the realization of potential, Faulkner time and again creates characters who are paralyzed in historical time, unable to move beyond the trauma of the South's defeat in the Civil War, and who spend their lives reenacting the past.[19] In *La hojarasca*, clock time does give way to a continuous present: the past invades the present, rendering it stagnant, too, while the future is either obviated or telescoped into the past through fatalism and foreshadowing. And the fatalism is at least partly self-inflicted and therefore self-fulfilling: Macondo moves teleologically and inexorably towards its doom, and at the same time becomes increasingly entrenched in its impotence. The townspeople have neither hope nor the possibility of change, that is, of a future that is anything other than an extension of the present. Their destinies become fixed and immutable; their lives are arrested partway through their development, placed on hold while they wait for their fates to catch up to them. And yet, the gradual putrefaction of the cadaver belies their belief in a continuous present and serves as a reminder that exterior time does still exist, and that change over time, even if it does only take the form of rot and decay, is still possible.

From *College Literature* 26, 2 (Spring 1999): 59-78. Copyright © 1999 by Westchester University. Reprinted by permission.

Notes

1. In their extremely important 1967 collection of interviews with and essays on the authors who were at that very moment defining the course of Latin American fiction, Luis Harss and Barbara Dohmann wrote that "If *La hojarasca* is a failure, it is largely because it is written in a borrowed idiom that never becomes a personal language. Its interwoven plots and subplots, overlappings and backtrackings, its involuted time play, are all more or less perfunctory devices that defeat the purpose they might be expected to serve" (1967, 233). Similarly, Michael Palencia-Roth has more recently written, "*La hojarasca* is the work of an insecure writer. . . . It is the work of a novice, written under the influence of other styles and other novelists. One of these styles, and the most influential, belongs to William Faulkner" (1987, 33; qtd. in Márquez 1995-1996, 94).

2. García Márquez (1980, 247). Except for the quotes from *Leaf Storm*, all translations are mine.

3. I speak here of Euro-American modernism to avoid confusion with the turn-of-the-century Latin American literary movement also known as modernism, or *modernismo*. Henceforth I will refer to the movement represented by William Faulkner, James Joyce, and Virginia Woolf, simply as "modernism."

4. The influence of Proust and, specifically, of his representation of time on García Márquez lies outside of the scope of this essay; however, for more information on this topic, consult McGowan (1982-83) and Craig (1990).

5. An exception to this tendency is to be found in Martin (1989), which identifies two stages in modern Latin American fiction: the 1920s through the early 1960s, which he sees as being dominated by Faulkner, and the years following the publication of Julio Cortázar's *Rayuela* (1963), in which he considers Joyce to be the dominant model. This division ultimately seems forced, though, rather than offering significant insights into the development of the modern Latin American narrative.

6. E.g., Coleman (1985) and Levine (1975).

7. See, for example, works by Bessière (1995-96), Davis (1985, 1979), Faris (1990), Fayen (1995), Frisch (1990), Irby (1956), Kulin (1975, 1979), Ludmer (1975), MacAdam (1983), Márquez (1995-96), Pothier (1995-96), Shapiro (1979), and Vargas Saavedra (1974). It is interesting to note that this subject has been almost exclusively the domain of scholars in the field of Latin American literature; the fact that an entire recent (double) issue of *The Faulkner Journal* was dedicated to the subject of "The Latin American Faulkner" (Vol. XI, 1 and 2, Fall 1995/Spring 1996) seems to indicate a growing reciprocal interest on the part of Faulknerists.

8. There are numerous important works which address various aspects of the role played by history, as well as by contemporary social and racial issues, in Yoknapatawpha County; many of these raise issues which dovetail with and may therefore also be used to elucidate the markedly historical orientation of recent Latin American fiction. I refer the reader to the following (limited) selection of works related to these topics for further investigation: for revisionist studies of patriarchy, authority, and the decline of the Old Order, see Dale (1992) and Porter (1995, 1987); for discussions of race, miscegenation, and the threat of social disorder, see Sherry (1989; this article also offers

strong discussions of other modes of dispossession and dehumanization), and Snead (1986); on the relationship of the reconstruction of history, narrative form and meaning, and the past's pervading of the present, see Brooks' chapter, "Incredulous Narration: *Absalom, Absalom!*" (1984) and Donnelly (1991); for more general discussions of Faulkner, southern history, and historiography, consult Lester (1995), Matthews (1989), Millgate (1977), Parker (1986), Rollyson (1984), and recent historical and intellectual biographies by Singal (1997) and Williamson (1993).

9. See, for example, works by Christie (1993), Corvalán (1981), Delay and de Labriolle (1973), Fields (1987), Levine (1975), Oberhelman (1975, 1978a, 1978b, 1980, 1987), Ramos Escobar (1985), Snell (1985), Tobin (1978), and Zamora (1982, 1989).

10. See especially works by Fields (1987), Tobin (1978), and Zamora (1982, 1989).

11. It is interesting to note the development of García Márquez's reworking of Faulkner's techniques by comparing his first novel (which often seems heavy-handed, mechanical, and even programmatic) to *El otoño del patriarca*, published twenty years later. The latter novel employs many of the same techniques as *La hojarasca*, including shifting perspectives, seemingly interminable sentences, the repetition and reworking of scenes, and narrative withholding and delayed disclosure of information (Vargas Llosa's "hyperbaton"). Also, in the same way that Faulkner traced the genesis of *The Sound and the Fury* to the single image of a little girl (Caddy Compson) with muddy drawers climbing a tree to look into the room where her dead grandmother was laid to rest (Faulkner 1959, 1, 17, 31), García Márquez has claimed that *El otoño del patriarca* began with the image of the solitary patriarch wandering through his palace, an image that the text begins and ends with, and returns to on numerous occasions throughout. And yet, while some critics might accuse *El otoño del patriarca* of being Faulknerian to a fault, it is nevertheless far from being derivative. There is no doubt but that García Márquez is speaking with his own voice here: this novel is a deliberately and self-consciously stylized, virtuoso performance in which the author emulates and acknowledges his models with a vengeance, and in which everything from his signature sense of humor to the images and episodes of Latin American history that he parodies and rewrites reflects an author much more at home with his originality and the creative process. The Colombian both accomplishes and, to a degree, spoofs Faulkner's desire to condense "everything into one sentence—not only the present but the whole past on which it depends and which keeps overtaking the present" (qtd. in Cowley 1966, 115), in the many sentences that run on for pages, literally encompassing the events of numerous centuries, and, in particular, in the final chapter, some seventy pages long, which consists of a single sentence and which narrates the rise and fall of the empire, beginning and ending with the death of the patriarch who was considered immortal, and whose reign was thought to be eternal. This condensation of time is, moreover, complemented formally by García Márquez's recourse, once again, to the structure of the novel-in-a-day.

12. Quentin's section is the day of his suicide, June 2, 1910; Jason Compson's is dated April 6, 1928; Benjy Compson's is April 7, 1928; and an unidentified third person narrator describes the events of Easter Sunday, April 8, 1928.

13. The only absolute date that she mentions, 1885, is an indirect quote of her father's delirious ramblings during his illness (García Márquez 1986, 145; 1972, 87).

14. Interestingly enough, while various critics have noted this distribution of historical perspective, none has addressed the fact that the story of the family's arrival in Macondo is not narrated by the Colonel, but, rather, by a multiply-marginalized character: Meme, the Indian servant who was cast out of the family's home and later socially ostracized, and who had simply disappeared from Macondo without a trace several years prior to the beginning of the novel, provides the first and most complete rendition of the family's odyssey, which is indirectly transcribed in one of Isabel's monologues.

15. Isabel observes that "El niño . . . levanta de pronto la cabeza, concentrado, atento, y me pregunta: '¿Lo oyes?' Sólo entonces caigo en la cuenta de que en uno de los patios vecinos está dando la hora un alcaraván. 'Sí', digo. 'Ya deben ser las tres', casi en el preciso instante en que suena el primer golpe del martillo en el clavo" (García Márquez 1986, 153; "The child . . . raises his head suddenly, concentrated, intent, and he asks me: 'Did you hear it?' Only then do I realize that in some neighboring courtyard a curlew is telling the time. 'Yes,' I say, 'It must be three o'clock already,' and almost at that precise moment the first hammer blow sounds on the nail" [1972, 93]). Her son, in turn, states that "Oigo otra vez el alcaraván y digo a mamá: '¿Lo oyes?' Y ella dice que sí, que deben ser las tres. Pero Ada me ha dicho que los alcaravanes cantan cuando sienten el olor a muerto. Voy a decírselo a mi madre en el preciso instante en que oigo ruido intenso del martillo en la cabeza del primer clavo" (1986, 158; "I hear the curlew again and I say to Mama: 'Did you hear it?' And she says yes, it must be three o'clock. But Ada told me that curlews sing when they get the smell of a dead man. I'm about to tell my mother just at the moment when I hear the sharp sound of the hammer on the head of the first nail" [1972, 96]).

16. See, for example, the following utterances in the narrative present, whose repetition indicates simultaneous monologues: the Colonel's comment that "'El Cachorro los habría hecho venir a correazos'" ("'The Pup would have made them come even if he had to whip them'"; narrated by the boy [García Márquez 1986, 132; 1972, 78], Isabel [1986, 137; 1972, 82], and the Colonel [1986, 146; 1972, 88]); the Colonel's declaration that "'De todos modos, lo que suceda tenía que suceder. Es como si lo hubiera anunciado el almanaque'" ("'In any case, whatever happens, it had to happen. It's as if it had been announced in the almanac'"; by the Colonel [1986, 150; 1972, 91] and quoted by Isabel [1986, 152; 1972, 92] and the boy [1986, 157; 1972, 95]); and the final entrance of the justice of the peace and his startling of the Colonel (by Isabel [1986, 142 and 144; 1972, 84 and 86], the Colonel [1986, 149; 1972, 90], and the boy [1986, 156; 1972, 94]). Examples of repeated flashbacks are as follows: the first supper with the doctor, when Adelaida asks the doctor "'¿Qué clase de hierba, doctor?' Y él, con su parsimoniosa voz de rumiante . . . : 'Hierba común, señora. De esa que comen los burros'" ("'What kind of grass, doctor?' And he in his parsimonious ruminant voice . . . :'Ordinary grass, ma'am. The kind that donkeys eat'"; by the Colonel [32 and 71; 1972, 17 and 41]); Meme's announcement of the arrival of the doctor (quoted by Isabel [1986, 49; 1972, 28] and the Colonel [1986, 56; 1972, 32]); and the townspeople's request that the doctor help the wounded on election night in 1918 (by the Colonel [1986, 27 and 148; 1972, 14 and 90]).

17. Vargas Llosa further observes that a limited number of formulae is repeatedly used to describe the characters' physical attributes, so that their outward appearances are, like their emotional states, reduced to the most basic and invariable qualities (1971, 273).

18. Root (1988) identifies the same historical and political principles as governing the structure of *Cien años de soledad*. He claims that critics who cast García Márquez as a "mythmaker" do so primarily on the basis that "his world is opposed to linear and conventional time." But, he continues, "myth itself does not adequately explain the use of time; even recurring time cannot free itself from history" (1988, 4)—an observation which applies equally to *La hojarasca*.

19. See Porter (1987) for a discussion of a parallel phenomenon in *Absalom, Absalom!* Essentially, Porter argues that characters such as Sutpen and Miss Rosa are associated with "a vertical transcendence of time" (1987, 64) whereby the former strives to extricate himself from history as a series of events and changes and instead seeks to make experience conform to an atemporal structure—the design—that he imposes on it, while the latter (like García Márquez's Adelaida) has been removed from the flow of linear time and immobilized in the past as a result of the affront inflicted on her by this same design (Judith, in contrast, is described as immersed in the horizontal movement of time precisely because she gives Bon's letter to Quentin's grandmother, hoping in that way to have her memory preserved by the community as it moves into the future). In the same way that Sutpen's "transcendence" of time fails to grant him access to the immortality that he so desired (through the perpetuation of either his name or of his lineage) while Miss Rosa remains trapped forever in that day forty-three years prior to her meeting with Quentin, as we have seen in *La hojarasca*, eternity—that is, exemption from the passage of time—is equated with stagnation and paralysis, and thereby similarly proves intranscendent.

Works Cited

Ashok, A. V. 1988. "Gabriel García Márquez's *Leaf Storm* and the Human Passage." *Literary Criterion* 23.3: 16-23.

Bessière, Jean. 1995-1996. "Carlos Fuentes vis-à-vis William Faulkner: Novel, Tragedy, History." *The Faulkner Journal* 11.1-2 (Fall-Spring): 33-42.

Brooks, Peter. 1984. *Reading for the Plot*. New York: Alfred A. Knopf.

Christie, John. 1993. "Fathers and Virgins: García Márquez's Faulknerian *Chronicle of a Death Foretold*." *Latin American Literary Review* 21.41: 21-29.

Cohn, Deborah. 1997. "'He Was One of Us': The Reception of William Faulkner and the U.S. South by Latin American Authors." *Comparative Literature Studies* 34.2: 149-69.

Coleman, Alexander. 1985. "Bloomsbury in Aracataca: The Ghost of Virginia Woolf." *World Literature Today* 59.4 (Autumn): 543-49.

Corvalán, Octavio. 1981. "Faulkner y García Márquez: Una aproximación." *Sur* 349 (July-Dec.): 71-88.

Cowley, Malcolm. 1966. Introduction to *The Faulkner-Cowley File: Letters & Memories, 1944-62*. New York: Viking Press.

Craig, Herbert E. 1990. "Proustian Time in *El amor en los tiempos del cólera*." *Confluencia* 5.2 (Spring): 55-59.

Dale, Corinne. 1992. "*Absalom, Absalom!* and the Snopes Trilogy: Southern Patriarchy Revision." *Mississippi Quarterly* 45 (Summer): 323-37.

Davis, Mary E. 1979. "William Faulkner and Mario Vargas Llosa: The Election of Failure." *Comparative Literature Studies* 16: 332-43.

_____. 1985. "The Haunted Voice: Echoes of William Faulkner in García Márquez, Fuentes, and Vargas Llosa." *World Literature Today* (Autumn): 531-35.

Delay, Florence, and Jacqueline de Labriolle. 1973. "Márquez: Est-il le Faulkner colombien?" *Revue de Literature Comparée* 47: 88-123.

Donnelly, Colleen E. 1991. "Compelled to Believe: Historiography and Truth in *Absalom, Absalom!*" *Style* 25.1 (Spring): 104-22.

Faris, Wendy. 1990. "Marking Space, Charting Time: Text and Territory in Faulkner's 'The Bear' and Carpentier's *Los pasos perdidos*." In *Do the Americas Have a Common Literature?*, ed. Gustavo Pérez Firmat. Durham: Duke University Press.

Faulkner, William. 1956a. *The Sound and the Fury*. New York: Random House.

_____. 1956b. Interview by Jean Stein vanden Heuvel. Reprint. In *Lion in the Garden*. Ed. James Meriwether and Michael Millgate. New York: Random House.

_____. 1959. *Faulkner in the University*. Ed. F. L. Gwynn and J. L. Blotner. Charlottesville: University of Virginia Press.

_____. 1968. *Lion in the Garden*. Ed. James Meriwether and Michael Millgate. New York: Random House.

_____. 1972. *Absalom, Absalom!* New York: Vintage Books.

Fayen, Tanya T. 1995. *In Search of the Latin American Faulkner*. Lanham, MD: University Press of America.

Fields, Wayne. 1987. "*One Hundred Years of Solitude* and New World Storytelling." *Latin American Literary Review* 15.29: 73-88.

Frisch, Mark. 1990. "Self-Definition and Redefinition in New World Literature: William Faulkner and the Hispanic American Novel." *Crítica Hispánica* 12.1-2: 115-31.

_____. (In Press). "Faulkner and Latin American Literature." *William Faulkner Encyclopedia*. Westport, CT: Greenwood Press.

García Márquez, Gabriel. 1972. *Leaf Storm and Other Stories*. Trans. Gregory Rabassa. New York: Harper Colophon.

_____. 1980. *Obra periodística. Vol. I: Textos costeños*. Ed. Jacques Gilard. Barcelona: Bruguera.

_____. 1986. *La hojarasca*. Barcelona: Bruguera.

García Márquez, Gabriel, and Mario Vargas Llosa. 1968. *La novela en América Latina: Diálogo*. Lima: Carlos Millá Batres/Universidad Nacional de Ingeniería.

Harss, Luis, and Barbara Dohmann. 1967. *Into the Mainstream: Conversations with Latin-American Writers*. New York: Harper & Row.

Irby, James East. 1956. "La influencia de William Faulkner en cuatro narradores hispano-americanos." M.A. Thesis. Universidad Nacional Autónoma de México.

Kulin, Katalin. 1975. "Razones y características de la influencia de Faulkner [*sic*] la ficción latinoamericana moderna." Trans. Aída Fajardo and Nilita Vientós Gastón. *Sin Nombre* 6.1 (julio-septiembre): 20-36.

_____. 1979. "Reasons and Characteristics of Faulkner's Influence on Juan Carlos Onetti, Juan Rulfo and Gabriel García Márquez." *Proceedings of the 7th Congress of the International Comparative Literature Association. Vol. I: Literatures of America*. Ed. Milan V. Dimic and Juan Ferraté. Stuttgart: Kunst und Wissen.

Lester, Cheryl. 1995. "Racial Awareness and Arrested Development." In *The Cambridge Companion to William Faulkner*, ed. Philip Weinstein. Cambridge: Cambridge University Press.

Levine, Suzanne Jill. 1975. *El espejo hablado: Un estudio de "Cien años de soledad."* Caracas: Monte Avila Editores.

Ludmer, Josefina. 1975. "Onetti: La novia (carta) robada (a Faulkner)." *Hispamérica* 9: 3-19.

MacAdam, Alfred. 1983. "Carlos Fuentes: The Burden of History." *World Literature Today* 57.4: 558-63.

Márquez, Antonio. 1995-1996. "Faulkner in Latin America." *The Faulkner Journal* 11.1-2 (Fall-Spring): 83-100.

Martin, Gerald. 1989. *Journeys Through the Labyrinth: Latin America in the Twentieth Century*. London: Verso.

Matthews, John. 1989. "Faulkner's Narrative Frames." In *Faulkner and the Craft of Fiction*, ed. Doreen Fowler and Ann Abadie. Jackson: University Press of Mississippi.

McGowan, John. 1982-83. "A la recherche du temps perdu in *One Hundred Years of Solitude*." *Modern Fiction Studies* 28.4 (Winter): 557-67.

Millgate, Michael. 1977. "Faulkner and History." In *The South and Faulkner's Yoknapatawpha: The Actual and the Apocryphal*, ed. Evans Harrington and Ann J. Abadie. Jackson: University Press of Mississippi.

Oberhelman, Harley. 1975. "García Márquez and the American South." *Chasqui* 5.1 (November): 29-38.

_____. 1978a. "Faulknerian Techniques in Gabriel García Márquez's Portrait of a Dictator." *Proceedings of the Comparative Literature Symposium, Vol. X: Ibero-American Letters in a Comparative Perspective*, ed. Wolodymyr T. Zyla and Wendell M. Aycock. Lubbock: Texas Tech University Press.

_____. 1978b. "William Faulkner's Reception in Spanish America." *The American Hispanist* 3.26: 13-17.

_____. 1980. *The Presence of Faulkner in the Writings of García Márquez. Graduate Studies* No. 22. Lubbock: Texas Tech University Press.

_____. 1987. "William Faulkner and Gabriel García Márquez: Two Nobel

Laureates." In *Critical Essays on Gabriel García Márquez*, ed. George McMurray. Boston: G. K. Hall.

Palencia-Roth, Michael. 1987. *Gabriel García Márquez: La línea, el círculo y las metamorfosis de mito*. Madrid: Editorial Gredos.

Parker, Robert D. 1986. "The Chronology and Genealogy of *Absalom, Absalom!*: The Authority of Fiction and the Fiction of Authority." *Studies in American Fiction* 14: 191-98.

Porter, Carolyn. 1987. "William Faulkner: Innocence Historicized." *William Faulkner's "Absalom, Absalom!": Modern Critical Interpretations*, ed. Harold Bloom. New York: Chelsea House Publishers.

_____. 1995. "*Absalom, Absalom!*: (Un)making the Father." In *The Cambridge Companion to William Faulkner*, ed. Philip Weinstein. Cambridge: Cambridge University Press.

Pothier, Jacques. 1995-96. "Voices from the South, Voices of the South: Faulkner, García Márquez, Vargas Llosa, Borges." *The Faulkner Journal* 11.1-2 (Fall/Spring): 101-18.

Ramos Escobar, J. L. 1985. "Desde Yoknapatawpha a macondo." *En el punto de mira: Gabriel García Márquez*, ed. A. M. Hernández de López. Madrid: Editorial Pliegos.

Rollyson, Carl, Jr. 1984. *Uses of the Past in the Novels of William Faulkner*. *Studies in Modern Literature* 37. Ann Arbor: UMI Research Press.

Root, Jerry. 1988. "Never Ending the Ending: Strategies of Narrative Time in *One Hundred Years of Solitude*." *The Rackham Journal of the Arts and Humanities* 1-25.

Rulfo, Juan. 1992. "Luvina." In *Juan Rulfo: Toda la obra*, ed. Claude Fell. Paris: UNESCO Colección Archivos. 107-12.

Shapiro, J. P. 1979. "Une histoire contée par un idiot . . . (W. Faulkner et J. Rulfo)." *Revue de Litterature Comparée* 53: 338-47.

Sherry, Charles. 1989. "Being Otherwise: Nature, History, and Tragedy in *Absalom, Absalom!*" *Arizona Quarterly* 45.3 (Autumn): 47-76.

Sims, Robert L. 1976. "García Márquez's *La hojarasca*: Paradigm of Time and Search for Myth." *Hispania* 59: 810-19.

Singal, Daniel. 1997. *William Faulkner: The Making of a Modernist*. Chapel Hill: University of North Carolina Press.

Snead, James A. 1986. *Figures of Division: William Faulkner's Major Novels*. New York: Methuen.

Snell, Susan. 1985. "William Faulkner, un guía sureño a la ficción de García Márquez." In *En el punto de mira: Gabriel García Márquez*, ed. A. M. Hernández de López. Madrid: Editorial Pliegos.

Tobin, Patricia Drechsel. 1978. *Time and the Novel: The Genealogical Imperative*. Princeton: Princeton University Press.

Vargas Llosa, Mario. 1971. *García Márquez: Historia de un deicidio*. Barcelona: Barral Editores, S.A.

Vargas Saavedra, Luis. 1974. "La afinidad de Onetti a Faulkner." *Cuadernos hispanoamericanos* 98.292-4: 257-65.

Weinstein, Philip, ed. 1995. *The Cambridge Companion to William Faulkner*. Cambridge: Cambridge University Press.

Williamson, Joel. 1993. *William Faulkner and Southern History*. New York: Oxford University Press.

Zamora, Lois Parkinson. 1982. "The End of Innocence: Myth and Narrative Structure in Faulkner's *Absalom, Absalom!* and García Márquez's *Cien años de soledad*." *Hispanic Journal* 4.1 (Fall): 23-40.

_____. 1989. *Writing the Apocalypse: Historical Vision in Contemporary U.S. and Latin American Fiction*. Cambridge: Cambridge University Press.

A "Gyrating Wheel"

Rosa Simas

> In a line of study inaugurated by the Uruguayan critic Emir Rodríguez Monegal, Rosa Simas examines the cyclical as well as synchronic patterns of time in *One Hundred Years of Solitude* through various perspectives: natural change and what a scholar calls the "variations, substitutions and transformations" of people and things in Macondo. She proves that the more things change, the more they remain the same. The novel is part of the dialectical struggle between civilization and barbarism at the heart of Latin America, the way the environment is at once hostile and beautiful. It owes a debt to the vision of the U.S. South offered by William Faulkner in his Yoknapatawpha County saga. According to Simas, the novel's first sentence already contains the central tenet of García Márquez's view on chronos— what Ricardo Gullón calls "the gyrating wheel." — I.S.

Summarizing the role of the artist in a 1954 interview, William Faulkner describes the dynamics of aesthetic creation and recreation when he affirms: "The aim of every artist is to arrest motion, which is life, by artificial means and hold it fixed so that one hundred years later, when a stranger looks at it, it moves again, since it is life."[1] Interestingly enough, "arrest motion" within a "one-hundred year" span is what the Latin American writer and 1982 recipient of the Nobel Prize for literature, Gabriel García Márquez, succeeded in doing so admirably in his acknowledged masterpiece *Cien años de soledad*. Whereas *Absalom, Absalom!*, along with most of Faulkner's work, is set in the fictional but quotidian reality of Yoknapatawpha County, Mississippi, and the Southern region of the United States, García Márquez sets his novel in the mythical and magical region of Macondo, the name of a banana plantation from his childhood in Colombia, and then proceeds to trace the development and destruction of this microcosm of Latin America. Combining fantastic elements with ordinary reality, *Cien años de soledad* tells the story of seven generations of the Buendía family, from the discovery and founding of Macondo to its final demise and obliteration from the face of the earth.

Grounded in the socio-historical reality of Latin America, therefore, *Cien años de soledad* projects itself beyond this diachronic frame to the synchronic level of archetypal myth and cosmological reality. Referring in general to the so-called "boom" generation of Latin American writers, the following observation by Katalin Kulin certainly holds true for this novel by Gabriel García Márquez: "The works of this generation, similar to their ideology, immerse their roots in their socio-historical experience, but project before the public a vision which, although inspired in these experiences, assumes an *a priori* totality of the world."[2] In the fancifully portentous mode of *Cien años de soledad*, this totality is simply rendered metaphorically when the patriarchal figure of the Buendía clan, José Arcadio Buendía, emerges from his imaginary voyage of discovery to affirm that "The world is round like an orange" (12). Speaking of *Cien años de soledad* specifically, Lucila Inés Mena contrasts the synchronic projection of this text with its diachronic framework when she observes: "That which on a diachronic level is presented as a succession of seven generations of a race and one hundred years of political repression within the life of a community, on a synchronic level becomes the vision of one of the infinite cosmic cycles within the history of the human race."[3] Vincenzo Bollettino, in his turn, speaks of the temporal dimensions of this novel as "historical, lucid and chronological time" in relation to "mythical, circular and achronological time."[4]

This tension between a chronological and linear conception of time and an achronological and circular conception is indeed basic to *Cien años de soledad* and the world it creates. At once a recreation of the socio-cultural trajectory of Latin American history and an expression of the existential solitude inherent to the human condition, this text weaves the history of the Buendía family into the magically real world of Macondo. So formed, this novel is a fancifully self-conscious recreation of the parameters which shape human experience and perception of time and history, a recreation molded by a New World perspective on the temporal and historical experience of the Western World. In this sense, therefore, *Cien años de soledad* helps to discover and uncover a whole "new world" of aesthetic and cultural expression which the rationalism and bourgeois tradition of Old World philosophy and history for centuries helped silence. While discussing the artistic expression of Hispanic America's "new novel" in relation to "our long history of lies, silences and empty speech," the Mexican author Carlos Fuentes speaks of the need to invent a new language in order to "say all that history has silenced"[5] in order to allow those peoples which the dominant mode of Western tradition and history has excluded, to tell their own story and write their own history. In *Cien años de soledad*, Gabriel García Márquez tells the story of Latin America and joins his hearty voice to the many that are writing and rewriting the history of this region and its people from a twentieth-century perspective.

Heir to Western tradition, nevertheless, *Cien años de soledad* patterns the story that it tells after the two historical paradigms which have traditionally formed and informed human experience: circular, cyclical motion and linear eschatological direction. While exploring the human search for and preoccupation with *Meaning in History*, Karl Löwith describes universal "approaches to the understanding of history" and explains just how fundamental these two geometric configurations are:

> it seems as if the two great conceptions of antiquity and Christianity, cyclical motion and eschatological direction, have exhausted the basic approaches to the understanding of history. Even the most recent approaches to an interpretation of history are nothing else but variations of these two principles or a mixture of both of these.[6]

The "new science" elaborated by Giambattista Vico during the first half of the eighteenth century, for example, combines these two historical paradigms, as it attempts to distinguish the analysis of socio/

cultural phenomena within the social sciences, from the analysis of physical nature within the natural sciences. Considering the "efforts of human beings to endow their world with meaning," and analyzing how tropes function in the discourse of the human sciences in his study *Tropics of Discourse*, Hayden White discusses the "deep structure" of Vico's *New Science* and also summarizes the noteworthy work of this historian, in terms of these two historical paradigms, when he observes that Vico's "employment of human history is elaborated on two levels: the Hebrew-Christian, which describes a progressive evolution of consciousness in the light of revealed truth; and the pagan, which describes a pattern of cyclical recurrence."[7]

Playfully orchestrating these two historical configurations, the narrative development of *Cien años de soledad* not only erases linear conceptions of time but actually reshapes its world according to the repetitive circularity of cyclical motion. Once again, the text is extremely forthright in expressing the temporal trajectory that forms and informs the world of Macondo; this time it is Úrsula, the matriarchal figure of the Buendía family, who reshapes the linear cliché which says that "Time passes," into cyclical temporal patterning. Due to her many years of experience, the aging matriarch "knows" the true nature of time, while her great-grandson José Arcadio Segundo must continue studying the magical manuscripts left by the gypsy Melquíades, because he has not yet succeeded in deciphering their enigmatic tale:

José Arcadio Segundo seguia releyendo los pergaminos. . . . Al reconocer la voz de la bisabuela, movió la cabeza hacia la puerta, trató de sonreir, y sin saberlo repitió una antigua frase de Úrsula:

—Qué queria—murmuró—, el tiempo pasa.

—Asi es—dijo Úrsula—, pero no tanto.

Al decirlo, tuvo consciencia de estar dando la misma réplica que recibió del coronel Aureliano Buendía en su celda de sentenciado, y una vez más se estremeció con la comprobación de que el tiempo no pasaba, como ella lo acababa de admitir, sino que daba vueltas en redondo. (291-2)

(José Arcadio Segundo continued re-reading the manuscripts. . . . Upon recognizing his great-grandmother's voice, he turned his head toward the door, tried to smile, and without knowing it, repeated an old phrase of Úrsula's.

"What can I say," he murmured. "Time passes."

"Yes, it does" said Úrsula, "but not so much."

Upon saying this, she was conscious of having received the same answer from Colonel Aureliano Buendía in his cell, and she once again shuddered with the certainty that time did not pass, as she had just finished saying, but that it went around in circles.)

Two other characters share this intuitive insight into the true nature of time: the elusive gypsy Melquíades and the concupiscent fortune teller Pilar Ternera. True to their natural tendency for overstepping temporal boundaries, Melquíades and Pilar, along with Úrsula, seem to live on and on as they overcome the traditional conception of the passage of time. In keeping with the magical margins which he inhabits, Melquíades actually dies and returns to life still wearing his "chaleco anacrónico" (164) ("anachronic vest"), "porque no pudo soportar la soledad" (50), because he could not bear the solitude of death. The two matriarchal figures—Úrsula the legitimate Buendía mother and Pilar, mistress and illegitimate mother to the clan—give birth to the first generation of the Buendía family, assist in periodic attempts at regeneration, and accompany the gradual degeneration of the Buendías and of Macondo. Coming full circle in the end, Úrsula is reduced to the shape and size of a decrepit old woman who looked newly born, until she finally dies, after having lived much beyond one hundred years. Joining the beginning to the end of the family, she is buried in a box only slightly larger than the cradle which holds her great-great-great grandson, the very last Buendía who attends her funeral as a baby. Uniting past and present, the archetypal matriarch, the ageless Úrsula Buendía, steps far beyond chronological time in appearance and attitude, in life and death:

Liegó a revolver de tal modo el pasado con la actualidad, que en las dos o tres ráfagas de lucidez que tuvo antes de morir, nadie supo a ciencia cierta si hablaba de lo que sentía o de lo que recordaba. Poco a poco se fue reduciendo, fetizándose, momificándose en vida, hasta el punto de que en sus últimos meses era una ciruela pasa perdida dentro del camisón. . . . Parecía una anciana recién nacida. . . . Amaneció muerta el jueves santo. La última vez que la habían ayudado a sacar la cuenta de su edad . . . la había calculado entre los ciento quince y los ciento veintidós años. La enterraron en una cajita que era apenas más grande que la canastilla en que fue llevado Aureliano. (297 & 298)

(She ended up confusing the past with the present to such an extent that, during the two or three lucid moments she had before dying, no one knew for sure if she was talking about what she felt or about what she remembered. Slowly she shrank, becoming like a fetus or a mummy, so that in her last months she looked like a raisin lost in her nightgown. . . . She looked like an old woman recently born. . . . She died on Holy Thursday morning. The last time that they had helped her calculate her age . . . they had figured it to be between one hundred fifteen and one hundred twenty two years. They buried her in a little box which was barely larger than the cradle which contained Aureliano.)

Pilar Ternera also gives up on calculating her age. Realizing that the young man who has just entered her brothel is her great-great grandson Aureliano, Pilar joins the past, present and future, as she prepares the last Buendía for his ultimate revelation and demise by telling him about the development, about the grandeur and misfortune of his family and of Macondo. The night Aureliano appears at her door:

. . . la espléndida y taciturna anciana que vigilaba el ingreso en un mecedor de bejuco, sintió que el tiempo regresaba a sus manantiales primarios, cuando entre los cinco que llegaban descubrió un hombre óseo, cetrino, de pómulos tártaros, marcado para siempre y desde el principio del mundo por la viruela de la soledad. . . . Estaba viendo otra vez el coronel Aureliano Buendía. . . . Era Pilar Ternera. Años antes, cuando cumplió los ciento cuarenta y cinco, había renunciado a la costumbre de llevar las cuentas de su edad, y continuaba viviendo en el tiempo estático y marginal de los recuerdos, en un futuro perfectamente revelado y establecido, más allá de los futuros perturbados por las acechanzas y las suposiciones insidiosas de las barajas. (342)

(. . . the splendid and taciturn old woman who watched the entrance in a wicker rocking chair, felt that time returned to its primordial origins, when among the five men who arrived she discovered a thin melancholy man with pale cheeks, marked forever and from the beginning of time by the virus of solitude. . . . She was seeing Colonel Aureliano Buendía again. . . . It was Pilar Ternera. Years before, when she reached one hundred forty five, she had renounced the pernicious habit of counting one's age, and continued living in the static and marginal time of memory, in a perfectly revealed and stable future, far beyond the bothersome future of waiting and of insidiously reading the cards.)

Throughout the novel and her long life, the ageless matriarch Úrsula Buendía repeatedly alerts the reader to the cyclical temporality which patterns and shapes *Cien años de soledad*. As Macondo "naufragaba en una prosperidad de milagro" ("floated lost in a sea of miraculous prosperity"), Úrsula accompanies this precarious progress by comparing it to previous phases and observing that "Ya esto me lo sé de memoria. . . . Es como si el tiempo diera vueltas en redondo y hubiéramos vuelto al principio" (173). ("I already know all this from memory. . . . It's as if time were revolving in circles and we had returned to the beginning.") Furthermore, as the strike and subsequent massacre of the banana plantation workers draw near, the intuitive matriarch feels tormented by "algo que ella misma no lograba definir pero que concebía confusamente como un progresivo desgaste del tiempo" (215) ("something which she herself could not define but which she perplexedly perceived as a progressive wearing down of time"). So attuned is Úrsula to the cyclical repetition which shapes the life of her family and house, that blindness only makes her more acutely aware of the physical "geography" of her house and of the static existence of her family:

> Nadie supo a ciencia cierta cuándo empezó a perder la vista. . . . Conoció con tanta seguridad el lugar en que se encontraba cada cosa, que ella misma se olvidaba a veces de que estaba ciega. En cierta ocasión, Fernanda alborotó la casa porque había perdido su anillo matrimonial, y Úrsula lo encontró en una repisa del dormitorio de los niños. Sencillamente, mientras los otros andaban descuidadamente por todos lados, ella los vigilaba con sus cuatro sentidos para que nunca la tomaran por sorpresa, al cabo de algún tiempo descubrió que cada miembro de la familia repetía todos los dias, sin darse cuenta, los mismos recorridos, los mismos actos, y que casi repetía las mismas palabras a la misma hora. (216)

> (No one knew for certain when she began to lose her sight. . . . She was so sure of where everything was, that she herself forgot sometimes that she was blind. Once, when Fernanda upset the whole house because she had lost her wedding ring, Úrsula found it on a shelf in the children's bedroom. While the others went carelessly from place to place, she simply watched them with her four senses so that they would never take her by surprise, and after some time she discovered that each family member unconsciously traversed the same distance, and repeated the same gestures and almost the same words at the same time each day.)

While repeated psychic obsession with Thomas Sutpen shapes the telling and retelling of his story in *Absalom, Absalom!*, recurrent cyclical repetition permeates every thread of *Cien años de soledad* as it weaves the story of the founding, development and final destruction of Macondo and the Buendía family. So fundamental is recurrent cyclicity, that the narrative fabric of this fanciful text actually thrives on excessive repetition, taking it to exaggerated proportions. The most obvious examples of this tendency are: the recurrent use of the same names and combinations thereof, especially "Aureliano" and "José Arcadio"; the inherited tendency toward existential solitude which *all* members of the family exhibit; as well as the overwhelming attraction toward physical incest which many experience. So basic is repetition to this novel, that many critics have discussed this characteristic. In his classic study of Gabriel García Márquez's work, *Historia de un deicidio*, the Peruvian writer Mario Vargas Llosa, for example, observes:

> In *Cien años de soledad*, many things apparently happen, a profusion of beings, objects and especially events, seems to be a characteristic of this fictional world: something is always happening. An objective reading shows us, however, that fewer things happen than would seem, for *the same things happen various times.*[8]

Josefina Ludemar, in her turn, finds *Cien años de soledad* to be a continuous play of variations, substitutions and transformations of certain signifiers and signifieds.[9] Perhaps one of the most blatant examples of fancifully exaggerated repetition is the case of Úrsula's 17 Aureliano grandsons, all fathered by her famous and solitary son Colonel Aureliano Buendía, during his twenty-year career in the civil wars which only served to leave him feeling "disperso, repetido, y más solitario que nunca" (149) ("scattered, repeated and more solitary than ever"). These seventeen sons, then, certainly do "scatter and repeat" the Colonel's solitude as García Márquez, true to his vocation of "providing a magnifying glass" in order to better reveal and see reality[10] through the use of the fantastic, transforms metaphorical and figurative images and situations into actual physical beings and circumstances. As news spreads of festivities honoring the Colonel's premature retirement, ordered by the government in power and contrary to the military leader's wishes, these sons arrive one by one, forming a living chronicle of the twenty years of civil war which have made Colonel Buendía retire more and more into his solitude and defeat.

> Entonces el coronel Aureliano Buendía quitó la tranca, y vio en la puerta diecisiete hombres de los más variados aspectos, de todos los tipos y colores, pero todos con un aire solitario que habría bastado para identificarlos en cualquier lugar de la tierra. Eran sus hijos. Sin ponerse de acuerdo, sin conocerse entre si, habían llegado desde los más apartados rincones del litoral cautivados por el ruido del jubileo. Todos llevaban con orgullo el nombre de Aureliano, y el apellido de su madre. Durante los tres dias que permanecieron en la casa, para satisfacción de Úrsula . . . Amaranta buscó entre antiguos papeles la libreta de cuentas donde Úrsula habia apuntado los nombres y las fechas de nacimiento y bautismo de todos, y agregó frente al espacio correspondiente a cada uno el domicilio actual. Aquella lista habría permitido hacer una recapitulación de veinte años de guerra. (190-1)

> (Colonel Aureliano Buendía then unlocked the door and came face to face with seventeen males of all aspects, types and coloring, but all with a solitary manner which would have been enough to identify them anywhere on earth. They were his sons. Without planning it, without knowing each other, they had come from the furthest regions of that coast, captivated by the festive plans. All were proud to be called by the name Aureliano and by their respective mother's surnames. During the three days they stayed in the house, in order to satisfy Úrsula . . . Amaranta found the account booklets where Úrsula had written down their names and dates of birth and baptism, and added the present address of each one in the corresponding space. That list would have permitted a recapitulation of twenty years of war.)

Having tired of the "circulo visioso de aquella guerra eterna" (149) ("the vicious circularity of that never-ending war"), Colonel Buendía retires to his workshop to make and melt and remake little goldfish, a "circulo vicioso exasperante de pescaditos de oro" (177). As evidenced by the solitary military figure, the Buendía "vicio de hacer para deshacer" (274), a "vice" of making and unmaking, of doing and undoing, marks other members of the family in what Raymond L. Williams calls "activity without substance . . . which indicates a rejection of linear movement."[11] Caught in her incestuous circle of solitude, Úrsula's only daughter and the Colonel's sister, Amaranta, weaves and unravels and reweaves her own burial shroud. Two generations later and after years of rain, Fernanda del Carpio, wife of Úrsula's great-grandson, Aureliano Segundo, watches her husband trying to avoid boredom by fixing various defects in the house. Observing him "montar picaportes y desconectar relojes, Fernanda se preguntó si no estaria incurriendo también en el vicio de hacer para deshacer, como el Coronel Buendía con los pescaditos de oro, Amaranta con . . . la mortaja . . . y Úrsula con los recuerdos" (274-5) ("installing latches and disconnecting clocks, Fernanda asked herself if he hadn't also caught the vice of doing in order to undo, like Colonel Buendía with his little gold fish, Amaranta with her shroud . . . and Úrsula with her memories").

Although Aureliano Segundo exhibits a spurious interest in restoring the Buendía house after the rains which lasted "4 years, 11 months and 2 days" (274), it is Úrsula who repeatedly preoccupies herself with the periodic renovation and restoration of the Buendía house. While in *Absalom, Absalom!* the fragile Ellen Coldfield is completely overcome by her husband's will and design, and the haunted Rosa Coldfield is caught in the narrative ripple pattern she initiates, in *Cien años de soledad* Úrsula Buendía is vigorous and enterprising and characteristically undaunted in her attempts at maintaining the physical structure and spiritual existence of the Buendía "house." Robert Lewis Sims speaks of this matriarch as "the Great Mother who nourishes her race" and observes that Úrsula "demonstrates an overpowering effort to encompass all the members of her clan . . . and is extremely active in keeping the family intact."[12] Úrsula's physical and spiritual space, the Buendía house, expresses and encompasses what Gaston Bachelard, in

---

his analysis of *The Poetics of Space*, calls the "maternal features of the house." Referring to the space of our birth, Bachelard goes on to say:

> in short, the house we were born in has engraved within us the hierarchy of the various functions of inhabiting. We are the diagram of the functions of inhabiting that particular house, and all the other houses are but variations on a fundamental theme.[13]

As if confirming the importance of this space, Gabriel García Márquez had originally entitled his masterpiece "La Casa," just as William Faulkner had originally called *Absalom, Absalom!* "The Dark House."

From the very beginning of Macondo and of *Cien años de soledad*, the house is Úrsula's, for she refused to leave it and Macondo behind because, as she tells her husband José Arcadio Buendía, "Aqui nos quedamos porque aqui hemos tenido un hijo" ("Here is where we will stay because it's where we have had a son"). When the introspective young patriarch replies that "Uno no es de ninguna parte mientras no tenga un muerto bajo la tierra" ("We are from nowhere until we have a dead one under the ground"), she simply retorts, "Si es necesario que yo me muera para que se queden aqui, me muero" (19) ("If it's necessary that I die so that we will stay here, then I'll die"). So central is Úrsula to the mythical founding and cyclical development of Macondo, that her activities, according to Sims, reach beyond "the matriarchal realm" as "the men abandon their patriarchal duties and she fulfills them in their absence."[14] Ironically, it is Úrsula who hinders her husband's exploratory projects to leave Macondo since, he laments, "nos hemos de pudrir en vida sin recibir los beneficios de la ciencia" (19) ("we will rot here without receiving the benefits of science"); yet, a few pages later, after a five-month search for her young son José Arcadio who had run away from Macondo with a band of gypsies, it is the hearty young matriarch who returns "excited and rejuvenated" and accompanied by a group of new faces, with the news that she had found "la ruta que su marido no pudo descubrir en su frustrada búsqueda de los grandes inventos" (38 & 39) ("the route which her husband had never been able to find in his frustrated search for great inventions"). At the moment that José Arcadio Buendía gives in to his wife's decision to stay, and begins to resettle into his own particular space within Macondo—his alchemy laboratory—"the center of power in the Buendía family," according to Michael Palencia-Roth, "passes invisibly and forever . . . from the husband to the wife, from the men to the women, from the alchemy laboratory to the maternal home."[15]

True to her maternal role, Úrsula occupies and preoccupies herself with the physical and existential space of the Buendía "house." Unlike the linear design of Thomas Sutpen's obsessive design, the pattern and shape of Úrsula's house is unequivocally cyclical and founded on the prolific reproductive and repetitive tendencies of the various Buendía generations. While her husband, José Arcadio Buendía, remains in his lab occupied with his discoveries and inventions—the most recent of which, at this point in the text, is an attempt to scientifically prove the existence of God through the use of daguerreotype—Úrsula watches her children grow older and ready to have children of their own. In order to keep them near her, she pools her resources and decides to expand the house. Extremely sensitive to the function of space and to the place of her family, Úrsula maintains "common sense" and acts as the cohesive force within an "extravagant house." As she is followed, during the reconstruction, by "docenas de albañiles y carpinteros . . . Úrsula ordenaba la posición de la luz y la conducta del calor, y repartía el espacio sin el menor sentido de sus límites" (55) ("dozens of masons and carpenters . . . Úrsula ordered the position of light and the channeling of heat, and divided space without any sense of its limits").

Periodically, then, as if following the natural cyclical renewal of the physical world, this perennial matriarch restores and rejuvenates the Buendía house in order to maintain and revitalize the Buendía family. When Colonel Aureliano actually escapes the firing squad after the civil wars, for example, Úrsula dedicates herself once again to the renewal of the house.

Con una vitalidad que parecía imposible a sus años, Úrsula habia vuelto a rejuvenecer la casa. "Ahora van a ver quién soy yo," dijo cuando supo que su hijo viviría. "No habrá una casa mejor, ni más abierta a todo el mundo, que esta casa de locos." . . . Decretó el término de los numerosos lutos superpuestos, y ella misma cambió los viejos trajes rigurosos por ropas juveniles. La música de la pianola volvió a alegrar la casa. (161)

(With a vitality which seemed impossible at her age, Úrsula was rejuvenating the house once again. "Now they're going to see who I am," she said when she heard that her son would be allowed to live. "There will be no greater or more open house in all the world, than this crazy house." . . . She ordered the end to mourning and herself exchanged the old stuffy outfits for young clothing. The music of the pianola once again brightened the house.)

The last time that she attempts to renew the family house, the aging matriarch is already blind and the house is suffering the ravages of 4 years, 11 months and 4 days of rain. Strong as Úrsula's invincible heart may be, the forces of nature which have thrived in the deluge are threatening and menacing, and will ultimately prove more vital and powerful. While the actual structure is eaten away by termites and the contents are destroyed by moths, the giant red ants which signal the beginning of the end, congregate. While Úrsula is physically blind,

el ánimo de su corazón invencible la orientaba en las tinieblas. . . . Ella no necesitaba ver para darse cuenta de que los canteros de flores, cultivados con tanto esmero desde la primera reconstrucción, habían side destruidos por la lluvia . . . y que las paredes y el cemento de los pisos estaban cuarteados, los muebles flojos y descoloridos, las puertas desquiciadas, y la familia amenazada por un espíritu de resignación y pesadumbre que no hubiera sido concebible en sus tiempos. Moviéndose a tientas por los dormitorios vacíos percibía el trueno continuo del comején taladrando las maderas, y el tijereteo de la polilla en los roperos, y el estrépito devastador de las enormes hormigas coloradas que habían prosperado en el diluvio y estaban socabando los cimientos de la casa. . . . "No es posible vivir en esta negligencia," decía. "A este paso terminaremos devorados por las bestias." (290 & 291)

(The life in her invincible heart oriented her in her darkness. . . . She didn't need to see in order to know that the flower beds, planted so carefully during the first reconstruction . . . had been destroyed by the rains . . . that the walls and cement floors were cracked, the furniture worn and discolored, the doors unhinged, and the family threatened by a resignation and gloom which would have been unthinkable in her day. Feeling her way through the empty rooms, she could hear the continuous din of termites eating away at the wood, the clipping sound of moths in the closets, and the devastating clamor of enormous colored ants which had prospered in the deluge and which were digging into the cracked cement of the house. . . . "It's impossible to live in this neglect," she would say. "At this rate, we will end up devoured by the beasts.")

Just like her great-great-great grandmother, Amaranta Úrsula, the last Buendía female, will once again restore and rejuvenate the house thirty pages later (327). All of this will prove futile, of course, for, as Úrsula's words quoted above predict, at this rate of negligence and resignation, the Buendía house and family do indeed end up devoured by nature.

The theme of civilization versus "barbarie," of human beings versus the forces of nature, is a recurrent theme in Hispanic-American literature. The short stories of Horacio Quiroga, Sarmiento's *Facundo: civilización y barbarie*, and Ribera's *La vorágine*, for instance, come to mind right away. Summarizing this perspective, Michael Wood writes that geographically, Latin America "is a beautiful but hostile landscape which earlier fiction always represented as a killer."[16] Whereas North American literature is ambivalent in its treatment of nature, caught between the great drive to conquer and control nature versus guilt for having violated the purity and innocence of the natural state, Hispanic-American literature presents nature as an overwhelming force that ultimately envelops and swallows human attempts at civilization, attempts which, in this region, have all too often resulted, not in civilization, but in cruelty, injustice, oppression and destruction. Extending his analysis of nature in *La nueva novela hispanoamericana* to include sociological implications, Carlos Fuentes calls nature "an enigma which devours, destroying will and purpose, diminishing dignity and leading to annihilation." Ultimately, this writer and critic affirms, nature is the protagonist of a literature and of a social condition in which "it is better to be devoured by the jungle than to suffer a slow death in a society which is enslaved and cruel and bloodthirsty."[17]

Caught in a vicious cycle of social injustice and oppression, Macondo is overwhelmed by the cycle of a voracious nature which acts as metaphor for the social condition of Latin America. At once the center of the family and of the town, Úrsula's house is finally destroyed by the apocalyptic winds which close the great cycle recreated by *Cien años de soledad*, a great cycle comprised of the original founding, the illusory development and the final destruction of Macondo and of the Buendías. "Like any human victim," says Palencia-Roth, "the house only waits for the 'biblical wind' which will wipe Macondo from the face of the earth, thereby completing the great circle of jungle-civilization-jungle." D. P. Gallagher says very simply, "Only nature is permanent. Ultimately, it is the cyclical rhythm of nature that predominates," while Robert Sims concentrates on the temporal element when he observes that "Nature assaults Macondo and separates it from time."[18] Perhaps the image that most graphically captures Úrsula's role within the cyclical pattern of nature and of the Buendía house, is the thread of blood which runs from the body of her dead son José Arcadio. (121) Like an umbilical cord searching for its source, the trickle of José Arcadio's blood threads its way from his recently shot body, through streets and corridors and rooms, until it finds the mother Úrsula, in the kitchen ready to break thirty-six eggs to make bread. Having found the body which gave it birth, José Arcadio's blood goes "in search of its origin" and returns to the dead body from which it flowed, thereby uniting the beginning and the end, and closing the cycle of life and death.

Although Úrsula Buendía is the character who is most aware of the cyclical patterning which shapes the story of her family and the life of Macondo, it is the fortune teller Pilar Ternera, the "other" mother figure, who provides the image of circularity and cyclical repetition which best illustrates the narrative movement and thematic development of *Cien años de soledad*. Making her as aware of this non-linearity as Úrsula is only toward the end of the story, Pilar's powers of divination finally give her the necessary insight to propose the image of a gyrating wheel which would have spun eternally were it not for the irreparable breakdown of its central axis. Having just recognized the great-great grandson Aureliano coming into her brothel, and feeling that "time returned to its primordial sources" (342), Pilar realizes her full potential as fortune teller to Macondo and unsanctioned matriarch of the Buendía clan, when she thinks:

> No había ningún misterio en el corazón de un Buendía, que fuera impenetrable para ella, porque un silo de naipes y de experiencias le había enseñado que la historia de la familia era un engranaje de repeticiones irreparables, una rueda giratoria que hubiera seguido dando vueltas hasta la eternidad, de no haber sido por el desgaste progresivo e irremediable del eje. (343)

> (There was no mystery in the heart of a Buendía which was beyond her insight, because a century of cards and of experience had taught her that the history of the family was a gear of irreparable repetitions, a gyrating wheel which would have spun eternally, were it not for the progressive but irreparable breakdown of its central axle.)

Pilar's sense of primordial time as the final moments of Macondo's existence approach, joins the end to the beginning, joins "la última madrugada de Macondo" (357) ("the last dawn of Macondo") to its primordial founding, when

Macondo era entonces una aldea de veinte casas de barra y cañabrava construidas a la orilla de un rio de aguas diáfanas que se precipitaban por un lecho de piedras pulidas, blancas y enormes como huevos prehistóricos. El mundo era tan reciente, que muchas cosas carecían de nombre, y para mencionarlas había que señalarlas con el dedo. (9)

(Macondo was then a village of twenty houses constructed of clay and wild cane on the edge of a river whose diaphanous waters rushed through a bed of polished rocks, enormous and white as prehistoric eggs. The world was so new, that many things lacked names and had to be indicated by pointing a finger.)

At once a fanciful parody of the Bible and of the Exploration of the New World, *Cien años de soledad* takes its characters to "la tierra que nadie les habia prometido" (27) ("the land no one had promised them"). Relating the founding of Macondo to the discovery of America, Robert Sims calls Macondo "a variant of the myth of the golden age," and says that its "story is written in the context of timelessness where the myth of Macondo as a golden age acquires a greater scope." Indeed, drawing on the ancient myth of a golden age and on the belief that this El Dorado lay in the Americas, García Márquez creates the myth of El Dorado unfulfilled or, as Laurence Porter terms it, "a lost paradise embodied in the family name Arcadio."[19] Tracing the trajectory of a human civilization according to the archetypal myth of creation-development-destruction, then, *Cien años de soledad* follows the cyclical pattern of Pilar's "gyrating wheel." Encompassing this mythical cycle, the gyrating wheel contains within its perimeter the vicious, repetitive circularity which characterizes the seven generations of the fantastic and fanciful Buendía family. Its de-centered axle, irreparably worn by continuous vicious revolution, becomes the point that unites these cycles into one all-encompassing and eternal instant, conducting the human experience of one hundred years of solitude and constructing the literary creation of *Cien años de soledad*.

William Faulkner, as described previously, struggled against the sequential nature of language by employing complex and convoluted syntactical structures as well as a narrative ripple pattern in *Absalom, Absalom!* Gabriel García Márquez, in his turn, neutralizes the linearity inherent in his simple, straightforward syntax, by employing fancifully exaggerated cyclical repetition and vicious circularity. Along with this cyclical patterning, which René Cuadra calls "the most existential and immediate way of living a-chronicity,"[20] *Cien años de soledad* recasts linear chronology and conceptions of time and history into a synchronic patterning characterized by perfect, atemporal coincidence of all "times." Describing both of these patterns, Emir Rodríguez Monegal affirms that this novel is "heir to a narrative tradition in which time is alive and capricious, sometimes turning on itself, biting its own tail furiously, and other times lying dormant and totally immobile." Gregorio Salvador, in his turn, describes a time which "goes around in circles, that bites its own tail, that shatters and fragments itself, stationary, curved and circular."[21] Just as Úrsula shapes the cyclical trajectory of the Buendía house and Pilar Ternera foretells the breakdown of the gyrating wheel, the third and most markedly "timeless" figure of the novel, Melquíades patterns the manuscripts of one hundred years of solitude according to the synchronicity of total and final existential revelation. While the two matriarchal figures embody cyclical time, the enigmatic gypsy Melquíades incorporates simultaneity and atemporality into his magical existence and his mysterious manuscripts. Written and contained within the room Úrsula had constructed especially for him when she originally expanded the house (69), the manuscripts of the magical gypsy partake of the eternal fraction of time which characterizes this room, where "it is always March and always Monday" (303).

During his many alchemical experiments and parodic discoveries, the patriarch of the family, José Arcadio Buendía, regretfully surmises that "la máquina del tiempo se ha descompuesto" (75) ("the machine of time had broken down"), since, as far as he can surmise, in Macondo every day is Monday. Fulfilling this patriarchal observation, Melquíades' room becomes the archetypal atemporal space within Úrsula's cyclical house. Consequently, when the young Aureliano and his uncle José Arcadio Segundo look in, they "see" the figure of the gypsy and an eternal fraction of time:

En el cuartito apartado, adonde nunca llegó el viento árido, ni el polvo ni el calor, ambos recordaban la visión atávica de un anciano con sombrero de alas de cuervo que hablaba del mundo . . . muchos años antes de que ellos nacieron. Ambos descubrieron al mismo tiempo que allí siempre era marzo y siempre el lunes, y entonces comprendieron que José Arcadio Buendía no estaba tan loco como contaba la familia, sino que era el único que habia dispuesto de bastante lucidez para vislumbrar la verdad de que también el tiempo sufria tropiezos y accidentes, y podía por tanto astillarse y dejar en un cuarto una fracción eternizada. (303)

(In the remote room, where neither dry wind, nor dust, nor heat ever reached, both remembered the ancient vision of an old man wearing a hat adorned with crows wings, who spoke of the world . . . many years before they had been born. At the same time, both discovered that in that room it was always March and always Monday. Then they understood that José Arcadio Buendía was not as crazy as the family said, but was the only one lucid enough to discern the truth, that time also stumbled and tripped, and that it could shatter and leave an eternal fraction within a room.)

This fanciful but profound negation of the most basic notion of temporal chronology, obliterates traditional Western conceptions of cause-effect relationships. Moreover, the broken time machine, which turns out to be the irreparably worn axle of Pilar's gyrating wheel, expresses the redundant reality of a people living on the forgotten edge of a world dominated by Occidental thought and existence. Simultaneously, this broken and negated time recreates the synchronic dimensions of total human perception and revelation, the eternal instant in which, as Jorge Luis Borges might say, a person truly "knows" totality of being. Traditionally depicted as the moment of death, this eternal moment of totality occurs at the end of *Cien años de soledad*, as the last Buendía finally achieves a total vision of the eternal manuscripts and dies, at the same moment that Macondo is wiped from the face of the earth.

While in *Absalom, Absalom!* each re-telling of the Sutpen story both differs from the previous telling and also defers interpretation and meaning, the trajectory of García Márquez's novel moves inexorably toward synchronicity, toward the totality of human perception and self-knowledge which occurs with the prophetic revelation of the final paragraph. As the Apocalyptic winds begin to blow at the very end of the narrative, Aureliano discovers his destiny by finally succeeding in deciphering the prophetic manuscripts left by the enigmatic Melquíades:

. . . entonces sabía que en los pergaminos de Melquíades estaba escrito su destino . . . empezó a descifrarlos en voz alta. Era la historia de la familia, escrita por Melquíades hasta en sus detalles más triviales, con cien años de anticipación. . . . Melquíades no había ordenado los hechos en el tiempo convencional de los hombres, sino que concentró un siglo de episodios cotidianos, de modo que todos coexistieron en un instante. . . . saltó once páginas . . . y empezó a descifrar el instante que estaba viviendo, descifrándolo a medida que lo vivía, profetizándose a si mismo en el acto de descifrar la última página de los pergaminos. (358-60)

(. . . he then knew that his destiny was written in the manuscripts of Melquíades . . . he began to decipher them out loud. It was the history of the family, written by Melquíades even in its most trivial details, one hundred years before. . . . Melquíades had not ordered the events within conventional human time, but had instead concentrated a century of daily episodes so that they coexisted within one instant. . . . he skipped eleven pages . . . and began to decipher the very instant he was living, deciphering it as he lived it, prophesying his own existence as he deciphered the last page of the manuscripts.)

Given the temporal simultaneity which characterizes the narrative discourse of *Cien años de soledad*, it is not surprising that this end (*present* time) of Macondo should be contained within the prophetic (*future*) writings of Melquíades, which simultaneously contain the origins (*past*) of Aureliano, the last Buendía, finally deciphering the last page of the enigmatic manuscripts within the last paragraph of the novel.

This macrocosmic simultaneity, which encompasses the total experience of a people, of a "race condemned to one hundred years of solitude," is recreated on a microcosmic and individual level through the very first sentence of the novel. In fact, the very first sentence of *Cien años de soledad* sets this precedent of temporal simultaneity by recreating a-historical synchronicity, as Colonel Aureliano Buendía re-lives a key *past* experience (his father taking him to see ice for the first time), which he will remember in the *future* whenever he recalls this moment in the *present*. Thus begins the story of "one hundred years of solitude": "Muchos años después, frente al pelotón de fusilamiento, el coronel Aureliano Buendía habia de recordar aquella tarde remota en que su padre lo llevó a conocer el hielo" (9) ("Many years later, facing the firing squad, Colonel Aureliano Buendía would remember that distant afternoon when his father took him to see ice for the first time"). This syntactical and temporal patterning recurs throughout the text, as the narrator refers to *key moments* in the various characters' lives, moments which live on in memory and consciousness, moments which unite past, present and future, moments of perfect existential coincidence.

In addition, this very first sentence sets the precedent followed throughout *Cien años de soledad* of rendering in a literal manner a metaphorical image, a technique mentioned earlier in this study with respect to the seventeen Aurelianos. In this first sentence, the image of ice is especially significant and noteworthy, for it congeals memory, i.e., human time, forever. The symbolic meaning of this element has been described by J. E. Cirlot as follows:

Given that water is the symbol of communication between the formal and informal, the element of transition between different cycles, it follows that ice represents principally two things: first, the change induced by the cold, that is, the "congelation" of its symbolic significance; and secondly, the stultification of the potentialities of water. Hence ice has been defined as the rigid dividing-line between consciousness and unconsciousness.[22]

Couched within a syntagm which, as has been discussed, depicts temporal simultaneity on a syntactical level, ice represents the mediating element between the conscious and the unconscious, between diachronic and synchronic perception, i.e., perceptive simultaneity on a symbolic level. Phenomenologically, it is the frozen moment of remembered experience which divides unconscious reality from conscious reality, which divides the a-historical origins of human existence from the historical past of the race. And thirdly, on a semantic level, the first sentence of this novel joins history—in a figure taken from the military ranks of Latin America's civil wars between liberals and conservatives, the liberal Colonel Aureliano—with the a-historical and archetypal—"that afternoon" of experiencing ice when "the world was so new" and Aureliano was an innocent child.

Numerous critics have pointed out the significance of this first sentence to the novel as a whole. René Cuadra, for example, observes that "the entire novel is structured according to the sentence which begins the story."[23] Mario Vargas Llosa speaks of this syntactical structure in circular terms and finds that its circularity is characteristic of the principal episodes and of the entire narrative structure of the novel:

Almost all the units (episodes in their own right) correspond to this circular temporal construction: movement to the future, movement back to a remote past and, from there, a linear trajectory until reaching the moment which opened the unit; the episode bites its own tail, begins and ends in the same place, suggests the notion of totality, of something finished and sufficient unto itself which inspires the circle.[24]

Zunilda Gertel finds, in her turn, that "the syntagmatic components of the initial paragraph function as crystallized, correlated paradigms throughout the novel, thereby closing the fundamental cycles of the novel." Viewing the novel in terms of the Colonel, she goes on to explain that three parallel paradigms occur exactly a) at the beginning of the book; b) at a crucial instant in the life of Colonel Aureliano (p. 115); and c) at his death, as nostalgic memory when he sees the gypsies for the last time (p. 229). According to Gertel, then, the novel would be divided into three paradigmatic cycles: a world of myth (pp. 9-115); an historical world (pp. 116-229); and the return to a world of myth (pp. 230-251), cycles which correspond to "three parallel and key moments in the life of Colonel Aureliano."[25] By utilizing a semiotic perspective and focusing on syntagmatic and paradigmatic parallelism, Gertel follows the cyclical trajectory of nature-culture-nature. The Cuban writer Alejo Carpentier seems to unite the cyclical and synchronic patterning I have been discussing, as he describes the world of Latin America by superimposing the natural cyclical patterning of the physical world onto a synchronic layering of different epochs. While describing the magically real, he affirms that in

> Latin America everything is outsized and disproportionate; towering mountains and waterfalls, endless plains, impenetrable jungles. An anarchic urban sprawl overlies breathless virgin expanses. The ancient rubs elbows with the new, the archaic with the futuristic, the technological with the feudal, the prehistoric with the utopic. In our cities skyscrapers stand side by side with Indian markets that sell totemic amulets.[26]

In addition, the cyclical motion and simultaneous patterning which characterize this text lead to final revelation and point to a recurrent theme within *Cien años de soledad* specifically, and within Latin American literature in general. While North American literature, as already discussed, is centrally concerned with innocence and loss of innocence, Latin American literature is predominantly concerned with the search for identity, on both an individual and collective level. Speaking of both *Pedro Páramo* by the Mexican Juan Rulfo and *Cien años de soledad*, Suzanne Jill Levine observes that "the search for identity that both novels present is not just a search for personal and family identity, but also for national and cultural identity."[27] The apparent obsession with history, with the retelling of the past in ways and modes that differ from traditional and officially sanctioned accounts is, indeed, an attempt to discover the personal and national identity of a people too long silenced by dominant Western rationalist culture, of a people too long resigned and passive and unable to find their own voice. Called "the great Latin American novel" by many, and "a metaphor for Latin America" by García Márquez himself,[28] *Cien años de soledad* is a search for identity which, within the magical space of Macondo and the mythical hundred-years' time, encompasses a continent and the life span of a civilization. Focused, of course, on the enigmatic manuscripts written by Melquíades in Sanskrit, one of the first languages within the Indo-European family of languages, this search becomes a search for "the origin of Spanish linguistic genealogy."[29] Throughout the novel, various of the Buendía male descendants occupy the gypsy's timeless room in order to attempt to decipher his elusive manuscripts. A mystery on both a linguistic and temporal level, the manuscripts prove indecipherable because they are written in the ancient language of Sanskrit and according to temporal simultaneity. Ultimately unlocking the origins of human expression and the totality of human experience, the last Buendía finally deciphers the prophetic manuscripts and discovers his personal and collective identity. Contained within a prophecy, moreover, this identity and history is transformed into a warning, a vision of a dark *future* contained within an ignoble *past* and *present*.

This fundamentally cyclical and synchronic patterning of narrative discourse is, nevertheless, in constant play with the diachronic dimensions of a novel which recounts the chronological trajectory of Macondo and of the Buendía family. In fact, the narrative development of this novel is apparently sequential, as it takes the reader through the various developmental phases of Macondo, phases which mirror the history of Colombia and, by analogy, the history of all Latin America. Contrary to the fragmented and unsequential piecing together of the past which creates the narrative ripples of *Absalom, Absalom!*, *Cien años de soledad* follows a sequential pattern that traces Macondo's history, from its primordial founding to its eventual apocalyptic destruction. Arriving in a "tierra que nadie les habia prometido" (27) ("land no one had promised them"), the Buendía patriarch and matriarch found a race whose history at once imitates biblical eschatological direction and parodies the story of Genesis to Apocalypse. In the end, the prophecy of *Cien años de soledad* reveals that, for Latin America, the discovery and founding of the Americas have not led, by any means, to a "new Jerusalem."

Briefly, the phases of Latin American history recounted within this novel can be listed and summarized as: the establishment of a patriarchal regime, led by José Arcadio Buendía; the instillation of civil and religious authorities; the breaking out of civil wars between liberals and conservatives; and the neo-colonial period of banana fever, based on the period from the establishment of the United Fruit Company in Colombia in 1899 to the violent repression of its workers' strikes in the region of Magdalena in 1928. Numerous critics have delineated and analyzed the diachronic dimensions of this novel, which is now "required reading in many Latin American history and political science courses."[30] Among them, Lucila Inés Mena presents a lengthy and informative analysis in her book *La función de la historia en Cien años de soledad* and Roberto González Echevarría, focusing on the Latin American novel's "obsession with history and myth," describes the historical trajectory of García Márquez's famous work in the following manner:

. . . there is lurking in the background of the story the overall pattern of Latin American history, both as a general design made up of various key events and eras, and in the presence of specific characters and incidents that seem to refer to real people and happenings. Thus we have a period of discovery and conquest, when José Arcadio Buendía and the original families settle Macondo. There is in this part of the book little sense that Macondo belongs to a larger political unit, but such isolation was in fact typical of Latin America's towns in the colonial period. Even the viceroyalites lived in virtual isolation from the metropolitan government. The appearance of Apolinar Moscoso and his barefoot soldiers is the beginning of the republican era, which is immediately followed by the outbreak of the civil wars in which Colonel Aureliano Buendía distinguishes himself. Though Colombia is the most obvious model for this period, nearly the entire continent suffered from civil strife during the nineteenth century, a process that led to the emergence of dictators and *caudillos*. This period is followed by the era of neocolonial domination by the United States and the struggle against it in most Latin American countries. These culminate in the novel with the general strike and the massacre of the workers. There are, unfortunately, countless models for this last, clearly defined period in the novel. After the flood, there is a time of decay before the apocalyptic wind that razes the town at the end.[31]

While Úrsula's house and Pilar's gyrating wheel express cyclical patterning, and Melquíades' manuscripts embody synchronic patterning, the image of the Buendía patriarch, José Arcadio Buendía, tied to the chestnut tree in the family yard depicts the fate of genealogy and linearity within *Cien años de soledad*, a novel which at once chronicles the founding of America and traces the family tree of its founders.[32] Called a "genealogical and a philological emblem" by Anibal González, the tree to which the founder of the Buendía line is tied, symbolizes the axis of the world and the presence of a center, along with representing the phallus as well as the virility and creative action of the male, according to Graciela Maturo.[33] Significantly, José Arcadio Buendía is forcibly tied to the tree when the discovery that in Macondo every day is Monday since the "máquina del tiempo" is broken leads him into a destructive rampage, indicative of the frustration which re-

Critical Insights

sults from the lack of scientific development and technological progress which characterizes some regions of the Americas.

Entonces agarró la tranca de una puerta y con la violencia salvaje de su
fuerza descomunal destrozó hasta conventirlos en polvo los aparatos de
alquimia, el gabinete de daguerrotipia, el taller de orfebrería, gritando como
un endemoniado en un idioma altisonante y fluido pero completamente
incomprensible. Se disponía a terminar con el resto de la casa cuando
Aureliano pidió ayuda a los vecinos. Se necesitaron diez hombres para
tumbarlo, catorce para amarrarlo, veinte para arrastrarlo hasta el castaño
del patio, donde lo dejaron atado, ladrando en lengua extraña y echando
espumarajos verdes por la boca. (76-7)

(He then grabbed the lock on one of the doors and, with a savage violence
proportionate to his unusual strength, destroyed his alchemy utensils, the
daguerreotype closet and the gold shop, crying insanely in a resonant and
fluid but totally incomprehensible language. He was about to destroy the
rest of the house when Aureliano asked the neighbors for help. It took ten
men to stop him, fourteen to tie him and twenty to drag him to the chestnut
tree in the yard, where they left him tied, barking in a strange language and
foaming at the mouth.)

While, as we have seen, genealogy and a "clean," i.e., "white," linearity define Sutpen's design and reason for being in *Absalom, Absalom!*, family lines and genealogy are put "outside" and out of the way
early in *Cien años de soledad*, only to be followed by prolific and pro-
miscuous procreation. Himself a searcher and researcher, José Arcadio's tirade can be interpreted as the frustrated scientist's reaction to
"a whole continent which resists assimilation into the Western race to
progress," as Patricia Tobin puts it, and into Western conceptions of
time and history. Speaking of a genealogical enterprise which is emp-
tied of authority by the language and style of *Cien años de soledad*,
Tobin goes on to say that "fatherhood is denied any metaphorical sig-

nificance in this text." As traditional historical and patriarchal systems break down, including the "vicious circularity of civil wars" (124) which traps Colonel Aureliano Buendía and the military, the ultimate patriarchal system, the novel, says Tobin, "is fused once more to organic life, as lived beyond and before paternal deliberation." By rejecting "the paternal guarantee of knowledge and by embracing the whole immediacy of everything," concludes Tobin, García Márquez "has severed the novel from its hidden alliance with knowledge and fused it once more to organic life, as it is lived beyond and before paternal deliberation." Affirming "circular rhythms of the cosmos over linear history,"[34] then, *Cien años de soledad* by Gabriel García Márquez expresses the reality and consciousness of Latin Americans for whom, according to Jaime Mejía Duque, "history is not linear."[35] In the end, the apparent chronology of this text proves, of course, to be illusory. Just as the Aureliano of the last paragraph re-lives the redundant and enlightening experience of totality that Colonel Aureliano experiences in the first sentence of the novel, the various generations of the Buendía family re-live varying experiences of redundancy and degrees of enlightenment. Tied to and devoured by nature, the Buendía family fulfill the prophecy of Melquíades' manuscripts in which, for a "prodigious instant," the beginning and the end is revealed to the last Aureliano, as he deciphers the magical phrase pronouncing the fate of the Buendía genealogical enterprise: *"El primero de la esuipe está amarrado en un árbol y el último se lo están comiendo las hormigas"* (358) ("The first of the line is tied to a tree and the last is being eaten by ants"). This revelatory phrase refers, of course, to Aureliano's great-great-great grandfather and to his and Amaranta Úrsula's infant son, born only to be eaten by the enormous colored ants.

Comparative analyses of the work of William Faulkner and Gabriel García Márquez have often devoted attention to *La hojarasca* (*Leaf Storm*), the Colombian writer's first novel, published in 1955. In this work, García Márquez first creates Macondo, a region whose narrative import will come to stand next to that of Yoknapatawpha County, and experiments with multiple narrators trapped in the circularity of their psychological labyrinths. Recalling *As I Lay Dying* as they revolve around the dead body of the town doctor lying in his casket awaiting burial, the interior monologues of the Colonel, Isabel and Isabel's young son represent three generations which together give narrative expression to their individual realities and to the history of Macondo. Having **discovered** the world of Macondo, Gabriel García Márquez's writing seems to **uncover** a "world of circularity," as it **recovers** a range of significance traditionally attributed to the circle.

The circle as a closed and static, stagnant space which traps and retards expresses the reality of Macondo from its creation within García Márquez's work. Macondo, of course, proves to be a world within which its citizens feel as if they are "flotando en circulos concéntricos dentro de un estanque de gelatina" ("floating in concentric circles within a pond of gelatin"), words which describe the condition of the Colonel and his wife desperately "rotting alive"[36] and waiting fifty years for his military pension which never arrives in *El coronel no tiene quien le escriba* (*No One Writes to the Colonel*) published in 1957. In *Cien años de soledad* ten years later, the feeling of being trapped within the vicious circularity of repetitive stasis and static repetition is expanded to express the redundant human experience of all "estirpes condenadas a cien años de soledad" (306) ("races condemned to one hundred years of solitude"). In García Márquez's famous novel, moreover, this vicious circularity is as much a result of oppressive socio-political regimes and foreign neo-colonial exploitation as it is a result of the passive forgetfulness and resigned acceptance of its people, as can be seen by Macondo's ready acceptance of the "official" proclamation denying the massacre of 3,000 banana plantation workers and by the insomnia plague during which everyone has to be reminded of the most elementary details of everyday life, like the fact that cows give milk which, when mixed with coffee, makes "café con leche." Macondo is certainly guilty of forgetfulness, the most unpardonable sin according to traditional belief and myth.[37]

The short story "Los funerales de la Mamá Grande" is the first work by this Colombian writer into which magical and fantastic elements are interwoven. Within this narrative, published in 1962, circularity becomes "una intrincada maraña de consanguinidad que convertió la procreación en un circulo vicioso" ("an intricate tangle of consanguinity which transformed procreation into a vicious circle"). The death and funeral of the long-lived and powerful matriarch around whom all creation revolved, prompts "algunos de los alli presentes . . . (a) comprender que estaban asistiendo al nacimiento de una nueva época"[38] ("some of those present to understand that they were present at the birth of a new era"), thereby reflecting the potential for renewal inherent to the cyclical motion of the circle. Five years later, the cyclical patterning of *Cien años de soledad* springs from the traditional paradigm of periodic renewal attributed to the cycle of nature and the physical world. Because "cyclical time is periodic," the final destruction and disappearance of Macondo "implies a new beginning,"[39] as Julio Ortega puts it. Although implied but not contained in the novel, renewal is so basic to cyclical motion that García Márquez himself quoted Faulkner's own Nobel acceptance phrase, "I decline to accept the end of men," as he himself accepted the Nobel Prize in 1982; he then ended by envisioning "a new and sweeping utopia of life, where no one will be able to decide for others how they die, where love will prove true and happiness be possible, and where the races condemned to one hundred years of solitude will have, at last and forever, a second opportunity on earth."[40]

Simultaneous to circularity as entrapment within vicious repetition and as potential for cyclical renewal, *Cien años de soledad*, the innovative and audacious novel which García Márquez published in 1967, presents circularity as the moment of total vision and perception, as the instant of complete self-knowledge and identity. Reflecting the existential preoccupation of other twentieth-century writers, this instant could be called "the ultimate epiphany" in James Joyce's terms, "the ultimate moment of being" for Virginia Woolf, the ultimate "momento privilegiado" for the Brazilian writer Clarice Lispector, or the perfect "Aleph of time"[41] for Jorge Luis Borges, the influential Argentinian writer whom many critics relate to García Márquez's writing and to twentieth-century Hispanic American writing in general. In his own work, Borges himself returns constantly to a traditional image of circularity, $\odot$, the point within a circle. A symbol which first appears, according to Georges Poulet, in "a pseudo-hermetic manuscript of the twelfth century," the circle with the point in the middle represents God, "a sphere whose center is everywhere and whose circumference is nowhere."[42] In discussing *Cien años de soledad*, critics have readily acknowledged its basic circularity and many have spoken in terms which recall the circle with the point in the middle. Ricardo Gullón, for example, says that "the novel has the circular and dynamic structure of a 'gyrating wheel'"; Robert Sims emphasizes this wheel's "immobile center" and "revolving perimeter," while Vargas Llosa describes "a great circle composed of numerous concentric circles, contained one within the others."[43]

However, the gyrating wheel of *Cien años de soledad* is characterized by a broken axle which ultimately causes it to spin itself into oblivion, i.e., causes the cyclical stasis of Macondo to spin off-center and disappear from the face of the earth. Whereas Faulkner's ripples de-center narrative circularity by multiplying and expanding circularity to infinite proportions, García Márquez's gyrating wheel spins off-center due to its vicious repetitive oscillations. Contained within a prophecy, this gyrating wheel obliterates human forgetfulness and unconsciousness of social injustice and evil, as it simultaneously becomes a warning to races which neglect and forget, races which accept official manipulation and political oppression. So constructed, it becomes "la máquina de memoria" (49) which José Arcadio had tried but failed to invent for his family and for Macondo; so shaped, it reflects the historical frustration and a-historical reality of human experience in Latin America. Uniting the beginning and the end, Genesis and Apocalypse, the dark point at the top of the diagram I propose represents the worn axle of an elliptical trajectory which ultimately obliterates time and space, in the guise of the Buendía family and the region of Macondo. At the same time, this point represents the all-encompassing *present* moment of temporal simultaneity and total self-knowledge, containing within itself all *past* and *future*. In its turn, the parameters of the larger outer circle expand to paradigmatic proportions through the magically archetypal evocation of "100 years," while the solitude of Latin American existence goes in circles endlessly, simultaneously following the trajectory of the seven generations of the Buendía family and tracing the various cycles of collective history which characterize this region. So dominant, however, is projection into the future, the narrative mode of a novel which is in the end a prophecy, a warning to be deciphered, that the circularity of *Cien años de soledad* "ends up" pointing to the possibility of natural cyclical renewal, the dotted line leading out of the atemporal point in my diagram.

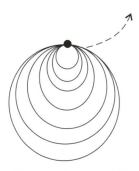

"una rueda giratoria"
Cien años de soledad

As with *Absalom, Absalom!*, the circularity of *Cien años de soledad* implicates the reader for, as the last Buendía succeeds in deciphering the prophetic manuscripts, the reader of this novel also participates in an "instant" of total vision, i.e., the completion of the novel. Contrary to the partial nature of the interpretative process in *Absalom, Absalom!*, then, the reader of *Cien años de soledad*, along with Aureliano, assumes the vantage point of paradigmatic synchronicity reflected in the circular totality of the eternal instant of revelation. From this vantage point, the reader also has a total vision and experience of the fundamental tension between the historical and a-historical dimensions of the text, as the novel unabashedly challenges its reader to participate in the pleasantly playful yet philosophically profound erasure of clear distinctions between "reality" and "fiction." Indicating just how central this ontological game is to his work, García Márquez himself, as noted in chapter 2, describes his greatest problem as that of "destroying the line separating what seems real from what seems fantastic."[44] Examples of the novel as game appear both in the title, where the word "SOLꓱDAD," written with a backward E, is "an invitation to play"[45] according to José Antonio Bravo, and within the text itself. As the last Aureliano becomes more and more enlightened, he realizes that literature is "el mejor juguete que se había inventado para burlarse de la gente" (337) ("the best game ever invented to make fun of people"). Ironically enough, it is the playful and fanciful aspects of this novel which have made it a literary phenomenon, "one of those very rare cases of a major contemporary work which everyone can read, understand and enjoy,"[46] as Vargas Llosa puts it.

Indeed, as circularity and simultaneity break down the barriers between history and synchronicity, and between "reality" and "fiction," the narrative discourse of *Cien años de soledad* plays with the reader by mixing historical figures, both human and numerical, with imaginary recreations. Exemplifying the former, García Márquez himself (336-49), his "real-life" wife Mercedes (394) and actual situations from his "real life" appear and participate in the novel, as do fictional characters from novels by the Latin American writers Alejo Carpentier, Carlos Fuentes and Julio Cortázar. An example of numerical play would be the very significant number of massacred strikers taken away after Macondo's banana strike, a number which is slowly forgotten by Macondo's survivors, as they passively accept the false but official story which "los historiadores habían admitido y consagrado en los textos escolares" (303) ("historians had admitted and made official within school textbooks"). In the end, the event is totally erased from the characters' minds, a case of fiction being erased from fictional characters' minds if we take into account the historically "real" sources of this important episode. In an interview, García Márquez explains how reality became fiction for this episode, and how, in true Márquezian circular fashion, fiction became reality once again:

> That episode didn't come from any story telling. It is, more or less based on historical reality. The reasons, the motives and the manner in which the events around the strike occurred were exactly as in the novel—though there were not 3000 dead, of course. There were very few deaths. If 100 people had been killed in 1928, it would have been catastrophic. I made the death toll 3000 because I was using certain proportions in my book. One hundred wouldn't have been noticed. I was also interested in achieving a certain imagery; I wanted the bodies to be taken away in a train, a train such as the ones that were loaded with clusters of bananas. I did research and found that to fill such a train, you'd need at least 3000 bodies. . . . Let me tell you something very curious about that incident. Nobody has studied the events around the real banana strike—and now when they talk about it in the newspapers, even once in the congress, they speak about the 3000 who died! And I wonder if, with time, it will become true that 3000 were killed.[47]

Affirming the precedence and predominance of the imaginary in yet another interview, and asserting its importance for the Latin American narrative, García Márquez declares: "Yo creo que este sistema de explotación de la realidad, sin prejuicios racionalistas, le abren a nuestra novela una perspectiva espléndida. Y no se crea que es un método escapista: tarde o temprano, la realidad termina por darle la razón a la imaginación." ("I believe that this system of exploiting reality, by forgetting rationalist biases, offers our novel a splendid perspective. And I don't believe this to be an escapist method: sooner or later, reality has to admit that the imagination is right [translated literally, 'that imagination has reason'].") Very simply, this writer says: "Lo único que sé sin ninguna duda es que la realidad no termina en el precio de los tomates."[48] ("All I know for sure is that reality doesn't begin and end with the price of tomatoes.")

As the reader participates in this real/fantastic game, the novel partakes of total circularity and shapes Latin American history according to the circular paradigm, retelling the history of this America in a different mode from that which has traditionally dominated the Western world, including North America, with its linear paradigm focused on progress and the future. Gerald Martin offers this appraisal of Latin American experience in relation to Occidental tradition and development, which are symbolized by the various objects mentioned:

> Conceived by Spain in the sixteenth century (the stranded galleon, the buried suit of armour), the characters awaken in the late eighteenth century Enlightenment (magnet and telescope as symbols of the two pillars of Newtonian physics), but are entirely unable to bring themselves into focus in a world they have not made.[49]

In his Nobel Prize acceptance speech, Gabriel García Márquez himself devotes special attention to this issue, which he calls "the lack of conventional means for expressing Latin American reality" as he relates it to the all-encompassing theme of *Cien años de soledad*, the theme of human solitude. Describing the "outsized reality" of Latin America, at the same time that he focuses the central concern and "quest for our own identity," he says that

> our crucial problem has been a lack of conventional means to render our lives believable. This, my friends, is the crux of our solitude. And if these difficulties, whose essence we share, hinder us, it is understandable that the rational talents on this side of the world, exalted in the contemplation of their own cultures, should have found themselves without a valid means to

interpret us. It is only natural that they insist on measuring us with the yard-stick that they use for themselves, forgetting that the ravages of life are not the same for all, and that the quest for our own identity is just as arduous and bloody for us as it was for them. The interpretation of our reality through patterns not our own serves only to make us ever more unknown, ever less free, ever more solitary.[50]

Isolated, then, within their individual and collective circle of soli-tude, Latin Americans live to the ultimate degree the universal human experience of solitude, of knowing that it is impossible to ever know a person completely.[51] Within a novel which makes its characters "bite into the bitter fruit of shared solitude," as Emir Rodríguez Monegal puts it, the "humorous and playful style" of this novel is paradoxically constructed from "the saddest, most solitary and most lucid gaze."[52] Trapping his unforgettable characters within the circle of human soli-tude, Gabriel García Márquez presents "a vision of humans abandoned to total earthly solitude,"[53] in the words of Zunilda Gertel. In so doing, he creates the "labyrinth of solitude" which the Mexican writer and thinker Octavio Paz had described in his classic study published in 1950, a labyrinth within which García Márquez's characters suffer the "sleep of one hundred years" of solitude, as Paz had put it seventeen years before *Cien años de soledad* was published. While describing the universal experience of solitude in our modern de-centered world, Paz joins Latin American experience to that of the Western World when he affirms that today "we are all at the edge, because the center has disap-peared."[54] As the gyrating wheel of *Cien años de soledad* describes its vicious circular trajectory, its central axle wears down and becomes de-centered, simultaneously spinning Macondo right off the face of the earth and creating an unforgettable circular experience of solitude in America and in the modern world.

Notes

1. Quoted in Richard Adams, *Faulkner: Myth and Motion* (Princeton UP, 1968) 12.

2. Katalin Kulin, *Creación mítica en la obra de Gabriel García Márquez* (Budapest: Akadémia Kladó, Editorial de la Academia de Ciencias de Hungría, 1980) 12.

3. Lucila Inés Mena, *La función de la historia en Cien años de soledad* (Barcelona: Plaza & Jones, 1979) 137.

4. Vincenzo Bollettino, *Breve estudio de la novelística de García Márquez* (Madrid: Playor, 1973) 95.

5. Carlos Fuentes, *La nueva novela en hispanoamérica*, 30.

6. Karl Löwith, *Meaning in History* (Chicago: U of Chicago P, 1949) 19.

7. Hayden White, *Tropics of Discourse. Essays in Cultural Criticism* (Baltimore, Maryland: Johns Hopkins UP, 1978) 5 & 216.

8. Mario Vargas Llosa, *García Márquez: Historia de un deicidio* (Barcelona: Barral Editores, 1971) 598-9. For examples and an analysis of repetition in *Cien años de soledad*, see especially pages 598-607.

9. Josefina Ludemar, *Cien años de soledad: una interpretación* (Buenos Aires: Editorial Tiempo Contemporaneo, 1972) 92.

10. Claudia Dreifus, "Interview: Gabriel García Márquez," *Playboy* 30.2 (Feb 1983): 74.

11. Raymond L. Williams, "El tiempo en la novela: observaciones en torno al tiempo en la novela colombiana Contemporanea," *Explicación de Textos Literarios* 11.2 (1982-83) 15.

12. Robert Lewis Sims, *The Evolution of Myth in Gabriel García Márquez* (Miami: Ediciones Universal, 1981) 111.

13. Gaston Bachelard, *The Poetics of Space*, trans. Maria Jolas (Boston: Beacon Press, 1964) 7 & 15.

14. Sims, 111.

15. Michael Palencia-Roth, *Gabriel García Márquez: La linea, el circulo y las metamorfosis del mito* (Madrid: Editorial Gredos, 1983) 92.

16. Michael Wood, "Review of *One Hundred Years of Solitude*," *Columbia Forum* 13.3 (summer 1970): 162.

17. Fuentes, *La nueva novela en hispanoamérica*, 10.

18. Palencia-Roth, 96; D. P. Gallagher, "Gabriel García Márquez," *Modern Latin American Literature* (London: Oxford UP, 1973) 157; and Sims, 123.

19. Sims, 142 & Laurence M. Porter, "The Political Function of Fantasy in García Márquez," *Centennial Review* 30.2 (1986): 200.

20. René Jara Cuadra, *Las claves del mito en Cien años de soledad* (Chile: Ediciones Universidad de Valparaiso, 1972) 18.

21. Emir Rodríguez Monegal, "Novedad y anacronismo de *Cien años de soledad*," *Homenaje a Gabriel García Márquez*, Helmy F. Giacoman, ed. (New York: Las Américas Publishing Co., Inc., 1972) 32, and Gregorio Salvador, *Comentarios estructurales a Cien años de soledad* (Las Palmas: Litografía Saavedra, 1970) 30.

22. J. E. Cirlot, *A Dictionary of Symbols* (New York: Philosophical Library, 1962) 148.

23. Cuadra, 13.

24. Vargas Llosa, 550.

25. Zunilda Gertel, "Tres estucturas fundamentales en la narrativa hispano-americana actual," *Nueva Narrativa Hispanoamericana* 5 (enero y sept, 1975): 219.

26. Luis Harss and Barbara Dohmann, *Into the Mainstream* (New York: Harper & Row, 1967) 39.

27. Suzanne Jill Levine, "*Pedro Páramo y Cien años de soledad*: un paralelo," *Homenaje a Gabriel García Márquez*, ed. Helmy F. Giacoman (New York: Las Américas, 1972) 283.

28. Rodríguez Monegal, 16 & Dreifus, 172.

29. Aníbal González, "Translation and Genealogy: *One Hundred Years of Solitude*," *Gabriel García Márquez: New Readings*, eds. Bernard McGuirk & Richard Cardwell (Cambridge: Cambridge UP, 1987) 73.

30. Gene H. Belle-Villada, "García Márquez and the Novel," *Latin American Literary Review* 13.25 (Jan-June 1985): 21.

31. Roberto González Echevarría, "*Cien años de soledad*: The Novel as Myth and Archive," *Modern Language Notes* 99.2 (March 1984): 358 & 369.

32. Iris M. Zavala, "*Cien años de soledad*: Crónica de Indias," *Homenaje a Gabriel García Márquez*, ed. Helmy F. Giacoman (New York: Las Américas, 1972) 205. Although García Márquez himself has said that the word Macondo comes from the name of a banana plantation in the region in which he grew up, Zavala goes on to say that "macondo" is the "popular word used in Colombia to indicate a hefty bombacacea tree, similar to the silk-cotton tree."

33. Graciela Maturo, *Claves simbólicas de García Márquez* (Buenos Aires: Fernando García Cambeiro, 1972) 116.

34. Patricia Drechsel Tobin, *Time and the Novel: The Genealogical Imperative* (Princeton UP, 1978) 188; 178; 183; 191 & 184.

35. René Jara and Jaime Mejía Duque, *Las claves del mito en García Márquez* (Valparaíso: Ediciones Universitarias de Valparaíso, 1972) 75.

36. Gabriel García Márquez, *El coronel no tiene quien le escriba* (México: Ediciones Era, 1961) 11 & 25-6.

37. Kulin, 187.

38. Gabriel García Márquez, "Los funerales de la Mama Grande," *Los funerales de la Mama Grande* (Barcelona: Plaza & Janes, 1976) 121 & 139.

39. Julio Ortega, "Exchange System in *One Hundred Years of Solitude*," *Gabriel García Márquez and the Powers of Fiction*, ed. Julio Ortega (Austin: U of Texas P, 1988) 5.

40. Gabriel García Márquez, "The Solitude of Latin America: Nobel Lecture, 1982," trans. Marina Castañeda, *Gabriel García Márquez and the Powers of Fiction*, ed. Julio Ortega (Austin: U of Texas P, 1988) 91.

41. Emir Rodríguez Monegal, "*One Hundred Years of Solitude*: The Last Three Pages," *Critical Essays on Gabriel García Márquez*, ed. George R. McMurray (Boston: G. K. Hall, 1987) 149.

42. Georges Poulet, *The Metamorphosis of the Circle* (Baltimore: Johns Hopkins UP, 1966) xi.

43. Ricardo Gullón, "García Márquez o el olvidado arte de contar," *Homenaje a Gabriel García Márquez*, ed. Helmy F. Giacoman (New York: Las Américas, 1972) 149; Sims, 139 and Vargas Llosa, 500.

44. Fernández-Braso, 96.

45. José Antonio Bravo, *Lo real maravilloso en la narrativa latinoamericana* (Lima: Editoriales Unidas, 1978) 43.

46. Mario Vargas Llosa, "García Márquez: de Aracataca a Macondo," *9 asedios a García Márquez* (Santiago de Chile: Editorial Universitaria, 1969) 127.

47. Dreifus, 76.

48. Fernández-Braso, 61 & 59.

49. Gerald Martin, "On 'Magical' and Social Realism in García Márquez," *Gabriel García Márquez: New Readings*, eds. Bernard McGuirk & Richard Cardwell (Cambridge: Cambridge UP, 1987) 104.

50. García Márquez, "Nobel," 89.

51. Dreifus, 176.

52. Rodríguez Monegal, "Novedad," 42 & 41.

53. Zunilda Gertel, *La novela hispanoamericana contemporanea* (Buenos Aires: Nuevos Esquemas, 1970) 157.

54. Octavio Paz, *El laberinto de la soledad* (México: Fondo de Cultura Económica, 1950) 18, 152 & 153.

The Dark Side of Magical Realism:
Science, Oppression, and Apocalypse
in *One Hundred Years of Solitude*_____

Brian Conniff

> Brian Conniff concentrates his attention on José Arcadio Buendía, the character in García Márquez's magnum opus who is obsessed with scientific discoveries and technological inventions. Inspired by the way the Chilean playwright and cultural commentator Ariel Dorfman analyzes popular culture, Conniff argues that in *One Hundred Years of Solitude* the playfulness of José Arcadio Buendía serves as a reminder that the Magical Realist style is marked by an unavoidable disappointment in progress, particularly in Latin America, where modernity arrived in unfinished fashion.   — I.S.

In criticism of the Latin American novel, "magical realism" has typically been described as an impulse to create a fictive world that can somehow compete with the "insatiable fount of creation" that is Latin America's actual history.[1] This concept of magical realism received perhaps its most influential endorsement in the Nobel Prize acceptance speech of Gabriel García Márquez. The famous Colombian novelist began this speech, suggestively enough, with an account of the "meticulous log" kept by Magellan's navigator, Antonia Pigafetta. In the course of this fateful exploration of the "Southern American continent," the imaginative Florentine recorded such oddities as "a monstrosity of an animal with the head and ears of a mule, the body of a camel, the hooves of a deer, and the neigh of a horse" (207). In the course of his Nobel speech, García Márquez recorded many less imaginative but equally improbable facts—"in the past eleven years twenty million Latin American children have died before their second birthday. Nearly one hundred and twenty thousand have disappeared as a consequence of repression. . . . A country created from all these Latin Americans in exile or enforced emigration would have a larger population than Norway" ("Solitude of Latin America" 208, 209)—on and on, as if he were trying to combat a plague of amnesia.

In such a "disorderly reality," García Márquez explained, the "poets and beggars, musicians and prophets, soldiers and scoundrels" of Colombia had been forced to respond to one of the saddest and most productive challenges in modern literature: "the want of conventional resources to make our life credible" (208-209). Fortunately, conventional resources were not everything. So, according to conventional wisdom, "magical realism" was born, offering the type of hope that García Márquez tried to provide, in that famous speech, when he said that the writer can somehow "bring light to this very chamber with his words" (208). Perhaps magical realism might allow the writer to create in his work a "minor utopia," like the one inhabited by Amaranta Úrsula and the next to last Aureliano at the end of *One Hundred Years of Solitude*, a fictive order that might somehow, like the birth of a child, affirm life in the face of the most brutal oppression. It was a novelistic act analogous to pulling a rabbit, or a child with a tail of a pig, out of a hat. It was magic.

Needless to say, critics have been quick to make use of such a powerful precept. "Magical realism" has typically been seen as the redemption of fiction in the face of a reality that is still becoming progressively more disorderly. But some critics have noted that the term, as it has most often been used, has always lent itself to certain simplifications. Most important, it has sometimes served as "an ideological stratagem to collapse many different kinds of writing, and many different political perspectives, into one single, usually escapist, concept" (Martin 102). Still, the overall optimism needs further qualification. In fact, there is another side of "magical realism," just as there is another side of magic. Not only can the conjuror make rabbits and flowers and crazed revolutionaries appear instantly, but he can also make them disappear, just as instantly. Although critics have not been quick to notice, García Márquez also sensed this darker side of magical realism. Unlike his "master" William Faulkner thirty-two years before, he could not "refuse to admit the end of mankind." Apocalypse, he was forced to admit, had become "for the first time in the history of humanity . . . simply a scientific possibility" ("Solitude of Latin America" 211). By the end of *One Hundred Years of Solitude*, apocalypse had become, perhaps for the first time in the history of the novel, just one more calamity on "this planet of misfortune" (211). When apocalypse does occur, García Márquez suggested, it will be pervaded, like so many events toward the end of *One Hundred Years of Solitude*, by a strange air of eternal repetition. It will be only the logical conclusion of the progress already brought by "advanced" ideas. In the disorderly modern world, magical realism is not merely an expression of hope; it is also a "resource" that can depict such a "scientific possibility." That is, it can depict events strange enough, and oppressive enough, to make apocalypse appear not only credible but inevitable.

On the first page of *One Hundred Years of Solitude*, such a strange event occurs, an event that will recur, over and over, like the ceaseless repetition—of names and incest, solitude and nostalgia, madness and failed revolutions—that haunts the house of Buendía: the gypsies come to Macondo. For a long time, they will come every year, always "with an uproar of pipes and kettledrums," and always with new inventions, until the wars make such trips too dangerous, and the natives become too indifferent; but their first appearance is the most impressive, and the most ominous. They first appear in a distant past, "when the world was so recent that many things lacked names, and in order to indicate them it was necessary to point" (11). Into this "primitive world" the gypsies bring an omen of the future, an invention of great wonder and potential: the magnet.

Melquíades, the "heavy gypsy with the untamed beard," calls this invention "the eighth wonder of the learned alchemists of Macedonia" (11). He drags it around, from house to house, so that everyone can see pots and pans fly through the air, nails and screws pull out of the woodwork, long-lost objects reappear. Like any great missionary of progress, Melquíades is concerned with enlightening the natives, so he also provides an explanation: "Things have a life of their own. . . . It's simply a matter of waking up their souls" (11).

But José Arcadio Buendía, the first citizen of Macondo, has an idea of his own. Prophet, patriarch, inventor, and murderer—José Arcadio is not a man to forsake progress. He is, in fact, "the most enterprising man ever to be seen in the village" (18). His "unbridled imagination" often takes him, along with anyone he can convince to follow, "beyond the genius of nature, and even beyond miracles and magic," just as he once led a handful of men and women on an "absurd journey" in search of the sea, the journey that resulted in the founding of their inland village (31-32). Confronted with the marvelous magnet, José Arcadio feels that it is necessary to discover a useful application. Whereas Melquíades is content to mystify the natives, José Arcadio must look, with a wonder of his own, toward the future. He comes up with an idea that is portentous, just as his technological imagination will be fatal. Through a process no one else seems to understand, he calculates that it must be possible to use this marvelous invention "to extract gold from the bowels of the earth" (12). A "brilliant idea," to a man like José Arcadio, should translate into a well-deserved profit.[2] Even though Melquíades is honest and tells him that this idea will not work, José Arcadio begins to search for "gold enough and more to pave the floors of the house." He trades in "his mule and a pair of goats for the two magnetized ingots" and explores "every inch of the region"; but he fails to find anything he considers valuable. All he finds is "a suit of fifteenth-century armor that had all of its pieces soldered together with rust and inside of which there was the hollow resonance of an enormous stone-filled gourd" (12). Searching for gold, José Arcadio finds the remains of Spanish imperialism.

The following March, when the gypsies next appear in Macondo, they bring a telescope and a magnifying glass, "the latest discovery of the Jews of Amsterdam." Once again, Melquíades provides an explanation—"Science has eliminated distance"—and, not surprisingly, he once again mystifies the natives (12). His theory of the elimination of distance, like his theory of magnetic souls, is a fusion of chicanery and "advanced" science—and it is just as prophetic as José Arcadio's accidental discovery of the suit of armor. Even though the natives, José Arcadio in particular, are unable to understand the principles of Melquíades's discoveries, they are all too willing to assume that it is because they are not "worldly" or "advanced" enough. Melquíades's perspective, unlike theirs, is "global"; he has circled the world many times; he seems to know "what there was on the other side of things" (15). Perhaps he even believes he is being honest when he tries to comfort them by promising that such a perspective will soon be available to everyone, through the wonders of science, with no disruption of domestic tranquility, without the inconvenience of travel: "in a short time, man will be able to see what is happening in any place of the world without leaving his own house" (12).

But Melquíades's "theoretical" approach to science, just like José Arcadio's "practical" approach, suffers from a fatal blindness. Both of them are willing to assume that science is essentially democratizing. They do not understand that José Arcadio's misdirected discovery of the rusted armor, and its "calcified skeleton," has already brought to Macondo a vision of "progress" that is both mystifying and applied—but not democratizing. Years later, after the prolonged senility and death of José Arcadio, after the innumerable deaths of Melquíades, Macondo will eventually see the outside world—which José Arcadio tried so hard to discover, which Melquíades leads them to believe he knows completely—and science will be responsible. But, by then, the chicanery of the gypsies will only be displaced by more sophisticated and more determined exploitation.

For the moment, however, José Arcadio is simply inspired by the magnifying glass, so he allows his fantasies to transport him, once again, closer to an "outside" reality that he badly misunderstands. After watching another of the gypsies' demonstrations, in which the magnifying glass is used to set a pile of hay on fire, he immediately decides that this invention has even greater potential than the magnet because it can prove useful as an "instrument of war." Ignoring the protests of Melquíades, and ignoring the legitimate fears of his wife, José Arcadio is compelled, once again, to invest in an invention. This time, he uses a more progressive currency, the two magnetized ingots and three "colonial coins." His enthusiasm prevents him from noticing that his currency is being debased. Many years later, gold, and even colonial coins, will be superseded by the banana company's scrip, which is "good only to buy Virginia ham in the company commissaries" (278); but José Arcadio will never be able to understand how the debasement of the currency helps support the domination of his people.[3] He is happy to dream of progress, to experiment, to burn himself, to almost set the house on fire, and to finally complete "a manual of startling instructional clarity and an irresistible power of conviction" (13)—thus linking, for the first time in the history of Macondo, and without noticing, scientific discovery and political rhetoric.

Then, in his zeal to improve his village, José Arcadio makes the greatest of his many misjudgments: he sends his manual to "the military authorities" (13). With it, he sends all the scientific evidence he considers appropriate, "numerous descriptions of his experiments and several pages of explanatory sketches" (13). He is determined to leave no doubt that he is ready to do his part for the perfection of military technology: if called upon, he will even "train them himself in the complicated art of solar war" (13). Nothing happens. At least, nothing happens in Macondo. But it is clearly not José Arcadio's fault that the government fails to respond. He has even anticipated Star Wars.

José Arcadio never quite recovers from his disappointment at having been denied the excitement of futuristic wars. Melquíades tries to console him with more "new" discoveries: an astrolabe, a compass, a sextant, and the alchemical equipment that Colonel Aureliano Buendía will later use to make the little gold fishes that will ultimately, and ironically, become the symbol of failed subversion.[4] José Arcadio does revive his spirits just long enough to prove that "The earth is round, like an orange" (14). By this time, however, his dedication to science only convinces Úrsula, and most everyone else, that he has lost what little was left of his mind. Later, when confronted with the marvel of ice, he will imagine an entire city constructed entirely of the fantastic substance; he will create a memory machine in an attempt to combat Macondo's plague of somnambulistic insomnia; he will spend sleepless nights trying to apply the principle of the pendulum to oxcarts, to harrows, "to everything that was useful when put into motion"; he will even try to execute a daguerreotype of God—but he will continue to lose faith in the reality of his fantasies. So his family must fight a losing battle, struggling to keep him from "being dragged by his imagination into a delirium from which he would not recover" (80). Finally, they all have to be content with his strange senility, interrupted only by prophecies in Latin.

The tragedy of José Arcadio Buendía is that his infatuation with science allows the government to exploit a passion that was, initially, a "spirit of social initiative." His first creations were the traps and cages he used to fill all the houses in the village with birds. He made sure that the houses were placed "in such a way that from all of them one could reach the river and draw water with the same effort" (18); he saw that no house received more sun than another. He was, from the start, a type of "model citizen," useful to his people. It is the appearance of "advanced" science in Macondo that makes him, virtually overnight, useful to authority: "That spirit of social initiative disappeared in a short time, pulled away by the fever of magnets, the astronomical calculations, the dreams of transmutation, and the urge to discover the wonders of the world" (18). That is how his faith in progress, and the faith of his people, is betrayed.

But more important than José Arcadio's tragic disappointment, more important than his invested doubloons—which Melquíades returns in any case—even more important than his final senility, is the fact that he resolves his debate with the gypsy. Throughout the rest of the novel, scientific discoveries will continue to serve two purposes: science will mystify the citizens of Macondo and will lead to their exploitation. The novel's arresting first sentence suggests that these two purposes have always been inseparable: "Many years later, as he faced the firing squad, Colonel Aureliano Buendía was to remember that distant afternoon when his father took him to discover ice" (11). But, perhaps, if his father had avoided such discoveries, Aureliano Buendía might never have wound up before a firing squad of his own government.

The equally arresting ending of the novel is a full-scale denial of José Arcadio's ill-begotten dream. The novel's "apocalyptic closure" is a denial of progress, as conceived by either the scientist or the politician, and a momentary glimpse of the world that might have been, if the great patriarch had not been so carried away with his idea of the future—if he had tried, instead, to understand history. Only Amaranta Úrsula and Aureliano, the last adults in the line of the Buendías, see "the uncertainty of the future" with enough demystified clarity to forsake progress, "to turn their hearts toward the past"; only they are not exploited (375). Their child, Aureliano, is "the only one in a century who had been engendered with love"—but by then it is too late (378). They cannot enjoy their primal, "dominant obsessions" for long; they cannot remain "floating in an empty universe where the only everyday and eternal reality was love" (374).[5] They are confronted, instead, with an end that is as ridiculous as their family's beginning: "The first of the line is tied to a tree and the last is being eaten by the ants" (381). The world has not progressed one bit. In fact, the key to understanding the present, and all of history, is not in the science so valued by José Arcadio but in Melquíades's ancient manuscripts, written in Sanskrit. Macondo is finally devoured by the "prehistoric hunger" of the ants, then obliterated by "the wrath of the biblical hurricane" (383).

Because he is the man of technology, the man of science-as-progress, who brings together, more than anyone else, mystification and exploitation, José Arcadio is never able to foresee this end, just as he is never able to turn his obsessive nature toward love, just as he is never able to admit the kind of association that occurs to Colonel Aureliano Buendía when he faces the firing squad. He never understands, as Úrsula does, that time is circular. He never really pays any attention to the suit of armor from the past, so he never learns that the rusted coat of armor anticipates the soldiers and machine guns that will support the banana company, that the imperialism of the past prefigures the imperialism of the future. In this sense, Úrsula is capable of learning; José Arcadio is not. Úrsula learns, at least, that her schemes for prosperity have set her up to be betrayed. Ultimately, José Arcadio cannot understand any of these things because his view of the world shares too much with the oppressors who will take over his village in the delirium of banana fever; in other words, whether he realizes it or not, his horizon is determined by the interests he serves. As John Incledon has written, José Arcadio's fascination with scientific inventions—as sources of wealth, power, control—"reveals a frantic desire to grasp and manage his world" (53).

The difference between José Arcadio and the other residents of Macondo—who think he is crazy, when they are not following him—is merely that he is a useful citizen of the active type, whereas they are useful citizens of the passive type. The only exceptions are Colonel Aureliano Buendía and his men, but their revolutions always take place outside Macondo. José Arcadio is doomed because he has convinced himself that "Right across the river there are all kinds of magical instruments while we keep on living like donkeys" (17). His greatest fear is that he might die "without receiving the benefits of science" (21). The village is doomed by the same belief that magic—in particular, advanced technology—is valuable in itself, uplifting, and the privileged possession of the outside world. Once the people believe that science, like all uplifting things, must come from elsewhere, that the outside world is better because it is more "advanced," then imperialism becomes much easier to justify. The gypsies' "discoveries" are always excessively foreign. Later, the residents of Macondo easily convince themselves of the innate superiority of Italian music and French sexual techniques. The Crespi brothers' business in mechanical toys, aided by their foreign looks and foreign manners, develops into a "hothouse of fantasy" (108).

If the government had only understood this inclination when they received José Arcadio's manual on solar war, it could have saved itself a lot of time. But José Arcadio's plans did not convince it that Macondo was a regular hothouse of applied fantasy; in this sense, it did not fully appreciate its "natural resources" until it learned from Mr. Brown and the Banana Company.

For their part, the villagers never understand what all these foreign wonders do to them. Like José Arcadio when he bumps into the suit of armor, they let their infatuation with the promises of the future render them incapable of uncovering their past: "Dazzled by so many and such marvelous inventions, the people of Macondo did not know where their amazement began" (211). They merely enjoy, with more moderation than José Arcadio, the excitement of closing the "technical gap" that has separated them from the "outside world."[6] The bearers of science are always exoticized. At the same time, the villagers' "primitive" past is rendered so insignificant that it is not worth remembering. To them, the important things have always happened somewhere else—and their future will be determined by somebody else.

Many years later, when the government massacres thousands of civilians in order to crush a union strike, no one except José Arcadio Segundo, great-grandson of the first José Arcadio, will even be capable of remembering "the insatiable and methodical shears of the machine guns" (284). As for the rest, they will remember only what they have been taught to remember by the technocrats and by the government that supports them: "Nothing has happened in Macondo, nothing has ever happened, and nothing ever will happen. This is a happy town" (287). In this "modern" world, things always happen somewhere else. The Banana Company, with the help of the government, is raising the village's standard of living, so it must be benevolent. It cannot be responsible for a massacre. The irony that José Arcadio Segundo has the name of his great-grandfather is just one of the novel's, and history's countless circles, one more indication that, despite their "progress"—or, in fact, because of their "progress"—the oppressed have been unable to learn what is really important.

The first José Arcadio has a quality of many characters in García Márquez's fiction: he is so strange, so absurd, that it seems he must be real. José Arcadio Segundo is, in this sense, his precise opposite. He sees the events of the government massacre with a clarity that suggests he is unreal. So when government troops enter the room where he has given up hiding, they cannot see him, even though they are looking right at the place where he believes he is sitting. Opposition, to such a government, must be invisible. It makes no difference that they did not actually kill him, that he jumped off the train on which the corpses had been "piled up in the same way in which they transported bunches of bananas" (284). He is merely left alone, once again, to decipher Melquíades's ancient manuscripts.

In the end, however, José Arcadio Segundo shares something important with the first José Arcadio. "The events that would deal Macondo its fatal blow"—the strike, the public unrest, the massacre, and its aftermath—take shape at the precise moment that the train begins to control the events of the novel (272). Transportation, in Colombia, has inescapable links to the desire for "progress." Aureliano Triste's initial sketch of Macondo's railroad "was a direct descendent of the plans with which José Arcadio Buendía had illustrated his project for solar warfare." Aureliano Triste believed that the railroad was necessary "not only for the modernization of his business but to link the town with the rest of the world" (209). Only Úrsula, who had seen so much of the suffering that results from such schemes, understood that "time was going in a circle"; only she knew enough to fear modernization that came from "the rest of the world" (209).

The train also allows Fernanda to travel back to the dismal, distant city of her birth. She has never stopped thinking of the villagers of Macondo as barbarians; and she is so intent on her desire to sequester her daughter in a convent, away from the "savagery" of the Caribbean zone, that she does not even see "the shady, endless banana groves on both sides of the tracks," or "the oxcarts on the dusty roads loaded down with bunches of bananas," or "the skeleton of the Spanish galleon" (273). At this point it is clear that she has failed in her attempt to colonize Macondo with the manners and rituals of the inland cities; but her "internal colonialism" has been superseded, without her noticing it, by the brutal imperialism of the Banana Company. When Fernanda returns to Macondo, the train is protected by policemen with guns. Macondo's "fatal blow" is under way. José Arcadio Segundo has already organized the workers in a strike against the Banana Company, and he has already been "pointed out as the agent of an international conspiracy against public order" (276). Fernanda's two rides on the train are opposite in direction, but tell of a single effect: "civilization," modernization, and progress are finally assured, even in Macondo—if not with "proper" manners and gold chamberpots, then with guns.

The train is, if anything, even more symbolic of this "progress" in Colombia than it is in Macondo. Under the dictatorship of General Rafael Reyes (1904-1909), "British capital was, for the first time, invested in Colombian railways in substantial amounts" (Safford 232). Not surprisingly, this period saw the completion of the railway between Bogotá and the Magdalena River; "Macondo" was irreversibly linked to the "outside world." But, of course, that was only the start: "As the transportation improvements of 1904 to 1940 began to knit together a national market, significant innovations occurred in other economic sectors," and it was the nationalization of Colombia's railways that made many such "innovations" possible (Safford 232-234). In the period of the strikes against the United Fruit Company, in particular, reorganization of the railroads was a central issue of American diplomacy in Colombia. The National City Bank and the First National Bank of Boston refused to extend short-term credits until a railroad bill was passed. By 1931, they demanded, in their negotiations with the Colombian government, an even greater control: "that the railroad system be taken out of the hands of the government and placed under the direction of professional management" (Randall 64). In his description of the banana strike, García Márquez makes the implications obvious: the same trains that send bananas and profits to the north transport the murdered bodies to the sea. There—both the government and the "professional management" hope—they will disappear, even from history.

The repeated follies of José Arcadio—like the name and hereditary stubbornness of his great-grandson, like Úrsula's pronouncements, like the end of the novel—are attempts on the part of García Márquez to assert that history is, in some sense, circular. The "primitive" past of Latin America, like that of Macondo, might have provided countless omens of Colombia's future, if anyone had paid attention—that is, if anyone had avoided the delirium of progress. From the first half of the nineteenth century, the combination of foreigners and trains was devastating, in Argentina, in Chile, in Guatemala, in Mexico, and in Uruguay. With their public services, especially the railroads, controlled by foreigners, or by governments serving foreigners—first from Paraguay, then principally from Britain, then principally from the United States—these countries faced extraordinary military expenditures, "a frenzied increase in imports," and growing debts, subject to inflationary manipulation. In Galeano's words, they "mortgaged their futures in advance, moving away from economic freedom and political sovereignty" (216-219). Later, in Colombia, the tendency to see railroads as "forerunners of progress" would be just one more failure to remember. For García Márquez, such an assertion of history's circularity is not merely a matter of philosophical speculation; it is a calculated attempt to make the outrages of oppression, ancient and recent, visible again; it is an attempt to make Colombian history credible.

After the massacre, when the train from which he has escaped slips off into the night, "with its nocturnal and stealthy velocity," on its way to dump more than three thousand murdered bodies into the ocean, José Arcadio Segundo cannot see it in the darkness; the last things he sees are "the dark shapes of the soldiers with their emplaced machine guns" (285).[7] Perhaps José Arcadio Segundo came to understand such progress as his great-grandfather could not, and perhaps that is why the government's search squad could not see *him*. For men indoctrinated by such a government, opposition must not exist.

For such men, the past must disappear. That is why they seem so improbable, and so real. That is why a "resource" like "magical realism" is needed to depict them. And that is why the novel's famous "apocalyptic closure" is not only credible but also anticlimactic. Apocalypse is merely the darkest side of "magical realism," in which the "magic" and the "realism" are most completely fused, in which the most unimaginable event is the most inevitable. The "biblical hurricane" that "exiles" Macondo "from the memory of men" is "full of voices from the past, the murmurs of ancient geraniums, sighs of disenchantment that preceded the most tenacious nostalgia" (383). The ceaseless repetitions of the novel lead to this final conviction that apocalypse is only one more "scientific possibility," which the "primitive world" understands only after it is too late. Apocalypse is only the logical consequence of imperialist oppression, supported by science. The "events" that bring about the end of Macondo were actually determined much earlier, even before the trains came. The end began the first time the gypsies appeared with their foreign discoveries.

From *Modern Fiction Studies* 36 (1990): 167-179. Copyright © 1990 by the Purdue Research Foundation. Reprinted by permission.

Notes

1. Gabriel García Márquez, in "The Solitude of Latin America: Nobel Address, 1982," describes Latin American history as such a fount (208). Gerald Martin provides a detailed and critical summary of this criticism in his essay.

2. I have borrowed this idea from Ariel Dorfman's *The Empire's Old Clothes*: "having a 'brilliant idea' is not only what allows a contestant to win in the game of life. It is also a sign that such a victory is well deserved" (35). In the United States, the belief in such radical insight is one component of our mystification of ideas, in particular our mystification of science. We want to believe that certain people have privileged access to the truth and that they have, therefore, a "natural" authority over those people who

lack such insight. Dorfman explains how the government of the United States has tried to cultivate this ideology in Latin America—even through such apparently innocuous vehicles as Donald Duck, the Lone Ranger, and Babar the Elephant—as part of our effort at domination. In *How to Read Donald Duck*, referring to the United States' assistance in the overthrow of the Allende government, Dorfman and Armand Mattelart write: "There were, however, two items which were not blocked: planes, tanks, ships, and technical assistance for the Chilean armed forces; and magazines, TV serials, advertising, and public opinion polls for the Chilean mass media" (9).

3. In his study of nineteenth-century European colonialism, Robert Schnerb writes of Latin America: "These republics' histories may be said to be that of the economic obligations they incur to the all-absorbing world of European finance," obligations that were quickly exacerbated by "inflation, which produces depreciation of the currency." Eduardo Galeano adds, "The use of debt as an instrument of blackmail is not, as we can see, a recent American invention" (217-218).

4. Perhaps it is no coincidence that Colonel Aureliano Buendía is both the revolutionary and the alchemist—that he is, like José Arcadio Segundo, the heir of both Úrsula's indomitability and Melquíades's manuscripts. For the Latin American who would resist domination, a knowledge of transformation, even alchemy, might be much more practical than it would at first appear. Galeano suggests such a connection, at least metaphorically, in his *Open Veins of Latin America*, a book that would be immensely popular in Colombia a few years after its initial publication in 1971: "Our defeat was always implicit in the victory of others; our wealth has always generated our poverty by nourishing the prosperity of others—the empires and their native overseers. In the colonial and neocolonial alchemy, gold changes into scrap metal and food into poison" (12).

5. The final situation of Amaranta Úrsula and Aureliano will become increasingly important as criticism begins to address García Márquez's recent novel, *Love in the Time of Cholera*. As Thomas Pynchon suggests, with some trepidation, in his review of that novel, critics will inevitably ask "how far" that novel, so dominated by love, has departed from the more "political" concerns of *One Hundred Years of Solitude* and *The Autumn of the Patriarch*: "we have come a meaningful distance from Macondo, the magical village in *One Hundred Years of Solitude*. . . . It would be presumptuous to speak of moving 'beyond' *One Hundred Years of Solitude*, but clearly García Márquez has moved somewhere else, not least into deeper awareness of the ways in which, as Florentino comes to learn, 'nobody teaches life anything'" (49).

6. I have borrowed the phrase "technical gap," as well as the basic idea of this passage, from Dorfman's reading of Babar the Elephant in *The Empire's Old Clothes*. Of course, there are systems—of ownership, of trade, of education—that keep the gap from actually closing, despite the useful illusion of progress. In this regard see Galeano, especially the section appropriately entitled "The Goddess Technology Doesn't Speak Spanish" (265-268). Dorfman's explanation of the capitalist's equation of childhood and underdevelopment is also worth noting, especially in reference to José Arcadio's later senility. Once he abandons his hope of reaching the "outside world's" level of civilization, José Arcadio destroys his scientific equipment and allows himself to lapse into his "second childhood," to be spoon-fed by Úrsula.

---

7. Later, José Arcadio Segundo would tell little Aureliano his "personal interpretation of what the banana company had meant to Macondo" (322). But no one would want to believe Aureliano, either; "one would have thought that he was telling a hallucinated version, because it was radically opposed to the false one that historians had created and consecrated in the schoolbooks" (322). In *Gabriel García Márquez: Writer of Colombia*, Stephen Minta provides a brief, useful summary of the surviving accounts of the 1928 strike against the United Fruit Company in Ciénaga. Accounts differ, of course, in their estimates of the number murdered. Cortes Vargas, who signed the decree that "declared the strikers to be a bunch of hoodlums" and "authorized the army to shoot to kill," and whose name appears unchanged in *One Hundred Years of Solitude*, wrote his own account, in which he claims that only nine were killed. Officially sanctioned accounts typically mention "the menace of Bolshevism." But perhaps the most telling document is a telegram from the Head of the U.S. Legation in Colombia to the U.S. Secretary of State: "I have the honor to report that the Bogota representative of the United Fruit Company told me yesterday that the total number of strikers killed by the Colombian military exceed one thousand" (171).

Works Cited

Dorfman, Ariel. *The Empire's Old Clothes*. Trans. Clark Hansen. New York: Pantheon, 1983.

Dorfman, Ariel, and Armand Mattelart. *How to Read Donald Duck*. Trans. David Kunzle. New York: International General, 1975.

Galeano, Eduardo. *Open Veins of Latin America*. Trans. Cedric Belfrage. New York: Monthly Review, 1973.

García Márquez, Gabriel. *Autumn of the Patriarch*. Trans. Gregory Rabassa. New York: Harper, 1976.

—————. *Love in the Time of Cholera*. Trans. Edith Grossman. New York: Knopf, 1988.

—————. *One Hundred Years of Solitude*. Trans. Gregory Rabassa. New York: Avon, 1970.

—————. "The Solitude of Latin America: Nobel Address 1982." McGuirk and Cardwell. 207-211.

Incledon, John. "Writing and Incest in *One Hundred Years of Solitude*." *Critical Perspectives on Gabriel García Márquez*. Ed. Bradley A. Shaw and Nora Vera-Godwin. Lincoln: Society of Spanish and Spanish-American Studies, 1986. 51-64.

McGuirk, Bernard, and Richard Cardwell, eds. *Gabriel García Márquez: New Readings*. Cambridge: Cambridge University Press, 1987.

Martin, Gerald. "On 'Magical' and Social Realism in García Márquez." McGuirk and Cardwell. 95-116.

Minta, Stephen. *Gabriel García Márquez: Writer of Colombia*. London: Cape, 1987.

Pynchon, Thomas. "The Heart's Eternal Vow." Review of *Love in the Time of Cholera*, by Gabriel García Márquez. *New York Times Book Review*. 10 April 1988: 1, 47-49.

Randall, Stephen J. *The Diplomacy of Modernization: Colombian-American Relations, 1920-1940*. Toronto: University of Toronto Press, 1976.

Safford, Frank. *The Ideal of the Practical: Colombia's Struggle to Form a Technical Elite*. Austin: University of Texas Press, 1976.

Schnerb, Robert. *Le XIXe siècle: l'apogée de l'expansion européenne, 1815-1914*. Paris: Gallimard, 1968.

Superstition, Irony, Themes _____
Stephen M. Hart

Stephen M. Hart organizes thematically his study of García Márquez's detective-novel-in-reverse, *Chronicle of a Death Foretold*. He
starts by focusing on the role superstition plays in the assassination
of Santiago Nasar. He stresses the use of irony in the narrative, then
moves to understand the way machismo motivates the assassins, a
pair of siblings, to take revenge for the apparent deflowering of their
sister Angela. Hart looks at themes such as falconry and the comparison between García Márquez's book and Sophocles' tragedy *Oedipus
Rex*.   — I.S.

Superstition

Superstition plays an important role in *Crónica de una muerte
anunciada* (*CMA*), which is only to be expected in the work of a
writer who believes in its power. As García Márquez has stated: 'las
supersticiones o lo que llaman supersticiones, pueden corresponder a
facultades que un pensamiento racionalista, como el que domina en
Occidente, ha resuelto repudiar' (*1*, p. 165). In his view certain objects
are associated with bad luck, such as snails behind doors, aquariums in
houses, plastic flowers, peacocks, 'mantones' from Manila, large black
capes, and dinner jackets. Some actions bring bad luck, such as inva-
lids playing musical instruments, smoking while walking around the
house in the nude, walking around in the nude but with your shoes on,
and making love with your socks on. Even words can bring bad luck,
especially technical terms such as 'level', 'parameter', 'context', 'and/
or', 'focus', and 'symbiosis' (*1*, p. 167). People can also bring bad
luck: García Márquez recalls the time he met the neighbour of the
apartment on the Costa Brava which he and his wife were checking
into. Because the woman was unlucky ('tenia pava'), he refused to
sleep in the apartment and had to go and stay with a friend nearby. He

also believes in premonitions. Once in January 1958 he was with Apuleyo Mendoza in Caracas and said that he had a feeling that something was about to happen; hardly had he finished speaking when the presidential palace was bombed, much to Mendoza's and indeed García Márquez's astonishment (8, pp. 166-70). He also claims to be telepathic.

Superstition operates in a variety of ways in *CMA*. The narrator's mother is telepathic (p. 36; I; 19) and knows what people are going to say before they finish speaking (p. 39; I; 21). Plácida Linero has a reputation for interpreting dreams (p. 10; I; 2). Superstition also surfaces in the 'pava' which surrounds certain characters. Ángela has an air of bad luck about her (pp. 52-53; II; 31), and she and her sisters are described as experts in the 'cult of death' (p. 51; II; 30). Equally ominous is the allusion to her 'martyrdom' (p. 62; II; 37). Other elements which add to the aura of superstition in the novel and which derive from García Márquez's private symbolism are the artificial flowers Ángela makes (p. 51; II; 30; p. 53; II; 31) which we know him to distrust (but which also imply Ángela's lost virginity, *103*, p. 107), the colour yellow with which the Vicario family paint their house in preparation for Ángela's wedding (p. 66; II; 40), and which García Márquez believes brings good luck, and is therefore used ironically in the novel, and the gold with which Bayardo is associated (pp. 45-46; II; 26-27), gold being something of which García Márquez has a pathological fear (*1*, p. 166).

Superstition also surfaces in the omens which predict Santiago's death. These range from the explicit, such as the opening sentence of the novel, to rather more veiled symbolism. On the morning he was murdered he seemed to have an air of death about him; Clotilde Armenta thought he already looked like a ghost (p. 27; I; 13), while Divina Flor said his hand felt like a dead man's (pp. 23-24; I; 12). Other omens operate ironically. Despite Santiago's mother's talent for interpreting dreams, she fails to see any ominous significance in the dream which Santiago has on two separate occasions before his death (p. 10; I; 2); she even goes as far as to interpret the dream in positive terms, arguing that dreams of birds stand for good health (p. 14; I; 4), and missing the allusion to premature death/imprudence contained in the reference to 'almendros' (p. 9; I; 2), a common symbol in Golden Age literature (*105*, 937). Her blindness to her son's fate is echoed when it emerges that she is the only person in the village who does not know what is in store for her son (p. 40; I; 21). Santiago is likewise blind to his fate since he failed to grasp the dream's ominous content (p. 10; I; 2). Equally ironic is Santiago's casual reference to his dislike of flowers at funerals: '"No quiero flores en mi entierro", me dijo, sin pensar que yo había de ocuparme al día siguiente de que no las hubiera' (p. 69; II; 42). There are also three symbolic omens which point to the barbarity of Santiago's death. The first occurs in the opening scene of the novel when Victoria Guzmán is feeding the rabbit innards to the dogs in the kitchen. Santiago is appalled, and Victoria later interprets the scene as an omen:

> Pero no pudo reprimir una ráfaga de espanto al recordar el horror de Santiago Nasar cuando ella arrancó de cuajo las entrañas de un conejo y les tiró a los perros el tripajo humeante.
>   —No seas bárbara—le dijo él—. Imagínate que fuera un ser humano. (p. 20; I; 8)

The omen proves to be accurate especially since the dogs attempt to eat his intestines as they had done only a few hours earlier with the rabbits (p. 118; IV; 73-74). The second omen is the abortive autopsy carried out by Father Amador since, although it occurred, chronologically speaking, after Santiago's death, it is narrated earlier in the text and therefore operates prophetically rather than retrospectively (p. 116; IV; 72). Once more it is Santiago's intestines which most suffer: 'el párroco había arrancado de cuajo las vísceras destazadas, pero al final no supo qué hacer con ellas, y les impartió una bendición de rabia y las tiró en el balde de la basura' (p. 123; IV; 76). Notice that precisely the same expression, 'arrancar de cuajo', is used here as to describe the rabbits' evisceration, which reinforces the parallels between the two events.

The third and least obvious omen is contained within the allusion to the manner of preparation of the bishop's favourite soup. One critic has noted that the cockerels are omens of death (*116*, p. 67), but the parallel lies more specifically in the bishop's bizarre habit of making soup out of the cockerel's crests and throwing the rest of the animal's body away (p. 64; II; 38), which is an oblique allusion to the autopsy and thereby to the destruction of Santiago's body. In both these cases Santiago's murder is parallelled with the slaughter of an animal (a rabbit and a cockerel). The animal with which Santiago is most often associated is, not surprisingly, given the Vicario twins' profession, a pig. Thus Santiago is 'destazado como un cerdo' (p. 10; I; 2). (García Márquez offers a further twist to this analogy since the murder takes on sacrificial connotations; the twins' pig knives are described as 'útiles de sacrificio' [p. 83; III; 51].) The various symbolic omens which predict Santiago's death, as we can see, are linked through the central image of animal sacrifice and demonstrate effectively the rigorous authorial control García Márquez achieved in *CMA*.

Irony

Irony is used so consistently in *CMA* that the novel could be seen as an exercise in irony. For our purposes irony will be defined as pertaining to an occurrence in which exactly the opposite of what was expected, or what normally occurs, happens. The single most important irony of the novel is that Santiago died for a crime he did not commit, and all the other instances of irony in the story spring from this one. One of the most significant structural ironies of the narrative is the twins' vain attempts to get themselves prevented from carrying out the murder (p. 81; III; 49). There are a number of events in the novel which are due to the irony of circumstance. First, had it not been for the bishop's visit, Santiago would have gone hunting that day (p. 12; I; 3), and had he been on the ranch, the twins' weapons would have been no match for his highly sophisticated guns of which we are given a detailed description (p. 12; I; 3). But Santiago is attacked when unarmed: the hunter becomes the hunted. Secondly, had Cristo Bedoya not called at the social club to confirm a domino match that evening on his way to warn Santiago (p. 175; V; 111), things might have turned out differently. The problem was compounded by Bedoya's erroneous belief that Santiago had gone to the narrator's house for breakfast, his search for him there, and his being held up by having to examine Próspera Arango's ailing father (p. 175; V; 111). But the most poignant example of circumstantial irony occurs when Plácida Linero believes her son to be already in the house and therefore bolts the door when she sees the twins approaching, thereby unwittingly causing her son's death: 'Desde el lugar en que ella se encontraba podía verlos a ellos, pero no alcanzaba a ver a su hijo que corría desde otro ángulo hacia la puerta' (pp. 186-87; V; 118-19). As we can see, García Márquez draws attention to so many points in the story where it might have turned out otherwise that the reader is aware at every turn of the operation of irony.

At times García Márquez's irony smacks of black humour. Examples are Pedro's rage when discovering that his sister is not a virgin, although he has just returned from the local brothel (p. 78; II; 47); the crowd of revellers who, at Santiago's instigation, sing to the newly-weds in their new home at 4.00 am, when the marriage is already finished (pp. 107-09; III; 66-68); and the bizarre contradiction in Father Amador's autopsy report:

> La masa encefálica pesaba sesenta gramos más que la de un inglés normal, y el Padre Amador consignó en el informe que Santiago Nasar tenía una inteligencia superior y un porvenir brillante. Sin embargo, en la nota final señalaba una hipertrofia del hígado que atribuyó a una hepatitis mal curada. "Es decir—me dijo—, que de todos modos le quedaban muy pocos años de vida." (p. 122; IV; 76)

One last type of irony ought to be mentioned: the ironic coincidence of life and literature. As already noted, this is mainly presented through the judge's perspective on the murder; he believes Santiago's murder to be more literary than literature itself (p. 159; V; 100), and gives the door outside which Santiago met his death a name worthy of a potboiler novel:

> Nadie podía entender tantas coincidencias funestas. El juez instructor que vino de Riohacha debió sentirlas sin atreverse a admitirlas, pues su interés de darles una explicación racional era evidente en el sumario. La puerta de la plaza estaba citada varias veces con un nombre de folletín: *La puerta fatal*. (p. 23; I; 10-11)

In a similar vein, the reunion of Ángela and Bayardo after seventeen years of separation is worthy of a nineteenth-century melodrama. Here, as elsewhere, García Márquez is clearly casting an ironic light on the melodramatic nature of the events he portrays. The final irony is the letter pushed under the door containing all the details about the murder to be committed:

> Alguien que nunca fue identificado había metido por debajo de la puerta un papel dentro de un sobre, en el cual le avisaban a Santiago Nasar que lo estaban esperando para matarlo, y le revelaban además el lugar y los motivos, y otros detalles muy precisos de la confabulación. El mensaje estaba en el suelo cuando Santiago Nasar salió de su casa, pero él no lo vio, ni lo vio Divina Flor ni lo vio nadie hasta que mucho después de que el crimen fue consumado. (p. 26: I; 12-13)

Within the narrative we thus have a text which tells its own story, rather like a play within a play. It is similar to the verbal message brought by the beggar women to Victoria Guzmán which is likewise not heeded (p. 24; I; 11). But once the murder takes place the letter is discovered and, as in an apocalyptic prediction, its meaning is fulfilled. As Jorge Olivares points out: 'As a written message whose reading and significance are strategically deferred until the very end, this anonymous note turns out to be a textual metonym of García Márquez's *Crónica*' (*97*, p. 486). Indeed, the author comes close to suggesting that the novel writes itself, a technique already used in *Cien años de soledad*, which is written by a character in the novel, Melquíades. It is certainly possible that the narrator was the author of the letter, in which case his reference to 'alguien que nunca fue identificado' would be a supreme example of being economical with the truth. Here García Márquez teases us with pseudo-solutions; his use of the letter shows him at his most playful with the reader.

The wedding in *CMA*, not surprisingly given the event on which it was based, is presented ironically. Hindsight allows it to be interpreted not as the celebration of the joyful union of Bayardo and Ángela but rather as a social feast preceding human sacrifice. The connection between the murder and the wedding is underscored at various points of the narrative. As Jaime recalls: 'Lo unico que recuerdo es que se oía a lo lejos un ruido de mucha gente, como si hubiera vuelto a empezar la fiesta de la boda, y que todo el mundo corría en dirección de la plaza' (p. 41; I; 22). This association is confirmed by another witness (p. 191; V; 122). Santiago is portrayed in terms of whiteness on two separate occasions, which reinforces the parallel between his death and the wedding (p. 11; I; 3; and p. 19; I; 8); indeed, as Peñuel suggests, the wedding is associated, via reference to Petronio San Román, with Trimalchio's banquet mentioned in Petronius's work, since both conclude with death (*35*, pp. 201-02). García Márquez's use of irony, to conclude, is not to be understood as a device which undermines his narrative; on the contrary, it operates as evidence of a teleological structure informing the apparent randomness of everyday events.

Machismo

Seen by most critics as a significant theme in *CMA*, *machismo* has been called the main theme of the novel by one critic (*16*). The author seems to share this view in that he states that *CMA* 'es sin duda una radiografia y al mismo tiempo una condena de la esencia machista de nuestra sociedad' (*1*, p. 159). When asked how he would define *machismo*, García Márquez did so, intriguingly enough, in non-sexist terms: 'Yo diría que el machismo, tanto en los hombres como en las mujeres, no es más que la usurpación del derecho ajeno' (*1*, p. 159). The novel focuses on the way in which the domination of one sex by the other is naturalized. In Ángela's family, for example:

> Los hermanos fueron criados para ser hombres. Ellas habían sido educadas para casarse. Sabían bordar en bastidor, coser a máquina, tejer encaje de bolsillo, lavar y planchar, hacer flores artificiales y dulces de fantasía, y redactar esquelas de compromiso. (p. 51; II; 30)

They are even more traditional than most since they are expert in looking after the sick, comforting the dying, and shrouding the dead (pp. 51-52; II; 31). On account of their capacity to suffer, they are seen as the stuff out of which perfect wives are made by the older generation (p. 52; II; 31). It is therefore not surprising, given this environment, that Ángela becomes an outlaw when her indiscretion is discovered. Her mother beats her non-stop for two hours when she is brought back by the groom, and her brother trembles with self-righteous rage (p. 77; II; 46-47). The novel makes clear that *machismo* is the belief-system shared by the whole community, and not just the Vicario twins.

Indeed, the brooding sexual tension which animates the town depicted in García Márquez's novel is redolent of the atmosphere which he builds up of Sucre in his memoirs (the city in which *CMA*, of course, is set). Wracked with guilt about sex, obsessed with revenge for lost honour, Sucre was a place where sexual misconduct was traditionally paid for in blood. García Márquez's father, for example, once publicly threatened to shoot anyone who touched his daughters: 'Al que se le ocurra tocar a cualquiera de mis hijas—gritó—va a llevar plomo del bravo' (*119*, p. 275). When García Márquez was discovered having an affair with a married woman, the aggrieved husband threatened him with the words: 'Las vainas de cama se arreglan con plomo' (*119*, p. 261) and, indeed, only let him off because the novelist's father had once cured him of gonorrhea. The latency of sexual desire within García Márquez's household—he recalls a highly sexually-charged dance he had with the maid's daughter which, as he recalls, 'me quitó la inocencia' (*119*, p. 88)—is transposed to form the backdrop for Santiago Nasar's innuendo-laced conversation with Divina Flor in *CMA* ('Ya estás en tiempo de desbravar', he comments to her in the kitchen, and her mother threatens him with a kitchen knife; p. 19; I; 8).

It is, indeed, because of the pervasive force of machismo that the inhabitants of the town appear to accept the inevitability of Santiago's revenge-murder. Instead of warning Santiago, they take up positions in the main square as if to watch a bull-fight: 'La gente que regresaba del puerto, alertada por los gritos, empezó a tomar posiciones en la plaza para presenciar el crimen' (p. 174; V; 116; see *36*, p. 177). During the murder scene the reference to 'los gritos del pueblo entero espantado de su propio crimen' (p. 189; V; 120) suggests that the onus of guilt lies with the town, an impression reinforced when the twins describe their deed in court as a legitimate action in defence of family honour (p. 79; III; 48), and in similar terms to the local priest:

Lo matamos a conciencia—dijo Pedro Vicario—, pero somos inocentes.
—Tal vez ante Dios—dijo el padre Amador.
—Ante Dios y ante los hombres—dijo Pablo Vicario.
—Fue un asunto de honor. (p. 80; III; 49)

Not only the judicial system (which gives the twins a reduced sentence of three years), and the Church (Father Amador saw their surrender as an 'act of great dignity'; p. 80; III; 49), but also the townswomen justify the crime. Pedro's fiancée, Prudencia Cotes, is enthusiastic about the murder and her mother goes as far as to encourage the two men to get on with the deed (pp. 101-02; III; 62-63).

The Honour Code

The Vicario twins justify their murder of Santiago Nasar by calling it 'homicide in legitimate defence of honour' and, as we have seen, they are not alone in regarding it as necessary for that reason. Interestingly enough, García Márquez is quoting here the language used in 1951 by the Chica brothers' defence lawyer who described their action as 'un clásico caso de defensa legítima del honor, no sólo del honor personal de los actores sino del honor de toda la familia' (*10*, p. 27; see *70*, pp. 40-42). The portrayal of the honour code in *CMA* can be studied from two complementary angles, first, as an unconscious moral code which regulates social conduct in Latin-American society (García Márquez has said that murder on account of a woman's lost honour is a quite common occurrence in Latin America; *1*, p. 38), and secondly, as a remanipulation of a common literary topos. An important literary precedent for *CMA* is the Calderonian honour play, and particularly his three wife-murder plays, *El médico de su honra, A secreto agravio, secreta venganza*, and *El pintor de su deshonra*, which, as Melveena McKendrick points out, all 'dramatize the predicament of the husband who becomes convinced that his wife is unfaithful'.[1] Thus the community deliberately does not intervene since matters of honour 'son estancos sagrados a los cuales sólo tienen acceso los dueños del drama' (p. 155; V; 98). The dramatic metaphor is not fortuitous here. Critics have pointed to some specific resonances of Golden Age drama in *CMA*; Gonzalo Díaz-Migoyo suggests a link between the novel and Calderón's *La vida es sueño* (*68*, p. 79), while other critics have suggested parallels with Lope de Vega's *Fuenteovejuna* (*36*, p. 175; *101*, reprinted in *35*, p. 208, n. 26; *89*). There are a number of similarities between *CMA* and the typical Golden Age honour play, which are: the crime (suspicion of a woman's extramarital relations), the punishment (death), and the avenger's reluctance to carry out what the honour code dictates (which in Calderón's play typically takes the form of the husband's protests and in *CMA* is expressed in the twins' disinclination to kill Santiago). But there are differences, for it is not Bayardo who metes out the punishment as would be the case in a Calderón-style plot but his brothers-in-law, and it is Santiago rather than Ángela who pays for her crime (although she is punished with what amounts to social death since she is banished from town and not allowed to re-marry). The allusion in *CMA* to the Calderonian honour code should be seen as another example of García Márquez's ironic wit.

Falconry

Like the honour code, falconry derives its conventions from an aristocratic world of the past. All the references in *CMA* to falconry centre on Gil Vicente's celebrated poem, 'Halcón que se atreve [. . .]'. (Gil Vicente is mentioned by García Márquez as one of his favourite writers, as noted above, which explains why he uses this particular text.) Fragments of the poem are scattered around the novel; lines 11-12 form an epigraph to the novel, and lines 1-3 are used by the narrator to portray Santiago's love for María Alejandrina: 'Nasar perdió el sentido desde que la vio por primera vez. Yo le previne: *Halcón que se atreve con garza guerrera, peligros espera*' (p. 105; III; 65). The basic metaphor evoked here and consistent with the rest of Gil Vicente's poem is that of the discomfiture of a man who attempts to seduce a woman who is too wild for him.[2] Santiago, like his father, is a womanizer, and the connection between the two men is underscored through their love of falconry (p. 16; I; 6). His description as a 'gavilán pollero' at various stages in the novel further enhances this association. Santiago's statement of the reason why he should seduce Divina Flor ('Ya estás en tiempo de desbravar'; p. 19; I; 8) makes clear that he understands his amorous exploits in terms of his hunting activities. Divina Flor's mother epitomizes his predatory nature when she refers to 'las garras del boyardo' (p. 110; III; 69) from which she strives to protect her innocent daughter. As we have already seen, the allusions to hunting are ironic, which suggests the same should be said of the literary allusion to 'Halcón que se atreve [. . .]'. Curiously, it is not only Santiago who is associated with predation, but Bayardo as well. The latter is described by Ángela as typical of those 'hombres altaneros' she does not much care for (p. 49; II; 29), which evokes the 'altanería' in the epigraph. Likewise, the phonetic similarity of Bayardo and 'boyardo' ('seigneur'; English translation, p. 69, as applied to Santiago) suggests a parallel is being drawn between the two men in terms of their rapacious attitude towards women. As already mentioned in Chapter 3, Bayardo sees Ángela as merchandise he can buy and dispose of at will. The ironic reversal of the falconry motif is confirmed towards the end of the novel when Santiago, once associated with a haughty falcon, is now no more than a 'pájaro mojado' (p. 183; V; 116), a deflationary image echoed by the early reference to the dream he had on the eve of his death in which he imagined that bird droppings were falling on him (p. 9; I; 1).

Oedipus

Gisela Pankow has argued that the events of the plot in *CMA* concerning a repudiated spouse and 'legitimate defence of honour' should be interpreted as the manifest material of an Oedipal conflict which afflicts Santiago on an unconscious level (*38*, p. 98; see also *78* and *80*). This would explain why the crime for which Santiago is punished gives rise to such vicious retaliation. To follow this line of reasoning, we should see Santiago's death as a displaced punishment for the heinous sin of incest. There are a number of elements which hint at the presence of this unconscious scenario in *CMA*; taken individually they would not amount to much, but when placed together they suggest a subliminal level of incest-anxiety at play. First is Plácida Linero's loving description of her son: 'Fue el hombre de mi vida' (p. 15; I; 5). Second, and much less circumstantial, is the symbolism surrounding the door outside which Santiago was hacked to death. It is well-known that *Oedipus Rex* is one of García Márquez's favourite literary works (see above, p. 16) and it is surely not fortuitous that, in the final scene of Sophocles' play when Oedipus's crime is finally revealed, the door is a crucial image: 'But, looking for a marriage-bed, he found the bed of his birth,/ Tilled the earth his father had tilled, cast seed into the same abounding earth;/ Entered through the door that had sent him wailing forth.'[3] As we have already seen, the door becomes an obsessive image in *CMA*, largely through the literary musings of the judge who called it 'la puerta fatal'. What makes the allusion to Oedipus irresistible is the fact that Santiago's death is caused by none other than his mother bolting the door ('corrió hacia la puerta y la cerró de un golpe'; p. 187; V; 119) as if, figuratively speaking, she were denying him access to the 'bed of his birth', to use Sophocles' expression. There is one further detail which needs to be mentioned in the context of Oedipus and this concerns the bar which is used to lock Santiago out of the house. The word 'tranca' is used only twice in *CMA*, once when Plácida Linero bolts the door in the scene referred to above ('Estaba pasando la tranca cuando [. . .]'; p. 187; V; 119), and once when the narrator goes to see María Alejandrina at the brothel ('había dejado sin tranca la puerta de la casa', pp. 110-11; III; 69), and this is surely significant. Given the similarities between the narrator and Santiago, which not only relate to their physical appearance but include their amatory exploits, we perhaps need to interpret the door as an image of the womb to which the narrator has access (through the person of his cousin) and from which Santiago is barred entry, as if to underscore that Santiago paid the price for a crime that the narrator committed. We ought not to forget, however, that the allusion to Oedipus's plight is oblique and certainly not overpowering in *CMA*; rather it works in the same unobtrusive way that allusion to other literary works such as Gil Vicente's 'Halcón que se atreve [. . .]' and the detective novel operates. Relevant in this context is the phrase used by the investigating magistrate on folio 382 of the brief 'La fatalidad nos hace invisibles' (p. 180; V; 114). It is applicable in a literal sense to Santiago when he is not seen by his mother as she looks out of the window, sees the Vicario twins running towards the house, and quickly closes the door, thereby sealing her son's fate. But it is also applicable in a metaphorical sense to the narrator who, throughout the novel, observes, but is not observed (*105*, p. 20). His physical appearance is never described, we do not know his name, and, if he were the perpetrator of the crime, which seems likely, then he would indeed have been the invisible agent of Fate.

It is important to underscore that *CMA* is a text which offers the reader a series of readings of its final 'meaning' and, in doing so, draws attention to how a sequence of events can be interpreted in mutually conflicting ways. Indeed all of these readings are legitimate 'pathways' into the text and none is pre-eminent. Since *CMA* offers so many different perspectives on the same event, as we shall see in Chapter 5, it ultimately leaves the reader in the dark as to which is the 'true' meaning (see *57*, *82* and *128*). *CMA* is an intrinsically ambiguous text simultaneously pointing in contradictory directions.

From *Gabriel García Márquez: Crónica de una muerte anunciada*, 50-62. Copyright © 2005 by Grant & Cutler Ltd. Reprinted by permission.

Notes

The edition used throughout this study is *Crónica de una muerte anunciada*, 16th impression (Barcelona: Bruguera, 1986). All page references in parentheses in the text are to this edition, but any reader using one of the three other editions will have no difficulty in locating quotations since the four editions have identical pagination. Since some readers may intend to consult the English translation, I have included the chapter number for each textual reference followed by a reference to *Chronicle of a Death Foretold*, trans. Gregory Rabassa (London: Picador, 1983).

1. *Theatre in Spain, 1490-1700* (Cambridge: Cambridge Univ. Press, 1989), p. 147.
2. *Poesías de Gil Vicente*, ed. Dámaso Alonso (México: Séneca, 1940), p. 33.
3. Sophocles, *Greek Plays in Modern Translation*, ed. Dudley Fitts (New York: Dial Press, 1949), p. 376.

Works Cited

1. Apuleyo Mendoza, Plinio, *Gabriel García Márquez. El olor de la guayaba. Conversaciones con Plinio Apuleyo Mendoza* (Barcelona: Bruguera, 1982). English translation: *The Fragrance of Guava*, translated by Ann Wright (London: Verso, 1983).

8. Rentería Mantilla, Alfonso, *García Márquez habla de García Márquez* (Bogotá: Rentería Editores, 1979).

10. Roca, Julio, 'Sí, la devolve la noche de bodas', *Al Día*, no. 3 (12 May 1981), 24-27.

16. Prescott, Peter S., 'Murder and Machismo', *Newsweek* (1 Nov. 1982), p. 8.

35. McMurray, George R. (ed.), *Gabriel García Márquez* (Boston: G. K. Hall, 1987).

36. Méndez, José Luis, *Cómo leer a García Márquez: una interpretación sociológica* (Río Piedras: Editorial de la Universidad de Puerto Rico, 1989).

38. Pankow, Gisela, 'L'Homme absurde et son espace', *Esprit*, 85 (Jan. 1984), 96-108.

57. Boling, Becky, '*Crónica de una muerte anunciada*: In Search of Authority', *Hispanic Journal*, 9 (1987), 75-87.

68. Díaz-Migoyo, Gonzalo, 'Truth Disguised: Chronicle of a Death (Ambiguously) Foretold', in *Gabriel García Márquez and the Powers of Fiction*, ed. Julio Ortega with Claudia Elliott (Austin: Univ. Press of Texas, 1988), pp. 74-86.

70. García Márquez, Eligio, *La tercera muerte de Santiago Nasar* (México: Editorial Diana, 1989).

78. Kerr, R. A., 'Archetropic Imagery in García Márquez's *Crónica de una muerte anunciada*', *Hispanófila*, 131 (2001), 85-92.

80. King, K. C., 'Voices in *Crónica de una muerte anunciada*', *Comparative Literature*, 43 (1991), 305-25.

82. López, François, '*Crónica de una muerte anunciada* de Gabriel García Márquez ou Le crime était presque parfait', *Bulletin Hispanique*, 96.2 (1994), 545-61.

89. Méndez Ramírez, H., 'La reinterpretación paródica del código de honor en *Crónica de una muerte anunciada*', *Hispania* (U.S.A.), 73 (1990), 934-42.

97. Olivares, Jorge, 'García Márquez's *Crónica de una muerte anunciada* as Metafiction', *Contemporary Literature*, 28 (1987), 483-92.

101. Penuel, Arnold M., 'The Sleep of Vital Reason in García Márquez's *Crónica de una muerte anunciada*', *Hispania* (U.S.A.), 68 (1985), 753-66.

103. Predmore, Richard, 'El mundo moral de *Crónica de una muerte anunciada*', *Cuadernos Hispanoamericanos*, 130 (1982), 703-12.

105. Rama, Angel, 'García Márquez entre la tragedia y la policial o crónica y pesquisa de la *Crónica de una muerte anunciada*', *Sin Nombre*, 13 (1982-83), 7-27.

116. Vargas Valentín, Ciriaco, & Ramón Núñez Hernández, *La Multiplicidad de sentidos en 'Crónica de una muerte anunciada'* (Santo Domingo: Editora de la Universidad Autónoma de Santo Domingo, 1985).

119. Gabriel García Márquez, *Vivir para contarla* (Barcelona: Mondadori, 2002).

128. Martin, Gerald, 'Spanish Narrative since 1970', in *The Cambridge Companion to Latin American Culture*, ed. John King (Cambridge: Cambridge Univ. Press, 2004), pp. 105-18.

Intertextualities:
Three Metamorphoses of Myth[1]
in *The Autumn of the Patriarch*_____
Michael Palencia-Roth

Michael Palencia-Roth focuses on the figures that, through the device known as intertextuality, acquire the unique resonances with
which García Márquez wants to infuse them in *The Autumn of the Patriarch*. The three myths are Julius Caesar, Christopher Columbus,
and Rubén Darío. Palencia-Roth suggests that the novel uses Julius
Caesar to explore power, Columbus to deal with issues of political and
cultural imperialism, and Darío to question the aesthetic and literary
life of Lautaro Muñoz, the novel's dictator. Palencia-Roth juxtaposes
quotations from these figures with samples from García Márquez's
book to show how, in a Pierre Menard fashion, words transposed
from one context to another acquire renewed meaning.   — I.S.

Although intertextuality has always been part of literature, it has not
always been part of literary theory. Its complex theoretical elaboration
is a relatively recent phenomenon. The diffusion of the theory of intertextuality, however, may today be considered to be worldwide. Like all
the best theories, it builds on what we "sense" to be true; and many critics have been "speaking intertextuality" all along, whether they realized it or not, much as Molière's Monsieur Jourdain spoke prose, to his
eventual surprise. The applicability of the theory of intertextuality is
exaggerated; for while it may explain the dynamics of some literary
works, one must always remember—as some French and American
critics seem to forget—that literature is not created ONLY from other
texts. Intertextuality is but one aspect of the creative process. It is, nevertheless, an important and fascinating aspect of certain authors' *ars
faciendi*; and this is especially true of García Márquez in his novel *The
Autumn of the Patriarch*.

Intertextuality exists every time a text is constructed—directly or indirectly—by means of another text.[2] There are three basic forms or kinds of intertextuality, as distinguished by Lucien Dällenbach.[3] First, there is "general" intertextuality, in which an author cites texts by other authors. Second, there is "restricted" intertextuality, in which an author cites from another work that he himself has written. Third, there is "autarchic" intertextuality, which occurs when the author cites from another portion of the text that he is in the process of writing. "Restricted" and "autarchic" intertextualities are, therefore, self-citations. This essay focuses on "general" intertextuality in *The Autumn of the Patriarch*.

Intertextuality transforms a previous text. When placed in a new context, words can acquire a different meaning. The tone is usually transformed as well, either into one of admiration or, more frequently, into irony, parody, and satire, all of which undermine the original text. In Latin American literature the most self-consciously ironic intertext is probably Jorge Luis Borges' "Pierre Menard, Author of the *Quixote*."[4] Menard is a twentieth-century author whose life-work consists, in part, of writing *Don Quixote*. With infinite care and patience, he composes a masterpiece of fiction which, word for word, is identical to the original *Don Quixote*. As the author of Pierre Menard's story of authorship, Borges cites texts from both Cervantes' and Menard's *Don Quixote*. In doing so he demonstrates, with inimitable Borgesian irony, how an early seventeenth-century text means something radically different when written in the twentieth century. The same words yield different meanings.

The Borges-Menard principle applies to the transformations of myth: any myth, placed in a different context, becomes a new myth. The dynamics of such transformations may be discussed under the general rubric of "metamorphosis." Whether the transformation is that of a text or a myth, a previous reality or entity becomes a new reality or entity as the old text becomes a new text, the person becomes a monster, the animal becomes a prince. Although the transformations in *The Autumn of the Patriarch* are not so radical, García Márquez exploits the following figures: Julius Caesar, Christopher Columbus, and Rubén Darío. Around each figure is gathered one of the central thematic complexes of the novel: García Márquez uses Julius Caesar to explore the concept of power; Christopher Columbus, issues of political and cultural imperialism; and Rubén Darío, questions of aesthetics and the literary life in relation to the aged dictator. Each figure affords us the opportunity of analyzing a concrete and extensive example of intertextuality. Together, they document how "mythical metamorphosis" works in García Márquez—how the new intertext is constructed.

I. Julius Caesar

at the mercy of omens and the interpreters of his nightmares[5]

In a 1977 interview with García Márquez, the Spanish novelist Juan Goytisolo asked him about the theme of the dictator in Latin American literature. García Márquez's response focused on the creation of his Patriarch:

> I learned a lot from Plutarch and Suetonius, as I did in general from all the biographers of Julius Caesar. That is only natural, since Julius Caesar is, in truth, the one character I should like to have created in literature. Because I couldn't do so, because, that is, it was already too late in my life, I had to make do with that crazy quilt which is the old Patriarch, stitched together as he was from all the dictators in the history of man.[6]

Julius Caesar is indeed "stitched" into *The Autumn of the Patriarch*. He is stitched both into the character of the Patriarch and into García Márquez's prose.[7] The Patriarch and his Roman predecessor are similar in that they both try to rearrange time and even to "redo it": the Patriarch tries to recalculate time arbitrarily according to his own "will";

Julius Caesar does so in accordance with the scientific knowledge of his day. Both are haunted by auguries or prophecies. While the Patriarch takes them so seriously that he often alters his life to accommodate them, Julius Caesar tries to ignore them and is eventually killed as prophesied. Both men are epileptics. During public meetings the Patriarch often tumbles from his throne in convulsions (*Autumn*, p. 43; *Otoño*, p. 47). According to Suetonius, Julius Caesar frequently fainted toward the end of his life, and twice epileptic fits surprised him during campaigns.[8] Both the Patriarch and Julius Caesar have trouble sleeping and are often awakened by fitful dreams and nightmares.

The two rulers are also reputed to be great lovers. In the Patriarch's case, the designation is ironic. In the case of Julius Caesar, writes Suetonius, "it is admitted by all that he was much addicted to women, as well as very extravagant in his intrigues with them, and that he seduced many illustrious women" (p. 29). Both dictators rule as though their every pronouncement were law. Examples of this attitude—and its abuse—are legion in the novel. Suetonius reports that Julius Caesar thought that "men ought to be more circumspect in addressing him, and to regard his word as law" (p. 42). We read in Plutarch that the Romans submitted to Julius Caesar only because they saw no other solution to their internecine wars and to the misery of their daily lives; the government of a single person, they thought, "would give them the time to breathe."[9] It was only because of these circumstances that Julius Caesar was named dictator for life. Plutarch, Suetonius, and García Márquez have commented that the conjunction of great power and extended rule leads almost inevitably to tyranny (see, for instance, Plutarch, p. 349; Suetonius, pp. 41-42). Both the Patriarch and Julius Caesar live with the threat of assassination. While the Patriarch survives every attempt on his life, Julius Caesar does not and is killed in a scene which has passed into literary immortality through its elaboration in Suetonius, Plutarch, and, of course, Shakespeare. Once dead, both the Patriarch and Julius Caesar are accorded divinity and perhaps for similar reasons. Their subjects somehow feel responsible for their deaths and want to render them in death the homage that they had in-sufficiently rendered them in life. Both the Patriarch and Julius Caesar, finally, are associated with the portents of nature, particularly with comets. The Patriarch thinks that his death has been prophesied to co-incide with the return of Halley's comet, but that does not occur. And for an entire week after the death of Julius Caesar, a great comet ap-peared every night, as if to remind the people of the greatness of their fallen leader (Plutarch, p. 364; Suetonius, pp. 49-50).

The great temptation of intertextual criticism is the unbridled appli-cation of the critic's imagination. That imagination must be based, if the analysis is to have any validity, on secure foundations. In the case of *The Autumn of the Patriarch*, fortunately, there is little danger of un-founded comparisons in Plutarch and Suetonius, for here García Már-quez's intertextual practice is blatant. Not only does he mention Sueto-nius in regard to that illustrious Latinist and precursor of the Patriarch, General Lautaro Muñoz ("an enlightened despot whom God keep in His holy glory with his Suetonius missals in Latin"–*Autumn*, p. 52; *Otoño*, p. 56), he also incorporates information on Julius Caesar from Plutarch and Suetonius to create a scene in which the Patriarch dreams of his own death. Following are the relevant scenes from Plutarch and Suetonius:

Plutarch:

But those who came prepared for the business inclosed him on every side, with their naked daggers in their hands. Which way soever he turned, he met with blows, and saw their swords levelled at his face and eyes, and was encompassed, like a wild beast in the toils, on every side. For it had been agreed they should each of them make a thrust at him, and flesh themselves with his blood; for which reason Brutus also gave him one stab in the groin. Some say that he fought and resisted all the rest, shifting his body to avoid the blows; and calling out for help, but that when he saw Brutus's sword drawn, he covered his face with his robe and submitted, letting himself fall, whether it were by chance, or that he was pushed in that direction by his murderers, at the foot of the pedestal on which Pompey's statue stood, and which was thus wetted with his blood. So that Pompey himself seemed to have presided, as it were, over the revenge done upon his adversary, who lay here at his feet, and breathed out his soul through his multitude of wounds, for they say he received three and twenty. And the conspirators themselves were many of them wounded by each other, whilst they all levelled their blows at the same person. (pp. 360-361)

Suetonius:

As [Julius Caesar] took his seat, the conspirators gathered about him as if to pay their respects, and straightway Tillius Cimber, who had assumed the lead, came nearer as though to ask something. When Caesar with a gesture put him off to another time, Cimber caught his toga by both shoulders. As Caesar cried, "Why, this is violence!" one of the Cascas stabbed him from one side just below the throat. Caesar caught Casca's arm and ran it through with his stylus, but as he tried to leap to his feet, he was stopped by another wound. When he saw that he was beset on every side by drawn daggers, he muffled his head in his robe, and at the same time drew down its lap to his feet with his left hand, in order to fall more decently, with the lower part of his body also covered. And in this wise he was stabbed with three and twenty wounds, uttering not a word, but merely a groan at the first stroke, though some have written that when Marcus Brutus rushed at him, he said in Greek, "You too, my child?" All the conspirators made off, and he lay there lifeless for some time, until finally three common slaves put him on a litter and carried him home, with one arm hanging down. (pp. 46-47)

The corresponding text in *The Autumn of the Patriarch* takes place during one of the Patriarch's dreams. (The words and phrases in italics refer to either Suetonius or Plutarch.) The Patriarch sees himself

in the big empty house of a bad dream *surrounded by pale men* in gray frock coats who were smiling and sticking him with butcher knives, *they harried him with such fury that wherever he turned to look he found a blade ready to wound him in the face and eyes*, he saw himself *encircled like a wild beast* by the silent smiling assassins who *fought over the privilege of taking part in the sacrifice and enjoying his blood*, but he did not feel rage or fear, rather an immense relief that grew deeper as his life trickled away, he felt himself weightless and pure, so he too smiled as they killed him, he smiled for them and for himself in the confines of the dream house whose whitewashed walls were being stained by my spattering blood, until *someone who was a son of his in the dream gave him a stab in the groin through which the last bit of breath* I had left *escaped*, and then *he covered his face with the blanket soaked in his blood so* that no one who had not been able to know him alive would know him dead and *he collapsed shaken* by such real death throes that he could not repress the urgency of telling it to my comrade the minister of health and the latter ended up by putting him in a state of consternation with the revelation that that death had already occurred once in the history of men general sir, *he read him the story of the episode in one of the singed tomes of General Lautaro Muñoz, and it was identical*, mother, so much so that in the course of its reading he remembered something that he had forgotten when he woke up and it was that while *they were killing him* all of a sudden and with no wind blowing all *the windows in the presidential palace opened up and they were in fact the same number as the wounds in the dream, twenty-three, a terrifying coincidence* which had its culmination that week with an attack on the senate and the supreme court by corsairs along with the cooperative indifference of the armed forces. . . . (*Autumn*, pp. 90-91; *Otoño*, pp. 94-95)

Prior to each of these scenes, the central character is haunted by prophecies. A soothsayer (named "Spurinna" in Suetonius; unnamed in Plutarch) has warned Julius Caesar to be wary of the ides of March. In Suetonius, in addition, a so-called "kingbird" flies in through one of the palace windows pursued by other birds which destroy it; in García Márquez's novel, that bird is transformed into one that sings above the Patriarch's head (*Autumn*, p. 90, *Otoño*, p. 93). In Suetonius' version, on the night before he is killed, Julius Caesar dreams that he is flying through clouds holding on to Jupiter by the hand. This detail anticipates the ending of García Márquez's novel and that way in which the Patriarch actually dies, "flying through the dark sound of the last frozen leaves of his autumn toward the homeland of shadows of the truth of oblivion, clinging to his fear of the rotting cloth of death's hooded cassock" (*Autumn*, p. 269; *Otoño*, p. 271). While in Suetonius and in Plutarch it is Julius Caesar's wife, Calpurnia, who senses the imminent death of her husband, in García Márquez's novel, the comparable role is played by the Patriarch's mother, Bendición Alvarado. After she finds an egg with two yolks, the Patriarch, trembling for his safety, changes the date of a public appearance (*Autumn*, p. 90; *Otoño*, p. 94).

The only fragment of the novel's manuscript which has been published is—quite fortuitously, for the purpose of this study—the facsimile of a draft of this crucial scene.[10] Perusing it reveals the care with which García Márquez works. On the margin of page 7, for instance, is the author's note to himself: "ojo: el texto de Plutarco (Suetonio). Ver" (Note: See the text of Plutarch [Suetonius]). Although some textual borrowings are obvious, others are subtle textual allusions. For instance, in Suetonius (though not in Plutarch) Julius Caesar, upon perceiving that one of his assassins is Marcus Brutus, cries out to him in Greek, "You too, my child?" (p. 47). In García Márquez, this cry is transformed from reality into dream, for the novelist relies on Plutarch (the detail is not in Suetonius) to specify the place where Brutus stabbed Caesar: "alguien que era hijo suyo en el sueño le dio un tajo en la ingle" ("someone who was a son of his in the dream gave him a stab in the groin").

On a more profound level, a reference in the manuscript not found in the printed version is of interest to anyone studying the creative process. Around the phrase "hijo suyo" (his son), García Márquez has drawn a circle and queried himself in the margin: "¿uno de sus 5,000 hijos?" (one of his 5,000 sons?). In so questioning himself about the

Patriarch's son, García Márquez is treating his character as though he had a life of his own, independent of his creator. These and other questions are a means by which García Márquez develops his character more fully and, from the knowledge gained by such private queries, creates a richer, more rounded, more convincing literary hero. For García Márquez, such a *modus operandi* is associated with Hemingway's. In an article published simultaneously in English in the *New York Times Book Review* (26 July 1981) and in Spanish in the Colombian newspaper *El Espectador*, entitled "My Personal Hemingway," García Márquez cites the American writer in a description, in part, of his own writing: "Writing in literature is only valid if—like the iceberg—it is supported beneath the surface by seven eighths of its volume." The dream sequence in *The Autumn of the Patriarch* has this kind of validity.

Julius Caesar seems to have interested García Márquez primarily as a well-defined and stable mythical legendary figure who could be used as a foil for his Patriarch. The Colombian author, however, did not change the legend or the myth significantly. Intertextuality, therefore, is accomplished without irony or parody. Structurally, the writings of Plutarch and Suetonius function as a kind of palimpsest on which the Patriarch's story is written. We should remember, however, that in the ancient palimpsests the original text (first erased and then written upon) normally had no relationship with the new text other than that of spatial contiguity. In terms of content, the palimpsest effect in *The Autumn of the Patriarch* resembles the iceberg effect. Plutarch and Suetonius' subtexts support the Patriarch's dreams and fears, giving them a density and a context (and, therefore, "meaning") they would not have otherwise had. The myth of the Patriarch—or the mythical, legendary being that the Patriarch becomes—is nourished by the mythic subtexts of Julius Caesar; it does not, however, represent a "modified" Julius Caesar or one adapted to Latin American reality. *The Autumn of the Patriarch* gains literary and symbolic weight and density by drawing sustenance from its classical subtexts.

2. Christopher Columbus

Unfortunate admiral

(Rubén Darío, "To Columbus")

Christopher Columbus belongs to Latin American reality, culture, and history in a way that Julius Caesar never can. With the passing centuries, Columbus, like George Washington, has increasingly become part of American consciousness, a figure surrounded by myth and legend. In the sixteenth century, however, Columbus was anything but a revered mythical or legendary hero. He died abandoned and poverty-stricken in Valladolid in 1506; during the entire sixteenth century he did not appear in a single work of Spanish literature. It is only during the early years of the seventeenth century, with the 1614 publication of Lope de Vega's play *El nuevo mundo descubierto por Colon* (*The New World Discovered by Columbus*), that the literary mythification of Columbus may truly have begun.[11] This mythification reaches its ironic apogee with *The Autumn of the Patriarch*. Although the myth of the Patriarch is based on the subtexts associated with Columbus,[12] as well as on those of Julius Caesar, García Márquez's treatment of the two is distinct; while he does not renovate the myth of Julius Caesar, García Márquez transforms the "myth of Columbus" to such an extent that our vision of him is altered forever.[13]

García Márquez is extremely knowledgeable about Columbus and his works. For him, the Admiral of the Ocean Sea is not only the first European to have landed on American shores, but also the first "American" writer. Upon being asked about magical realism in Latin American literature, García Márquez once answered:

The first masterwork of the literature of magical realism is the *Diary of Christopher Columbus*. From the first it was so contaminated by the magic of the Caribbean that even the history of the book itself makes an unlikely story. Its most moving moments, the moments, that is, of the discovery itself, were written twice, and we do not possess either version directly. A few nights before he returned to Spain on the first voyage, a tremendous storm lashed his ship near the Azores. He thought that none of his crew would survive the gale and that the glory of his discovery would belong to Martin Alonso Pinzón, whose ship was sailing ahead. In order to make sure that the glory would belong to him alone, Columbus hastily wrote down a history of his discoveries, placed the sheaf of papers in a water-proof barrel, and commended it to the waters. He was so mistrustful that he did not confide in a single one of his sailors but instead made them believe that the barrel contained a prayer to the Virgin Mary to make the storm abate. One surprising thing is that the storm did abate, and another is that the barrel was never found, which means that if Columbus' ship had gone down, his account would never have seen the light of day. The second version, written at greater leisure, has also been lost. What we know as *The Diary of Columbus* is, in reality, its reconstruction by Father Las Casas, who had read the original manuscript. However much Las Casas may have added to the manuscript, and however much he may have taken out, the truth is that the text is the first work of the magical literature of the Caribbean.[14]

A follow-up question asks how García Márquez could consider the diary to be a *literary* work, and a magical one at that, when it purports to be both a general and personal account of the "real" discovery of America. García Márquez responded:

[I consider the diary as such] because in it one reads of fabulous plants, of mythical animals, and of beings with supernatural powers which could not possibly have existed. Columbus, probably, was a con man above all else, for everything he said was intended to excite the King and Queen so that they would continue to finance his expeditions of discovery. In any case, however, this text is the first work of the literature of the Caribbean.[15]

García Márquez is also unusually knowledgeable about Columbus' life, what he was like, what legends surrounded him, and what happened to his cadaver:

> The second work [of the literature of the Caribbean] is the life of Columbus himself, full as it was of mysteries which he himself encouraged. He has so often been depicted as impoverished, as wandering from pillar to post, as departing emotionally charged from the monastery of La Rábida in the company of his son Diego, and as dying in chains and in misery, that no one can imagine what he was truly like.
>
> And what was he like?
>
> He was a very tall man, a red-head, and covered with freckles; he had blue eyes and he was balding, something that bothered him so much that during his voyages he searched for magical anti-baldness elixirs. Nothing, however, is perhaps as fantastic as what happened to his cadaver. He is perhaps the only man in history for whom there are three tombs in different parts of the world, and no one knows for certain in which of the three his cadaver is really to be found. There is a tomb in the Cathedral in Santo Domingo, one in Havana, and another in Seville.[16]

Columbus' frequent appearance, usually as a character but once as a "text," further demonstrates the iceberg effect in García Márquez's work. First let us note some of García Márquez's allusions to Columbus the man. The Patriarch seems to have known him personally, for the Admiral of the Ocean Sea (the official title granted him by the King and Queen for his discoveries) has given the Patriarch a golden spur to be worn on the left heel as a sign of the highest authority (*Autumn*, pp. 176-177; *Otoño*, p. 179). At three different points in the novel are passages which deal with Columbus's three tombs and with his posthumous existence:

. . . and the granite promontory of the empty mausoleum for the admiral of the ocean sea with the profile of the three caravels which he [the Patriarch] had built in case he [Columbus] wanted his bones to rest among us . . . (*Autumn*, p. 100; *Otoño*, pp. 101-104)

. . . I had had a tomb built for an admiral of the ocean sea who did not exist except in my feverish imagination when I myself with my own blessed eyes had seen the three caravels anchored across the harbor from my window . . . (*Autumn*, p. 123; *Otoño*, p. 125)

. . . they said he [Columbus] had become a Moslem, that he had died of pellagra in Senegal [note the "restricted intertextuality" here, for the echo is to Melquíades in *One Hundred Years of Solitude*], and had been buried in three different tombs in three different cities in the world although he really wasn't in any of them, condemned to wander from sepulcher to sepulcher until the end of time because of the twisted fate of his expeditions . . . (*Autumn*, p. 256; *Otoño*, p. 258)

There are other, briefer references to Columbus: to "the flagship of the first admiral of the ocean sea just as I had seen it from my window" (*Autumn*, p. 247; *Otoño*, p. 248); to Columbus' incipient baldness, to his poverty, and to the three caravels (*Autumn*, pp. 255-256; *Otoño*, p. 258). One day, from the window of his presidential limousine (particularly note the deliberately syncretistic conjunction of centuries), the Patriarch recognizes Columbus in the crowd, "disguised in a brown habit with the cord of Saint Francis around his waist swinging a penitent's rattle" (*Autumn*, p. 256; *Otoño*, p. 258), a detail so bizarre to most twentieth-century readers that it would seem to have been invented. In fact, however, Columbus did dress in a Franciscan habit after his second voyage and again just before his death.

The most important allusion, however, is not to Columbus but rather to his famous—or infamous—diary. A long passage found at the end of the first chapter of *The Autumn of the Patriarch* is concretely based on

Columbus' diary entries of the twelfth and thirteenth of October, 1492, the moments, therefore, of the discovery of America. Following are the relevant portions from the diary:

[Friday, October 12]: I, says he [Columbus, for this is a direct transcription from the diary by Las Casas], in order that they might develop a very friendly disposition towards us, because I knew that they were a people who could better be freed and converted to our Holy Faith by love than by force, gave to some of them red caps and to others glass beads, which they hung on their necks, and many other things of slight value, in which they took much pleasure. They remained so much our [friends] that it was a marvel . . .

. . . it appeared to me that these people were very poor in everything. They all go quite naked as their mothers bore them; and also the women, although I didn't see more than one really young girl. All that I saw were young men, none of them more than 30 years old, very well built, of very handsome bodies and very fine faces; the hair coarse, almost like the hair of a horse's tail, and short. . . . Some of them paint themselves black (and they are of the color of the Canary Islanders, neither black nor white), and others paint themselves white, and some red, and others with what they find. And some paint their faces, others the body, some the eyes only, others only the nose. They bear no arms, nor know thereof; for I showed them swords and they grasped them by the blade and cut themselves through ignorance. They have no iron. Their darts are a kind of rod without iron, and some have at the end a fish's tooth and others, other things. They ought to be good servants and of good skill, for I see that they repeat very quickly whatever was said to them. I believe that they would easily be made Christians, because it seemed to me that they belonged to no religion.

[Saturday, October 13]: At the time of daybreak there came to the beach many of these men, all young men, as I have said, and all of good stature, very handsome people. Their hair is not kinky but straight and coarse like horsehair; the whole forehead and head is very broad, more so than [in] any other race that I have seen, and the eyes very handsome and not small, They themselves are not at all black, but of the color of the Canary Islanders; nor should anything else be expected because this is on the same latitude as the island of Ferro in the Canaries.[17]

In the corresponding passage from *The Autumn of the Patriarch*, the words and phrases which are derived from the diary (primarily from the entries cited above) are in italics. Also worthy of note are Rabassa's archaizing touches in the translation which reflect both García Márquez's original text and Columbus' fifteenth-century Spanish (Morison's translation cited above is a modernized version):

... and contemplating the islands he evoked again and relived that *historic October Friday* when he [the Patriarch] left his room at dawn and discovered that everybody in the presidential palace was wearing *a red biretta*, that the new concubines were sweeping the parlors and changing the water in the cages wearing *red birettas*, that the milkers in the stables, the sentries in their boxes, the cripples on the stairs and the lepers in the rose beds were going about with the *red birettas* of a carnival Sunday, so he began to look into what had happened to the world while he was sleeping for the people in his house and the inhabitants of the city to be going around wearing *red birettas and dragging a string of jingle bells* everywhere, and finally he found someone to tell him the truth general sir, that *some strangers had arrived who gabbled in funny old talk because they made the word for sea feminine and not masculine, they called macaws poll parrots, canoes rafts, harpoons javelins*, and when they saw us going out to greet them and *swim around their ships* they climbed up onto the yardarms and shouted to each other look there *how well formed, of beauteous body and fine face, and thick-haired and almost like horse-hair silk*, and when they saw that we were painted so as not to get sunburned they got all excited like wet little parrots and shouted look there *how they daub themselves gray, and they are the hue of canary birds, not white nor yet black, and what there be of them*, and we didn't understand why the hell they were making so much fun of us general sir since we were *just as normal as the day our mothers bore* us and on the other hand they were decked out like the jack of clubs in all that heat, which they made feminine the way Dutch smugglers do, and they wore their hair like women even though they were all men and they shouted that *they didn't understand us in Christian tongue* when they were the ones who couldn't understand what we were shouting, and then they came toward us in their *canoes which they called rafts, as we said before*, and they were amazed that our *harpoons had a shad bone for a tip which they called a fishy tooth*, and we traded everything we had for these *red birettas and these strings of glass beads that we hung around our necks* to please them, and also for *these brass bells* that can't be worth more than a penny and for chamber pots and eyeglass and other goods from Flanders, *of the cheapest sort* general sir, and since we saw that *they were good people and men of good will* we went on leading them to the beach without their realizing it, but the trouble was that among the I'll swap you this for that and that for the other a wild motherfucking trade grew up and after a while everybody was swapping his parrots, his tobacco, his wads of chocolate, his iguana eggs, everything God ever created, because they took and gave everything willingly, and they even wanted to trade *a velvet doublet* for one of us to show off in Europeland, just imagine general, what a farce, but he was so confused that he could not decide whether that lunatic business came within the incumbency of his government, so he went back to his bedroom, opened the windows that looked out onto the sea so that perhaps he might discover some new light to shed on the mixup they had told him about, and he saw the usual battleship that the marines had left behind at the dock, and beyond the battleship, anchored in the shadowy sea, he saw *the three caravels*. (*Autumn*, pp. 40-42; *Otoño*, pp. 44-46)

The *fact* of the intertextuality is undeniable. Of interest is the *way* in which García Márquez has retold this famous discovery. He introduces the scene by using the mythic pattern of the eternal return: the Patriarch "evoked *again* and relived" the day of discovery. In the mythical conception of the world,[18] *everything* can live anew, and historical events that are so repeated come to be considered (and are, in a sense) "mythic" events. The "historic October Friday" is willed to exist again in the Patriarch's mind and experience, and in the world of the novel. Columbus first gives the Indians some "red caps," and these naturally are the first things that the Patriarch notices upon leaving his room at daybreak. Surprised, the Patriarch tries to find out what had happened in the world (a phrase that echoes similar ones in *One Hundred Years of Solitude* and other works) while he has slept. The description which follows can, then, be considered the result of the Patriarch's investigations. At the end of the chapter, as though to reaffirm the truth of the radical transformation of the indigenous night into the dawn of the European day in the New World, the Patriarch looks out of his palace window and sees, at anchor, the sight which seals the fate of the Indians and inaugurates the new era: the three caravels. In the New World in 1492 these were probably as bizarre as spaceships from another galaxy would be today.

On the one hand, it is surprising that the Spaniards were not immediately killed. On the other, the Spanish presence in the New World was seen as a sign from heaven, and such messengers are usually well received. According to Columbus, although one wonders how he could understand a language he had never heard before, the natives shouted to one another, "Come and see the men who come from the sky, bring them food and drink" (Diary entry for October 14). Cortés, incidentally, was also initially protected by a similar native belief. The attitudes of Columbus and, later, Cortés and the advantage each took of the native naïveté are but two examples of the cultural arrogance which characterized the European incursions into the New World.[19] Such arrogance is often apparent when a first-world country comes in contact with a third-world country, and Latin America as a whole has only recently begun to emerge from beneath this attitudinal yoke. One of the ways García Márquez casts off this yoke in *The Autumn of the Patriarch* is by changing the perspective from which the discovery of America is viewed. With this shift in perspective comes a simultaneous shift in attitude, in cultural arrogance. For García Márquez, the superior culture belongs to the native Americans, *el pueblo* (the people), and the Patriarch, symbolically converted for the rest of the scene into an Indian chief. García Márquez satirizes European attitudes toward native peoples and the New World, and he describes the Spaniards as if *they* were the bizarre creatures: "some strangers had arrived who gabbled in funny old talk" (p. 41). Ironically, the modern Spanish of the New World is considered more correct than that of fifteenth-century Spain.

The incomprehension is mutual. Neither culture understands the other's language, dress, customs, or value system: "[The Spaniards] shouted that they didn't understand us in Christian tongue when they were the ones who couldn't understand what we were shouting." Columbus' diary gives the impression that the arrival of the Spanish in the New World was the beneficent act of a superior culture, and that the resulting transformation of simple native lives was part of a necessary civilizing process. García Márquez consistently undermines the cultural superiority of the Spaniard. For instance, when the natives, courteously adhering to their customs for receiving strangers, swim out to the Spanish ships, the sailors scurry up the yardarms and chatter at each other like monkeys, getting as excited as "wet little parrots." These images hardly befit those of a conquering and culturally superior nation. The Spaniards are startled by the nudity of the natives. The latter, however, are even more surprised at the stupidity of the Spaniards who, in the tropical heat, are "decked out like the jack of clubs." Another piece of clothing emphasizes the cultural abyss between the Europeans and the native Americans. On October 11 Columbus had promised the first man to sight land a velvet doublet, a valuable item for Europeans. In the novel, that velvet doublet is suggested as being equivalent in value to a native American. The native reaction is appropriate: "what a farce." It is a farce not only to exchange a human being for an article of clothing, but also to wish to barter with a useless item. A velvet doublet, reaching from the neck to the waist and worn snugly against the body, seems hardly the best apparel for the humidity and warmth of the Caribbean. Moreover, it is superfluous in a culture in which everyone is naked. Another native practice—the use of body paint—is also misunderstood. Whereas the natives use it to protect themselves against the sun, the Spaniards see it only as decoration, and bizarre decoration at that, not as something useful or socially significant.

García Márquez's irony at the end of this opening chapter of *The Autumn of the Patriarch* could not be more profound. It is as though he wishes *both* to rid Columbus' enterprise of all its heroic and legendary content *and* to destroy its historical validity. Through parody, through the reversal of the hermeneutical perspective, García Márquez brings us face to face with the *other* side of the history of the New World. That other side possesses its own truth and, although it too may be culturally conditioned, it at least has a right to be heard and to exist alongside the dominant ideological interpretation of the discovery of America. The point is not that Columbus has invented the reality of what he discovered or that he has lied. The point is, rather, that he cannot help but see "American reality" through the prism of his European consciousness. And since his is the dominant culture, American reality is primarily defined through the European prism."[20] In emphasizing the other side of the events of 1492, García Márquez makes Columbus one of his principal antagonists. The Admiral of the Ocean Sea, therefore, is unlike Julius Caesar in this regard. Perhaps because of Columbus' position in the exploitation of the New World and because of his place in the thematics of *The Autumn of the Patriarch*, García Márquez said that the historical figures he disliked most were "Christopher Columbus and the general Francisco de Paula Santander."[21] Perhaps, for García Márquez, Columbus is indeed, in Rubén Darío's words, a "hapless admiral."

3. Rubén Darío

the forgotten poet
(*Autumn*, p. 5; *Otoño*, p. 8)

García Márquez once said that "there has never been an homage to Rubén Darío like that in *The Autumn of the Patriarch*. The book includes entire verses of Darío. It is written in Rubén Darío's style. It is full of gestures to the connoisseurs of Rubén Darío. I tried to figure out who was the great poet in the era of the great dictators, and it was Rubén Darío. Darío even makes an appearance as a character."[22] García Márquez later commented: "I even think that it is more of a poem than a novel. [The text] has been worked on more in the manner of poetry than that of fiction."[23] The novel may, therefore, be read either as an homage or as a poem.

The first direct allusion to the so-called "poet of America"—the sobriquet itself is a hint of Darío's legendary importance to Latin American literature and culture—may be found on page 5: ". . . one Sunday many years ago they had brought him [the Patriarch] the blind man on the street who for five cents would recite the verses of the forgotten poet Rubén Darío and he had come away happy with the nice wad they paid him" (*Otoño*, p. 8). In Latin America, Darío is recited in perhaps the same way Homer was recited in his time. As a character, the poet of America makes a cameo appearance in the era of Leticia Nazareno, who invites him to recite his verses in the National Theatre. At that time he is considered not the "forgotten poet" but "the well-known poet" (p. 183, *Otoño*, p. 185), and he is received as though he were a god:

> . . . in through the open balconies came the crowd's hymns of jubilation that had previously been sung to exalt his glory as they knelt under the burning sun to celebrate the good news that God [Rubén Darío] had been brought in on a ship general sir, really, they had brought Him on your orders, Leticia, by means of a bedroom law . . . (*Autumn*, p. 176; *Otoño*, p. 178)

The visit of the Nicaraguan poet is so special that the presidential house is painted white and decorated with new lamps. On the evening of the poetry reading, the Patriarch accompanies Leticia Nazareno to the National Theatre and listens to America's poet recite his verses.

As a character, Rubén Darío is decidedly minor. It is his poetry, however, that is important in *The Autumn of the Patriarch*. The "Dariano" setting and mood are apparent almost immediately, as the Patriarch's body seems to be discovered during the epoch of Darío. Upon entering the palace prior to discovering the cadaver, the people enter "the atmosphere of another age" (*Autumn*, p. 2; *Otoño*, p. 5), a decadent one of colored mushrooms and pale irises, of ancient carriages, coaches, and limousines, all "under the dusty cobwebs and all painted with the colors of the flag" (*Autumn*, p. 2; *Otoño*, p. 6). "The atmosphere of roses" wafts among the "camellias and butterflies" (ibid.), but beneath it all, in a very "un-Darian" way, we smell the cow-dung and the stench of urine belonging to the cows and the soldiers, and, in a flash, Darío's world—or rather the world of his early poetry, the world of roses, long-necked swans, ballrooms, and sad princesses—has disappeared.

Some of the descriptions in *The Autumn of the Patriarch* refer to that world of the early Darío, to the poet of *Azul* (*Blue*) and *Prosas profanas* (*Profane Hymns*).[24] The following description, for example, relies on the early Darío:

[During trips on "the eve of his autumn" the Patriarch's train would "creep" and "crawl"] about the cornices of his vast mournful realm, opening a path through orchid springs and Amazonian balsam apples, rousing up monkeys, birds of paradise, jaguars sleeping on the tracks . . . [and as it went along it would leave] a wake of player-piano waltzes in the midst of the sweet fragrance of gardenias and rotting salamanders of the equatorial tributaries, eluding prehistoric dragons in their leather gun cases, providential isles where sirens lay down to give birth . . . (*Autumn*, pp. 15-16; *Otoño*, pp. 19-20)

There are two other brief intertextual moments concerning Darío in *The Autumn of the Patriarch*. One day, during the last years of the Patriarch's rule, the blind declaimer of Rubén Darío sits down in the shade of the palace's dying palm trees and, thinking that the cows going by are marching soldiers, "recited those lines of poetry about the happy warrior who came from afar in a conquest of death, he recited them with full voice and his hand outstretched toward the cows who climbed up to eat the balsam apple garlands on the bandstand with their habit of going up and down stairs to eat" (*Autumn*, p. 218; *Otoño*, p. 220). The subtext here is Darío's famous "Sonatina" (1895), and the stanza in question reads as follows:

> "Hush, Princess, hush," says her fairy godmother;
> "the joyous knight who adores you unseen
> is riding this way on his wingèd horse,
> a sword at his waist and a hawk on his wrist,
> and comes from far off, having conquered Death,
> to kindle your lips with a kiss of true love!"[25]

Corresponding to the theory of intertextuality, the same words in a different context mean something different. The novel literally repeats a phrase from the penultimate line of this poem, *vencedor de la muerte*, "conqueror of death," a phrase which neither the translator of García Márquez nor that of Rubén Darío has rendered with total accuracy, thus making possible and even likely the loss of the intertextual reference. In any case, here García Márquez is being doubly parodic, as he undermines both the "precious" world of the "Sonatina" and the decadent world of the Patriarch. The first world comments on the second, for the escapist sentiments of "Sonatina" contrast sharply with the sordid reality of a senile and melancholy dictator. In the novel it is not a "joyous knight" who climbs the stairs but a few cows. Many years ago there was a sad princess in the Patriarch's world. Her name was Manuela Sánchez. Now there is no one even remotely resembling her.

Moreover, the Patriarch himself is not, in the end, the "conqueror of death" (although at times during his reign he seems to have been), and it has been years—if indeed it ever occurred—since he "kindled" with his lips "a kiss of true love."

Another example of "general intertextuality" in the novel is when the Patriarch, having but a few hours to live, follows his customary nocturnal routine. Toward the end of that routine, after eating a spoonful of honey, he places the honey jar once more in the

> hiding place where there was one of his little pieces of paper with the date of some birthday of the famous poet Rubén Darío whom God keep on the highest seat in his kingdom, he rolled the piece of paper up again and left it in its place while he recited from memory the well-aimed prayer of *our father and celestial lyrophorous master* who keepeth afloat airplanes in the heavens and liners on the seas . . . (*Autumn*, p. 265; *Otoño*, p. 267)

The italicized words belong to the first line of Rubén Darío's poem, "Responso a Verlaine," which reads, in Spanish, "*padre y maestro mágico liróforo celeste*" (it is quoted verbatim in the novel). Darío's poem not only "celebrates" Verlaine; it "deifies" him. Placed in the context of the novel, Verlaine becomes, ironically, a kind of God to the Patriarch. It is ironic not only that a poet should be worshipped by a man like the Patriarch, who is totally ignorant of literature and who, until the last few years of his life, remains illiterate; but also that the poet should be French (a language and culture of which the Patriarch has no clue). The only character in the novel to whom such an act of worship might have seemed "natural" is, of course, General Lautaro Muñoz, a Latinist and, like many presidents of Colombia, a man of letters.

Thematically, the poetry of Rubén Darío is also important to García Márquez's vision of "love" in the novel. This is to be expected, for, as Pedro Salinas points out, in *La poesía de Rubén Darío* (Buenos Aires: Losada, 1948), "love" is Darío's most constant theme. Here García

Márquez exploits the man as well as his poetry. For example, there were three important women in Darío's life: Rafaela Contreras (his first wife, idealized as "Stella" in the poetry); Rosario Emelina Murillo (his second wife, known as "la garza morena"—"the dark heron"); and Francisca Sánchez (his "companion" of many years, 1899-1914). And there are three central women around the Patriarch: Bendición Alvarado (his mother),[26] Manuela Sánchez (his "inviolate" love), and Leticia Nazareno (his wife). The name of Rubén Darío's last great love, Francisca Sánchez, is split into two in the novel and is shared by two women loved, however briefly, by the Patriarch: the peasant woman *Francisca* Linero (Darío's last love was also a peasant) and Manuela *Sánchez*.

Like Aldonza Lorenzo (or "Dulcinea") in *Don Quixote*, Manuela Sánchez is idealized, now into an "untouchable maiden" (*Autumn*, p. 77), now into a "queen" (p. 78). The air surrounding her is perfumed with roses. Hopelessly in love with this Beauty Queen, the Patriarch visits her house in the slums, wondering, while he waits for her, "where is your rose, where your love" (*Autumn*, p. 74; *Otoño*, p. 77). When she enters the room, she bears a rose, and when he leaves, the rose is dead. During the many months of almost daily visits, the relationship does not progress beyond the platonic. He is unable to seduce her, and she is unable to summon any sympathy for this toothy old man (*Autumn*, p. 75; *Otoño*, p. 78), tolerating him only because he is the President of the Republic. Finally, one day as they watch an eclipse together, she disappears before his eyes, vanishing into air as easily as Remedios the Beauty in *One Hundred Years of Solitude* ascends into heaven. Manuela Sánchez's disappearance brings to mind Darío's poem entitled "To Margarita Debayle" (1907-1908), in which a princess disappears when she tries to find—and catch—a star in the sky. After losing Manuela Sánchez, the Patriarch becomes obsessed by her "absent presence," by his memory of her, and, especially, by her flowery fragrance. Transformed into a ghost, she haunts him in his bedroom, passing through the walls at will. "Extinguish that rose," the Patriarch moans

(*Autumn*, p. 67; *Otoño*, p. 70), for he associates Manuela Sánchez with failure and with unrequited love.[27]

It is not surprising that Rubén Darío and the Patriarch have opposite attitudes to roses, for in García Márquez's novelistic universe, the two men are polar opposites. Darío was loved by the "people" of Latin America; the Patriarch was tolerated, at best, by his countrymen. Darío lived almost his entire life in the public eye, surrounded by friends and acquaintances; the Patriarch lived in aloof isolation. Darío was a poet; the Patriarch, an illiterate. Darío belonged to the world of letters; the Patriarch, to that of politics. Darío was a man without "power" (in the conventional sense of that term); the Patriarch, a man for whom power was both a fact and an obsession. Darío died at a relatively young age (forty-nine); the Patriarch, as we know, lived to an incredibly advanced age.

These contrasts are the basis for the most elaborate and extensive Darío-García Márquez intertextuality in the novel. One of the poems which the Patriarch hears recited at the poetry reading in the National Theatre is the famous "Marcha triunfal" (1895), the "Triumphal March." This becomes part of a beautiful textual mosaic in the novel. Since García Márquez systematically incorporates numerous phrases from Darío's poem into this scene of *The Autumn of the Patriarch*, it is worthwhile to reproduce the entire poem:

> The procession is coming!
> The procession is coming! You can hear the clear trumpets,
> and the swords flash in the sun:
> the procession of the paladins, gold and iron, is coming.
>
> The solemn glory of the standards,
> borne in the strong hands of heroic athletes,
> is passing beneath tall arches adorned
> with figures of Mars and white Minerva,
> triumphal arches where Fame lifts her long bugle.

You can hear the clattering weapons of the knights,
the bold war horses champing their bits,
their hooves wounding the earth,
and the drummers
beating out the step with martial rhythms.
Thus the fierce warriors pass
beneath the triumphal arches!

The clear trumpets sound their music,
their sonorous song,
their fervent chorus,
surrounding the august pomp of the flags
with a golden thunder.
It speaks of struggle, wounded vengeance,
the rough manes of the horses,
rude crests, the pike and spear,
and blood that watered the earth
with heroic crimson;
of the black mastiffs
which death urges forward, which battle governs.

The golden sounds
announce the triumphant
arrival of Glory;
leaving the peak that guards their nests,
unfolding their enormous wings to the wind,
the condors arrive! Victory has arrived!
The procession is passing.
A grandfather points out the heroes to his grandson.
See how the old man's beard
surrounds the child's gold ringlets with its ermine.
And beautiful women are fashioning crowns of flowers,
their faces under the porticoes are roses,

and the loveliest of them

smiles at the fiercest of the warriors.

Honor to him who brings the strange banner he captured,

honor to the wounded, honor to the faithful soldiers

who were slain by alien hands.

Trumpets! Laurels!

The noble swords of the glorious past

salute the new crowns and triumphs from their panoplies:

the old swords of the grenadiers, who were stronger than bears,

the brothers of those lancers who were centaurs.

The warlike trumpets resound,

The winds are filled with voices—

Hail to those ancient swords,

those illustrious arms

that embody the glories of the past,

and hail to the sun that shines on these new-won victories,

to the hero leading his cluster of fierce young men,

to the soldier who loves the ensign of his native land,

to the soldier who, his sword in hand,

defied the sun through long red summers

and the wind and snow of cruel winters,

the night, and the frost,

and hatred, and death, immortal servant of the homeland—

the heroes are hailed by the brazen voices

that sound the triumphal march![28]

The relevant passage from *The Autumn of the Patriarch* follows, with the references to Darío's poem italicized:

[During the evening the audience] saw no one else in the presidential box [besides the Patriarch's young son and Leticia Nazareno], but during the two hours of the recital we [the people] bore the certainty that he was there, we felt the invisible presence that watched over our destiny so that it would not be altered by the disorder of poetry, he regulated love, he decided the intensity and term of death in a corner of the box in the shadows from where unseen he watched the heavy minotaur whose voice of marine lightning lifted him out of his place and instant and left him floating without his permission in *the golden thunder of the trim trumpets of the triumphal arches of Marses and Minervas* of a glory that was not his general sir, he saw *the heroic athletes with their standards the black mastiffs of the hunt the sturdy war-horses with their iron hooves the pikes and lances of the paladins with rough crests who bore the strange* flag *captive to honor* arms that were not his, he saw the troop of *fierce young men* who had *challenged the suns of the red summer the snows and winds of the icy winter night and dew and hatred and death* for the eternal splendor of an *immortal nation* larger and more glorious than all those he had dreamed of during the long deliriums of his fevers as a barefoot warrior, he felt poor and tiny in the seismic thunder of the applause that he approved in the shadows thinking mother of mine Bendición Alvarado this really is a parade, not the shitty things these people organize for me, feeling diminished and alone, oppressed by the heavy heat and the mosquitoes and the columns of cheap gold paint and the faded plush of the box of honor, God damn it, how is it possible for this Indian to write something so beautiful with the same hand that he wipes his ass with, he said to himself, so excited by the revelation of written beauty that he dragged his great feet of a captive elephant to the *rhythms of the martial beat of the kettledrums*, he dozed off to the rhythm of the voices *of glory of the cadenced chant of the calorific choir* that Leticia Nazareno recited for him in the shade of the *triumphal arches* of the ceiba tree in the courtyard, he would write the lines on the walls of the toilets, he was trying to recite the whole poem by heart in the tepid cowshit olympus of the milking stables when the earth trembled from the dynamite charge that went off ahead of time in the trunk of the presidential automobile parked in the coach house . . . (*Autumn*, pp. 192-193; *Otoño*, pp. 194-195)

The importance of these references lies not solely with the existence of intertextuality and with the great number of Darío's verses incorporated into the novel, but with the Patriarch's reaction to these verses and the thoughts they trigger amidst his discomfort in the presence of "poetry" and/or "culture." For the first time in his life, the Patriarch finds himself face to face with an astonishing, poetic, and personal phenomenon, and he begins to be conscious of the great abyss which exists between a beloved "man of the people" and a dictator, between poetry and politics, between literature and the exercise of power. The text signals that abyss through a series of negations. In other words, the poetic world of Mars and Minerva concerns a "glory that was not his." The war-horses, the paladins, and the captive flag honor "arms that were not his." The "eternal splendor" of that world celebrates a nation "larger and more glorious than all those he had dreamed of." The poetic imagination, at least in this scene of the novel, proves to be more powerful than political activism—literature more powerful than life. In the face of Darío's world, a world of which the Patriarch was previously unaware, the Patriarch feels impotent; in the presence of the poet himself, diminished and alone, impoverished and small. The adoration of the poet makes the Patriarch realize the inauthenticity of the people's celebrations in his honor, and this insight only further diminishes his own sense of self-worth. In addition, the elevated rhetoric of Darío's discourse (in the original) contrasts sharply with the Patriarch's crudeness. In fact, it is fully in character for him to react to the unexpected beauty of the poetry by asking himself how "the Indian" could write such verses "with the same hand that he wipes his ass with."

The incongruity in linguistic ability and culture between the poet and the Patriarch represents a double parody. On the one hand, if one considers the Patriarch to be the archetypal representative of the caudillo in Latin American history, then that figure is—as a type—rude, crude, and despised. The Patriarch, unable to appreciate Darío's poem on an aesthetic level, expresses his "appreciation" in an obscene way. On the other hand, the Patriarch's reaction also demonstrates the great distance between the world of poetry and his own world and, by extension, how far Darío is from the present realities of Latin America. It is probably for this reason that Darío is introduced in the novel as the "forgotten poet," as simply being irrelevant to the way the Latin American people today must live and love and work.

Hypnotized by his experience that evening, the Patriarch tries for a while to live "poetically." He moves his elephantine feet to the rhythms of Darío's martial music. Leticia Nazareno reads him to sleep at night with Darío's verses. Having at long last learned how to read and write, the Patriarch writes Darío's words on bathroom walls, perhaps symbolically and unconsciously returning the poetry to the only world he had been able to call upon in reacting to the poetry in the first place.

In light of this reaction, the Nicaraguan *pater noster* which the Patriarch much later recites to Verlaine every night (*Autumn*, p. 265; *Otoño*, p. 267) is ironic. By then, however, senile and near death, the Patriarch has lost control over his memory, and he has forgotten Darío just as, earlier, he had forgotten even his wife.

Why should the Patriarch have been so affected—for a while at least—by the poetry reading? Was it because he discovered a "New World," a world which he, like Columbus, had never dreamed of? Was it because of the incredible and unexpected sounds and rhythms of a language he thought he knew? Perhaps. Perhaps, however, he was shocked by the people's reaction, by their spontaneity, by their exuberance, by, above all, the sincerity of their love. The affection shown Darío was not affection by decree; it came from the heart and made the Patriarch aware that the true ruler of the people is the one who controls their hearts, rather than the one who controls their bodies. In Latin America, it is usually the poet, not the president, who speaks for the people. This is why literature is much more powerful in the national life of Latin American countries than it is, for example, in the United States or in Canada. This is why so many poets have been presidents of their country, why the voice of García Márquez himself is so influential, and why Darío can be considered, both with and without irony, the "poet of America." It is indeed fitting that Darío be singled out for special homage in *The Autumn of the Patriarch*.

More than homage is being rendered to the Nicaraguan poet; the text announces, or reminds us, of his apotheosis. The religious phrase "the good news" ("gospel" is another translation) occurs but twice in the novel. One use is at the very end, when the world is informed of "la buena nueva" (which Rabassa mistranslates, in my opinion, as "the jubilant news") that the Patriarch has died. The "gospel" here announces the death of a tyrant, not the coming of a messiah. The other occurrence of the phrase is associated with messianic thinking. Many years before, the crowds which had been singing hymns exalting the Patriarch got down on their knees in the hot sun and, kneeling all the while, began to "celebrate the good news that God had been brought in on a ship general sir" (*Autumn*, p. 176; *Otoño*, p. 178). The God being celebrated is Rubén Darío. This deification, given the history of Latin America, is in part ironic.

The Patriarch's literary genealogy is impressive. Through intertextual methodology and the transformation of prior myths, García Márquez associates him with classical literature, history, with one of the most famous prototypes of the dictator (Julius Caesar); with the history of the New World, with the beginning of Latin American literature (Christopher Columbus); and, finally, with one of the demigods of that literature itself (Rubén Darío). The practice of intertextuality does not ensure literary greatness. What distinguishes García Márquez's practice from that of so many others is the degree of thematic, stylistic, and symbolic integration which his subtexts achieve in the undeniably brilliant product. Although it is possible to read the novel with pleasure without being aware of its subtexts, they enrich our experience of the novel profoundly and deepen our understanding of the Patriarch, a character who, after all is said and done, holds an honorary position in the literary history of the tyrant in Latin America.

From *Gabriel García Márquez and the Powers of Fiction*, Julio Ortega, ed., 34-60. Copyright © 1988 by The University of Texas Press. Reprinted by permission.

Notes

1. I analyze a number of mythical metamorphoses in my recent book entitled *Gabriel García Márquez: La línea, el círculo y las metamorfosis del mito* (Madrid: Gredos, 1983), from which I freely translated and adapted the present essay. I am grateful to Gredos for allowing me to publish a translation and revision of part of my book.

2. See, for example, Julia Kristeva, *Semeotiké: Recherches pour une sémanalyse* (Paris: Editions du Seuil, 1969) and Jeanine Parisier Plottel, ed., *Intertextuality: New Perspectives in Criticism* (New York: New York Literary Forum, 1978).

In *The Pursuit of Signs* Jonathan Culler lucidly defines intertextuality in a way that emphasizes its dual nature. "On the one hand," writes Culler, intertextuality "calls our attention to the importance of prior texts, insisting that the autonomy of texts is a misleading notion and that a work has the meaning it does only because certain things have previously been written. Yet in so far as it focuses on intelligibility, on meaning, 'intertextuality' leads us to consider prior texts as contributions to a code which makes possible the various effects of signification. Intertextuality thus becomes less a name for a work's relation to particular prior texts than a designation of its participation in the discursive space of a culture: the relationship between a text and the various languages or signifying practices of a culture and its relation to those texts which articulate for it the possibilities of that culture" (*The Pursuit of Signs: Semiotics, Literature, Deconstruction* [Ithaca: Cornell University Press, 1981], p. 103).

In relation to García Márquez, Culler's definition means not only that prior texts are important to the "meaning" of *The Autumn of the Patriarch*, but also that the use of Julius Caesar, Christopher Columbus, and Rubén Darío in the novel says something significant about Latin American culture and the way it views its dictators and men of power. For instance, the association of presidents with poets is a fairly natural one for Latin Americans. Colombia, after all, has had at least eight presidents who were also published poets.

3. See Lucien Dällenbach, "Intertexte et autotexte," *Poétique* 27 (1976): 282-296. This special issue of *Poétique* is entirely devoted to the theme of intertextuality.

4. Jorge Luis Borges, "Pierre Menard, Author of the *Quixote*," in *Labyrinths: Selected Stories and Other Writings*, ed. Donald A. Yates and James E. Irby (New York: New Directions, 1962), pp. 36-44. (Originally published as "Pierre Menard, autor del *Quijote*," in *Ficciones*, 1944.)

5. Gabriel García Márquez, *The Autumn of the Patriarch*, trans. Gregory Rabassa (New York: Harper and Row, 1976), p. 90. See *El otoño del patriarca* (Barcelona: Plaza y Janés, 1975), p. 93. Wherever possible, I either cite from English translations of the works in question or supply my own. Where it seems advisable to cite the original text in the body of this essay I do so. Hereafter, each reference to either the Spanish original or the English translation is included in parentheses in the body of my text.

6. Eva Norvind, "Intelectuales interrogan a GGM," in *García Márquez habla de García Márquez*, ed. Alfonso Rentería Mantilla (Bogotá: Rentería Editores, 1979), p. 152 (my translation). (This article was originally published in the magazine *Hombre de Mundo*, Mexico City, 1977.)

7. García Márquez has alluded to several of the other Caesars as well. To cite but two examples: Caligula forced parents to be present at the executions of their own children. When one of the fathers protested, insisting that he was too ill, Caligula ordered that the man be brought to the execution on a litter. The Patriarch demonstrates this kind of cruelty in the episode of the children's lottery. Also, the Caesar named Galba suffered so from gout that he could not even wear shoes on his swollen feet. The Patriarch's feet are described as those "of an elephant," and he suffers similarly.

8. See Suetonius, *The Lives of the Twelve Caesars*, trans. and ed. Joseph Gavorse (New York: Random House, 1931), p. 27. All citations from Suetonius are taken from this edition and translation.

9. See Plutarch, *Lives: The Translation Called Dryden's*, corrected and rev. A. H. Clough, vol. 4 (New York: Bigelow, Brown and Co., 1911), p. 349. All citations from Plutarch are taken from this edition and translation.

10. See Rentería, *García Márquez habla de García Márquez*, pp. 114-15.

11. See J. H. Elliott's summary of how, and how belatedly, Columbus acquired his posthumous fame, in *The Old World and the New (1492-1650)* (Cambridge: Cambridge University Press, 1970), pp. 10-12.

12. Ironically, for our purposes, Columbus himself also "fed" on prior myths and legends. During his first voyage, for instance, the legend of the Great Khan was constantly with him, and, in preparation for meeting the oriental potentate, he took along translators (no one, however, who knew either Chinese or Japanese) and letters of introduction. Columbus thought for a while that Cuba was part of the Khan's kingdom, and during the second voyage he forced his sailors to swear solemnly that Cuba was indeed part of the mainland and part of the Khan's kingdom. During the third voyage Columbus sought the Earthly Paradise, and believed he had found its entrance (it was in truth the mouth of the Orinoco River).

13. When *The Autumn of the Patriarch* was first published, critics largely ignored García Márquez's use of Columbus. Only Graciela Palau de Nemes had developed this theme in her brief but intelligent review of the novel, "Historicidad de la novela," *Hispamérica* 4, nos. 11-12 (1975): 173-183. Since then, other critics have looked at this aspect of the novel, the most recent being Martha Canfield. In the closing pages of her article on García Márquez's patriarch, she comments on both Columbus and Rubén Darío ("El patriarca de García Márquez: Padre, poeta y tirano," *Revista Iberoamericana*, nos. 128-129 [1984]: 1017-1056).

14. Rentería, *García Márquez habla de García Márquez*, p. 196 (my translation).

15. Ibid.

16. Ibid. There are a number of biographies of Columbus. The most complete and the best for English readers is Samuel Eliot Morison's *Admiral of the Ocean Sea*, first published in 1942.

17. Samuel Eliot Morison, trans. and ed., *Journals and Other Documents on the Life and Voyages of Christopher Columbus* (New York: The Heritage Press, 1963), pp. 64-66.

18. For a more detailed account of the mythical conception of the world, and of the function of repetition in it, see the introduction to my book on García Márquez (pp. 13-24).

19. The actions of Columbus, Cortés, and others were supported by an ideology of conquest which owed a great deal to the wars against the Moors for the reconquest of Spain. Concrete action in the New World was backed by theory, a theory which evolved, however, in response to the differences in the realities encountered. See J. H. Parry's brief but lucid exposition, *The Spanish Theory of Empire* (Cambridge: Cambridge University Press, 1940); and also the recent work by Tzvetan Todorov, *The Conquest of America* (1982, English translation by Richard Howard, New York: Harper and Row, 1983).

20. For greater detail on the comparison of the New World consciousnesses of Columbus and García Márquez, see my forthcoming article entitled "Prisms of Consciousness," in *Critical Perspectives on García Márquez* (Lincoln: University of Nebraska Press).

21. Rentería, *García Márquez habla de García Márquez*, p. 156 (my translation).

22. In an interview with Manuel Pereira, originally published in *Bohemia* (Cuba, 1979); reprinted in Rentería, *García Márquez habla de García Márquez*, p. 207 (my translation).

23. Interview, published first in "El Manifesto" (Bogotá, 1977); reprinted in Rentería, *García Márquez habla de García Márquez*, p. 166 (my translation).

24. Wherever possible, I have relied on Lysander Kemp's translations, published in *Selected Poems of Rubén Darío* (Austin: University of Texas Press, 1960).

25. Ibid., p. 53.

26. In her article entitled "Apuntes sobre el mito dariano en *El otoño del patriarca*," *Cuadernos Hispanoamericanos* 340 (October 1978): 71, Michèle Sarrailh states that the surname of Bendición Alvarado comes from one of Darío's aunts: Rita Darío de Alvarado.

27. The ghostly presences of both Manuela Sánchez and (at the very end) the figure of Death are reminiscent of a similar episode in Rubén Darío's life, described in his *Autobiografía* (1912). In that never forgotten nightmare, Darío saw himself reading late at night in the small living room of his home. To his right, there was a door which led to the bedroom. Through the open door Darío saw, at the end of the room, a ghostly figure. After looking away to clear the vision from his mind, Darío looked again. There, in the depths, he saw a white-robed figure; it was shrouded, as cadavers are, and it walked toward him. He screamed, but no one heard him. He screamed again, and still no one heard. He tried to flee, but the presence of the figure paralyzed him. He saw that it had no face but a human trunk. It had no arms but was about to embrace him. It had no legs but still it "walked." The odor of dead flesh permeated the room. Darío, in self-defense, tried to bite the ghost and suddenly he awakened, drenched in sweat. See Rubén Darío, *Obras completas* (Madrid: Afrodisio Aguado, 1950) 1: 34-35.

28. *Selected Poems of Rubén Darío*, trans. Kemp, pp. 73-75. Reprinted by permission from the University of Texas Press. Darío's poetry, admittedly, does not translate well. What is eloquence in Spanish tends toward bombast in English. The martial rhythms, so carefully worked out in the original, are almost impossible to replicate in translation. The epic vocabulary of the Spanish, which for every native speaker carries connotations of military music and stories of legendary exploits, pales in translation and loses much of its evocative power.

Biblical Justice and the Military Hero in Two Novels of Gabriel García Márquez_____

Lourdes Elena Morales-Gudmundsson

Lourdes Elena Morales-Gudmundsson addresses the concepts of justice and human rights expounded in the Judeo-Christian tradition as adapted by García Márquez in his novella *No One Writes to the Colonel* and the so-called dictator's novel, *The Autumn of the Patriarch*. Her discussion of the former focuses on the corruption of the world surrounding the protagonist, the cock as the embodiment of collective hope, and the waiting for a messianic letter that will redeem him. In her examination of the latter work, she meditates on the dictator's physical and spiritual dimensions, his God-like qualities, and his role as Antichrist and even as a Leviathan. In that respect, she analyzes the sea imagery in the book. Morales-Gudmundsson suggests, in somewhat forced fashion, that García Márquez, in his novels, builds what amounts to "a theology of justice."   — I.S.

Mikhail Bakhtin has most eloquently drawn attention to the multiplicity of sociolinguistic elements present and orchestrated in the novel. This is certainly a fundamental acknowledgment to make when studying the novels of Gabriel García Márquez who, like few others, has known how to "dialogue" effectively with the full gamut of human life. This study analyzes the ways in which two García Márquez novels—*No One Writes to the Colonel* and *The Autumn of the Patriarch*—dialogue with the concept of justice as it is present both in the Bible and in Latin American liberation theology.[1] García Márquez's definition of justice, though certainly not purposely Christian, does contain many important elements implicit in the biblical, Judeo-Christian understanding of that concept. The Colombian novelist finds in the Bible ready-made images and symbols that he will use to deconstruct received sociopolitical structures in order to build his case for the application of justice and love to broken human beings. Drawing on many of the fundamental tenets of liberation theology, he consistently breaks down human hypocrisies and uncovers individual and corporate injustice. Employing the biblical concept of justice and selected teachings of liberation theology, I will look at the manner in which García Márquez handles the theme of justice in these two novels and thereby extract his understanding of the concept.

Liberation theology begins with Moses at the burning bush, the point of departure for the story of Israel's deliverance from unjust captivity and the establishment of God's covenant with Israel, which is associated with the exercise of justice and mercy both by God and humanity (Motthabi 6). Liberation theologians also understand Christ's work on earth as one of liberation. Citing Paul, Gustavo Gutiérrez states that Christ frees us so that we may enjoy freedom (Gal. 5:1). Liberation from sin is important as a freeing from an egocentric withdrawal into oneself ("un repliegue egoísta sobre sí mismo"). Sin separates humanity from God, and it is the ultimate cause of all misery, injustice, and oppression in which human beings live (Gutiérrez, *Teología* 66). These facts reveal, furthermore, that behind every unjust structure, there is a personal or collective will responsible for injustice, a will to reject God and one's neighbor. In general, justice, as understood by liberation theology, "comprises not merely the cardinal virtues as inherent in persons, but the comprehensive moral rectitude of society and humankind, expressing itself in social order as opposed to disorder, particularly the radical disorder of the denial of human dignity . . . together with the radical disorder of neglect of the common good" (Clarke 59). In Latin America the fundamental assumption of liberation theology is that the present social order is founded on a principle of injustice: the exploitation of the many by the moneyed few. If the kingdom of God is to be ushered in by Christians, then they must contribute to bringing justice to society.

For liberationists, the axiomatic injustice at the heart of poverty calls for the Christian's highest virtue, love, a concept espoused by Gutiérrez and other Latin American theologians. José Porfirio Miranda argues that perhaps one of the most devastating mistakes of Christianity, under Greek influence, was to differentiate between love and justice. In fact, says Miranda, the Bible calls "justice" what later Christianity called the act of Christian love, "almsgiving" (14). He further points out that in the Magnificat ("He has filled the hungry with good things and sent the rich away empty" [Luke 1:53]), God is partial to the poor, a notion quite distant from the Greek idea of justice's blind impartiality (Miranda 17).

Finally, liberation theology picks up on the eschatological/soteriological as well as apocalyptical dimensions of this process of liberation/salvation in the Judeo-Christian tradition. Liberation at either the individual or the collective level is a type of the ultimate liberation for all who practice justice and mercy on the earth. The final liberation will occur, according to Revelation, with the entrance into the heavenly dispensation, a new heaven and a new earth, where justice and mercy will reign forever and ever. Salvation as understood in the Bible moves inexorably to a final conflagration of all that is unjust (Rev. 20:11-15).

García Márquez, always in tune with the realities surrounding him, enters into dialogue with the Christian concepts of justice as they are present in the Scriptures and in Latin American liberation theology. In his recently published biography of García Márquez, Bell-Villada points to the importance of the Bible in the novelist's formation as a thinker and writer. In a 1982 interview with the biographer, García Márquez said that he had begun to read the Bible as a teenager and that he was fascinated by "all the good stories" to be found there. His youthful journalistic work reveals that he was already experimenting with parodic uses of Biblical stories and figures as early as 1948 (Bell-Villada 75).

It is evident that García Márquez does not necessarily believe that the Christian gospel is the answer to social injustice, but neither is he reluctant to take from the Judeo-Christian system of thought what he can use to give a more universal character to the struggles of humanity for justice. By his own admission, García Márquez is interested in the

Bible as a primitive and gutsy text in which "fantastic things" happen (Mendoza 7). But he also seems interested in the durable structures, symbols, and themes that this text offers him as he searches for a useful framework for his treatment of some fundamental issues of human existence. Indeed, García Márquez seems very interested in what the Bible, as a document of Judeo-Christian culture, has to say about how the human being relates to the call of the higher virtues.

In his concern for human rights as the rights of the poor, García Márquez enters the flow of thinking that emanates from liberation theology every bit as much as from Marxism. Although García Márquez is a man who has always been politically committed to socialism, Camilo Torres Restrepo—one of his closest friends and the priest who baptized his son Rodrigo—was a liberation theologian and eventually a Marxist revolutionary. Certainly García Márquez's combined concern for justice and love—his persistent search for the important links between them—reveals that he was not unconscious of how the liberation theologians had already linked them.

Justice lies at the heart of the basic predicament of *No One Writes the Colonel*, a short novel whose protagonist is a retired colonel who is still waiting after many years for his well-deserved veteran's pension check. At the core of the novel is a biblical-liberationist theme: the plight of a poor man who seeks justice. Despite his having fought nobly for a worthy cause, those in a position to deal justly with the colonel have ignored him for years and, as if to add insult to injury, they have been responsible, directly or indirectly, for the death of his only son.

Regina Janes suggests that the original for many of the novelist's beaten old men was his grandfather, Colonel Nicolás Márquez Iguarán, who served under the Liberal General Rafael Uribe during the War of a Thousand Days (1899-1902) (10). Although Janes considers the War of a Thousand Days to be the ostensible setting for *No One Writes the Colonel*, Stephen Minta places the story somewhere around 1956 when Colombia had suffered through ten or more years of "la violencia," a period (approximately between the years of 1946 and 1966) of interminable wars between Liberals and Conservatives.[2] That the protagonist is a war veteran who is also a survivor of postwar political conflict is evident in the colonel's matter-of-fact observation, as he prepares to attend a funeral, that this is the first death by natural causes in his city for many years. In the story of a retired colonel, García Márquez has found both a typical and specific political-historical situation that breeds injustice in Latin America.

As opposed to the implied violence that surrounds and sporadically affects the decaying backwater town in which he lives, the colonel's life of implacable waiting is the only significant "activity." Waiting, in the novel, is a silent yet spiritually dynamic quest. On the surface, the colonel is simply waiting for a letter and a pension check for his services to his nation. However, two images with biblical resonances exacerbate the frustration and despair of the waiting and suggest some larger implications: the dead son and the fighting cock. The colonel's only treasured possession is a fighting cock that once belonged to his son, who died a martyr's death at the hands of ruthless government henchmen: he was distributing clandestine antigovernment flyers at a cockfight when he was gunned down. The colonel's tenacious insistence on keeping the cock, even when, at the end of the novel, the cock refuses to fight, and even if keeping it means starvation for him and his wife, represents his refusal to give up on justice.

Robin W. Fiddian uncovers some important aspects of the novel by which we may see how themes of caring for one's neighbor and the injustice of poverty are given form. Two of the three Christian elements he finds in the novel are of interest for our discussion: the idea of a corrupt and fallen world and the messiah figure (389). The idea that "the world is corrupted," enunciated early on in *No One Writes to the Colonel* (13), is associated with the hopeless waiting for the "Messiah" (justice in the colonel's particular case and overall collective and individual justice). Fiddian believes that the subsequent reference to the civil war fought in Macondo by Colonel Aureliano Buendía suggests that the defeat of the Liberal cause in the War of a Thousand Days reenacted the fall of the world. Yet the suggestion of continued violence throughout the novel implies that the time in which the colonel is holding his implacable vigil for justice continues to belong to that apocalyptical time in which the world is predominantly corrupt and evil, and thereby ready for deliverance.

The corrupt world motif reappears when the colonel goes to sell the cock to Don Sabas. The reference to the "sky falling" indicates a present apocalypse (45), characterized by indifference to the neighbor and injustice toward the poor. The messiah theme is inevitably linked with the theme of waiting for deliverance from injustice when the colonel expresses his hope that there may be incorrupt elections this year. The doctor who hears him replies: "Don't be so naïve, colonel. . . . We're too old now to be waiting for the Messiah" (66). But justice is foremost in the mind of this forgotten military hero, obsessed with the arrival of a letter of exoneration and his pension check, precisely because he is that "neighbor" to whom justice is due. His hope for deliverance from poverty and death and for justice to return to the earth is a hope for the return of the Messiah; waiting for the letter is a type of the other more significant waiting for justice.

Why is this waiting so intensely painful? The answer arises out of the colonel's keen sense of the injustice and his awareness of himself as a victim. This realization is made all the keener by its obvious links to liberation theology's concept of the individual. The individual possesses a kind of authenticating creativity, the freedom of the authentic person, a privilege that ought not be limited to the wealthy and the powerful. The poverty-ridden colonel refuses to succumb to an inevitable destiny. Just as he fought on the battlefield for collective justice, so now the dispossessed military man fights for personal justice, as well as for a larger justice in which his son is implicated. In the end, the colonel's fight for justice takes the form of his refusal to sell the cock in the face of hopeless poverty and cruel government indifference.

As to the meanings that can be attached to the cock, it should be noted that Mario Vargas Llosa was among the first to see the cock as the embodiment of the people's collective hope for change. But, as Minta aptly points out, the long-awaited cockfight (where change was to begin) is anticlimactic: neither the colonel's cock nor the other one want to fight (78). If the cock represents hope for change, the failure to fight reveals the hopelessness and beaten will of the people. However, Fiddian argues persuasively that the cock represents rather the dead son, as messiah, given the other New Testament elements that complement the theme. He suggests that the dead son is an allusion to the hope for a risen messiah (390-92).

The cock reveals the government's treason and so becomes a two-pronged symbol of justice: justice for the colonel and justice for a nation rife with political wars. At the historical level, within the fiction of the novel, the colonel who has fought bravely for a just cause is waiting to receive his just reward. The inherent injustice in futile waiting is exacerbated by the death of his son, another courageous "soldier" in the battle for justice. But García Márquez will go one step further to suggest that one death—the death of the son with all its biblical echoes—can bring collective life in that it keeps hope for justice alive. At the mythic-biblical level, that death is hope-filled, in that it is a vicarious one that must come so that new seed may grow into the sturdy plants of justice. At this level, waiting for the messiah is concomitant with an indestructible hope in the triumph of personal, social, and political justice.

But does García Márquez believe in such a sweeping triumph?[3] The novelist seems to echo the determined optimism both of Scripture and liberation theology. The prophetic literature of the Old and New Testaments attests to an ultimate liberation. Comfort and hope offered to the poor in Isaiah is always given in light of the call to obedience (implying the exercise of love and justice in the present) which in turn brings on the reward, understood as restoration and eternal life. Gutiérrez certainly believed in the abolition of the exploitation of human beings by human beings, and Miranda picks up on the biblical *eschaton* implicit in history by stating that every small effort in favor of justice contributes to the consummation of all things (296). The final, defiant stance of the colonel in the face of crass injustice suggests that the author, too, shares a similar belief in victory for good on the earth.

The Autumn of the Patriarch is the work in which García Márquez most successfully merges biblical images with liberationist themes to expose the fundamental sinfulness at the heart of the human struggle for power that creates human injustice. He works out this multifaceted problem by using familiar biblical figures and motifs to reveal the crass selfishness and pathetic frailties that lead to injustice. The apocalyptic setting for the nefarious career of the dictator protagonist, through his early years of popular idolatry to his demise in utter isolation, is seen from the perspective of "judgment," a view that allows for hope in an otherwise hopeless review of Mind brutality. The textual association of the dictator with the biblical antichrist (8) clearly places the events of the novel in a kind of time-prior-to-consummation that precedes the introduction of a new and presumably better era. Here again the author draws on received Christian eschatological notions that serve him well to organize events and employ evocative images to characterize the dictator and his people.

The military figure here is none other than the Latin American general as dictator. García Márquez has said that the dictator is the only mythological figure that Latin America has ever produced (Minta 95). Unwilling to create yet another unilateral monster, like the dictators of other Latin American novelists, García Márquez employs parodic biblical figures and themes to demythologize the dictator. The confrontation of the people with their dictator appeals to a fundamentally liberationist theme: the obligation of political leaders to be the guardians of social justice. The entire book is the story of a people's liberation from their tyrant through the gradual revelation of the true nature, not only of political slavery, but of human selfishness, the antithesis of human love. This revelation is set out in terms of various parodied biblical and Christian motifs that underscore the cosmic dimensions of the battle: the dictator as patriarch, almighty god, and messianic figure is juxtaposed to the dictator as satanic antichrist and apocalyptic beast. The author also plays with the concept of the Trinity to reveal the futile attempts of the dictator to create a kind of triune godhead, under his command, who will rule the world made in his image.

The ultimate meaning of justice is suggested in the very structure of the novel, divided up into chapters introduced repeatedly by the same scene: the people discover the rotting body of the dictator in what remains of his once-luxurious palace. Somehow the horror that seems to cling to every page is mitigated by this persistent reminder that justice will triumph over the ill-gotten glory of humanity, a recurrent theme in García Márquez's novels. More importantly, for our study of justice, the entire book is organized around biblical sea imagery, very closely related in the biblical writings with Satan (as sea monster) and the chaotic dwelling place of evil. The dictator's betrayal of the "royal covenant" with his people is given in terms of biblical images associated with the biblical king-messiah—often portrayed in Scripture as winning victories for the people by slaying the dragon of the deep or quelling the turbulent sea.[4] As a kind of human-satanic antichrist, the dictator-patriarch, on the one hand, takes on the sea as his private property to dispose of as he wills. On the other hand, the satanic antichrist becomes a victim of that sea, a drowning man.

The dictator as godlike figure is everywhere in the novel. According to popular opinion, he can make the world stop at his command or be omnipresent, if he so chooses. It is later discovered that his reputed omnipresence is a ploy to confuse people into thinking that he is a god: he has hired a perfect "other" in the form of Patricio Aragonés, his double. The link with the biblical deity becomes evident in the implied "covenant" with the people that the patriarch-god has not kept. The Old Testament concept of justice is one of liberation from spiritual servitude—"You shall have no other gods before me" (Ex. 20:3)—as well as from sociopolitical injustice and slavery. It is precisely in this relationship to his people that the dictator is seen as having violated a covenant of trust at both the personal and political levels.

The idolatry inherent in his ascent to deity is, ironically, fashioned by those he most disdains. In the early years, when he still believes that the people love him, he basks in the servility with which the men, women, and children of the city leave what they are doing to shout his praises as the royal coach rolls by. He is referred to as the "nameless patriot who sits at the right hand of the Holy Trinity" (16). Later, he is no longer a mere aristocrat, but a veritable god figure. So convinced is he of his godlike status that he is amazed that when he dies (in the person of his double, Patricio Aragonés) the sun rises the next day and life continues as usual (34). Rhonda Buchanan, in a Jungian reading of the novel, sees the dictator as an impotent man hounded by a serious moral and psychological affliction that Jung calls "psychic inflation" (77). In his desperate search to be omnipotent, the patriarch compensates for his inadequacies by identifying with his office—he is the government. His deep-seated sense of personal deficiency, however, leads constantly to anxiety about the loss of power. The turning point in his delusions of grandeur is the disappearance of Manuela Sánchez, the beauty queen who disdains his love. He suddenly feels "older than God" (83), and begins to cultivate the solitude that will alienate him from others and even from himself.

The dictator clearly reveals a very human need for love, but his inability to give it or receive it on anybody's terms but his own is consistently underscored. Martha Canfield describes the dictator here as a pathetic being who establishes a relation of possessive love with the people, a man engaged in an obsessive search for a response to his love, but unable to understand the give and take inherent in the love relationship (1020). The multivoiced narration, which changes back and forth between the voice of the people and that of the other characters, is careful to point out the decay of the dictator in terms of his increasing unwillingness to give love as well as to take it. Hours before his death, he will suddenly assume the arbitrary prerogatives of an angry and vengeful god who invokes his creative powers to quell his fears of death (268), but now there is nobody to follow his commands.

With respect to the dictator's "infidelity" to his people, we are re-minded of the liberationist concept of covenant. Assman, for example, sees God's covenant as having "life" and "human life" as its funda-mental reason for being. Therefore, God has entrusted human beings with the mission of perpetuating, enriching, and protecting life (10). In the novel, the covenant relationship of the patriarch to the poor is vio-lated in his unwillingness to see his neighbor as a true "other" rather than as a mere extension of his inordinate ego. The closest he comes to a sense of the other is when he allows room in his life for his favorites—Patricio Aragonés, Rodrigo de Aguilar, Leticia Nazareno, and finally the ruthless José Ignacio Sáenz de la Barra—all of them, as it turns out, mere Jungian shadow archetypes or moral reflections of the egocentric personality of the dictator (Buchanan 77) and eminently expendable. Indeed, he ignores the poor's right to think for themselves and refuses to acknowledge their inalienable autonomy. He has succeeded, like the exploiters of whom liberationists so insistently complain, in separating ethics from politics and social life, so that he is free to manipulate the people for his purposes.

The messianic figure is the most eloquent allusion to liberation in the novel. The biblical Messiah comes to save the poor and enslaved from their oppressors. In the novel, the patriarch as an inversion of the biblical Messiah appears in the context of the structural violence that characterizes his domain of power. Liberationists understand "struc-tural violence" to mean a social order that by necessity allows the few to receive the fruits of the work of the many, an "order" that ironically guarantees political disorder on the one hand, and powerlessness of the victims on the other. Violence, not freedom, is the mechanism used to maintain the status quo and effect change (García 27).

Liberationist analysis shows how the most effective way for oppres-sors to achieve a semblance of social order is to make the poor accept the present state of affairs as natural. The slow process of "desengaño" or disillusionment, the realization that their myth is being dismantled before their eyes, is set against the people's credulity and their acceptance of the status quo dictated by their betrayer. The dictator's messianic character is in fact attributed to him by the people, at first, and later by his adulators, who cooperate with him in rewriting and recreating reality as well as history for the people. The biblical patriarch ostensibly elicits admiration and suggests heroic pioneering on behalf of the people. But the messianic role of liberation and justice is consistently countermanded by the dictator's self-serving attempts to set up a comfortable trinity consisting of himself as a kind of God the Father and Son rolled into one, his mother, Bendición Alvarado, as a kind of Virgin Mary (she is believed to have conceived him without the intervention of man [47]), and his political favorites who carry out his commands, as a kind of Holy Spirit.

Unable to have his almighty will done on earth, the patriarch turns to a kind of matriarchal idolatry that serves as a means of private "salvation." There are clear echoes of the Virgin Mary in the "immaculate" mother figure to whom the dictator confesses his joys and woes (48-53) and whom he invokes to strengthen him in his isolated battle to retain power: "he passed by the windows with a heavy heart crying out mother of mine Bendición Alvarado illuminate me with your wisest lights . . ." (247). But this mother worship is yet another outgrowth of his self-serving exercise of what he understands love to mean. The savior role and its concomitant ushering in of a just world are undermined consistently by the dictator's incapacity to understand how love saves.

Perhaps one of the easiest associations to make between the dictator and Christian concepts is that of the antichrist. The Christian understanding of this figure originates in Saint Paul's references to "that man of sin" who must come before Christ's return to earth at the end of time. Although the concept is not always clearly delineated, there is a connection between apocalypse and antichrist in all Catholic Christian thinking. Siemens has already studied the antichrist figure as García Márquez employs it in this novel (113-21), but it is important to remember that in Christian thought the antichrist is a satanic formulation. García Márquez attempts not only to depict the dictator in the role of an optimally evil man (like the antichrist), but to project the dictator's character and actions onto the larger setting of the satanic or evil forces that ever fight against good on this earth. To achieve this larger connection in the mind of the reader, García Márquez depicts the dictator in exaggeratedly grotesque lines. What emerges is a larger-than-life caricature who takes on the cosmically evil qualities of a Satan figure, even as he assumes the pathetic doom of a defeated antichrist.

On the one hand, we are given the physical and "spiritual" dimensions of the dictator through the "official" elementary school textbooks—a kind of beneficent giant who loves children and birds and whose secret potion heals lepers and the lame. He is a miraculous being "who had the virtue of being able to anticipate the designs of nature, who could guess a person's thought by one look in the eyes, and who had the secret of a salt with the virtue of curing lepers' sores and making cripples walk" (46). Those same textbooks tell how he is the product of an immaculate conception, his mother discovering his "messianic destiny" in a dream (47). However, as the reader is introduced to the truly weak, pathetically clownish, and endemically evil nature of the patriarch, the ironic messianic/redemptive imagery gives way to animalistic and diabolic associations. The relentless references to the man as a slow-moving, heavy-footed, elephant-like beast place him squarely in the animal realm and, more importantly, in the metaphoric lineage with such biblical monsters as Behemoth, a ferocious-looking but mild-mannered land beast somewhat like the hippopotamus or the prehistoric mastodon. However, the dictator is more obviously associated with another of the biblical monsters, namely Leviathan, a kind of twistingly sinister sea monster (Isa. 27:1). When John refers to Satan as a dragon in Revelation, he is drawing on this Old Testament association between the sea, the sea monsters, and Satan, who will be destroyed at the end of the world (cf. Ps. 74:13-15).

That we are meant to associate the dictator with Leviathan is evident in the patriarch's insignia: a dragon. Furthermore, the dictator's cold-blooded reptile-like eyes (154), which blink while still open (124), draw on the reptilian imagery (in this case, the reptile is an iguana) that so often is associated with the biblical devil. The indifference with which he assassinates army generals and children alike (115) and his penchant for vengeance (238) underscore the unfeeling, satanic nature of this military prince of implacable injustice.

We have already seen, how the satanic is often associated with the sea in biblical literature. The conflict Yahweh of the Old Testament and the Christ of the New wage with the satanic adversary is a common thread that runs through the entire Bible into later Christian theology. In that context, the appearance of the dragon in the sea is a common combat image. The powerful and comprehensive way García Márquez uses the sea motif reveals a more than casual understanding of its biblical form and function. As in its biblical context, the sea/waters imagery in the novel is associated with the eventual triumph of justice over the powers of evil.

The sea imagery is set out like the two faces of a coin: the sea as the arena of confusion (the biblical dwelling place of Satan, cf. Ps. 104:2-9) and the sea as masses of peoples (Dan. 7:2-7, 16-17; Rev. 13:1). García Márquez uses the confusion model to structure *The Autumn of the Patriarch*. Like a monstrous satanic creature, the dictator exercises his power in the midst of a seemingly endless confusion of people who are treated like marketable wares. His indulgence in egocentric acts of aggression against the people places the dictator in direct line with biblical associations between evil and the sea. The author seems aware of the biblical sea, with all of its implications of evil and peoples and salvation, when he lets his protagonist die the victim of a drowning.

As we begin the novel, the nature of the dictator's death slowly becomes evident to us. We are first told that it was commonly believed that the dictator's demise would coincide with a number of cataclysmic events: "on the day of his death the mud from the swamps would go back upriver to its source, that it would rain blood, that hens would lay pentagonal eggs, and the silence and darkness would cover the universe once more because he was the end of creation" (125). Prophecy here, however, is equivalent only to mere superstition. In the end, the dictator dies in spite of prophecies and quite differently from the dramatic way it was commonly predicted he would die.

What, then, is the significance of his death by drowning, a kind of death emphasized by the repeated description of the corpse opening each chapter? The visual image is that of a cadaver tossed on a lonely shore where we are allowed to stand and look out over the dark, chaotic waters in which the narrators and their dictator have lived out their life. The dictator's habitation of the sinister deep is hinted at early on when we are told what happens when he takes his siesta. A wave washes over the city and the nation when he sleeps the sleep of a "solitary drowned man" floating "face down on the lunar waters of his dreams" (9-10). After his death, the people find that his body "was sprouting tiny lichens and parasitic animals from the depths of the sea" (6). Later, as they prepare the body for burial, they will have to scrape off with fish scalers the "deep-sea shark suckers" from the body (166). The characterization of the dead dictator as a parasite-infested waste product of the sea clearly points to his role as insidious destroyer whose apocalypse has arrived so that the reign of justice can now begin.

The biblical imagery of the sea as peoples or nations is related to the last and worst offense of the dictator: the sale of the sea to foreign interests. Throughout the story, the patriarch is depicted as having a special love for the Caribbean sea that his palace overlooks—a precarious love, as it turns out, similar to the "love" he has for his people. Again, this love is revealed as self-serving in that when he must give it up to preserve his power, it, too, is expendable. The sea, just as his people, can be sold for a price. This trafficking in masses of people through the sale of the sea is rich with apocalyptic overtones, in that it constitutes the supreme act of injustice.

The absence of the sea has echoes of the other meaning of the biblical sea. After the general desolation of the earth and the destruction of the dragon or Satan, John finally sees in a vision a new earth, and he observes that "there was no longer any sea" (Rev. 21:1). The betrayal of his people by the dictator-antichrist-Satan reaches its climax in this supreme act of utter egotism. At this point, the sea ceases to be the dictator's dominion and becomes his executioner. Those same people whom he would so easily betray will take their sweetest revenge on their dictator by outliving him and taking up life after his "eternal" reign. This pivotal victory is at the core of a book that reveals García Márquez's faith in the eventual triumph of love and justice.

In both *No One Writes to the Colonel* and *The Autumn of the Patriarch* the Colombian novelist uses various biblical and liberationist concepts to build his own theology of justice. He has chosen the military man as the focus of these stories of injustice because the latter's privileged position within Spanish-American society allows for a more comprehensive understanding of what is heroic and demonic in Latin American society as it relates to the underlying theme of justice.

On one hand, in the *Colonel*, the liberationist idea of rediscovering the biblical neighbor complements the focus on the injustice of poverty, and both concepts are set in the context of apocalypse, a time of supreme wickedness that culminates a long period of waiting and precedes deliverance. The colonel's determination to have justice is firmly rooted in his faith in the essential dignity of the individual and the possibility of transforming society. The affinity with Latin American liberationists is also seen in the blame placed on negligent political leaders who ignore those whom they have been called to serve. On the other hand, to depict the universal implications of human injustice, García Márquez employs the biblical Christ/Son figure and the cock to capture the deep betrayal inherent in injustice in general and in the particular injustice being perpetrated on the poverty-stricken war hero. The persistence of injustice contrasts with the colonel's uncompromising faith in the eventual triumph of justice; the cock as symbol of the indomitable human spirit makes waiting for the cause of the messianic, sacrificed son bearable and even heroic.

In both novels, García Márquez sets forth liberationist ideas and ideals through a reworking of biblical motifs with the ultimate purpose of communicating his own understanding of justice. There is a clear underlying optimism in both novels, but they are laid out in less-than-rose-colored terms. The evil at the core of political-military power denies the colonel justice; the evil at the core of the dictator denies justice to an entire nation. In both novels, the struggle for justice is not limited to the political arena—it launches into the moral and spiritual realms of human selfishness that are set against the exercise of human love. The dialogue with biblical images and liberationist themes is the indispensable means by which the author first understands the parameters of the problem, then sets it out for the reader's consideration: How can human love grow in a context of blatant injustice, even if it has been accepted as the status quo? In the end, García Márquez clings to his faith in the victory of good over evil, love over selfishness, while still recognizing the wretchedness of the human heart.

From *Postcolonial Literature and the Biblical Call for Justice*, Susan VanZanten Gallagher, ed., 60-73. Copyright ©1994 by the University Press of Mississippi. Reprinted by permission.

Notes

1. *El coronel no tiene quien le escriba* (1961) was first published in English as *No One Writes to the Colonel* in 1968. The first English edition of *El otoño del patriarca* (1975) appeared as *The Autumn of the Patriarch* in 1976. Subsequent references are made parenthetically to these English editions.

2. Minta has carefully researched Colombian political history. Quoting James Payne, he states, "On a scale of political deaths per generation, Colombia has one of the highest levels of political conflict in the world" (5-6). In the first century of its independence, Colombia went through thirteen periods of violent political strife, some lasting four to five years. R. W. Ramsey, according to Minta, called this prolonged struggle, the "western hemisphere's largest internal war in the twentieth century [which has] led to ¼ of a million deaths" (6).

3. Janes aptly summarizes the novelist's political optimism: "García Márquez calls himself a revolutionary socialist, and it might be said that his confidence in the eventual triumph of a socialism that permits the bourgeois liberty of the imagination is as chimerical as levitating with cups of chocolate: neither seems to be occurring in the immediate present. . . . But the belief in a future order that is to transcend the present,

curing all our social, political, and economic ills, freed him from the internal compulsion and the external obligation to render those ills in a realistic mode, while the belief in the necessity of such a transformation keeps him anchored in our world where those ills are all too apparent" (9).

4. Gen. 1:2; Job 9:5-14; Ps. 74:12-17; 89:10-15; and Isa. 51:9-11. Forsyth traces the combat myth in the Bible from its pagan source through St. Augustine's "Genesis." The conflict between God and the adversary is a common thread that runs through the entire Bible into later Christian theology. In that context, the appearance of the dragon in the sea is a common combat image (44-66). Prophetic literature portrays nations as beasts that arise out of the tumultuous "sea," a reference to peoples or multitudes (Dan. 7:2-7, 16-17; Rev. 13:1). The sea as "mythological enemy" (Forsyth 256) and as peoples serves the novelist well as a means to contextualize the final triumph of justice. It also allows him to do what the Book of Revelation does: it lets him project political repression onto the cosmic stage (Forsyth 257) in order to work out the apocalyptic victory of good over evil.

Works Cited

Assman, Hugo. *Practical Theology of Liberation*. London: Search P, 1975.

Bakhtin, Mikhail M. *The Dialogical Imagination: Four Essays by M. M. Bakhtin*. Ed. Michael Holquist. Trans. Gary Saul Morson and Caryl Emerson. Evanston: Northwestern UP, 1989.

Bell-Villada, Gene H. *García Márquez: The Man and His Work*. Chapel Hill: U of North Carolina P, 1990.

Buchanan, Rhonda L. "The Cycle of Rage and Order in García Márquez' *El otoño del patriarca*." *Perspectives on Contemporary Literature* 10 (1984): 75-85.

Canfield, Martha L. "El patriarca de García Márquez: Padre, poeta, tirano." *Revista iberoamericana* 50.128-129 (1984): 1017-56.

Clarke, Thomas E. "Spirituality, Justice, and Cultural Evangelization." *Religious Education* 83.1 (1988): 53-66.

Fiddian, Robin W. "Two Aspects of Technique in *El coronel no tiene quien le escribe*." *Neophilologus* 69.1 (1985): 386-93.

Forsyth, Neil. *The Combat Myth*. New Haven: Yale UP, 1990.

García, Matías. *La iglesia, el cristiano y la política*. Madrid: Ed. HOAC, 1968.

García Márquez, Gabriel. *The Autumn of the Patriarch*. Trans. Gregory Rabassa. New York: Harper, 1976.

――――――. *No One Writes to the Colonel*. Trans J. S. Bernstein. New York: Harper, 1968.

Gutiérrez, Gustavo. "Criticism Will Deepen, Clarify Liberation Theology." *Liberation Theology: A Documentary History*. Ed. Alfred T. Hennelly. Maryknoll, NY: Orbis, 1990. 419-25.

The Holy Bible, New International Version. Colorado Springs: International Bible Association, 1983.

Janes, Regina. *Gabriel García Márquez: Revolutions in Wonderland*. Columbia: U of Missouri P, 1981.

Mendoza, Plinio Apuleyo. *El olor a la guayaba*. Buenos Aires: Ed. Sudamericana, 1982.

Minta, Stephen. *Gabriel García Márquez: Writer of Colombia*. London: Jonathan Cape, 1987.

Miranda, José Porfirio. *Marx y la Biblia*. Salamanca: Ed. Sígueme, 1972.

Motthabi, Mokgethi. "Liberation Theology: An Introduction." *Liberation Theology and the Bible*. Ed. Pieter G. R. de Villiers. Pretoria: U of South Africa P, 1987.

Siemens, William L. "The Antichrist-Figure in Three Latin American Novels." *The Power of Myth in Literature and Film*. Ed. Victor Carrabino. Tallahassee: UP of Florida, 1980. 113-21.

Vargas Llosa, Mario. Interview. *Die Zeit* 30 March 1990: 17-18.

The Dangers of Gullible Reading:
Narrative as Seduction in García Márquez'
*Love in the Time of Cholera*_____

M. Keith Booker

> M. Keith Booker's argument is that the saccharine flavor readers might experience after delving into *Love in the Time of Cholera* is only a surface response, and that embedded in the narrative are a series of traps about duplicity and power. Booker compares the novel with Flaubert's *Madame Bovary* as well as with Nabokov's *Lolita*. He argues that García Márquez's novel is not only about romance but also about politics and history. He focuses on the way Doctor Juvenal Urbino approaches things differently from the septuagenarian lovers Florentino Ariza and Fermina Daza.   — I.S.

Initial critical reaction to Gabriel García Márquez' *Love in the Time of Cholera* has been positive, even rhapsodic, and most readers have found the book to be an uplifting affirmation of the human spirit, the author's kindest and gentlest work. Gene Bell-Villada is typical: even while recognizing that overly romantic attitudes are sometimes the subject of satire in the book, he still concludes that *Love* is basically "a good old-fashioned love story" (191). Indeed, Bell-Villada goes on to applaud García Márquez for his "courage and originality in writing a novel of love (a subject traditionally thought of as the preserve of younger authors) when on the verge of old age" (202). But *Love* is a complex work, and as García Márquez himself has said of it in an interview, "you have to be careful not to fall into my trap" (Williams 136). *Love in the Time of Cholera* is indeed a novel of love, but it is also much more, and Mabel Moraña probably gets closer to the heart of the matter when she suggests that it is "like other texts in the narrative saga of García Márquez, a reflection on power" (40).

The theme of love in the novel focuses on the lifelong fascination of Florentino Ariza with Fermina Daza, a fascination that is strongly informed by Ariza's own excessively romantic attitude toward life. This attitude derives largely from Ariza's gullible reading of bad literature, and the echo here of Flaubert's *Madame Bovary* is surely more than accidental. But there are more links between the texts of Flaubert and of García Márquez than this obvious one. In particular, the association with Flaubert provides a useful entry point into *Love* as a meditation on power as well as an exploration of romanticism. Near the end of *Madame Bovary* the sinister and self-promoting pharmacist Homais compiles a list of the credentials that he believes qualify him for the cross of the Legion of Honor, which he will in fact eventually win. Among these accomplishments, he congratulates himself for the "devotion" he showed doing his professional duty "in the time of the cholera" (253).[1] Perhaps one should not make too much of the fact that García Márquez verbally echoes this passage from Flaubert in the title of his novel, especially as the title functions on a number of levels within García Márquez' own text.[2] The echo may even be coincidental. But in the richly intertextual work of García Márquez such correspondences often bear surprising fruit when harvested carefully, even when the seeds have not originally been planted by the author. For example, García Márquez himself has identified "allusions" in *One Hundred Years of Solitude* to works he had not even read at the time he wrote his book (Janes 7). In any case, it is clear that *Madame Bovary* is of major importance as a source for *Love*, and the illumination provided by reading García Márquez through Flaubert is considerably enriched by bringing Homais into the picture, since Flaubert's manipulative pharmacist-vulgarian calls attention to the quests for power and domination that constitute a central theme of García Márquez' novel as well.

Most obviously, Homais is a representative of the philistine impulses that Flaubert so abhorred in the society of his contemporary France. But more than that, he is a generalized figure of the bad aspects of Enlightenment thinking. He prides himself on his education, his knowledge, and his scientific approach to things, and—following the Baconian dictum that "knowledge is power"—he puts his talents to use in furthering his own ambitions and in manipulating those around him for his own ends. As such he recalls the critique of Enlightenment thinking put forth by Max Horkheimer and Theodor Adorno in *The Dialectic of Enlightenment*. Horkheimer and Adorno suggest that the scientific impetus of the Enlightenment is informed by a quest not for a liberating truth, but for a power that ultimately enslaves: "What men want to learn from nature is how to use it in order to wholly dominate it and other men" (*Dialectic* 4). In particular, they suggest that the emphasis on the power of the individual in Enlightenment thought is related to a drive to dominate nature, a drive that inevitably turns back upon itself and leads to the formation of individuals who are internally repressed and of societies consisting of individual subjects who strive for domination of each other.

The Horkheimer/Adorno critique of the Enlightenment is also clearly relevant to the concerns of García Márquez' fiction. In *One Hundred Years of Solitude* José Arcadio Buendía insists on putting the scientific knowledge of the gypsy Melquíades to work for practical technological use, but his attempts to dominate nature through science invariably fail—and often in ways that recall Horkheimer and Adorno quite directly. For example, when José Arcadio attempts to use the gypsy's magnets to locate gold he finds instead an ancient suit of Spanish armor, with its associated echoes of imperial domination. In general, the citizens of Macondo find technological progress to be not liberating, but enslaving.[3] Science and technology also figure as negative forces in *Love*, particularly in the way that technological "progress" has led to the degradation of Colombia's natural environment and to the destruction of the Great Magdalena River that figures so centrally in the book. But García Márquez is no Luddite, and his argument is not with technological progress per se.[4] Instead, the link to Horkheimer and Adorno (courtesy of Flaubert's Homais) indicates that the real target of García Márquez' criticisms of the negative side of progress is the kind of ideology of domination that informs not only Enlightenment science, but a whole variety of other mechanisms of power as well, including imperialism, totalitarianism, and the Latin American tradition of *machismo*. A look at *Love* through the optic of these issues shows a book far more complex than the sweetly sentimental love story it is often perceived to be.

The character in *Love* whom Homais resembles most is Dr. Juvenal Urbino. Urbino is, on the surface at least, a rather admirable figure, if a little stiff and conventional. He is intelligent, educated, successful, an image of the kind of enlightened man who might bring hope of a better life to the benighted inhabitants of García Márquez' fictionalized Colombia. But a comparison with Homais helps to reveal certain ominous cracks and fissures in the surface of this depiction of Urbino. For example, one begins to wonder whether Urbino's rise to social and professional prominence might partake of some of the ruthlessly self-serving ambition that drives Homais onward toward the cross of the Legion of Honor. Indeed, Urbino himself is not above accepting honors, including being granted the rank of Commander in that same Legion (43). Finally, especially if Homais is read through Horkheimer and Adorno, aspects of Urbino's character such as the fact that he is so thoroughly "in control of his nature" begin to take on undertones of a drive for domination that may inform all of the good doctor's activities (105).

When we first meet Urbino at the beginning of the book we learn that he is a man very much accustomed to being in charge of whatever situation he may encounter. He arrives on the scene of the suicide of his friend Jeremiah de Saint-Amour, bullies the police inspector, and orders that the press be told that the death occurred due to natural causes (5-6). These actions, of course, can be interpreted as a perfectly understandable attempt to protect the memory of his friend, though it is telling that Urbino refuses to intercede with the Archbishop so that Saint-Amour can be buried on holy ground. And Urbino shows another negative side to his character when he reads Saint-Amour's suicide note and learns that his friend had been not a political exile as he had thought, but an escaped convict. Further, he discovers that Saint-Amour had been carrying on a clandestine sexual relationship for years. These revelations offend Urbino's self-righteous sense of propriety, and he shows not understanding, but disgust, rejecting his friend's memory. And when Urbino's wife Fermina Daza expresses sympathy for the dead Saint-Amour, Urbino violently explains to her the reason for his revulsion: "What infuriates me is not what he was or what he did, but the deception he practiced on all of us for so many years" (32). In short, what angers Urbino is the knowledge that he has been duped, that he has not been so thoroughly in charge of matters as he has believed—and of course there is the irony of the fact that Urbino himself has a past clandestine sexual history of which he may not want to be reminded.

Being in charge is clearly important to Urbino. Though he conducts numerous civic projects that are to the benefit of the local community it is not at all clear that he does so out of purely selfless motives. He does not hesitate, for example, to utilize the fire department that he has organized on European models for personal needs such as catching his escaped parrot. Urbino shows his typical imperious style when he sends for the firemen: "Tell them it's for me," he says (25). Indeed, in looking at Urbino's organization of the fire department one might keep in mind that Flaubert's Homais tops off the list of his own projects with which he lays claim to the cross of the Legion of Honor by noting that "there is always the assistance I give at fires!" (253).

It is also worth noting that not just the fire department, but all of Urbino's innovations tend to be based on European models. In *Love*, as in *One Hundred Years of Solitude*, scientific knowledge is something that comes to Colombia from the outside, as a sign of European technical and cultural superiority. But García Márquez consistently suggests in his work that such European imports often result not in improvement, but in degradation of living conditions in Colombia. The local aristocracy in *Love* are mocked for their fascination with European consumer goods (an image of foreign economic domination), even though those goods may be useless and out of place in Latin America. On her various trips to Europe even the practical Fermina Daza buys massive amounts of commodities in an attempt (again echoing Emma

Bovary) to fill the emptiness in her life. Most of these goods (like heavy European coats) simply get stored in trunks and closets when she returns to Colombia. And García Márquez indicates the dehumanizing impact of this invasion of commodities in Fermina's own attitude: "she was dismayed by the voracity with which objects kept invading living spaces, displacing the humans, forcing them back into corners" (301).

In this vein it is important to note that, though Urbino reads extensively, he has no interest in the literature of his native Latin America. Instead, he read the latest books ordered from Paris and Madrid, "although he did not follow Spanish literature as closely as French" (8). This sense of disengagement from his local context perhaps shows up most clearly in Urbino's style of dealing with the local cholera epidemics that he must combat in the course of his professional duties. Urbino's father, Dr. Marco Aurelio Urbino, had become so passionately and personally involved in the treatment of cholera victims that he himself contracted the disease and died from it (112-13). After this death, Juvenal Urbino becomes obsessed with battling against cholera, the very existence of which seems to stand as an affront to his personal mastery and as a challenge to his ability to dominate nature through science. Urbino shows a strong disdain for his father's methods, "more charitable than scientific," and himself takes a detached scientific approach to the battle, putting his efforts into the institution of new scientific public health projects such as the ones he has observed in France rather than into hands-on treatment of disease victims. These projects include the construction of the first local aqueduct, the first sewer system, and a covered public market, and they are no doubt of benefit to Urbino's fellow citizens. However, many of these projects also smack of the kind of self-promoting activities that might be undertaken by Flaubert's Homais, such as when the pharmacist encourages the disastrous surgery on poor Hippolyte not so much for the benefit of the clubfoot as to prove the extent of his own enlightened knowledge.

Urbino's reliance on European models clearly participates in García

Márquez' ongoing critique of the way in which Latin America has contributed to its own exploitation through its acceptance of the myth of
foreign superiority. This link between Urbino and the imperialist domination of Latin America further clarifies the drive for power and dominance that is so central to Urbino's personality. At the death scene of
Saint-Amour, Urbino speaks to the police inspector "as he would have
to a subordinate," and indeed Urbino tends to treat everyone like sub-
ordinates, including his wife Fermina Daza. It is in his relationship
with Fermina, in fact, that Urbino's style of relating to others through
domination shows itself most clearly.

When he first begins his courtship of Fermina, Urbino does so very
much in the manner of a military siege, and his early letters, though
composed in an apparently "submissive spirit," already show an "im-
patience" that the independent-minded Fermina finds unsettling (124).
And to press the courtship Urbino mobilizes whatever forces are at his
command. Fermina's father, Lorenzo, hungry for the social legitima-
tion that would come to his daughter through a marriage to Urbino,
eagerly encourages the courtship. Even more tellingly, Fermina has
been expelled from her convent school for reading love letters from
Florentino Ariza during class hours, and Urbino manages to induce the
school to offer to reinstate Fermina if she will only entertain his ad-
vances.

Urbino's domineering style of courtship continues into the marriage, and despite certain indications early in the book that the Urbino-
Daza marriage is nearly ideal, it becomes clear as the narrative progresses that the relationship is seriously flawed. Urbino's own rage for
order and control can be seen in his unromantic proclamation that "the
most important thing in a good marriage is not happiness, but stability"
(300). Indeed, this practical attitude seems to form the very foundation
of the marriage. Urbino marries Fermina though she is well below his
social class, and he apparently does so because he believes that she will
be a good and useful wife to him. As McNerney puts it, "She is a useful
adornment, as befits the wife of a man like Urbino" (82).

But one suspects that Urbino marries below his social class at least partially because such a marriage gives him the leverage that he needs to feed his desire for dominance in the relationship. In any case, Fermina herself often feels trapped and constrained within a life that is clearly Urbino's more than hers. Late in the marriage she realizes that she is little more than a "deluxe servant" under Urbino's command:

> She always felt as if her life had been lent to her by her husband: she was absolute monarch of a vast empire of happiness, which had been built by him and for him alone. She knew that he loved her above all else, more than anyone else in the world, but only for his own sake: she was in his holy service. (221)

Indeed, Urbino is so overbearing that when he is forced to take a laxative he demands that his wife take one as well, so that she must share in his alimentary inconvenience (222).

That the private reality of the Urbino-Daza marriage is so different from the public perception of it is one of the strategies used by García Márquez in the book to indicate the seductiveness (and potential duplicity) of narrative. That the marriage is perfect makes a good story, and so the gullible townspeople generally accept that interpretation without question. But the construction of *Love*, in which the original presentation of the Urbino-Daza marriage is gradually undermined by the accumulation of additional details, makes the point that appearances can be deceiving and that one should not leap to interpretive conclusions hastily. This point is made most clearly by an interesting inconsistency in the narration of the book. Early on, when the marriage is still being presented as ideal, we are treated to a somewhat amusing anecdote from that marriage, in which Urbino's complaint that Fermina has failed to keep the bathroom stocked with soap mounts into a tempest-in-a-teapot crisis that is of course successfully resolved. And, we are told, this minor incident was the most critical problem that had ever arisen in the relationship: "When they recalled this episode, now they had rounded the corner of old age, neither could believe the astonishing truth that this had been the most serious argument in fifty years of living together" (29).

The very triviality of this argument reinforces the notion that the marriage is one without important difficulties. But there may be a good reason why "neither could believe" that this episode was their most serious marital problem. Late in the book we are suddenly told of Urbino's serious mid-life affair with the mulatta Bárbara Lynch, an affair of which Fermina learns and to which she reacts by moving out and going to live with her Cousin Hildebranda on her provincial ranch. Urbino finally convinces Fermina to return to him after a lengthy separation, but the incident has clearly posed a serious threat to the marriage. The jarring disjunction between the earlier account of the soap incident and this later story of Urbino's affair with Bárbara Lynch brings the reader to a sudden realization that the narrator of *Love* may not be entirely reliable and that we should be cautious about accepting anything we are told in the book at face value.

This emphasis on unreliable narration is reinforced at several points in the book, as when the newspaper *Justice* publishes (after Urbino's death) what is apparently an entirely fictitious account of an alleged love affair between Urbino and Fermina's friend Lucrecia del Real del Obispo. It may indeed be justice that this account is published, since the affair with Miss Lynch went undetected, but the fact that the quickly suppressed story finds believers (including Fermina herself) is a further warning against gullibility in reading. Of course, the most gullible reader of all in *Love* (and the most obvious link to Flaubert) is the hopeless *bovaryste* Florentino Ariza. Ariza's gullibility is established early in the book in his attempts to recover the treasure from a Spanish galleon that is rumored to have been sunk in the Caribbean just off the Colombian coast. Despite warnings that the attempt is folly, Ariza employs Euclides, a twelve-year-old boy, to dive for the treasure. Amazingly, the boy apparently finds the ship and begins to return with bits of jewelry supposedly recovered from the wreck. Ariza is about to mount a major salvage campaign when his mother (an experienced pawn broker) determines that the jewelry is fake and that Ariza has been duped by the boy.

Fermina treats the galleon episode as another example of Ariza's "poetic excesses," and it is true that Ariza is exceedingly susceptible to romantic fantasies in general. As with Emma Bovary, this susceptibility shows up most clearly in Ariza's reading of literature. The young Ariza devours the various volumes of the "Popular Library," a massive compilation of works that observes no distinctions of national origin or literary quality, including "everything from Homer to the least meritorious of the local poets" (75). At first glance, there is considerable potential in this compilation. From the point of view of Mikhail Bakhtin, one might find a source of carnivalesque energy in this conflation of "high" and "low" culture, a conflation that might potentially undermine the pretensions to seriousness and superiority of the European classics. Indeed, this combination of voices from official and from popular culture is reminiscent of the polyphonic intertextual voicing in García Márquez' own texts. But the point of the Bakhtinian carnival (or of the rich mixture of cultural voices in García Márquez) is to celebrate difference and diversity and to bring them out in the open. The totally indiscriminate compilation of the Popular Library, on the other hand, acts more to efface difference entirely, especially as it is read by Ariza, who "could not judge what was good and what was bad," knowing only that he prefers verse to prose, especially verse with predictable patterns of rhythm and rhyme that make it easy to memorize (75). The works in this library are mere commodities, all reduced to the same level of interchangeability.

Not only is Ariza an undiscriminating reader, but he is unduly influenced by what he reads, attempting to live his life in a way that is patterned after the poetry he reads. Thus, the poems he reads in the Popular Library became "the original source for his first letters to Fermina Daza, those half-baked endearments taken whole from the Spanish romantics" (75). Indeed, Ariza, though a poet of sorts, is so absorbed in the poetry of others that he is capable of writing only in the most imitative of fashions. When he employs his poetic skills to write love letters for others he writes not only in a style that mimics the poets he has read, but even in a handwriting that reproduces that of the supposed writers of the letter. And he is so successful in his imitations that lovers seek out his services to the point that he sometimes finds himself writing both sides of the communication and therefore producing entire simulated courtships.

Like Flaubert's Emma Bovary (and León Dupuis) Ariza identifies wholly with the books he reads, replacing the characters with real people he knows, "reserving for himself and Fermina Daza the roles of star-crossed lovers" (142). But despite this conflation of art and reality, Ariza uses poetry not to engage the world, but to escape from it. When he attempts to employ his skills as an imitator of styles to the writing of business letters, he fails completely. Throughout his career he suffers professionally because he is unable to write even the simplest business letter without ascending into an inappropriate lyricism. Even in matters of love Ariza's poetic bent can act as a wall between himself and reality, as when he immerses himself in love poetry in the midst of a "transient hotel" while remaining virtually oblivious to the activities of the prostitutes who surround him (75-76).

Fermina Daza provides a focal point at which Dr. Juvenal Urbino and Florentino Ariza converge, and there is an obvious element of dialogue between the science of Urbino and the poetry of Ariza that results from this convergence. But, as with the similar dialogue that occurs in *Madame Bovary* between Homais and Emma Bovary, this clash of discourses is highly complex. García Márquez, who depicts even the dictator in *Autumn of the Patriarch* with a sympathy that is often quite touching, shows his typical equanimity by presenting neither Urbino nor Ariza as an entirely negative figure. Urbino's science does a great deal to improve the lot of the local populace, and Ariza's excessively romantic visions are in the end rewarded as he finally consummates his lifelong fascination with Fermina Daza. Still, Urbino's focus on science leads to a tunnel vision that cuts him off from genuinely human interactions and leads to his treatment of other people as objects for his own domination. And Ariza's absorption in poetry leads to a similar dehumanizing blindness, since he often treats others not as real people but as literary characters. For example, he seduces América Vicuña, a fourteen-year-old girl who has been entrusted to his guardianship, then summarily drops her when Urbino dies, making Fermina accessible to Ariza once again. The suggestively named América Vicuña then commits suicide, a victim of her own sheep-like gullibility and a symbol of the rape of Latin America by foreign powers.

Ariza's relationship with this girl is not that unusual in the fictional world of García Márquez, as the autumnal patriarch's fascination with young school girls amply illustrates. But Ariza's *bovarysme* invites comparison with literary models, and this particular autumn-spring relationship inevitably recalls that between Nabokov's Humbert Humbert and Lolita. Humbert, like Ariza, bears many similarities to Emma Bovary, and like Ariza his projection of his own aestheticized fantasies into the real world allows him to absorb other people within those fantasies, leaving them thoroughly objectified and "safely solipsized" (*Lolita* 62). Indeed, one suspects that Ariza has operated in this mode with all of the 622 "long-term liaisons" he has conducted during his "patient" wait for Fermina. Despite repeated suggestions in the text that Ariza has an unequalled capacity for love and that each of these 622 relationships is special and unique, enough is enough, and it seems clear on reflection that Ariza's initiation of new relationships at a clip of one per month for over fifty years bespeaks a lack of real emotional engagement in any of them. García Márquez' narrator describes a number of Ariza's affairs, apparently in an attempt to convince us of the sincerity and authenticity of Ariza's affections for his numerous conquests. And this attempt almost succeeds, despite the clear evidence that the affairs are simply too numerous for this sincerity to be possible. Narrative is a very seductive form, García Márquez seems to be telling us, and even the wisest of us must be on guard against gullibility in reading.[5]

The link to Nabokov helps to clarify this ongoing attack on gullibility. Humbert Humbert is a pervert, a rapist, and a murderer, and we are reminded repeatedly in *Lolita* of his mental and physical cruelty. Yet he is also a master of language who constructs a narrative so charming and so brilliant that many readers are seduced into sympathy with his position and are able to accept his claims that his relationship with Lolita was purely aesthetic. Similarly, Ariza's numerous love stories (especially the central one involving Fermina) make such attractive narratives that we are tempted to read him as the ideal lover he apparently thinks himself to be, not as a manipulative womanizer who jumps from one bed to another, causing considerable suffering and multiple violent deaths among the objects of this insatiable sexual appetite. Indeed, like Nabokov, García Márquez sprinkles his text with reminders of the sinister side of Ariza's sexual exploits—and exploitation. Perhaps the most telling of these concerns Olimpia Zuleta, a married woman whom he seduces after an extended siege. Afterwards, he marks his conquest by painting the woman's belly with the words "This pussy is mine" (217). That same night, her husband discovers the inscription and cuts her throat, whereupon Ariza's principal reaction is not remorse but simply fear that the husband might discover his identity and come after him as well.

It is true, as most critics have realized, that the confrontation between Urbino and Ariza represents not just a competition between rivals in love but also a clash of competing worldviews. Moraña seems to have understood this clash most fully:

> Vitalism and rationalism, modernization and tradition, Europeanization and popular culture, integration and marginality thus constitute poles in an ideological complex basically composed of Utopian projects that raise the question of the imposition of or resistance to foreign models. (40)

However, Moraña, like most other critics, goes on to conclude that *Love* privileges the romantic pole of this opposition, thereby offering a critique of the kind of modernization represented by Urbino. Yet the poet Ariza is just as domineering and manipulative as the scientist Urbino, and in many ways the two are not opposites but merely two sides of the same coin, just as Emma Bovary's love of literature is revealed by Flaubert to be a vulgar commodification of art that is merely the flipside of her insatiable materialism.

Both Ariza and Urbino make the same mistake—they accept the narratives that inform their lives without question, and this blind acceptance allows them to justify their lack of regard for others. And—like the patriarch, who becomes a prisoner of his own propaganda—both become the victims of their own narratives. Urbino fully accepts the standard nineteenth-century narrative of progress through scientific and technological advancement, and this acceptance not only blinds him to his own pompous and tyrannical attitudes but also to the destruction being wrought in South America by an unchecked and irresponsible development that is destroying natural resources such as the Magdalena River. Similarly, Ariza so fully accepts the narrative of the romantic lover that he cannot see the harm he is doing to others through his inveterate romancing.

Both Ariza and Urbino are, in short, gullible readers, and García Márquez' portrayal of them in *Love* constitutes a powerful indictment of such gullibility. But the book's most powerful statement on gullible reading occurs in the mechanics of the text itself, which seductively lures readers into reading it as a beautiful, poignant, and touching love story while ignoring the many textual instabilities that so clearly undermine such a reading. As with his earlier use of magical realism in works such as *One Hundred Years of Solitude*, García Márquez demonstrates in *Love* that a well-told story can make readers accept almost anything. Despite the instances of unreliable narration in which the narrator seems to be caught in out-and-out lies, despite the radical disjunction between the content of the book and the romantic *follétin* form on which it is based, and despite the subversive Rabelaisian humor of the book, *Love* still makes for a terrific story.

García Márquez reinforces such readings in a number of ways, most obviously by constructing a story that most readers will *want* to read in a positive way, due to the undeniable affirmation of humanity contained in readings of the book that emphasize the romance of the Ariza-Daza relationship. Indeed, the consummation of this relationship after over fifty years of waiting can be read to offer a commentary on the nobility of the human spirit, and on one level the book clearly serves to affirm the validity of love and sexuality even in old age. Yet this apotheosis of romance is undermined by the text in a number of ways. For one thing, the entire culminating riverboat trip is shadowed by certain ominous notes, including the death of América Vicuña and the reported murder of another couple of aged lovers, also on a boat. Even the long-awaited climax of the courtship turns out to be an anti-climax. When the couple first goes to bed together, Ariza—the sexual adventurer *extraordinaire*—assures Fermina that he has remained a virgin throughout his life because of his devotion to her. Fermina does not believe this outrageous lie, because Ariza's "love letters were composed of similar phrases whose meaning mattered less than their brilliance" (339). Still, that such dishonesty is a standard feature of Ariza's discourse hardly makes it more excusable. Then, the first time the couple attempts to make love, Ariza is totally impotent, and he leaves Fermina's cabin in "martyrdom" (340). Later, when Ariza finally does make love to Fermina, he does so hastily and clumsily, completely without romance or regard for her feelings. She doesn't even have time to undress as he practically assaults her in a scene in which his penis is significantly described as a "weapon" being displayed as a "war trophy." Afterwards, we are told, Fermina "felt empty" (340).

Such scenes hardly support readings of *Love* as a celebration of septuagenarian sexuality, though it seems clear that the target of such episodes is not sex in old age, but overly romanticized notions of sexuality in general. One could also argue that the point of the Ariza-Daza relationship is not sex, but love, though the book tends to suggest that the two are not neatly separable. But even the romance of the ending, in which Ariza envisions Fermina and himself travelling endlessly up and down the Magdalena River, is seriously undermined by other elements of the narrative.[6] In particular, the river has been ravaged by industrialization and "progress," and has become virtually unnavigable. Ariza's final fantasy of endlessly cruising the river, like most of his fantasies, is an impossible one that fails to take reality into account, and perhaps the message is that such unrealistic romantic visions have themselves contributed to the demise of the river by blinding the local populace to what is really going on in their country.

One of the most striking features of *Love* is that it can remain so seductive as a story of romance in spite of the way in which the text continually self-destructs as a romantic narrative. Much of this effect can be attributed to García Márquez' brilliance as a storyteller, of course, but much of it has to do with the nature of the narrative itself. *Love* very clearly suggests a complicity between the desire of Florentino Ariza for Fermina Daza and the reader's desire for a successful consummation of the text. But the book works its seductive magic in other ways as well, some of which are highly significant as aspects of the ongoing attack on gullible reading. One of the more interesting techniques employed in the book is the frequent use of real historical personages and events, whose appearance in the text tends to create an air of verisimilitude. When we read that Jeremiah de Saint-Amour has played chess with Capablanca (32), or that Juvenal Urbino studied with the father of Marcel Proust (114), or that Fermina Daza was chosen to greet Charles Lindbergh when he visited Colombia (306), there is a tendency for the entire plot to seem more realistic. Similarly, one of the reasons that Ariza is so easily duped by the boy Euclides in the episode of the Spanish galleon is that the story of the sunken ship is made more believable by the existence of specific historical information. For example, Ariza finds records which indicate that a fleet of ships led by the flagship San José had arrived in Colombia from Panama in May 1708, and is even able to find documentation concerning the number of ships, their exact route, and the circumstances under which they were sunk (90-91).

Yet there is also evidence that the entire story of the sunken ships was fabricated by a dishonest viceroy in an effort to hide his own thefts from the Spanish Crown (93). Likewise, *Love* is pure fiction, and a careful inspection shows that many of the concrete historical details in the book are impossible, anachronistic, or simply fictionalized. In short, history can be faked, and the reader who unquestioningly accepts official narratives of historical events is liable to be just as deceived as is Florentino Ariza in his reading of bad romantic poetry. Indeed, *Love* is principally a book not about romance, but about history and politics. Totalitarianism and imperialism thrive on the blind acceptance of their official narratives, and the gullible reading of these narratives by an unsuspecting populace makes their domination all the easier. The saccharine surface of *Love in the Time of Cholera* conceals a series of diabolical textual traps in a dynamic of duplicity very similar to that so familiar to victims of domination and dictatorship everywhere. García Márquez presents a narrative so seductive as to be almost irresistible, yet so complex as to be largely lost on those who fall prey to its seduction. The message is clear: even the best readers (and the most alert citizens) are ever in danger of being duped by a good story, whether that story be contained in a book of fiction or in the proclamations of a tyrant.

From *Studies in 20th Century Literature* 17, no. 2 (Summer 1993): 181-195. Copyright © 1993 by *Studies in 20th Century Literature.* Reprinted by permission.

Notes

1. Paul de Man's update of the Marx Aveling English translation of this passage reads "having at the time of the cholera distinguished myself by a boundless devotion" (253). The translation is quite literal, Flaubert's original French reading "s'être, lors du choléra, signalé par un dévouement sans borne" (408).

2. García Márquez' title presumably refers to the fact that the aged lovers Floren-

tino Ariza and Fermina Daza end the book, together at last, sailing endlessly up and down the Great Magdalena River on a riverboat which flies a cholera flag to discourage other passengers from coming aboard. There is a secondary resonance in the title which indicates the way that love sometimes endures despite negative developments (such as cholera epidemics) in the world around it. But the incongruous juxtaposition of "love" and "cholera" in the title also functions as a hint that the book's love story may not be quite what it appears.

3. On this aspect of *One Hundred Years of Solitude* see Conniff.

4. Note, for example, his enthusiasm over the impetus given to his career in recent years through a switch to a personal computer for the composition of his texts (Williams 134).

5. It is, of course, quite possible that the unreliable narrator of *Love* has himself exaggerated the number of Ariza's affairs.

6. See Fiddian for a further discussion of the ambiguity of this ending (198).

Works Cited

Bell-Villada, Gene H. *García Márquez: The Man and His Work*. Chapel Hill: U of North Carolina P, 1990.

Conniff, Brian. "The Dark Side of Magical Realism: Science, Oppression, and Apocalypse in *One Hundred Years of Solitude*." *Modern Fiction Studies* 36 (Summer 1990): 167-79.

Fiddian, Robin. "A Prospective Post-Script: Apropos of *Love in the Time of Cholera*." In *Gabriel García Márquez: New Readings*. Ed. Bernard McGuirk and Richard Cardwell. Cambridge: Cambridge UP, 1987. 191-205.

Flaubert, Gustave. *Madame Bovary*. Lausanne: Éditions Rencontre, 1965.

_____. *Madame Bovary*. Trans. Paul de Man based on the translation by Eleanor Marx Aveling. New York: W. W. Norton, 1965.

García Márquez, Gabriel. *Love in the Time of Cholera*. Trans. Edith Grossman. New York: Penguin, 1989.

Horkheimer, Max, and Theodor W. Adorno. *Dialectic of Enlightenment*. Trans. John Cumming. New York: Seabury P, 1972.

Janes, Regina. *Gabriel García Márquez: Revolutions in Wonderland*. Columbia: U of Missouri P, 1981.

McNerney, Kathleen. *Understanding Gabriel García Márquez*. Columbia: U of South Carolina P, 1989.

Moraña, Mabel. "Modernity and Marginality in *Love in the Time of Cholera*." *Studies in Twentieth-Century Literature* 14 (Winter 1990): 27-43.

Nabokov, Vladimir. *The Annotated Lolita*. Ed. Alfred Appel, Jr. New York: McGraw-Hill, 1970.

Williams, Raymond Leslie. "The Visual Arts, the Poeticization of Space and Writing: An Interview with Gabriel García Márquez." *PMLA* 104 (1989): 131-40.

Lessons from the Golden Age in Gabriel García Márquez's *Living to Tell the Tale*_____

Efraín Kristal

> Efraín Kristal suggests that García Márquez sanitizes his past in his first volume of memoirs, as memoirists often do, to showcase the way his "intentions as a novelist, journalist and political activist constitute a coherent project." Kristal revisits some themes in *Living to Tell the Tale*: the author's adventures in bordellos; his journey, along with his mother, to sell his childhood house in Aracataca; his debt to his mentor, *el sabio catalán* Don Ramón Vinyes; the way his political education was defined by the assassination of the liberal leader Jorge Eliécer Gaitán; and his love for the Spanish Golden Age literary classics. Kristal's conclusion is that in spite of this autobiographical confession of more than four hundred pages, García Márquez is impossible to pin down.   — I.S.

One April day in 1950 the 22-year-old writer, eaten up with nerves, offers the rough typescript of his first novel to the old Catalan dramatist, Don Ramón Vinyes, leading spirit of their bohemian group. Putting on his spectacles, Don Ramón smooths the pages out on the café table and reads, without any variation in his expression, the opening section of what would become *Leaf Storm*. Then, replacing his spectacles in their case, and the case in his breast pocket, he makes a few comments on the novelist's handling of time—which was, as García Márquez admits here, 'my life-or-death problem'; without doubt, the 'most difficult of all'.[1]

Resolving the Problem of Time

This portrait of the artist as a young man is no late, lazy memoir but a literary work in its own right, which recounts—or recreates—the process of García Márquez's formation as a writer within a highly wrought temporal framework. *Living to Tell the Tale* opens two months earlier, *in medias res*, as the author's mother, in mourning garb, threads her way lightly between the tables of the Mundo bookshop in Barranquilla, a stone's throw from Don Ramón's café, to confront her errant son with a mischievous smile: 'before I could react she said, "I'm your mother." And next, in her customary, ceremonial way: "I've come to ask you to please go with me to sell the house"' (*Living to Tell the Tale*, p. 3).

From here, time will double forward and back. The slow journey towards the old family home in Aracataca opens up vistas onto the past:

> The Sierra Nevada de Santa María and its white peaks seemed to come right down to the Banana plantations on the other side of the river. From there you could see the Arawak Indians moving in lines like ants along the cliffs of the sierra, carrying sacks of ginger on their backs and chewing pellets of coca to make life bearable. As children we dreamed of parched, burning streets. For the heat was so implausible, in particular at siesta time, that the adults complained as if it were a daily surprise. From the day I was born I had heard it said, over and over again, that the rail lines and camps of the United Fruit Company had been built at night because during the day the sun made the tools too hot to pick up. (*Living to Tell the Tale*, p. 5)

But it also, of course, anticipates the future—the moment in 1965, still ten years ahead at the end of this book—when, driving his family to Acapulco on holiday, García Márquez finds one of the twentieth-century's most famous first sentences forming in his head: 'Many years later, facing the firing squad, Colonel Aureliano Buendía was to remember that distant afternoon when his father took him to discover ice.'[2] He turns the car round and roars back to Mexico City, locks himself in his room for eighteen months, smoking cigarettes stump to tip, and writes *One Hundred Years of Solitude*.

Yet in another sense, *Living to Tell the Tale* begins long after the wind at the end of that novel has blown everything away. The old house in Aracataca has gone to rack and ruin by the time García Márquez and his mother arrive there, peopled by unevictable tenants; they are unable to make a cent from it. Echoing one of the most recurrent, indeed predictable, patterns in García Márquez's fiction, what was intended is not fulfilled as one had expected, but as destiny wills. Instead of money, the journey provides García Márquez with his principal literary inspiration. He sees the arid little square in Ciénaga where, in 1928, the Colombian army had mown down the striking banana workers—in his grandfather's version, as recounted in *One Hundred Years of Solitude*: the three thousand men, women and children motionless under the savage sun, as the officer in charge gives them five minutes to clear the streets. He hears the stories of his parents' courtship—the beautiful daughter of the élite Liberal family pursued by an ambitious Conservative telegraph operator; his colleagues conspiring to tap out love messages down the wires, as her parents whisk her to safety—that inspired both *Leaf Storm* and *Love in the Time of Cholera*. He recalls his close relationship with his grandfather, who had fought in Colombia's devastating civil wars and who resurfaces in several fictional characters, including *No One Writes to the Colonel*. Gazing from the train window as they pull slowly through the green silence of the banana groves, García Márquez is taken with the name of an old plantation, 'Macondo', which will feature as the tropical town in so many of his tales and novels.

The centrepiece of the journey back is a Proustian experience, as he and his mother are invited to lunch at the home of the poor but dignified family doctor:

> From the moment I tasted the soup, I had the sensation that an entire sleeping world was waking in my memory. Tastes that had been mine in childhood and that I had lost when I left the town reappeared intact with each spoonful, and they gripped my heart. (*Living to Tell the Tale*, p. 39)

But if the raw material for his fiction was to be the *real maravilloso* of the Colombian Caribbean, what of its form? García Márquez has often told the story of discovering, in Kafka's 'Metamorphosis', the same impassive narration of the extraordinary that he remembered from his maternal grandmother's tales. There is further homage to Tranquilina Iguarán here, as to his aunts and to Doña Juana de Freytes, who would retell stories for the children drawn from the *Odyssey*, *Orlando Furioso*, *Don Quixote* and *The Count of Monte Cristo*. The 'popular memory' of Aracataca's inhabitants, he found, would often correct or contradict official accounts of historical events. At school and college, first in Barranquilla and then Bogotá (where 'an insomniac rain had been falling since the beginning of the sixteenth century'), his time was devoted to 'reading whatever I could get my hands on, and reciting from memory the unrepeatable poetry of the Spanish Golden Age' (*Living to Tell the Tale*, p. 301).

In the Shadow of Poetry

After 1948, fleeing the violence and repression that swept Bogotá following the assassination of the Liberal leader Jorge Eliécer Gaitán, García Márquez returned to Barranquilla, one of the safest cities in the country. It was at this stage that he fell in with the group around Don Ramón Vinyes. 'It is difficult to imagine the degree to which people lived then in the shadow of poetry' (*Living to Tell the Tale*, p. 311), he writes here of his literary education:

> We not only believed in poetry, and would have died for it, but we also knew with certainty—as Luis Cardoza y Aragón wrote—that 'poetry is the only concrete proof of the existence of man'. The world belonged to the poets. Their new works were more important for my generation than the political news, which was more and more depressing. (*Living to Tell the Tale*, pp. 301-2)

Of equal importance were the Modernist writers, newly available to a Spanish reading public in the translations produced by Jorge Luis

Borges and his circle in Buenos Aires—'we waited for the traveling salesmen from the Argentine publishers as if they were envoys from heaven' (*Living to Tell the Tale*, pp. 246-7; see also p. 352). Faulkner, Woolf, Conrad, Graham Greene, Joyce, Gide, Kafka, Mann and Borges himself were devoured by the Barranquilla group, along with the Greek classics that would inform, for example, the Sophoclean *Chronicle of a Death Foretold*.

It was here in Barranquilla under the vicious regime of Laureano Gómez that García Márquez began to develop his *métier* as a writer, published his first short stories and gained his initial literary reputation, while eking out an existence as a journalist. His life as a reporter became progressively more difficult as, under Rojas Pinilla, the censorship increased still further. In 1954, his serialized 'Story of a Shipwrecked Sailor'—an account of a Colombian navy vessel that had sunk on its way back from Alabama—attracted the wrath of the authorities. According to the official version, the ship had been wrecked in a terrible storm, and the drowned sailors were made national heroes. On interviewing a survivor, however, García Márquez discovered that there had been no storm; but the officers had so overloaded the boat with contraband household appliances that it had capsized, leaving the Everyman hero adrift on his raft in the ocean. García Márquez and his editor at *El Espectador* were both aware that the articles would embarrass the armed forces; but the reaction was more sordid than anticipated. García Márquez was dogged by a man who claimed to admire his writing but warned that 'he was doing a disfavour to his country by supporting the Communists' and that his informant had 'infiltrated the Armed Forces in the service of the Soviet Union' (*Living to Tell the Tale*, p. 569). *Living to Tell the Tale* takes the story up to 1955 when, after a series of such incidents, García Márquez leaves Colombia for a four-year exile in Europe, where he would write *In Evil Hour*. It ends with a cliff-hanger that points towards the life to come in Volume Two: the letter of reply from Mercedes Barcha, his future wife.

Many of these details—the family history and its recreation in his later work; initiations into literature, sex, journalism and politics; the insights about his creative methods—have already been documented, in *The Fragrance of Guava* and elsewhere.[3] But the portrait of the writer that emerges remains an engaging one, steady and self-assured; even the most intimate admissions reveal a man content with a life he considers well lived. From the vantage point of his seventy-five years, García Márquez pays homage to friends, lovers and mentors; makes some disarming confessions regarding his phobias and manias; and gracefully settles a few old scores.

There are many fond memories of the bordellos where he would carouse with friends and colleagues, and of the kindness of the prostitutes with whom he shared the town's cheapest hotel. Sex, and its free celebration, constitute an important part of García Márquez's self-identity, as of his vision of political liberation. Though he objects to his father's and grandfather's patriarchal attitudes towards their daughters—whose own sexuality is reduced to a matter of paternal honour—he applauds their virility in siring innumerable children, before and after wedlock, with the grudging acquiescence of their wives; both of whom eventually welcomed these illegitimate offspring into their households. But his claim that women 'sustain the world while we men mess it up with our historical brutality' (*Living to Tell the Tale*, p. 89) can scarcely suffice as a politically aware account of the mass degradation forced upon lower-class Colombian women by the population displacements of the civil wars and *La Violencia*; and now again, with Uribe's counterinsurgency and fumigation campaigns. Keenly aware of the plight of the young men who came to peaceful Barranquilla as political refugees from the violence of other cities, García Márquez seems to overlook that of their sisters—many of whom became prostitutes as widows or orphans as a result of the same repression, driven from their homes to fill the bars and brothels he frequents.[4]

In many places, *Living to Tell the Tale* reads like a novel—fashioned with the same humour, themes, structures and poetic inflections as García Márquez's narrative fiction. If some of the rhetorical devices feel a little stale—there must be over a hundred uses of 'not this, but that' constructions to emphasize the unexpected—there are passages here as riveting as any that he has put on paper. Perhaps even more so, in his account of the assassination of Gaitán or of his own struggles against censorship, where the urgency of the historical moment, the combined sense of personal risk and social significance, is not mitigated or diffused by the subterfuges of magical realism. There is something refreshing about these sections, which deploy García Márquez's considerable literary resources stripped of any flights of fancy.

García Márquez's Magical Realism

In general, though, it is the aesthetic of magical realism that is exemplified; underscoring García Márquez's claim that, in Latin America and the Caribbean, 'artists have had to invent very little, and perhaps their problem has been the exact opposite: to make their reality credible'.[5] Many of the characters he recalls from childhood hold the wildest fantasies as firm beliefs, while he affects a tone, tiresome at times, of accepting them as reality himself; or of having experienced a few fantasies of his own. Yet as Fredric Jameson has suggested for the works of fiction, this brand of magical realism was born in an environment in which precapitalist and nascent capitalist modes overlap, involving—and this is another insight on García Márquez's handling of time—'the articulated superposition of whole layers of the past within the present'[6]: Indian or pre-Colombian realities, the colonial era and slavery, the Bolivarian struggle for independence, *caudillismo*, the War of a Thousand Days, the period of direct American domination. Indeed, the story of Aracataca and of his family can be understood only in terms of the false sense of progress brought by the United Fruit Company, before it devastated the region's economy and ecology.

One might extend Jameson's point by suggesting an activist intention of sorts, perhaps underwritten by García Márquez's own emphasis on the Spanish classics. This brand of magical realism could be seen as a political secularization of a central theme of Golden Age literature—in *Don Quixote* of course, but in Baroque poetry as well: the realization that, if life is a dream, nevertheless the blurring of boundaries between fantasy and reality does not exonerate humanity from its moral commitments. It goes without saying that morality, for García Márquez, translates into social and political rather than religious terms. But the point can still be made: for García Márquez, literature is a vehicle through which to understand a given reality; his brand of magical realism is informed by his political commitment. How he first began to make connexions between the two is one of the underlying themes of this memoir.

The Political Education

Elements of García Márquez's political education are powerfully reconstructed here. A visceral anti-imperialist sentiment was implanted early, by his grandfather's descriptions of the 1928 massacre of the striking United Fruit Company workers. The same viewpoint underlies his interpretation of Colombia's geopolitical predicament:

> Colombia had always been a country with a Caribbean identity which opened to the world by means of the umbilical cord of Panamá. Its forced amputation condemned us to be what we are today: a nation with an Andean mentality whose circumstances favour the canal between two oceans belonging not to us but to the United States. (*Living to Tell the Tale*, p. 538)

At the boarding school in Zipaquirá, on the outskirts of Bogotá, García Márquez recalls some of his progressive teachers as living expressions of magical realism—Manuel Cuello del Río, for example, a radical Marxist who 'admired Lin Yutang and believed in apparitions of the dead' (*Living to Tell the Tale*, p. 232). One of them lent him a book in which he found a citation, attributed to Lenin, that he would never forget: 'if you do not become involved in politics, politics will eventually become involved in you' (*Living to Tell the Tale*, p. 249). At this stage, however, literature still appeared as an escape from a depressing social reality, rather than an engagement with it. In retrospect at least, Pablo Neruda's arrival in the late 1940s—bringing to Bogotá the conviction that 'poetry had to be a political weapon' (*Living to Tell the Tale*, p. 305)—was a challenge to this quietism. García Márquez considers it 'a heartening symptom of the power of poetry during those years' (*Living to Tell the Tale*, p. 305) that the satirical sonnets Neruda composed in Bogotá on the subject of local intellectuals were taken so seriously; especially those that poked fun at Laureano Gómez's reactionary politics, even before he became Colombia's head of state.

But it was the events of 9 April 1948 and after that would signal his political coming-of-age. The most gripping section of *Living to Tell the Tale* is its account of Gaitán's assassination on that day, which triggered the furious protests and brutal repression of the *Bogotazo*—one of the defining moments of the decades palsied by *La Violencia*, during which at least 200,000 people were reputed killed (García Márquez suggests the figure might be much higher). Hobsbawm and others have argued that the conflicts can only be understood in the context of a frustrated social revolution—when 'revolutionary tensions are neither dissipated by peaceful economic development, nor redirected to create new and revolutionary structures. The armies of death, the scores of uprooted, the physically and mentally mutilated, are the price Colombia has paid for that failure.'[7] Though García Márquez would come to interpret the events along similar lines, he had initially been sceptical— 'I had allowed myself the arrogance of not believing in Gaitán' (*Living to Tell the Tale*, p. 331), as he puts it; but on hearing him speak, 'I understood all at once that he had gone beyond the Spanish country and was inventing a lingua franca for everyone' (*Living to Tell the Tale*, p. 331). The 20-year-old, then a cub reporter on the Bogotá *Espectador*, took part in the 'march of silence' against government repression, organized by Gaitán some months before the assassination—his first political act: 'I had come without political conviction, drawn by the curiosity of the silence, and the sudden knot of tears in my throat took me by surprise' (*Living to Tell the Tale*, p. 333). With hindsight, he sees Gaitán as having radicalized his election campaign of the previous year in a way

> that went beyond the historic division of the country into Liberals and Conservatives, [to make] a more realistic distinction between the exploiters and the exploited. With his historic slogan, 'Let's get them!', and his supernatural energy, he sowed the seeds of resistance even in the most remote places with a gigantic campaign of agitation that continued gaining ground until . . . it was on the verge of being an authentic social revolution. (*Living to Tell the Tale*, p. 330)

Gaitán had been on his way to lunch with *El Espectador*'s editor on the morning of the assassination. García Márquez heard the news within minutes and rushed to the scene of the crime. Angry bootblacks were already using their wooden boxes to bang down the gates of the chemist's shop where the police had locked the assailant, to protect him from the mob. 'A tall man, very much in control of himself and wearing an irreproachable grey suit as if he were going to a wedding, urged them on with well-calculated shouts'—and was driven away in a 'too new' car, as soon as Gaitán's apparent killer had been dragged off by the crowd.

It was only later that 'it occurred to me that the man had managed to have a false assassin killed, in order to protect the identity of the real one' (*Living to Tell the Tale*, p. 338). García Márquez recalls the rebellion that ensued:

> The smoke from the fires had darkened the air, and the clouded sky was a sinister blanket. Maddened hordes, armed with machetes and all kinds of tools stolen from the hardware stores, set fire to the businesses along Carrera Séptima, with the help of mutinous police officers. . . . Wherever we went we stumbled across household appliances, over bottles of expensive brands of whisky and all kinds of exotic drinks that the mobs beheaded with their machetes. (*Living to Tell the Tale*, p. 338)

Government troops raked the Plaza de Bolívar with machine-gun fire. A group of Gaitán supporters from the University proclaimed themselves a revolutionary *junta*. The Communists—'the only ones who seemed to act with any political sense' (*Living to Tell the Tale*, p. 346)—directed the crowd, 'like traffic police', towards the centres of power. In this chaos, who should appear but the 20-year-old Fidel Castro, in Bogotá as a University of Havana delegate to a progressive students' congress, and with an appointment to meet Gaitán that afternoon. Castro, who can do no wrong in García Márquez's eyes, is presented as a sensible pragmatist, trying to help stop the killings in the streets: 'One would have to know him to imagine his desperation' (*Living to Tell the Tale*, p. 356). He rushes to a pro-Gaitán police division, holed up in their garrison, and tries to persuade them, without success, that any force that stays in its barracks is lost: 'He proposed that they take their men out to struggle in the streets for the maintenance of order and a more equitable system' (*Living to Tell the Tale*, p. 357).

The Image of a Literary Life

Living to Tell the Tale suggests that García Márquez's intentions as a novelist, journalist and political activist constitute a coherent project; but a lot is left unsaid, and much might be read between the lines. The official image is of the most famous of all living Latin American writers, who has happily reconciled his literary vocation and global prestige with his political commitments: Caribbean *joie de vivre* goes hand in hand with a broad sense of compassion for hunger, poverty, human misery and social injustice. To the right-wing media—enamoured of his fiction but contemptuous of his affiliations—he has written: 'as a man, I am indivisible and my political position reflects the same ideology with which I write my books'.[8] But although he has often declared himself a sympathizer of the Colombian Communist Party, García Márquez has also wanted to maintain a safe distance from political militancy—explaining, in *The Fragrance of Guava*: 'My relationship with the Communists has had many ups and downs. We've often been at loggerheads because every time I adopt a stance they don't like, their newspapers really have a go at me. But I've never publicly condemned them, even at the worst moments.'[9]

Another, still more sanitized reading could show him as a man who values friendship over politics, and whose public interventions have stressed 'reconciliation' in the interests of peace. There are anecdotes here to suggest that his Nobel Prize status has made him a statesman of sorts, with access to political *players* across the spectrum from Castro to Kissinger and Clinton. It is clear that he wants to be seen as a man who has been able to reach—by virtue of his craft or prestige—spheres that might have otherwise been averse to the significance of his underlying message. And if he sometimes plays the naïve by leaving hidden the full thrust of his political views, he has been sanctioned in so doing by the most important leaders of the Latin American Left. There is a telling moment in the early 1950s when Gilberto Vieira—'the most prominent of the founders of the Communist Party . . . the man most wanted by the country's secret services'—contacts García Márquez from his clandestine hideout in Bogotá to let him know that he has been reading his newspaper articles with great attention, and has even identified the young journalist's anonymous pieces in order to 'interpret their hidden meanings'. It is from Vieira himself that García Márquez is exonerated from joining the Party, or from any direct political involvement: 'he agreed that the best service I could offer the country was to continue in the same way without compromising myself with anyone in any kind of political militancy' (*Living to Tell the Tale*, p. 556).

But if several meanings can be read from García Márquez's statements of his political positions, it is impossible to pin him down. Though he makes little of the years he spent as a law student it is clear that he is also mounting a preemptive defence in *Living to Tell the Tale* against those who might accuse him of either too much or too little radicalism. Perhaps something similar could be said of his literary achievements which, if one reads carefully between the lines, can be interpreted either as what Gerald Martin has described, in *Journeys Through the Labyrinth*,[10] as depictions of 'the prehistory before the dawn of proletarian consciousness'; or as wild expressions of the Latin American imagination, if one would prefer.

Notes

1. Gabriel García Márquez, *Living to Tell the Tale*, trans. Edith Grossman (New York: Knopf, 2003), p. 142.

2. Gabriel García Márquez, *One Hundred Years of Solitude*, trans. Gregory Rabassa (London: Picador, 1978), p. 9.

3. Plinio Apuleyo Mendoza, *The Fragrance of Guava: Conversations with Gabriel García Márquez*, trans. Ann Wright (London and Boston: Faber & Faber, 1988).

4. For a sobering picture of the exploitation and abuse of Colombian prostitutes in the 1950s see Saturnino Sepúlveda Niño, *La prostitución en Colombia: Una quiebra de las estructuras sociales* (Bogotá: Editorial Andes, 1970).

5. Gabriel García Márquez, 'Fantasía y creación artística', *Notas de prensa, 1980-1984* (Bogotá: Editorial Norma, 1988), p. 147. All translations from the Spanish are my own.

6. Fredric Jameson has speculated that magical realism 'depends on a content which betrays the overlap or the coexistence of precapitalist with nascent capitalist or technological features. [. . .] Not a realism to be transfigured by the "supplement" of a magical perspective but a reality which is already in and of itself magical or fantastic. Whence the insistence of both Carpentier and García Márquez that in the social reality of Latin America, "realism" is already "magical realism". [. . .] the articulated superposition of whole layers of the past within the present (Indian or pre-Columbian realities, the colonial era, the wars of independence, caudillismo, the period of American domination [. . .]) is the formal precondition of this new narrative style.' See Fredric Jameson, 'On magical realism in film', *Critical Inquiry*, 12 (Winter 1986), p. 311.

7. E. J. Hobsbawm, 'La anatomía de "La violencia" en Colombia', in Hobsbawm, *et al.*, *Once ensayos sobre La Violencia* (Bogotá: Centro Gaitán, 1985), p. 23.

8. Gabriel García Márquez, *Notas de prensa, 1980-1984*, p. 112.

9. Plinio Apuleyo Mendoza, *The Fragrance of Guava: Conversations with Gabriel García Márquez*, p. 97.

10. Gerald Martin's *Journeys Through the Labyrinth: Latin American Fiction in the Twentieth Century* (Verso, London and New York, 1989) is arguably the most compelling case for reading the Latin American novel as a response to social and political

predicaments, and the high point of the book is the analysis of *One Hundred Years of Solitude*. Martin argues that García Márquez's novel signals 'the end of primitive neocolonialism, its conscious or unconscious collaborators, and an epoch of illusions' (p. 233). The famous deciphering episode of a parchment in Sanskrit, at the end of the novel, which links Aureliano (the decipherer) and his friend Gabriel (García Márquez writes himself into the novel to indicate his complicity with a character whose understanding of the world is taken to be wild fantasies by all those around him) signifies, for Martin, nothing short of 'the prehistory before the dawn of proletarian consciousness' (p. 233). And indeed, Martin rounds off his main contention by indicating the implicit, optimistic hope that the new Latin American novel 'itself was proof of the end of neocolonialism and the beginning of true liberation' (p. 233).

RESOURCES

Chronology of Gabriel García Márquez's Life_____

1928	Gabriel José García Márquez is born on March 6 in Aracataca, Colombia, to Gabriel Eligio García and Luisa Santiaga Márquez Iguarán; he spends the first eight years of his childhood with his maternal grandparents.
1936-1940	When García Márquez is eight years old, his grandfather dies, and he goes to live with his parents in Sucre. He is sent to boarding school in Barranquilla.
1947	García Márquez enters the Universidad Nacional in Bogotá to study law. His first short story, "La tercera resignación" ("The Third Resignation"), is published in *El Espectador*, a Bogotá newspaper.
1948	Liberal Colombian presidential candidate Jorge Eliécer Gaitán is assassinated, and civil war—known as *la violencia*—erupts. García Márquez moves to Cartagena, continues his law studies, and writes a column for the newspaper *El Universal*.
1950	García Márquez quits law school; he moves to Barranquilla and begins writing a column for *El Heraldo*.
1953	García Márquez quits journalism temporarily and travels around Colombia working various jobs.
1954	García Márquez returns to Bogotá and begins writing articles and film reviews for *El Espectador*.
1955	García Márquez wins a national prize for a short story and publishes his first novel, *La hojarasca* (*Leaf Storm*). He writes an account of Luis Alejandro Velasco's survival at sea for *El Espectador* and travels to Geneva as a correspondent. The government closes down *El Espectador*, and García Márquez stays in Europe.
1956	Living in Paris, García Márquez writes *La mala hora* (*In Evil Hour*) and *El coronel no tiene quien la escriba* (*No One Writes to the Colonel*).

1957	García Márquez travels to East Germany, Czechoslovakia, Poland, Russia, and Hungary. He moves to Caracas to work for the newspaper *Momento*.
1958	García Márquez marries Mercedes Barcha. He writes almost all of the stories that will later appear in the collection *Los funerales de la Mamá Grande* (*Big Mama's Funeral*).
1959	García Márquez's first child, Rodrigo, is born.
1959-61	During and after the Cuban Revolution, García Márquez works for Cuba's news agency Prensa Latina in Bogotá, Cuba, and New York.
1961	García Márquez resigns from Prensa Latina. He makes an "homage to Faulkner" bus trip across the American South to Mexico City, and he receives the Colombian Esso Literary Prize for *In Evil Hour*.
1962	*Big Mama's Funeral* and *No One Writes to the Colonel* are published. A censored *In Evil Hour* is published in Spain. García Márquez's second son, Gonzalo, is born.
1963	García Márquez works for an advertising agency and writes films.
1965	García Márquez goes into seclusion to write *Cien años de soledad* (*One Hundred Years of Solitude*).
1966	The authorized version of *In Evil Hour* is published in Mexico.
1967	*One Hundred Years of Solitude* is published in Buenos Aires. García Márquez moves to Barcelona, Spain.
1968	*No One Writes to the Colonel* is published in the United States.
1969	*One Hundred Years of Solitude* wins the Chianchiano Prize in Italy and is named the Best Foreign Book in France.
1970	*One Hundred Years of Solitude* is published in English and chosen as one of twelve best books of the year by U.S. critics.
1971	García Márquez receives an honorary doctorate of letters degree from Columbia University.

1972	García Márquez is awarded the Rómulo Gallegos Prize and the Books Abroad/Neustadt Prize. *La increíble y triste historia de la cándida Eréndira y de su abuela desalmada* is published, and *Leaf Storm and Other Stories* is published in New York.
1974	García Márquez founds *Alternativa*, a leftist magazine, in Bogotá.
1975	*El otoño del patriarca* (*The Autumn of the Patriarch*) is published in both Spanish and English. García Márquez returns to Mexico.
1977	*Operación Carlota*, essays on Cuba's role in Africa, is published.
1978	*Innocent Eréndira and Other Stories* is published in the United States.
1979	English translation of *In Evil Hour* is published in the United States.
1981	*Crónica de una muerta anunciada* (*Chronicle of a Death Foretold*) is published. García Márquez is awarded the French Legion of Honor. When he returns to Colombia from Cuba, the government accuses him of financing a guerrilla group, and he flees and seeks political asylum in Mexico. *Textos costeños*, the first of five volumes of García Márquez's journalistic writings, edited by Jacques Gilard and titled *Obra periodística*, is published.
1982	García Márquez is awarded the Nobel Prize in Literature. *El olor de la guayaba: Conversaciones con Plinio Apuleyo Mendoza* (*The Fragrance of Guava: Plinio Apuleyo Mendoza in Conversation with Gabriel García Márquez*) is published. García Márquez writes *Viva Sandino*, a screenplay about the Nicaraguan revolution. *Chronicle of a Death Foretold* is published in the United States.
1983	García Márquez returns to Colombia from his exile in Mexico.
1984	*Collected Stories* is published in the United States.
1985	*El amor en los tiempos del cólera* (*Love in the Time of Cholera*) is published.

1986	*La aventura de Miguel Littín, clandestino en Chile* (*Clandestine in Chile: The Adventures of Miguel Littín*), a work of nonfiction, is published. *The Story of a Shipwrecked Sailor*, the tale of Luis Alejandro Velasco's survival, is published in the United States.
1987	*Clandestine in Chile: The Adventures of Miguel Littín* is published in the United States.
1988	*Love in the Time of Cholera* is published in the United States.
1989	*El general en su laberinto* (*The General in His Labyrinth*) is published in Argentina, Colombia, Mexico, and Spain. A year later the English translation is published in the United States.
1992	*Doce cuentos peregrinos* (*Strange Pilgrims: Twelve Stories*) is published in Madrid; the English translation is published in the United States a year later.
1994	*Del amor y otros demonios* (*Of Love and Other Demons*) is published in Barcelona; it appears in the United States a year later.
1996	*Noticia de un secuestro* (*News of a Kidnapping*) is published; it is published in English translation the following year.
1998	García Márquez is a guest of Fidel Castro during Pope John Paul II's historic visit to Cuba.
1999	García Márquez purchases the Colombian newsmagazine *Cambio*. He is diagnosed with lymphatic cancer.
2002	The first volume of García Márquez's memoirs, titled *Vivir para contarla* (*Living to Tell the Tale*), is published; it appears in the United States the following year.
2004	*Memoria de mis putas tristes* (*Memories of My Melancholy Whores*) is published; it is published one year later in the United States.

Works by Gabriel García Márquez

Fiction

La hojarasca, 1955 (novella; translated as *Leaf Storm* in *Leaf Storm and Other Stories*, 1972)

El coronel no tiene quien le escriba, 1961 (novella; translated as *No One Writes to the Colonel* in *No One Writes to the Colonel and Other Stories*, 1968)

Los funerales de la Mamá Grande, 1962 (*Big Mama's Funeral*, stories included in *No One Writes to the Colonel and Other Stories*, 1968)

La mala hora, 1962 (revised 1966; *In Evil Hour*, 1979)

Cien años de soledad, 1967 (*One Hundred Years of Solitude*, 1970)

Isabel viendo llover en Macondo, 1967 (*Monologue of Isabel Watching It Rain in Macondo*, 1972)

No One Writes to the Colonel and Other Stories, 1968

Relato de un náufrago, 1970 (*The Story of a Shipwrecked Sailor: Who Drifted on a Liferaft for Ten Days Without Food or Water, Was Proclaimed a National Hero, Kissed by Beauty Queens, Made Rich Through Publicity, and Then Spurned by the Government and Forgotten for All Time*, 1986)

La increíble y triste historia de la cándida Eréndira y de su abuela desalmada, 1972 (*Innocent Eréndira and Other Stories*, 1978)

Leaf Storm and Other Stories, 1972

El otoño del patriarca, 1975 (*The Autumn of the Patriarch*, 1975)

Todos los cuentos de Gabriel García Márquez, 1975 (*Collected Stories*, 1984)

Crónica de una muerte anunciada, 1981 (*Chronicle of a Death Foretold*, 1982)

El amor en los tiempos del cólera, 1985 (*Love in the Time of Cholera*, 1988)

El general en su laberinto, 1989 (*The General in His Labyrinth*, 1990)

Collected Novellas, 1990

Doce cuentos peregrinos, 1992 (*Strange Pilgrims: Twelve Stories*, 1993)

Del amor y otros demonios, 1994 (*Of Love and Other Demons*, 1995)

Memoria de mis putas tristes, 2004 (*Memories of My Melancholy Whores*, 2005)

Nonfiction

La novela en América Latina: Diálogo,1968 (with Mario Vargas Llosa)

Cuando era feliz e indocumentado, 1973

Chile, el golpe y los gringos, 1974

Crónicas y reportajes, 1976

Operación Carlota, 1977

De viaje por los países socialistas: 90 días en la cortina de hierro, 1978

Periodismo militante, 1978

Obra periodística, 1981-1999 (Jacques Gilard, editor; 5 volumes: *Textos costeños*, 1981; *Entre cachacos*, 1982; *De Europa y América, 1955-1960*, 1983; *Por la libre, 1974-1995*, 1999; *Notas de prensa, 1961-1984*, 1999)

El olor de la guayaba: Conversaciones con Plinio Apuleyo Mendoza, 1982 (*The Fragrance of Guava: Plinio Apuleyo Mendoza in Conversation with Gabriel García Márquez*, 1983)

La aventura de Miguel Littín, clandestino en Chile, 1986 (*Clandestine in Chile: The Adventures of Miguel Littín*, 1987)

Noticia de un secuestro, 1996 (*News of a Kidnapping*, 1997)

Por un país al alcance de los niños, 1996 (*For the Sake of a Country Within Reach of the Children*, 1998)

Vivir para contarla, 2002 (*Living to Tell the Tale*, 2003)

Bibliography

Alèthea 13 (Spring-Summer 1984). "Gabriel García Márquez: The Man and the Magic of His Writings" (special issue). Ed. Ricardo Pastor.

Alvarez-Borland, Isabel. "From Mystery to Parody: (Re)readings of García Márquez's *Crónica de una muerte anunciada*." *Symposium* 38.4 (Winter 1984-85): 278-86.

Bell, Michael. *Gabriel García Márquez: Solitude and Solidarity*. New York: St. Martin's Press, 1993.

Bell-Villada, Gene H. *García Márquez: The Man and His Work*. Chapel Hill: University of North Carolina Press, 1990.

_____. *Gabriel García Márquez's "One Hundred Years of Solitude": A Casebook*. New York: Oxford University Press, 2002.

Bloom, Harold, ed. *Gabriel García Márquez: Modern Critical Views*. New York: Chelsea House, 2007.

Boldy, Steven. "*One Hundred Years of Solitude* by Gabriel García Márquez." *The Cambridge Companion to the Latin American Novel*. Ed. Efraín Kristal. New York: Cambridge University Press, 2005. 258-69.

Brushwood, John S. "Reality and Imagination in the Novels of García Márquez." *Latin American Literary Review* 13.25 (1985): 9-14.

Fiddian, Robin, ed. *García Márquez*. New York: Longman, 1995.

Fuentes, Carlos. *Gabriel García Márquez and the Invention of America*. Liverpool, England: Liverpool University Press, 1987.

_____. "Gabriel García Márquez: La segunda lectura." *La nueva novela hispanoamericana*. Mexico City: Joaquín Mortiz, 1969. 58-67.

Guibert, Rita. "Gabriel García Márquez." In *Seven Voices: Seven Latin American Writers Talk to Rita Guibert*. Trans. Frances Partridge. New York: Knopf, 1973. 305-37.

Hart, Stephen M. *Gabriel García Márquez: Crónica de una muerte anunciada*. London: Grant & Cutler, 2005.

_____. "Magical Realism in the Americas: Politicised Ghosts in *One Hundred Years of Solitude*, *The House of the Spirits*, and *Beloved*." *Tesserae: Journal of Iberian and Latin American Studies* 9.2 (December 2003): 115-23.

Janes, Regina. *Gabriel García Márquez: Revolution in Wonderland*. Columbia: University of Missouri Press, 1981.

Kerr, R. A. "Patterns of Place and Visual-Spatial Imagery in García Márquez's *Del amor y otros demonios*." *Hispania* 79.4 (December 1996): 772-80.

Kutzinski, Vera M. "The Logic of Wings: Gabriel García Márquez and Afro-American Literature." *Latin American Literary Review* 13.25 (January-June 1985).

Latin American Literary Review 13 (January-June 1985). "Gabriel García Márquez" (special issue). Ed. Yvette E. Miller and Charles Rossman.

López-Mejía, Adelaida. "Women Who Bleed to Death: Gabriel García Márquez's 'Sense of an Ending.'" *Revista Hispánica Moderna* 52.1 (June 1999): 135-50.

Lutes, Tod Oakley. *Shipwreck and Deliverance: Politics, Culture, and Modernity in the Works of Octavio Paz, Gabriel García Márquez, and Mario Vargas Llosa.* Lanham, MD: University Press of America, 2003.

McGuirk, Bernard, and Richard Cardwell, eds. *Gabriel García Márquez: New Readings.* New York: Cambridge University Press, 1987.

McMurray, George R. *Gabriel García Márquez.* New York: Ungar, 1977.

McNerney, Kathleen. *Understanding Gabriel García Márquez.* Columbia: University of South Carolina Press, 1989.

Marting, Diane E. "The End of Eréndira's Prostitution." *Hispanic Review* 69.2 (Spring 2001): 175-90.

Minta, Stephen. *Gabriel García Márquez: Writer of Colombia.* London: Jonathan Cape, 1987.

Oberhelman, Harley D. *The Presence of Faulkner in the Writings of García Márquez.* Lubbock: Texas Tech Press, 1980.

_____. *The Presence of Hemingway in the Short Fiction of García Márquez.* Fredericton, NB: York Press, 1994.

Ortega, Julio. *Gabriel García Márquez and the Powers of Fiction.* Austin: University of Texas Press, 1988.

Pelayo, Ruben. *Gabriel García Márquez: A Critical Companion.* Westport, CT: Greenwood Press, 2001.

PEN America: A Journal for Writers and Readers 3.6 (2005). "Gabriel García Márquez: Everyday Magic" (tribute section).

Pérez García, Diana. "Apocalypse Now: Joyce's 'Cyclops' and Márquez's 'Big Mamma.'" *Irish Studies Review* 10.1 (April 2002): 63-73.

Santos-Phillips, Eva. "Power of the Body in the Novella *The Incredible and Sad Tale of Innocent Eréndira and of Her Heartless Grandmother* and the Film *Eréndira.*" *Literature Film Quarterly* 31.2 (2003): 118-23.

Shaw, Bradley A., and Nora Vera-Goodwin, eds. *Critical Perspectives on Gabriel García Márquez.* Lincoln, NE: Society of Spanish and Spanish-American Studies, 1986.

Shiffman, Smadar. "Someone Else's Dream: An Approach to Twentieth Century Fantastic Fiction." *Journal of the Fantastic in the Arts* 13.4 (2003): 352-67.

Simas, Rosa. *Circularity and Visions of the New World in William Faulkner, Gabriel García Márquez, and Osman Lins.* Lewistown, NY: Edwin Mellen Press, 1993.

Stone, Peter. "Gabriel García Márquez." *Writers at Work: The Paris Review Interviews—Sixth Series.* Ed. George Plimpton. New York: Viking Press, 1984. 313-39.

Vargas Llosa, Mario. *García Márquez: Historia de un deicidio.* Barcelona: Barral Editores, 1971.

Williams, Raymond L. *Gabriel García Márquez.* Boston: Twayne, 1984.

Wood, Michael. *Gabriel García Márquez: One Hundred Years of Solitude*. New York: Cambridge University Press, 1990.

Zamora, Lois Parkinson. "Apocalypse and Human Time in the Fiction of Gabriel García Márquez." *Writing the Apocalypse: Historical Vision in Contemporary U.S. and Latin American Fiction*. New York: Cambridge University Press, 1989.

CRITICAL
INSIGHTS

About the Editor

Ilan Stavans is Lewis-Sebring Professor in Latin American and Latino Culture and Five College-Fortieth Anniversary Professor at Amherst College. A native of Mexico, he received his doctorate in Latin American literature from Columbia University. Stavans's books include *The Hispanic Condition* (1995), *On Borrowed Words* (2001), *Spanglish* (2003), *Dictionary Days* (2005), *The Disappearance* (2006), *Love and Language* (2007), *Resurrecting Hebrew* (2008), and *Mr. Spic Goes to Washington* (2008). He has edited *The Oxford Book of Jewish Stories* (1998), *The Poetry of Pablo Neruda* (2004), *Isaac Bashevis Singer: Collected Stories* (3 volumes, 2004), *The Schocken Book of Sephardic Literature* (2005), and *Cesar Chavez: An Organizer's Tale* (2008). He is also the editor of two anthologies published in 2009: *Becoming Americans: Four Hundred Years of Immigrant Writing*, from the Library of America, and *The Norton Anthology of Latino Literature*, from W. W. Norton. His play *The Disappearance*, performed by the theater troupe Double Edge, premiered at the Skirball Cultural Center in Los Angeles and has been staged around the United States. His story "Morirse está en hebreo" was made into the award-winning film *My Mexican Shivah* (2007), produced by John Sayles. Stavans has received numerous awards, among them a Guggenheim Fellowship, the National Jewish Book Award, an Emmy nomination, the Latino Book Award, Chile's Presidential Medal, and the Rubén Darío Distinction. His work has been translated into a dozen languages.

About *The Paris Review*

The Paris Review is America's preeminent literary quarterly, dedicated to discovering and publishing the best new voices in fiction, nonfiction, and poetry. The magazine was founded in Paris in 1953 by the young American writers Peter Matthiessen and Doc Humes, and edited there and in New York for its first fifty years by George Plimpton. Over the decades, the *Review* has introduced readers to the earliest writings of Jack Kerouac, Philip Roth, T. C. Boyle, V. S. Naipaul, Ha Jin, Jay McInerney, and Mona Simpson, and published numerous now classic works, including Roth's *Goodbye, Columbus*, Donald Barthelme's *Alice*, Jim Carroll's *Basketball Diaries*, and selections from Samuel Beckett's *Molloy* (his first publication in English). The first chapter of Jeffrey Eugenides's *The Virgin Suicides* appeared in the *Review*'s pages, as well as stories by Edward P. Jones, Rick Moody, David Foster Wallace, Denis Johnson, Jim Shepard, Jim Crace, Lorrie Moore, Jeanette Winterson, and Ann Patchett.

The Paris Review's renowned Writers at Work series of interviews, whose early installments include legendary conversations with E. M. Forster, William Faulkner, and

Ernest Hemingway, is one of the landmarks of world literature. The interviews received a George Polk Award and were nominated for a Pulitzer Prize. Among the more than three hundred interviewees are Robert Frost, Marianne Moore, W. H. Auden, Elizabeth Bishop, Susan Sontag, and Toni Morrison. Recent issues feature conversations with Salman Rushdie, Joan Didion, Stephen King, Norman Mailer, Kazuo Ishiguro, and Umberto Eco. (A complete list of the interviews is available at www.theparisreview.org.) In November 2008, Picador will publish the third of a four-volume series of anthologies of *Paris Review* interviews. The first two volumes have received acclaim. *The New York Times* called the Writers at Work series "the most remarkable and extensive interviewing project we possess."

The Paris Review is edited by Philip Gourevitch, who was named to the post in 2005, following the death of George Plimpton two years earlier. Under Gourevitch's leadership, the magazine's international distribution has expanded, paid subscriptions have risen 150 percent, and newsstand distribution has doubled. A new editorial team has published fiction by Andre Aciman, Damon Galgut, Mohsin Hamid, Gish Jen, Richard Price, Said Sayrafiezadeh, and Alistair Morgan. Poetry editors Charles Simic, Meghan O'Rourke, and Dan Chiasson have selected works by Billy Collins, Jesse Ball, Mary Jo Bang, Sharon Olds, and Mary Karr. Writing published in the magazine has been anthologized in *Best American Short Stories* (2006, 2007, and 2008), *Best American Poetry*, *Best Creative Non-Fiction*, the Pushcart Prize anthology, and *O. Henry Prize Stories*.

The magazine presents two annual awards. The Hadada Award for lifelong contribution to literature has recently been given to William Styron, Joan Didion, Norman Mailer, and Peter Matthiessen in 2008. The Plimpton Prize for Fiction, given to a new voice in fiction brought to national attention in the pages of *The Paris Review*, was presented in 2007 to Benjamin Percy and to Jesse Ball in 2008.

The Paris Review won the 2007 National Magazine Award in photojournalism, and the *Los Angeles Times* recently called *The Paris Review* "an American treasure with true international reach."

Since 1999 *The Paris Review* has been published by The Paris Review Foundation, Inc., a not-for-profit 501(c)(3) organization.

The Paris Review is available in digital form to libraries worldwide in selected academic databases exclusively from EBSCO Publishing. Libraries can contact EBSCO at 1-800-653-2726 for details. For more information on *The Paris Review* or to subscribe, please visit: www.theparisreview.org.

Contributors

Ilan Stavans is Lewis-Sebring Professor in Latin American and Latino Culture and Five College-Fortieth Anniversary Professor at Amherst College. His books include *The Hispanic Condition* (1995), *On Borrowed Words* (2001), *Spanglish* (2003), *Dictionary Days* (2005), *The Disappearance* (2006), *Love and Language* (2007), *Resurrecting Hebrew* (2008), and *Mr. Spic Goes to Washington* (2008).

Roy Arthur Swanson is Professor Emeritus of Classics and Comparative Literature at the University of Wisconsin-Milwaukee. His publications include *Heart of Reason: Introductory Essays in Modern-World Humanities*, *Odie et Amo: The Complete Poetry of Catullus*, *Pindar's Odes*, *Pär Lagerkvist: Five Early Works*, and *Blue Margin: Versions of Rhetoric*. Lines from his translation of Catullus were used in the motion picture *Cleopatra* and in the HBO television series *Rome*.

Caitlin Roper is the managing editor of *The Paris Review*.

Amy Sickels is an MFA graduate of Pennsylvania State University. Her fiction and essays have appeared or are forthcoming in *DoubleTake*, *Passages North*, *Bayou*, *The Madison Review*, *LIT*, *Natural Bridge*, and *The Greensboro Review*.

Amy M. Green is in her final year of studies as a Ph.D. student in literature at the University of Nevada, Las Vegas. Her work has appeared in *Popular Culture Review*, *Papers on Language and Literature*, *The Shakespeare Bulletin*, and *The Mark Twain Annual*. Her dissertation focused on the influence of Shakespeare on the works of Henry James and Mark Twain.

John Cussen is Associate Professor in the Department of English and Theater Arts at Edinboro University of Pennsylvania. He has published scholarly articles in *Religion and the Arts*, *Journal of Modern Literature*, *Yeats: An Annual of Critical and Textual Studies*, *Interdisciplinary Literary Studies*, *Studies in Travel Writing*, *The CEA Critic*, *The New Hibernian Review*, *The Journal of Kentucky Studies*, *The Yeats Journal of Korea*, and *The Journal of the Modern Fiction Society of Korea*. He has also published fiction in *Fiction*, *Confrontation*, *The Cream City Review*, *Cincinnati Magazine*, *Ascent*, and *Ambergris*.

Gene H. Bell-Villada is the author of *García Márquez: The Man and His Work*, *Gabriel García Márquez's* One Hundred Years of Solitude: *A Casebook*, and *Conversations with Gabriel García Márquez*. He is also the author of *Art for Art's Sake and Literary Life: How Politics and Markets Helped Shape the Ideology and Culture of Aestheticism, 1790-1990* (1996), a finalist for the National Book Critics Circle Award.

Moylan C. Mills is Professor Emeritus of Integrative Arts at the Pennsylvania State University. He has published essays in both journals and edited volumes, including *Contemporary Irish Cinema*; *Studies in Latin American Popular Culture*; *Literature Film Quarterly*; *JAISA:The Journal of the Association for Interdisciplinary Studies in the Arts*; and *The Art World and Its Audience*.

Enrique Grönlund taught at Pennsylvania State University. His publications include contributions to *Film and Literature: A Comparative Approach to Adaptation* (1988), *Studies in Latin American Popular Culture*, and *Literature Film Quarterly*.

Deborah Cohn is Associate Professor of Spanish and Portuguese and Associate Professor and Director of the American Studies Program at Indiana University. Her books include *History and Memory in the Two Souths: Recent Southern and Spanish American Fiction* (1999) and *Look Away! The U.S. South in New World Studies* (coedited with Jon Smith, 2004).

Rosa Simas is the author of *Circularity and Visions of the New World in William Faulkner, Gabriel García Márquez, and Osman Lins* (1993).

Brian Conniff is Dean of the College of Humanities and Behavioral Sciences at Radford University. He has contributed articles to a number of books and journals, including *W. H. Auden: A Legacy* (2002), *Literature and Law* (2004), *Prose and Cons: New Essays on Contemporary U.S. Prison Literature* (2005), *Christianity and Literature*, *African American Review*, *Midwest Quarterly*, *Modern Fiction Studies*, and *American Literature*.

Stephen M. Hart is Professor of Hispanic Studies at University College London. He has published widely on Latin American film and literature, including the books *Contemporary Latin American Cultural Studies* (2003) and *A Companion to Latin American Film* (2004).

Michael Palencia-Roth is Trowbridge Scholar in Literary Studies and Professor of Comparative and World Literature at the University of Illinois. His books include *Gabriel García Márquez: La línea, el círculo y las metamorfosis del mito* (1984), *Myth and the Modern Novel* (1987), and *The Narrow Bridge: Beyond the Holocaust* (2000). His essays and articles have appeared in a wide variety of journals, including *Modern Language Notes*, *Journal of European Studies*, *Contemporary Literary Criticism*, *World Literature Today*, *Comparative Civilizations Review*, and *Philosophy and Literature*.

Lourdes Elena Morales-Gudmundsson is Chair of the Department of World Languages and Professor of Spanish at La Sierra University. In 2007 she published *I Forgive You, But . . . .*

M. Keith Booker is Professor of English at the University of Arkansas. He is the author of numerous articles and books on modern literature, literary theory, television, and film, including *Joyce, Bakhtin, and the Literary Tradition: Toward a Comparative Cultural Poetics* (1995), *Ulysses, Capitalism, and Colonialism: Reading Joyce After the Cold War* (2000), *The Post-Utopian Imagination: American Culture in the Long 1950s* (2002), *The Chinua Achebe Encyclopedia* (2003), *Science Fiction Television* (2004), and *From Box Office to Ballot Box: The American Political Film* (2007).

Efraín Kristal is Professor of Comparative Literature at the University of California, Los Angeles. He has published numerous essays on Latin American literature and intellectual history. His books include *The Andes Viewed from the City: Literary and Political Discourse on the Indian in Peru* (1987), *Temptation of the Word: The Novels of Mario Vargas Llosa* (1998), *Invisible Work: Borges and Translation* (2002), and *The Cambridge Companion to the Latin American Novel* (2005).

Acknowledgments_____

"Gabriel García Márquez" by Roy Arthur Swanson. From *Cyclopedia of World Authors, Fourth Revised Edition*. Copyright © 2004 by Salem Press, Inc. Reprinted with permission of Salem Press.

"The *Paris Review* Perspective" by Caitlin Roper. Copyright © 2010 by Caitlin Roper. Special appreciation goes to Christopher Cox and Nathaniel Rich, editors for *The Paris Review*.

"The Master of Aracataca" by Ilan Stavans. From *Art and Anger: Essays on Politics and the Imagination*. 41-67. Copyright © 1996 by the University of New Mexico Press. Reprinted by permission.

"The Master of Short Forms" by Gene H. Bell-Villada. From *García Márquez: The Man and His Work*. 119-138. Copyright © 1990 by The University of North Carolina Press. Reprinted by permission.

"Magic Realism and García Márquez's Eréndira" by Moylan C. Mills and Enrique Grönlund. From *Literature Film Quarterly* 17, no. 2 (1989): 113-122. Copyright © 1989 by Salisbury State University. Reprinted by permission.

"'The Paralysis of the Instant': The Stagnation of History and the Stylistic Suspension of Time in Gabriel García Márquez's *La hojarasca*" by Deborah Cohn. From *College Literature* 26, no. 2 (Spring 1999): 59-78. Copyright © 1999 by Westchester University. Reprinted by permission.

"A 'Gyrating Wheel'" by Rosa Simas. From *Circularity and Visions of the New World in William Faulkner, Gabriel García Márquez, and Osman Lins*. 95-127. Copyright © 1993 by Edwin Mellen Press. Reprinted by permission.

"The Dark Side of Magical Realism: Science, Oppression, and Apocalypse in *One Hundred Years of Solitude*" by Brian Conniff. From *Modern Fiction Studies* 36 (1990): 167-179. Copyright © 1990 by the Purdue Research Foundation. Reprinted by permission.

"Superstition, Irony, Themes" by Stephen M. Hart. From *Gabriel García Márquez: Crónica de una muerte anunciada*. 50-62. Copyright © 2005 by Grant & Cutler Ltd. Reprinted by permission.

"Intertextualities: Three Metamorphoses of Myth in *The Autumn of the Patriarch*" by Michael Palencia-Roth. From *Gabriel García Márquez and the Powers of Fiction*. Julio Ortega, ed. 34-60. Copyright © 1988 by The University of Texas Press. Reprinted by permission.

"Biblical Justice and the Military Hero in Two Novels of Gabriel García Márquez" by Lourdes Elena Morales-Gudmundsson. From *Postcolonial Literature and the Biblical Call for Justice*. Susan VanZanten Gallagher, ed. 60-73. Copyright ©1994 by the University Press of Mississippi. Reprinted by permission.

"The Dangers of Gullible Reading: Narrative as Seduction in García Márquez'

Love in the Time of Cholera" by M. Keith Booker. From *Studies in 20th Century Literature* 17, no. 2 (Summer 1993): 181-195. Copyright © 1993 by *Studies in 20th Century Literature*. Reprinted by permission.

"Lessons from the Golden Age in Gabriel García Márquez's *Living to Tell the Tale*" by Efraín Kristal. From *A Companion to Magical Realism*. Stephen M. Hart and Wen-chin Ouyang, eds. 88-97. Copyright © 2005 by Editors and Contributors. Reprinted by permission.

Index

Cortázar, Julio, 3, 21, 38, 57, 63, 133, 168, 209

Crónica de una muerte anunciada. See *Chronicle of a Death Foretold*

Cuadra, René, 194, 198

Cuban Revolution (1959), 22, 26, 54, 60

Culler, Jonathan, 279

Darío, Rubén, 267

Daza, Fermina (*Love in the Time of Cholera*), 5, 29, 58, 301, 306, 311

De viaje por los países socialistas (García Márquez), 53, 70

"Death Constant beyond Love" (García Márquez), 126

Death theme, 43, 113, 119, 158, 196, 234, 288, 296

Del amor y otros demonios. See *Of Love and Other Demons*

"Día después del Sábado, Un." *See* "One Day After Saturday"

Dictators, 8, 22, 26, 58, 116, 121, 202, 250, 267, 278, 289, 291

Doce cuentos peregrinos. See *Strange Pilgrims*

Dohmann, Barbara, 168

Don Quixote de La Mancha (Cervantes), 4, 35, 70, 95, 249

Donoso, José, 3, 62

Dorfman, Ariel, 229

Dos Passos, John, 4, 38, 48

Faulkner, William, 4, 7, 13, 20, 30, 47, 104, 148, 154, 161, 167-168, 176, 194, 204

Fiddian, Robin W., 286

Fish in the Water, The (Vargas Llosa), 62

Flores, Angel, 134

Fragrance of Guava, The (García Márquez and Apuleyo Mendoza), 37, 324, 329

Fuentes, Carlos, 3, 21, 23, 38, 44, 57, 138, 164, 178, 191, 209

Funerales de la Mamá Grande, Los. See *Big Mama's Funeral*

Gaitán, Jorge Eliécer, 7, 46, 325

Galeano, Eduardo, 228, 230

Gallagher, D. P., 191

García Márquez (Vargas Llosa), 29, 37, 51, 60, 159, 184

García Márquez, Gabriel; on the Bible, 285; childhood, 7, 12, 19, 39; education, 7, 43; European years, 8, 53; influences on, 7, 13, 20, 149, 322; memoirs, 320; Nobel Prize, 9, 14, 27, 30, 206, 211, 216, 330; political views, 27, 54; screenwriting, 44; short fiction, 53, 103; on writing, 9, 12, 14, 25; writing career, 3-4, 7, 13, 35, 49; writing style, 48, 58

Gass, William H., 60

General en su laberinto, El. See *General in His Labyrinth, The*

General in His Labyrinth, The (García Márquez), 29, 50, 80

Gertel, Zunilda, 199, 212

Gilard, Jacques, 48, 77

González Echevarría, Roberto, 201

Guerra, Ruy, 138, 142, 145

Gullón, Ricardo, 207

Hamsun, Knut, 4, 118

"Handsomest Drowned Man in the World, The" (García Márquez), 124

Harss, Luis, 42, 54, 168

Hart, Stephen M., 136, 141, 145

Hemingway, Ernest, 4, 14, 38, 48, 104, 123, 256